Born to Coach

*For their inspiration, laughter, support, love, and random goofiness,
I dedicate this with much love and gratitude to my late parents,
Frank Clerici Sr. and Carol Hunt-Clerici; my late brother,
David Clerici; and my brother, Frank Clerici Jr.*
—**Paul C. Clerici**

*I dedicate this to my family—Sally Squires, Mary Susan Squires,
Bill Squires Jr., Gerry Squires; and to all the athletes I have been
blessed with—from the greats to the almost-greats—who all paid the
price for improvement. I tried to give my best each time, as they
did in their performances. Amen.*
—**Bill Squires**

PAUL C. CLERICI

BORN TO COACH

THE STORY OF BILL SQUIRES
THE LEGENDARY COACH OF THE GREATEST
GENERATION OF AMERICAN DISTANCE RUNNERS

Foreword by DICK BEARDSLEY,
National Distance Running Hall of Fame Inductee

MEYER & MEYER SPORT

British Library Cataloguing in Publication Data

A catalogue record for this book is available from the British Library

Born to Coach

Maidenhead: Meyer & Meyer Sport (UK) Ltd., 2020

ISBN: 978-1-78255-196-6

© 2020 by Meyer & Meyer Sport (UK) Ltd.

Aachen, Auckland, Beirut, Cairo, Cape Town, Dubai, Hägendorf, Hong Kong, Indianapolis, Maidenhead, Manila, New Delhi, Singapore, Sydney, Tehran, Vienna

Member of the World Sports Publishers' Association (WSPA), www.w-s-p-a.org

Printed by: C-M Books, Ann Arbor, MI, USA

ISBN: 978-1-78255-196-6

Email: info@m-m-sports.com

www.thesportspublisher.com

CONTENTS

FOREWORD

I first met Coach Bill Squires in August of 1980. As an elite athlete, I'd been getting shoes and running gear from the New Balance Shoe Company, beginning in November of 1979. Other than a sales rep for NB, I'd never met anyone else there. NB brought me out to meet them, and since it was the weekend of the Falmouth Road Race, they thought I might want to run it. I had heard of Coach Squires before, but had never met him. On the plane with me was a runner from Minneapolis named Mike Slack, who NB was trying to sign. When we got to the gate, there to meet us was Coach, who worked with NB. Mike knew him well, but I was awestruck! I schlepped all our bags while Coach and Mike were talking and walking in front of me. We dropped Mike off at his hotel and now it was just me and Coach! What a treat! We headed for the NB office, where Coach introduced me to everyone.

We then got into his car and headed for Falmouth, where Coach said he knew some folks who said we could stay at their place which is what runners often did then. I was nervous because I had the Falmouth race the next morning and the house was full of non-runners partying. I finally went upstairs to find a room to sleep in, but they were all taken. I found an extra pillow and blanket and found a spot on the hallway floor to sleep. About 2 a.m., Coach apparently got up to use the bathroom and saw me sleeping there and woke me up and told me to go take his bed and that he'd find another place to sleep. I told him I was fine, but he insisted. I fell back to sleep right away in the bed and got up around 4 a.m. to use the bathroom. I walked in and flipped the light on and there was Coach, sound asleep in the bathtub with a small towel over him as a blanket! I couldn't believe it!

After the race, Coach took me to the airport and told me that if I was interested, he'd be happy to coach me since I was now part of Team New Balance.

I couldn't believe that he wanted to coach me! Before he got his final word out of his mouth, I said, "Yes!" I had never been so excited in my life. Here I was, going to be coached by one of the greatest distance-running coaches in not just our country but around the world.

We started working together right away. We had only two months before the New York City Marathon, but Coach had me as ready as I could be under his tutelage for such a short period. I'd never gone out with the leaders before, but Coach gave me the confidence to do so. Halfway across the Queensboro Bridge, I made a long, hard surge and came down onto First Avenue, leading the race by about 150 yards! The crowd noise was deafening. I then noticed someone off to my right, sprinting to keep up with me. I looked over and it was Coach! His next words were, "Dickie, what in the hell are you doing?" I said, "Coach, I'm winning the New York City Marathon!" I didn't win, but finished ninth and ran a new PR of 2:13:56. I knew after that race that great things were going to happen with Coach Squires coaching me.

I was in the NB office one day, chatting with Coach and a few other runners, when Coach said he had to go run some errands. About an hour later, we happened to be looking out the window when Coach drove up and got out of his car. When he got out, we noticed he had a full head of hair—apparently he had got a toupee. As he walked across the street towards the NB building, a gust of wind came up and his toupee turned sideways on his head, but Coach didn't know it. He walked in and came up to where we were and when he walked in and that toupee was sideways on his head, I've never heard a group of guys ever laugh so hard! Coach was great about it and laughed along with us.

Coach Squires is one of the most giving people I've ever met, and in my opinion the best distance coach in the world. He knows his athletes and cares for them dearly. When I worked with Coach, iPhones and home computers were not even thought of yet. With me in Minnesota and Coach in Boston, we communicated via phone and slow mail. Coach would send me my workouts once a week and we'd talk once or twice a week via phone. When I ran my first Grandma's Marathon in Duluth, Minnesota, in 1981, Coach sent me a note with another note that said, "Don't open till after the race." I was fortunate to win the race and ran 2:09:36. When I got back to my room, I opened the envelope and Coach had written, "You'll run between 2:09-2:10." Talk about a coach that knows his athlete!

In late summer of 1981, Coach and I decided it was time for me to run the Boston Marathon. From that point on, every mile I ran and every race I ran was to get ready for Boston. About two weeks before Boston, I flew out and stayed with Coach so I could do some training on the course. After I arrived at his home, he said, "Dickie, help yourself to anything in the fridge if you get hungry." I was training so hard then that in the middle of the night I'd always have to get up to have something to eat as I'd be hungry. I went to the fridge and the only thing in it was a jar of pickles!

Coach took me up to Hopkinton one morning to run the first 15 miles of the course as he was driving next to me in his car. At one point as we were about to go down a hill, he slowed down, stopped, and dropped a tennis ball out the window and said, "Follow that ball. It will give you the quickest way to run." I still remember that run vividly! I felt like I was floating the entire time. Coach kept telling me to slow down, but it felt so effortless! To have Coach in his car next to me was amazing.

On race day I was nervous and excited, but also knew I'd never been more ready for a race than at that point. Coach instructed me to not lead or do any surging for at least the first half but to be in that lead pack. He also gave me a white NB painter's cap to wear so it would reflect the bright sun. He had instructed me that if I was in that lead group when we got to the hills to run up and down them as hard as I could. I honestly trusted Coach so much that I would have banged my head against the wall 10 times if he told me to! Well, at 17 miles, when we got to the hills, it was just me and Alberto Salazar. And I did exactly what Coach told me to do, but I couldn't shake Alberto. It finally came down to a hundred-meter sprint and I got out-kicked. Alberto and I both broke 2:09, which was the first time that two men had ever done that in the same race. Alberto ran 2:08:52 and I ran 2:08:53.6 rounded up to 2:08:54. Coach was so proud of me and I was so proud and honored to have him as my coach.

I retired from high-level training in 1988 but continue to run every day. I can't begin to say enough wonderful things about Coach Squires. He is a great coach. But as great of a coach he is, he's even more of a caring person. After I retired from competitive running, I moved back to my Minnesota dairy farm and milked cows and continued my fishing guide business. On November 13, 1989, I got into a terrible farm accident. I almost lost my left leg and had numerous other broken bones and injuries. I was in the hospital for multiple weeks. Coach was one of the first people to reach out to ask how he could help. He even sent money out of his own pocket to help with my medical bills. Then, after more surgeries and other accidents, I became addicted to narcotic pain pills and once again Coach reached out to offer help.

I'm so happy that now the world will know about this remarkable man through this book. He brought me to a point in my running that I had only dreamed about, but more importantly, he helped shape me to be the person I am today; and for that I'll be forever grateful. Coach, you're the best of the best!

–**Dick Beardsley**
Marathon CR-winner—Grandma's, co-London, Napa Valley
Hall of Fame—National Distance Running, and Road Runners Club of America

ACKNOWLEDGMENTS

A book such as this could never be made without the help and assistance of many others.

First and foremost, my sincere thanks and great appreciation to Bill Squires for living to the fullest the interesting life that is depicted in these pages; and to Dick Beardsley for his warm, amusing, heartfelt, and caring foreword. I would also like to thank my late parents, both of whom were voracious readers—my mother, Carol Hunt-Clerici, who as the first line of editing, read every word before anyone else and provided valuable guidance; and my father, Frank Clerici Sr., for his continual support and interest in these endeavors.

Thank you to: Jack Authelet, Dick Campbell, Tim Evans, the late Richard Schnorbus, for their formative direction throughout my writing development; the late Bob Levitsky, for his fine comments and diligent assistance; Jill Beardsley, Kathleen Doherty, Mark Duggan, Jeff Johnson, Jack McDonald, Ashley Mitchell (USATF), *New England Runner* (especially Bob Fitzgerald, Michele LeBrun), NIKE, Charlie Rodgers, Rick Shannon, Bill Squires, Paul Sutton, for their photographic contributions; the former John Hancock Hotel & Conference Center in Boston, Mass., especially Warren "Bud" Carroll, Richie Dattoli, Charlie Grant, Terry Lee, for their company and sustenance; Louisa Clerici, Rick Clerici, Scott Douglas, Lorraine Moller, Dennis O'Rourke, Ken Reed, Bob Ryan, Marc Songini, for their deft insight and direction from within; Richard Benyo, Jan Colarusso Seeley, for their long-running support, advice, and foresight; Richard M. Fruci, Denali Granholm, Dave Kellogg, Chris Lotsbom, Gerald J. McTernan, Jean Nelligan, Blake Russell, Bob Sevene; Ambrose "Amby" Burfoot, Tom Derderian, Jack Fleming, Richard Johnson, Tim Kilduff, Stephen Lyons, Dave McGillivray, Guy Morse III, Gloria Ratti, Roger Robinson, Bill Rodgers, Kathrine Switzer, Fred Treseler III, who all provided supportive words of encouragement and various avenues of pursuit throughout the process; Cheryl Clerici, Fred Doyle, Mark Duggan, Beverly Jaeger-Helton, Barbara Lee, Christine Lee, Stephanie Lee, Gigi Turgeon, for their own infectious enthusiasm for this book when mine needed a boost; and Tom Doherty, Liz Evans, Dani McCormick, Thomas McLean, and everyone at Meyer & Meyer Sport Publisher and Cardinal Publishers Group for making it happen!

Regarding research—in addition to Coach's scribbles and notes on scraps of paper, and the colorful recollections and memories stashed "between his ears"— there were many people, published reports and records, and websites to whom and which I turned to confirm facts and figures and whatnot.

Websites included *Athens News* newspaper; Athletics Canada, especially director of public relations and corporate services Mathieu Gentes; Athletics Ireland; Athletics Ontario, especially communications and public relations manager Anthony Biggar, technical services director Roman Olszewski; *Athletics Weekly*'s gbrathletics.com; Atlanta Braves; Baseball Digest; Bill Rodgers Running Center; Biographical Directory of the United States Congress; Bob Hodge Running Page; Boston Athletic Association (B.A.A), especially former communications manager Thomas "T.K." Skenderian; Boston Bruins; Boston Celtics; Boston College Athletics; *Boston Globe* newspaper via boston.com; *Boston Herald* newspaper via bostonherald.com; Boston Public Library; Boston Red Sox; Boston State College via the University of Massachusetts Boston; Boston University Alumni *Bostonia*; Boston University Athletics; Bowdoin College; Brookline High School Alumni Association; Cambridge Running Club; Canadian Broadcasting Corporation (CBC); Canadian Masters Athletic Association (CMAA), especially the late Ed Whitlock; CBSSports.com; *Chicago Tribune* newspaper; CNN.com; College of Optometrists; College of William & Mary Athletics; Commonwealth Games Federation (CGF); Concord-Carlisle Regional High School; Dartmouth College Athletics; Dave McGillivray Sports Enterprises (DMSE); Debbie Reynolds Official Website; Delhi Police; Dick Gregory Global Watch; Dictionary of American Naval Fighting Ships (DANFS), Department of the US Navy, Naval Historical Center; Digital Deli Online; Drake Relays: America's Athletic Classic, presented by Cowles Library, Drake University.

Dwight D. Eisenhower Presidential Library and Museum; Epilepsy Foundation; Fairfield Half-Marathon; Falmouth Road Race, Inc.; GlobalSecurity.org; Golden Temple, Amritsar; Government of Nova Scotia; Greater Boston Track Club

(GBTC); Greek Royal Family Office, especially Aliki Strongylos; Hamilton Indoor Games & Sports Festival; Hamilton Public Library in Hamilton, Ontario, Canada, especially archivist Margaret Houghton of local history & archives; *Hamilton Spectator* newspaper in Hamilton, Ontario, Canada, especially Tammie Danciu of library archives; *Harvard Crimson*, Harvard University; *The Hour* newspaper, Norwalk, Conn.; *The Independent* newspaper (United Kingdom); Indiana University Athletics; International Association of Athletics Federations (IAAF); International Boxing Hall of Fame; International Olympic Committee (IOC); Iona College Alumni Online Community; JesseOwens.com; John F. Kennedy Presidential Library and Museum; Johnny Mathis Official Website; The Journal of Sport History via the LA84 Foundation website; Labatt Brewing Company; Liberty Athletic Club; *LIFE* magazine; London Marathon.

Madison Square Garden; Maine Running History; MarathonGuide.com; Massachusetts Bay Transportation Authority (MBTA); Massachusetts Broadcasters Hall of Fame; Massachusetts Department of Conservation and Recreation; Massachusetts Historical Society; Massachusetts State Track Coaches Association (MSTCA) Athletes Hall of Fame, especially Robert L'Homme, Frank Mooney, Lou Tozzi; *The Mass Media*, University of Massachusetts Boston; Masters Athletics; Matignon High School; Memorial University of Newfoundland; Michigan State University Athletic Communications, especially Vince Baker; Military.com; Minnesota Twins; The Morris Inn; Mount Washington Road Race; myguideIreland.com via Irish Tourism.com; The Naismith Memorial Basketball Hall of Fame; Natalie Wood Official Website; National Association of Intercollegiate Athletics (NAIA), especially sports information & media services manager Amanda C. Dahl; National Distance Running Hall of Fame; National Oceanic and Atmospheric Administration (NOAA); National Track and Field Hall of Fame at The Armory Foundation; NBA.com; Netaji Subhas National Institute of Sports (NSNIS); New Advent Catholic Encyclopedia by Kevin Knight; Newfoundland and Labrador Heritage; *New Mobility* magazine; New York City Marathon; *New York Times*; New Zealand Ministry of Culture and Heritage; Northeastern University Athletics; Northwestern University Athletics.

Official Finnish Tourist Board, especially Niina Aalto of VisitFinland; Official Muhammad Ali Website; Official Site of the Allstate Sugar Bowl; Official Site of Jack Dempsey; Official Website of District Patiala; Official Website of Shiromani Gurdwara Parbandhak Committee, Amritsar; Our Lady of Grace

Parish, Chelsea-Everett, Mass.; Paddington Recreation Grounds via Westminster. gov.uk; Penn Relays; Philly.com; Quinnipiac University Athletics; Racing Post; Rosa & Raymond Parks Institute for Self Development; Running USA; Saint Joseph's College of Maine Athletics; Society of the Little Flower; Southern Illinois University Carbondale Athletics; *Sports Illustrated*, SI Vault; Sports Museum of Finland; Sports Reference/International Society of Olympic Historians; St. Coletta of Wisconsin; Suffolk Downs; Therese Neumann of Konnersreuth website; thisisFINLAND website via the Finland Promotion Board, Ministry of Foreign Affairs, Department of Communications and Culture; *TIME*.com; *Times of India*; Time-to-Run online running magazine; Tornado Project.com; *Track & Field News* magazine, especially the editorial department; TRACS, Inc., especially Fred Treseler III; Transportation Corps Aviation Association; Tufts University Athletics.

United States Coast Guard (USCG) Station Nahant; United States Department of Labor, Office of the Assistant Secretary for Administration and Management; University of Massachusetts Boston Athletics; University of Massachusetts Boston Athletics Communications, especially Daniel Campagna; University of Massachusetts Boston Joseph P. Healey Library (yearbooks); University of Notre Dame Archives, especially Angela Kindig, Charles Lamb; University of Notre Dame Monogram Club, especially Mark LaFrance; University of Notre Dame Sports Information Office, especially Carol Copley; University of Texas at Austin Athletics, especially assistant athletics media relations director Ashley Walker; USA Track & Field (USATF); US Army Fort Dix; US Army Fort Eustis; US Library of Congress—Congressional Records; US Navy New London; US Track & Field and Cross-Country Coaches Association (USTFCCCA), especially communications manager Tom Lewis; Wakefield High School Athletics; Wheaton College Athletics; Wikipedia (for first references only); Zamperini Distance Carnival.

Published materials of record in book/paper form include the *Boston Globe* newspaper; *The Boston Marathon: A Century of Blood, Sweat, and Cheers* by Tom Derderian (Triumph Books, 2003); *Boston Marathon: Year-by-Year Stories of the World's Premier Running Event* by Tom Derderian (Skyhorse Publishing, 2017); *Fast Tracks: The History of Distance Running* by Ray Krise and Bill Squires (The Stephen Greene Press, 1982); *The History of the US Olympic Trials: Track and Field: 1908-2000* by Richard Hymans, ATFS (USA Track & Field, 2004); *If This*

Is Heaven, I Am Going to Be a Good Boy: The Tommy Leonard Story by Kathleen Cleary (iUniverse, Inc., 2005); *Images of America: Greater Boston's Blizzard of 1978* by Alan R. Earls (Arcadia Publishing, 2008); *Improving Your Running: 52 Weekly Sessions from Jogging to Fun Runs to 3-mile to 6-mile to Marathon Runs!* by Bill Squires (Running Systems, Inc., 1979); *Long Distance Log* magazine, the Official Publication of the United States Track and Field Federation.

Bill Squires would like to acknowledge and thank his late parents, Florence and Murt Squires, "who taught me to respect all people; and to be true, honest, and kind"; the late Dr. Edward Carroll Sr., "who saved my life when I was a kid"; the late Charlie Leverone, "who was the one in school that got me into running"; the late coach William "Doc" McCarthy, "who taught me to warm up, get out fast, own second place and hold it until your sprint to the finish"; the late John "Deke" DiComandrea, "the one who got me back into the sport"; the late Rev. Thomas J. Brennan, "who taught me things at Notre Dame I still use today"; all his coaches, "who gave me a chance to use my ideas"; Fred Doyle, Mark Duggan, Scott Graham, Kirk Pfrangle, Lou Ristaino, the late Bruce Lehane, "former athletes of mine who have all stayed close over the years"; and Paul Clerici, "with the guidance of a fine writer, the world can now read how the old coach ticks."

INTRODUCTION

"I'll clue ya!" Anyone who knows—or has met—Bill Squires has heard this declaration from him when he's about to dispense knowledge. And it is true. He will clue you. He will tell you something you didn't know and need to know.

Bill Squires is truly an enigma—puzzling; mysterious; contradictory; difficult to understand; a genius; possessing exceptional and natural ability; distinctive; a guardian spirit; and much more. This is a story of a man born with a late-diagnosed defective heart who suffered great childhood hardship and stunted growth, yet remained focused and determined enough to blossom to the world arena and who touched many lives with his coaching talent and selfless benevolence that despite successfully sacrificing his own fame for those of his charges, nevertheless is rightfully revered and honored to this day.

The process used for this book to capture decades of living was a journey unto itself. It began pedestrian enough with countless interviews, calls, follow-ups, editing, and over 124 hours of detailed conversations that unearthed everything contained "between [his] ears." It was immensely revealing—previously forgotten tales from his youth; hidden stories of greatness; training secrets and myths— some even he had thought lost; an emotional catharsis; and the humorous and comical. To prepare for each interview, I would explain the time period we were going to cover next so he could focus and prepare for that time frame. His attention would be laser-pointed. But throughout this adventure of revelation, he lived with an uncertain future in regard to his health, which he at first kept to himself. He grew weak. He was in a hurry. He was so focused on 80 years' worth of details that this endeavor consumed him. So intense were our talks and so intent was he to get all of this on record that within a month after we finished our initial last interview, he suffered a stroke. When I visited him at the hospital the day after he was admitted, I asked about the last thing he remembered. He recalled that the night before the stroke, he was thinking of how the book could end. The irony of his own comment lost on a stroke-affected mind, I asked if we could have a different ending. He laughingly agreed.

It amazes me still that the funny, gregarious, outgoing, boisterous man he is today grew from a weak, sickly, shuttered, shy presence of a boy he once was. That he survived an early undetected (then misdiagnosed) heart malfunction, and physical, social, and emotional pain as a child, to grow into adulthood and flourish as a teacher and instructor of international champions is beyond the scope of possibilities most—he included—would have predicted. And, of course, there were more stories, anecdotes, happenstances, and comical situations that one person should have had the pleasure of in a lifetime. I wanted him to open up and opine, which he did with great honesty, emotion, and candor. He is such a fount of wisdom that I decided to feature only his voice instead of also that of others. I thought it best to hear it all from the horse's mouth. And that was bountiful, too, as my original draft was around 235,000 words!

As he often prophesizes and is quoted in his 1979 *Improving Your Running* training book, "Success is that place on the road where preparation and opportunity meet, but too few people recognize it because it comes disguised as sweat and work. Have a good sense of humor, a big dose of patience, and a dash of humility, and you will be rewarded many-fold throughout your running career." It is hoped that the serious and the humorous convey the totality of the man in such a way that not only will you be entertained, but perhaps you will unapologetically also learn something. Because through it all is an amazing person who has affected many lives. It doesn't matter who a person is—rich, poor, male, female, famous, common, talented, novice—they're all important to him.

Also important to me—as a former newspaper editor, no doubt—was the accuracy of every fact and story herein. Originating from a man in his eighties, every effort was then made via official records, sources, websites, and published coverage and reports, to verify, confirm, and corroborate all names, locations, dates, events, times, records, and anything else featured. If any of that research failed in any way, I then relied and drew upon the recollections of that man in his eighties in the hopes it is understood from where it came. In addition, there are some events included about which have been previously dissected and widely written. Such events are not rehashed in an effort to repeat what has already been described, but rather to offer a fresh view from a man whose own presence and opinion had yet to be fully mined. I once joked to him that he has forgotten more about coaching than most of us will ever know ourselves; to wit he responded with the Squireism, "Yeah, but I'll remember it later." Fortunately, he remembered it now.

CHAPTER 1

"BULLCRAP! WE WANTED TO BEAT THEM ALL."

To date, 1975's Boston Marathon field was the largest ever recorded in its historically-massive canon. Within that field were five former champions and a handful of writers and historians of the sport. It was Patriots' Day, the Massachusetts state holiday named in recognition of the start of the American Revolutionary War in Lexington and Concord between British soldiers and the local Minutemen. It was Monday, April 21, the 79th edition of the race, filled to the brim with 2,340 runners. There was a semi-seasoned future national Hall of Fame coach eyeballing his local charge—a relative "newcomer" who belonged to a relative new club—wearing bib number 14 for his place in the previous year's Boston. While this was the runner's sixth overall marathon start, which included a pair of course-record (CR) victories, it was also his third attempt at Boston, of which he dropped out in 1973. Along with a new brand of running shoes on his feet from Oregon Nike rep Steve Prefontaine—mailed to him two weeks before Boston; five weeks before the legendary Pre's untimely death—a 27-year-old Bill Rodgers also wore dark shorts, white headband, white gloves, and a short-sleeve T-shirt. His blue-collar outfit stood out among the slick singlets and bare hands and foreheads of the favorites. He also stood out as a member of the budding 20-month-old Greater Boston Track Club (GBTC), coached by 42-year-old Bill Squires, already a proven commodity in the world of running.

Squires knew there was great potential in Rodgers, of course. Six weeks prior to Boston, Rodgers returned from the International Association of Athletics Federations (IAAF) World Cross-Country Championships in Morocco, as the third-best 12K runner in the world, and also just set a 30K CR in March. The Thursday before Boston, Squires last met with Rodgers and offered him the final pieces of advice before Marathon Monday. "I told him there's a carbohydrate diet, so stick with it. No beer, no mayonnaise crap—geez, he used to like mayonnaise—no pickle juice. None of that stuff. Just carbohydrates, like pasta. And forget the meatballs. No salad, no juice the morning of the race. A pancake and a half, a waffle and a half, is good. No coffee. Just water." As for the race itself, "I told him I want him to feel loose and to *use* these people. *Use these people*! They're better, they've been down the road, and usually they are *going*! I told him if he sees some crazy guy and he sees the other flock of foreign guys going, you know, be smart! I told him that's how he got his 14th—he picked off better guys who over-raced the course. He's run this course enough, there was no problem with that, and he's run it quick."

For the benefit of the local media and competitors, Squires downplayed expectations. He did not want a target on Rodgers's back, so he often informed the press that he thought Rodgers would be in the top 10, perhaps top five. He kept glossing over his runner's talent, despite the 34:20 a month earlier at the IAAF 12K, and the two CR wins at the 1973 Bay State Marathon and 1974 Philadelphia Marathon. "I said to the press we were kind of aiming for fifth. Bullcrap! Aiming for fifth? We wanted to beat them all!"

Sealed in an envelope and locked in the glove compartment of his car, Squires prior to the start scribbled on a piece of paper his prediction for Rodgers. It simply read "First place. 2:11:05." This was quite ambitious, since it was more than eight minutes faster than the personal record (PR) Rodgers set at the previous year's Boston, and just 35 seconds over the current CR of 2:10:30 set in 1970 by Ron Hill, who, in 1975, was wearing bib number one alongside Rodgers. During the race, Squires planned to first see Rodgers in Wellesley at around 15 miles, and then again six miles later at the bottom of the Boston College (BC) hill, near Lake Street, at the Chestnut Hill campus in Brookline where GBTC trained. "I didn't care about seeing him at 10K because I knew he'd know enough to just float. And I had told him to listen to what I tell him each time I see him."

Just prior to Newton Lower Falls, at around 15 miles—and the first of the little rumblings of hills before the big ones in Newton—Squires saw Rodgers as the runners exited Wellesley via the Route 128 highway overpass and headed toward the Newton-Wellesley Hospital at around 16.5 miles. "He was in fourth or fifth place then, and I think Jerome Drayton was in first. He was cruising then, and I yelled, 'Good, good, good, Bill!' and did the illegal thing and I go out there with water," recalled Squires, whose delivery of water at the time was technically against the rules as coaches and their athletes weren't to interact during competition. However, at this point in the race, Rodgers was running alone, just behind the small group of leaders, which afforded Squires the accessibility without interfering with other runners. "I always tell my runners how many seconds back they are. You always see me with a fresh watch." This was a strategic place on the course for Squires because he trained his runners to begin their race near the overpass. After mile 16, there is a slight incline over the highway, followed by a flat recovery period near the hospital and along the Woodland Golf Club in Auburndale, which leads to the right-hand fire-station turn onto Commonwealth Avenue and *the* hills. "I'd give the times there because that's when my guys can start to beat the other people. That's where we do the surge-and-pickups in training. The minute they get over that hill at Route 128, I'd have them bang away from the hospital to the fire station. Then a cool hill, and then *bing, bing, bing*, up the big ones."

Rodgers dug in on Commonwealth Avenue and the Newton Hills, particularly Heartbreak Hill, the 88-vertical foot, 600-meter rise at the most inopportune location between miles 20 and 21. He was in a zone, all race long, having carefreely stopped to drink water and to tie his shoelaces. This was his moment. "At the bottom of the hill, he's flying. He's coming off the hill, and I go, 'Cruise! Cruise! Put it in cruise control. And then roll over the remaining smaller hills.' We had talked about the rolly hills; to roll in there. I had hoped he would be in first place by then or be no more than third. I told him he would be in control by then and be able to know from the crowd how far back the runners are because that's when they didn't have crowd control. It was crazy."

Rodgers fed off the crowd. He was a local runner with many New England ties—born in Connecticut; graduate of Wesleyan University; resided just outside of Boston; and was about to receive his master's at BC. So he felt right at home on these roads. And fortunately, as Squires hoped and planned, all eyes were on Hill and Drayton. Since Squires last saw Rodgers with about four miles to go, and he himself made his way to the finish, Rodgers continued to create more distance from the rest of the field. He was in total control and on record pace. Due to the fact the race's homestretch of Boylston Street—and its location to the entire area of the finish line—was obviously closed to vehicular traffic, Squires illegally parked his car several blocks behind the finish line, near the Eliot Lounge, part of the historic Eliot Hotel at the corner of Commonwealth and Massachusetts avenues. The lounge, which featured its own separate entrance on Massachusetts Avenue, as well as an entryway from inside the hotel, was a popular runners' cathedral of libation with a name not reflective of its running memorabilia-laden interior décor. It's where Squires often frequented and occupied his well-worn Coach's Corner seat at the end of the bar from where he routinely dispensed his words of wisdom.

"There weren't any credentials for the finish area, but I knew enough to wear my AAU (Amateur Athletic Union) jacket with the shield on it, which meant something. And I was already head of the officials association, so I could get myself right out to the finish line." In 1975, however, although police and officials tried their best, crowd control was still at a minimum. On Boylston, cheering spectators stood dozens deep, which created a boisterously noisy funnel to the finish. It was equally congested at the finish line for the leader, who oftentimes barely recognized when to stop running until he was nearly on top of the painted line. Police on motorcycles and horseback added to the thickness of the masses, as spectators and officials blended together like an ocean of humanity and equine, pointing the way to the end of the race.

"I heard on the radio he had broke away, but I didn't know by how much. Then, at the fire station on Boylston that was near Hereford Street, the firefighter guys got out there and they started getting all the people crazy, with their bells and sirens," noted Squires of the point in the race several blocks from the finish where runners turn onto Boylston en route to the finish. "They were listening to it on the radio." Rodgers indeed broke away, so convincingly and resoundingly, that he set a new CR and an American record (AR) in 2:09:55. He chipped off 35 seconds from the four-year-old Boston mark. He also destroyed his previous PR. Having only about 18 months with Rodgers—as he eagerly prospected what he could do with even more time together—Squires watched with great pride as his pupil became only the ninth different American to win Boston since Clarence DeMar's record-setting seventh and final victory 45 years earlier in 1930. "I was in the back row and I saw Billy finish, and I think I watched the top 10 finish. I congratulated him. Then," Squires recalls with a laugh, "they put on these frigin' horse blankets—they were old surplus army blankets. They were the itchiest bitches in the world."

Rodgers won by just under two minutes over second place, and by more than three minutes over Hill in fifth, whose CR he just broke. Squires ventured toward the lower-level parking garage under the Prudential building where runners were directed after finishing. After a brief visit, he exited the celebratory hoopla, as was his wont. "When I was leaving, a radio guy wanted me to talk to him," said Squires, who while live on the air was asked what he was going to do now and where he was headed. "I said that I left my car down by the Eliot. And of course, the Eliot went nuts [to hear him mention them on the radio]. Billy also said that on the radio [in a separate interview]. Then Billy came in later and ordered some drink, a Blue Whale, whatever that was," he recalled of the cocktail of vodka, Blue Curacao liqueur, rum, gin, and a cherry or two that he recollects was the creation of Eliot bartenders Fran Coffey and Ed Jones. "The regular TV people came in, and then it became *the* place."

Squires avoided the post-race media attention and awards ceremony, and eventually returned to his car, which, thankfully, did not have a parking ticket. The early exit was typical of Squires, who rather than for himself, preferred his runners receive the attention. "You know what? If I go there, that means *I* get press. I'd get as much press as them. But I want the story to *be* them." And Rodgers was certainly *the* story. But he was so new to the majority of those covering the race that in the newspaper he was incorrectly referred to as Will Rogers. Even more confusing was no one seemed to have understood what was written on his T-shirt. Just prior to the start, his wife handwrote with a marker the word BOSTON in large uppercase letters and below it the initials GBTC for the newfound running club.

Squires sat in his car after the long day, which began early in the morning, and reflected upon his young club. He reached over to the glove compartment and dug out that piece of paper that read: "First place. 2:11:05." While off by 70 seconds, he was spot on about the place.

CHAPTER 2

"I'VE GOT WINGS NOW!"

William Joseph Squires was the first of his family to have bestowed upon him natural United States citizenship when he was born at Carney Hospital in South Boston, Mass., on November 16, 1932. Several decades earlier, in 1898, was born his mother Florence, the eldest of nine children of the Trainor family, in the city of County Cork in Ireland. Those from *Corcaigh*, on Ireland's southern shores, are infused with the rebellious, survival, and hearty nature from the creation and evolution of their land, as legend purports it was founded around the turn of the sixth to seventh centuries upon the search-and-destroy mission of St. Finbarr to kill the last dragon in Ireland. Following similar dreams of generations before her, Florence, in 1902, was four years old when the family traveled to England. After a year of work, they could afford only the storage-class level of a coal ship for the seven-day trip to its first stop in Newfoundland.

The first name of William came from Florence's father, a trained carpenter who in his early twenties, with two other men, built the chapel in his village. The middle name of Florence's first born was in recognition of St. Joseph, husband of the blessed Mary, mother of Jesus. A patron saint of many designations, St. Joseph is the patron saint against doubt and hesitation. Florence's father, known to most as Captain Bill, had also built a 50-foot freighter to assist Newfoundlanders caught in the rough, icy waters of the Atlantic Ocean, and to move families to other parts of the island. These waters are marked by the majestic daggers of floating chunks of ice seared off of glaciers from nearby Greenland to the north. Icebergs silently glide along the eastern shores of Labrador and Newfoundland for thousands of years, so steadily and dependable that the passageway along the coast is known as Iceberg Alley. "My mother said…sometimes she'd see animals on them. And from the first of May to the last sighting sometime in June, the radio station would have a contest that if you could pick the time it would go by here or go by there, you'd win a prize. They also had a contest for the last one of the year. If you guessed when it was, you'd win a grand prize."

Florence's family moved to the fishing community of Admiral's Cove in Cape Broyle Harbour, just south of the Newfoundland capital of St. John's, on the Avalon Peninsula, the most southeastern portion of Newfoundland. One cold, April evening when Florence was 14 years old, she and her family of five were asleep when they awoke to the penetrating, alarming wails of warning sirens along the shore. It was April 15, 1912. Four hundred miles to the east, three days after sailing from Southampton, England, for New York, the Royal Mail Ship (RMS) *Titanic* hit an iceberg and telegraphed distress calls to the Marconi wireless station on Cape Race, on the Avalon Peninsula. These calls, which reportedly began at 10:25 p.m. Cape Race time—12:15 a.m. on the passenger liner—were to be relayed to her originally-scheduled destination of New York City. Florence's father and his five-man crew took his freighter, with food and assistance, to the chilly Atlantic. The current was strong in that area, and some of the sinking ship's debris and victims made their way to the shores of Newfoundland. The Canadian Navy advised him to "pick up any remains of anything" and bring them to the dock. It was soon realized that his main purpose was recovery. "He never told my mother if he brought back bodies, but there were tons of them in the water. The children were not allowed to go down to the docks because they [bodies] started floating in," Squires recalled being told of the hundreds of victims.

Around this time, Florence, after the eighth grade, attended a separate school and learned to be a nanny. Squires's father, coincidentally, also learned a trade or two—carpentry, fixing motors—in a similar school, run by the Congregation of the Irish Christian Brothers. "They were poor, but the Irish Christian Brothers were over there, and they knew that these were the poor Irish people who would probably never leave there. And they all had big families of eight, nine people."

Murt Squires, in Ireland, was born two years after his future wife, Florence Trainor, in 1900, and settled as a youth in Renews (later known as Renews-Cappahayden), a small fishing village south of Admiral's Cove in Newfoundland. Florence, who by her mother, a nurse, was named after women's nursing pioneer

Florence Nightingale, had not met Murt, but knew of him because he played in a band. Murt played since the fifth grade. His school held musical instruments tryouts and students tried different ones until they found one they could play. Murt played the accordion, saxophone, and trumpet, all by ear. "In those days, the people in the band would play at the dances. And the dances were big. I mean, what else did they have? They didn't have movies then. They had them in America—the silent movies—but they didn't have them there. So they would have the dances, and the girls would make little sandwiches and decorations, and they'd have tea and whatever. The junior band would play between 7:00 p.m. to 8:30 p.m., and then get home to mind their brothers and sisters. Then the senior band, which were the older guys, would play. And what they did was, as the older men got better, everyone passed down their instruments to the school."

Just prior to Murt's 16th birthday, his father, a heavy smoker, died. He was in his 50s. When Murt did turn 16, the age at which work papers could be obtained, the teenager worked 10-hour days on a whaling ship for five months. "They go right out until the thaw lets the ship back in. They were big—like factory ships. He said they'd catch the whales and he'd have shears and they'd be there cutting it up. Whatever was left, they'd throw over the sides and other fish would eat the stuff. The minute the light came up, he was working. And he put in a few hours late at night just to get the stuff always settled for the next day. For lunch, they'd carry it on their person because they were working and working and working. But that was a big sum of money when he came home. That took care of the family for way more than a year for the five months he was out." When Murt's brother opened a grocery store and became the family provider, Murt traveled to the United States. He sailed through Ellis Island en route to New York, where he became a trolley car driver in Brooklyn. Still in his late teens, he was on his own. "He finds a one-room place to live where there were a lot of Irish in Brooklyn. I mean, the brogue! Anywhere else, they'd correct the way they'd speak. But not where there's all these Irish. So their brogues intensified."

Eighteen-year-old Florence, at around the same time as Murt, in 1916, left Newfoundland for New York. She became a nanny on upscale Fifth Avenue. While not a live-in nanny, she found a room within the Irish community in Brooklyn, and attended the social occasions put together by those immigrants from Ireland by way of Newfoundland and environs. At one local dance, this petite woman from County Cork noticed this handsome man from a town outside of Dublin, and they began to talk. "Both of them were kind of shy people, but somehow they go, 'You from…?' 'Yeah. You from…?' 'Yeah.' And he played his accordion in the band for food or some drinks, and everyone sang along to the Irish songs because they all knew them." Prior to their encounter in Brooklyn, the paths of Florence Trainor and Murt Squires had previously been near hits, as they lived no more than 140 miles apart in Ireland, and less than 20 miles from each other in Newfoundland. Within a couple years of when they first met, they married in Brooklyn in the fall of the start of the Great Depression. They moved to the heavily Irish settlement of South Boston, Mass., and lived atop a drugstore pharmacy on Broadway. Located along Dorchester Bay, *Southie* is dense with Catholic churches, Irish pubs, and Irish-American social clubs. Its Irish residents were well represented by a fire and police force filled with fellow countrymen. And political offices in Boston City Hall and the Massachusetts State House also held their ear. Their most well-known political representatives included Fitzgerald family patriarch John Francis "Honey Fitz" Fitzgerald, Boston's mayor and the state's governor; Honey Fitz's grandson, John Fitzgerald Kennedy, a House representative, United States senator, and the 35th president of the United States; and James Michael Curley, governor of Massachusetts and four-time mayor of Boston.

Florence for years worked as a nanny for a direct-descendant family of Declaration of Independence signer Robert Treat Paine. Murt became a Merchant Seaman and found work on freighters. With South Boston an ideal port, there was plenty of work for a man who did not mind the sea and did not mind the work. "And whatever it was, he wanted to finish it off. That was one thing he always said to me—'You start something, Billy, you finish it.' And I have." And so respected was Florence that upon her departure from the Paine's, she received $500 from the family. "That was during the Depression! You buy houses with that!" He joked of his own arrival, "It was a goodbye present that was given because Sir William was born."

For her son's entrance into the world, Florence on November 13, 1932, made her way to New England's first Catholic hospital with her first cousin, Madeline, her maid of honor. It was a dangerous birth, as the boy was a breech baby, having turned himself around to greet the world bottom-end first. After a second day of labor, and since Murt was a seaman and out to sea at the time, counselors from the Chelsea Naval Hospital were summoned. "She said they all came in with their white uniforms on and everything. She said she was so weak; and she weighed

104 pounds. She said I came down the wrong way." He laughs. "At that time, they didn't do the C-section. They were afraid she'd bleed to death. They didn't know what to do with my mother. So, they cut her to get me, and held on that she wouldn't bleed to death. My aunt said they extracted me after just under 74 hours, and she looked just like a ghost. She said I was all rosy cheeks with big, blue eyes, and everyone in the nursery goes, 'Oh, he's the cutest little thing. And he looks so healthy.' That's how I came in." Two-and-a-half weeks later, the Squires clan returned home as a family of three. They later moved from South Boston to the Dorchester section of Savin Hill, where the young boy prepared for first grade as a typical seven-year-old. At the required school physical examination, however, the doctor, who visited the school to perform exams one class at a time, detected a heart anomaly. "After the test, he told my mother we'd have to see a doctor on Beacon Street in Boston. We had to go see a specialist. He told my mother that I had a bit of a problem. I had something wrong with my heart. It wasn't working right."

There was not an immediate conclusive diagnosis, but it was advised that the boy stay home for four months with little to no activity in an attempt to rest his heart. Four months in the top of the three-story house in which they lived turned into eight months, his entire first grade of school. He was now home-schooled. "Then the doctor said to don't have me walk too much, but we could use the [baby] carriage. Geez, I can imagine what I was like then. I was above average in height, and just imagine the kids looking at me in the carriage. I remember my mother would take me down to get an ice cream, and the kids would look at me." It was a lonely, difficult time for a young boy to be so confined to a baby carriage or his room. No social or physical interaction or development with other kids his age, no fresh air or skinned knees. No real kid-oriented entertainment on the radio at that time. And, of course, no television then, circa 1938 to 1940. It was a punishing, solitary existence for a boy who could not feel what was ailing him. All he knew, as it was explained to him, was that he had a weak heart. "I'd listen to the radio, and I'd look out the windows. I watched the kids coming home from school and wanted to be out there. Now and then [as an adult] I can go back in my mind, I can go look at that window, and I swear to God I have flashbacks at the frigin' boringness of my life." He recalls taking a well-known cure-all at the time called Father John's Medicine, billed as cough medicine, but whose legend grew to possess great healing qualities for many ills. "I'd drink this crap all the time. There was a picture of this priest on the bottle, so you'd probably think this guy was a straight arrow. Any minister, rabbi, or anyone in those days—a pious person—you didn't question anything."

In school he was behind as well. He lacked math and number skills, and an example of his spelling being for the longest time cat would be spelled with a *k*, as he focused more on the phonetics than the spelling. Second grade was similar in that Florence picked up the lessons from school to be taught at home. They soon moved to Arlington Heights, near Symmes Hospital in Arlington, Mass. "A lot of hospitals were way up on hills. They looked at it as fresh air, but they didn't realize more people got heart attacks going up those hills, for crissakes! And that's why where we lived was called Cardiac Hill. They had chairs as you walked up so you could sit down and rest. From Arlington Heights, I'm looking down at all these buildings in Boston. We were that high up on the hill." On September 21, 1938, Squires experienced the most devastating hurricane to hit New England in nearly 70 years, known simply as the Great Hurricane of 1938. While those around him understood the inherent danger—with reported 100 mph winds and heavy rain that left nearly 700 people dead and 100,000 homeless—this young, sheltered boy viewed the natural disaster as fun and excitement. "We're up on the third floor, and from my room I watched the hurricane. Trees were coming down, shingles were coming off—this was the most entertainment I had since I lived there, and I told my mother I didn't want to leave! The landlady of the place was banging with pans, saying, 'Come down, Flo, and bring the boy! And bring some pillows and clothing!' We all went down to the cellar. We kept hearing the wind and lots of noise, but we didn't know what we were hearing. Then, no lights. To me, it was adventure. We go out the next day and, *wow*! All the big trees were banged in, houses were damaged, and the playground I used to look at [from the window] to see the kids play was filled with all these massive trees. And I said, 'Good.'" He laughed, since he was unable to play there anyway.

Within a year, a second boy, John Leonard Squires, was added to the family. And two years later, the United States entered World War II. Similar to when Florence heard the sirens in Newfoundland about the *Titanic*, her firstborn while he retrieved foul balls for 10 cents at town baseball games, heard an alarm in Arlington. "We heard the siren from the fire station and wondered what was going on. One of the cops comes by and says, 'We're at war with the Japanese.' I didn't know any Japanese. We knew the Chinese. The only guy we knew was the

Chinese guy who did the shirts." Florence worried about her son—who wanted to be a soldier, as kids that age said without realizing their words; and her husband—who at the time was out at sea with the Merchant Marine. In early 1942, Murt, who knew he could not be drafted because he was not an American citizen, went to enlist into the US Coast Guard but was turned away due to his age and his family of two young children. After his Merchant Marine duty, Murt worked on various fishing boats at the Fore River Shipyard in Quincy, and also as a rigger and electrical helper. Gas was rationed during the war, and he drove to and from work, so he always had stories to tell his family about what new buildings were being erected or anything else he could provide as sort of a tour guide. Because the family rarely went on trips during the war, these tales were exciting to the boys.

In 1943, when Billy was 11, and Johnny 4, Florence took her eldest to another specialist, Dr. Edward Carroll Sr., a Boston College grad. He was housed across the street from St. Agnes Parish, their church in Arlington, but mother and son still took the bus route that circumvented the hills so Billy could avoid the inclines. After being treated by so many doctors and adults, and never really having his health issues explained to him, for the first time in his young life, Billy felt he was being addressed on what he perceived as equal footing. "I come in and he goes, 'Hi, how are ya?' And he gives me a handshake, treating me like a real guy, and I go [in amazement], 'What?'" Florence explained the situation to the doctor, who ran the boy through several physical tests in the office that included jumping up and down on one foot and then with both, and some short spurts of running across the room. "He said, 'Okay, Mrs. Squires. This is a healthy young man. He has a heart murmur. Most heart murmurs go away at age 16. Now, from what I get, his pulse has gone down because of inactivity. Let him play, but within reason,'" Squires recalled of that glorious day. "Well, that was…I wanted to marry the guy! Geez! *I've got wings now*! I was out of the friggin' room—I wanted to play!"

So it was off to the playground and back to school. Several times a day he ran back and forth to home, climbed up the big hill of his street to his house, ran down the hill to school. He ran to school in the morning, ran home for lunch, back to school, and then home again. "Longing to play, I ran the big hill halfway up. In the spring, I ran all the way up. It's 700 yards long and steeper than Heartbreak Hill [of the Boston Marathon]." But as the eight-year-old entered third grade, there was still a problem academically. Those two years of basic isolation had stunted his educational growth. "I go back to school and I am lost. Lost! I am way behind.

I am like a mute. I was a mute from the time I was nine years old until the TV flashbulbs started at 20 at big meets in track and field [in college]. I was shell-shocked." Squires during those dozen years maintained an internal dialogue that took college life to become external and enable him to properly communicate. "I would say things that I was always saying to myself, internally. I would talk to my internal self, but I would never say it out loud. I think I was by myself for so long in that room, it made me withdraw. I had my head down so much, that's why I could always find money on the streets." He laughs. "But I'm telling you, I was a nerdling. Second-most shy in my high school class."

But with his brother, it was playtime. He liked being the big brother, and without even realizing it at the time, that connection, that sibling relationship, helped bring Billy out of his shell. But most of all, it was fun. "I was the oldest, so I tried to bring him along to things. I enjoyed it. He played sports with us [kids], and I tried to show him what I was doing, teach him things—passing the puck, shooting baskets. He was quick. And he was very, very sharp mentally. He'd pick things up fast. And he'd always ask questions, which I enjoyed because that's how I'd be. I always enjoyed that with him."

While still shy at school, to compensate, and to deflect any personal attention—whether in or out of school—he agreed with people even if he had no idea about the subject. "I pretended I understood. I became the biggest bluff in school. I wrote poorly because my spelling was not the best. I wasn't bad in math, but when it got to algebra and trigonometry and geometry, I would earn a C." Socially, at first, he hung around other students, but not necessarily forging deep friendships. Eventually, though, he made friends and played the typical boyhood games. He expanded his social horizons as a youngster during the war years. And as most boys did at that time, games were war-related in theme. One particular afternoon, in an unfinished basement of a neighborhood house being built, the kids played "parachute commando," where they jumped off elevated levels in the cellar to mimic soldiers who parachuted into battle. "I jumped down and there were two boards crossed over each other. I go down and I hit a two-by-four, and one of them swings up and hits me in the face." One end flipped up and slammed into his nose and left eye. Blood gushed out of his obviously broken nose, and so violently was the board's impact that it pushed his left eye inward with so much force he instantly lost his sight. The trauma severely damaged the cornea. His friend's mother brought him to the nearby hospital, while his buddy ran down the street to get Florence, who had to walk to see her son. At the hospital, his nose required 35 stitches, but it was feared the eye would be lost.

"They call the priest in because they may have to remove the eye. My mother's there, crying, and the priest comes in and he has a little flower relic. My mother always used to say, 'Praise the little flower,'" noted Squires of his mother's devotion to St. Therese, a 24-year-old French woman who died in 1897 and reportedly possessed great spiritual love for God, and had loved flowers so much that she often said she was the "little flower of Jesus" in God's garden. "He put this flower, or a piece of wood she touched or something like that, on my eye. I had a red eye, a black eye, and a real good shiner for months. And I had a patch over my eye when I went back to school, which screwed me up more. I had more trouble when I tried to breathe. And then they were putting glasses on me, but I didn't need glasses because my other eye was stronger. So I took that off when I could. As an adult, I have hardly any vision in that [damaged] eye. Someone sitting right next to me is a blur. I wouldn't know who it was [looking] through that eye."

While all of this—heart murmur, broken nose, lost eyesight—occurred by the time he was 11, he was more concerned about his mother and how she coped with these emergencies. "I got through that crisis, but my mother had [to worry about] my heart, which was one thing, and then being blind in one eye was another. But I never made anything out of this [injured] eye. I didn't want my mother to worry. I always told her I could see great. But I couldn't see." At the time of the eye accident, Murt was away at sea. When he returned home shortly after his son's two-week stay in the hospital, "I can remember my mother telling him that I look a little different. Then my father goes, 'What? Holy…! Flo, what the heck is this?'" I had a black eye, my nose was all zigzag and it has a bandage on it. But I would make jokes about it, like I looked like a pirate with the eye patch, or there was a [1932] movie called 'Scarface,' so I would say that was me. And she'd go, 'Oh, you were a beautiful baby,' like mothers do."

Squires continued to run back and forth to school, and up and down the big hill on his street. But Florence worried that he was not getting in enough playtime, as per doctor's orders, so another move was contemplated. Around the same time, his longtime playmate, who was with him in the cellar during parachute commando, moved away. That forced Squires to travel even farther away each time to find another kid with whom to play. He made his way down the hill to play, and as a result, often returned home late due to the extra time involved. So the Squires family moved about a mile south to East Arlington, near Spy Pond. "My mother decided the hill was too damn much for me. She was a wheeler-dealer—I mean, she turned the 500 [dollar] down payment from the Robert Treat Paine family and ended up selling our house for the cost of a new Cape home after telling the realtor they had to sell her house before she bought a new one. And she bought this home that was a mecca [for a kid]! Within about a half-mile away, I found out, on my way home from school on the first or second day, about these three kids on Beacon Street. They'd cut down on Beacon Street [en route to and from school] and I'd have another half-mile to go. They were nice kids. They'd wait for me and we'd go walk down together. They asked me to come and play, and I'd say I had to be home at quarter to six. And all their mothers were like alarm clocks, between 5:30 and quarter to 6. So I'd leave myself another eight or 10 minutes so I'd be home on time. And my mother liked them"

Squires caddied at Winchester Golf Course, near Upper Mystic Lake, and played ice hockey, which he loved. He played among a group of kids at The Rink, an outdoor open area of stagnant water connected to Lower Mystic Lake. It was naturally flooded, and firefighters applied a surface skim when they tested the hydrants or hoses. The kids also pitched in two dollars each and parents drove them to the Skating Club of Boston. It was primarily a figure skating club, but to earn extra money the club scheduled ice time for hockey. Some of the neighborhood boys, who called themselves the Beacon Street Bums, were good enough to play in school and they often beat teams from neighboring towns. They played mostly early weekend mornings, before the juniors, high school teams, and figure skaters. Surrounded by junior-high kids his own age with whom he felt comfortable, Squires opened up more through sports, where he participated and excelled yet also blended in with a group. He was still quiet, but nevertheless became just one of the kids and not that secluded boy in the baby carriage at whom everyone seemed to stare. And when not on the ice, there was a local cornfield that served as a gridiron when the farmer's maze was removed.

He was like a kid in a candy store; that candy store being outdoor life. With the go-ahead from the doctor, his free time was filled with sports and games. The kids had also told him about a Boy Scouts of America camping trip to the woods of Bedford, just beyond Hanscom Air Force Base. "They said we'd be outdoors in tents just like in the army, and I go, 'Wow, that's great!' I didn't have to join, but the leader, the guy, was a Marine from the war and when he came back he was asked to help out the kids in the neighborhood. And he'd take kids on the camping trips even if they weren't Scouts." A few of the Beacon Street kids, including Squires, joined the group and traveled the dozen or so miles to the campsite. After a few visits, Squires was hooked. He enjoyed the "primativeness" of the excursions of hiking, cooking, building tents. He learned to swim, and even won a boxing match. By the time of his third camping trip, in the May before his high school freshman year, Squires joined the Scouts and was familiar with the surroundings and responsibilities, enough so that they thought he had leadership qualities. "I don't know why." He laughs. "But I listen and I respect people in authority—which is from my parents—and I did what they said when they ran the camp. And I liked reading the books they had to get badges. You read the books and they told you how to get badges. Anything I started, I finished. That's a discipline I have had passed down to me from my parents."

The kids learned different lessons for subsequent badges, one of which involved an ax to cut down dead trees. During a lunch break, Squires and a fellow Scout cut down some extra trees and when he swung down the ax, "Bang!" Squires describes. "It goes right through my ankle. I didn't even know it." The blade was so sharp that after the cut sliced through his left boot and ankle, Squires handed the ax to his friend so he could make a few more chops at the tree, as he failed to immediately realize what had just transpired. "I felt nothing. Nothing! I hand the ax to the guy, and of course there's blood on it. He looks at it, and then all of sudden out of my boot, blood was starting to squirt out." It was a severe injury. As he was transported to the hospital, "I hear them say 'We're bringing this kid and he's got his leg cut off.' I remember hearing that. I'm going, 'Is my leg cut off?' I'm not feeling any pain. Nothing!" When they released the tourniquet, "All of a sudden it starts pulsating again, and I saw all the white towels all bloodied." With no anesthesia for Squires, a surgeon repaired the cut ligaments and nerves with nearly 80 stitches. The cut was so deep that it nearly hit the bone. The doctor explained the situation to Florence, and said her boy required a special shoe and that he would drag his foot a lot. After about a week in the hospital, Squires began to put pressure on the foot and started to walk again, dragging his foot along the way. "*Then* it hurt."

He missed more school, was unable to play hockey and football, and the ankle became incredibly sensitive to the touch and tight shoes, which contrasted the advice of the doctor who wanted him to wear boots for the support. But the boy continued his physical therapy, such as it was then, and focused on returning to athletics.

CHAPTER 3

IRISH SOD

Attending Arlington High School in Massachusetts was an awakening. Still behind academically—seemingly always trying to catch up—he grew and matured as an athlete. Despite his malformed heart, one legally-blind eye, broken nose, and nearly-severed ankle, the introverted soft-spoken "monk"—as he often described himself—won three state championships in the mile; set the school mile record indoors (4:22.6) and outdoors (4:22.8); and was named to the 1952 *Parade Magazine* All-American Team. He was so successful that as an upperclassman, a large paper shopping bag was used to contain all the college mail he received from interested coaches. The final decision was the University of Notre Dame.

With a scholarship and $150 in his pocket, Squires on September 15, 1952, first stepped foot on Midwest Irish sod, and was assigned Zahm Hall on the North Quad, one of only four dorms on the Indiana campus. For regular freshmen, the average of a 15-hour, five-course workload was the norm. As a student-athlete, however, it was recommended to take a 12-hour, four-course semester of general introductory core courses such as English, history, math, science (in addition to the scheduled times for games/meets, practices, training, travel). Student-athletes could begin 15-hour, five-course schedules in their second semester freshman year. If a student missed one, there was summer school to maintain the path to graduation. "And we had a crazy thing for freshmen at Notre Dame. Athletes had to get at least a 77, which would be a C+, to graduate. For everyone else, the passing grade was 70. Seventy! We had to average a 77! It was like a weeding-out process."

Before he met any of his professors, Squires greeted his future track coach, Alex Wilson. A four-time Canadian Olympic medalist and All-American Irish alum, Wilson had returned to the university in 1950 after nearly 20 years as a coach at Loyola University Chicago. Only the fifth track coach in Notre Dame history—the first of whom in 1916 was Knute Rockne—Wilson had months earlier with Arlington High coach William "Doc" McCarthy, visited Squires at his home and sold Notre Dame to Florence. Wilson inherited a below-average team which in two months' time was minus an exodus of athletes who had wanted to run specifically for E.R. "Doc" Handy, who Wilson replaced. Squires noticed, "There wasn't too much hope for this team. The guys that came with me said they'll run cross-country, and Wilson said okay if they wanted to come along, but they might be the junior varsity group. We had to go around and do a figure-eight run. I was so far ahead of everyone else, and I had only done two weeks of work. And there were two seniors there!"

Unlike most runners at the time, the approach to cross-country and track and field competition that Squires brought with him was an outlook previously unseen in such an organized, methodical, procedural manner. For example, he warmed up before he ran, and when asked about it said it made him feel better. This was at a time when most runners were unaware of its merits. "I got that from Doc McCarthy. He said the proper way to warm up was at least a 20- to 25-minute run—slow—and then work your way up. I might be doing a seven-minute pace and I'd be down to actually run five minutes because I could run under 4:21 in high school, so running five minutes was easy. That was my warm-up. Then I did my strides—two or three 100-yard strides. And then I'd wash my mouth out with water. A lot of times I'd even carry my own bottle of water. There were no plastic bottles like now. Everything was glass or a jar." Squires marveled that other runners did not warm up. "You had these jokers that said, 'Save it for the race.' I used to say, 'Ever start a car on a cold day?' You let it run for at least 30 seconds. Let the oil go through. That was old Doc's theory. Your muscles are cold. And Doc said you could walk slow right after your race for 50, 60 yards—don't walk too far—and then run for about five to six minutes to warm down. He said you want to have your muscles at least relaxed from the hard race. And he said there's a difference between a runner and a racer. A runner is in the race and he's fine and he does well. A racer makes the race—he's up there in the top three spots. And the longer he stays there, he'll never be worse than third, and he should be either first or second. He told me to don't be afraid of feeling very tired at the end of a race. 'You're expending yourself, but as time goes on, you're going to get stronger and you'll be getting closer to the finish line without feeling very tired.' So those attributes I used in high school and against the college kids I ran against."

Even as a collegiate freshman, there was something about Squires toward which Wilson gravitated. The work ethic and leadership Squires imbued from McCarthy impressed Wilson. "He said to me, on the side, 'Between you and I, we're going to have a special program. I've got this guy...' And so on. He had this plan. And after that first run, the other guys were asking me about what kind of training I did. They asked about the distances I ran and any fast runs." Almost immediately, Squires became the center of attention. He possessed a seemingly dormant level of confidence that searched for a way out. While he may have seen himself as quiet and shy, those around him recognized leadership qualities and even a coaching mentality. "I guess they liked what I did. I warmed up, I ate very little before a competition, and they would laugh at me at first. You see, at home in high school, my mother would make me eggs and ham and stuff, and I would almost get sick on it after I ran. So I learned. When we'd go on the road [in college], we'd get $15 to eat, and I'd put it in my pocket and spend it after I ran. I used to envision that steak and all that crap in my stomach, so I had Jell-o or tea and toast. The guys would look at me, but I was right."

Cross-country competed weekly, except freshman year when there were only four regular meets—two home, two away—plus one open championship tournament to fill out the season, in accordance with National Collegiate Athletic Association (NCAA) rules that freshmen were ineligible to compete on the varsity. The reduced schedule was intentional in order to allow underclassmen more time for studies. When asked about the half-mile, Squires informed Wilson that he had run the event only twice—once in 1:56—and a third-place finish in the 1000 yards at Boston Garden in his first competitive event at that distance. Wilson, an undefeated half-mile Irish "thinclad" from 1928-1932, was again impressed. Practices consisted of running on the nearby golf course and the incorporation of long intervals and repeat miles because of the five-mile distance of the course. Squires, for his part as a freshman, ran five-minute miles with short rest periods. A typical program example was a 4:55 first mile, followed by another sub-5:00 mile—near 4:58—and so on. "I could do it because I had some of that from Doc. But many of my teammates, first of all, didn't warm up enough, and I had to do all the leading. I wasn't trying to break them. I knew enough that I wanted a person to help me carry the load. You want to do it right so you can get more in the workout. And we'd work with the varsity, but only two days a week because we were freshmen."

Squires trained for speed, not endurance. He lived at the track. "I was always speed. I ended up being one of the most speed-trained outstanding athletes. Not many people beat me. And I'm doing it off 28 to 31 miles a week. Killing myself running three to five times on weekends. And Mondays and Wednesdays were bloodbaths with pure speed all on the track with short rests." One of the biggest differences Squires noticed between high school and college cross-country, other than the talent level, of course, was the terrain. It was *all* on grass, as opposed to high school courses of grass, roads, paths, trails. And harriers always wore spikes in college because they'd be pulling on the fairway grass. But by the time the regular season ended, he was confident and "seasoned," as best a freshman could be. He came in third in his first national-level collegiate competition, the 1952 Junior AAU Cross-Country Championships—open to anyone under 20 years of age—in a raw, windy, cold five-miler at Tam O'Shanter Golf Course, in Illinois.

Academically, Squires's first semester was rough. He earned a 72. He needed to do better. Much better. He found support in study groups. "The professors would speak quickly, and on the boards in the classrooms were all the material. When you came to class, the boards would slide back and forth with all the stuff written on it, and he'd go at it with a pointer. You had to keep up. That's what killed me my freshman year. Because I was a slow reader, I was behind. And I knew I had to do something. I eventually had to take a speed-reading course. I had to do it!"

For indoor track, Wilson incorporated runoffs—trial tryouts—for freshmen as a way to provide rookies with a chance to compete. Squires's first indoor experience was the relays at Michigan State University, home to a flat, eight-laps-to-a-mile cinder track. "The place was built in 1902. It was a good, solid track. The cinders were rolled, and it was dusty. The basketball court was inside the track, and when they would pound the ball, all the dust would move. Knute Rockne also jumped the pole vault there. He held the record, too."

Squires ran the last leg of the sprint medley relay (SMR). He ran the half-mile on its own, but a different approach was required when part of a relay. And with an eight-lap-to-a-mile track, he had to plan out four laps. "I figured out myself to go over to the side when you start; don't take the inside lane. You run extra, but I get to see everything. There's freedom there. You've got control. I just thought of that myself. I never heard of other people doing it. I'd just do things. With almost everything I do, I have to go through logical reasoning. I'll clue ya, I'm very good at it. I look at it and I always have options A, B, and C. I know if *this* is happening, then *this* will happen. I call it lane one-and-a-half. I would figure out the number of feet that I would lose if I'd go there on the outside on a 50-yard corner. I figured out that I'm losing probably two-and-a-quarter to three strides a lap. That's nothing. You see, you get a roll in lane two so when you're three-quarters of the way through, you get a roll where you can get moving again and push. I can determine the force on the corners, particularly on an indoor track. But it's totally different in a relay. What I had to do was almost put my head down for the first 50 yards to get really rolling and try to catch up. By nature, I'm not supposed to be a quarter-miler, but Wilson manufactured me into a very-short-distance man. He did give me really good speed, but he didn't give me the foundation to hold it through. I could run a better half in college than the mile."

When Squires received the baton, the Irish were in fourth. "He came up on me fast. I remember Coach had said to me, 'When he hits that line [before the exchange zone], you keep your eye on that line, stay in your lane, and *go!*' So, he comes in and *bang*—he's right up on my butt. Now, he doesn't slow down for me, I have to keep up to him. That's how you do it in a relay. You've got about 15 yards to do all of this in the exchange zone." They also used color codes as verbal signals during the exchange. They'd yell out commands of "red" or "green" as the situation warranted. And surprisingly, his bad eye did not affect Squires's ability to handle the exchanges. "I was about 12 yards back when I got the stick. And I made up about 12 yards in the first quarter-mile. It took me about 300 yards to get into second place. The kid from Kansas still had about six yards on me, but I couldn't catch him. They had a big lead. They beat us by a good 10 yards." The frosh Irish won silver. "That was big. Some conferences did have a freshmen championship. We were in the Central Collegiate Conference—which was so big with, like, 26 schools—and we were allowed to go and run the Michigan State Relays." (In the years after Squires graduated, Notre Dame became part of the Intercollegiate Association of Amateur Athletics of America—aka the ICAAAA or IC4A; and the NCAA eventually allowed freshmen to compete in varsity.)

For away meets, Notre Dame traveled with approximately 40 to 45 athletes, which included walk-ons who wouldn't be turned down. "You filled up the bus with whatever freshmen who came out. But we'd have runoffs on Tuesday and the top ones would come. And if you were really working at it, Coach would be good enough to give a guy at least one trip. But later, when you came out for the varsity team, it was more cutthroat. But we only had about four freshmen on scholarships, and all the other kids were walk-ons—and some very good walk-ons. When you get some good kids in, that can actually develop these walk-ons. The work ethic works."

During his second semester, the toll of running affected his study-group attendance. Plus, he felt he no longer needed it. "It was tough. The workload was way above my capacity. It was such a mental drag. I was worn out. It was easier for me to do the running—the fatigue wasn't there. But the classroom! For me, it was like I'd put things off. I didn't want to go to these things in the evenings—the lectures, the library, the reading, the groups. It got to the point where I couldn't study." The increased stress of running and studying also started to show. He lost weight to the point where he was given extra meal tickets to "beef up" at the dining hall (Squires began at 168 pounds and graduated 13 pounds lighter). Because of his first semester 72, he required at least an 81 to squeak by for the year. But he fell short. "A 73," he recalls of an academic dean's letter he received in the mail at home. "It said I was on probation, and if I do not attend summer school, which I could in my area, I'd flunk out." When he read that letter, his shoulders sank, his cheeks warmed, his eyes closed. It was the worst news he could receive. The only thing he could possibly do now was find out which schools around Arlington offered the class and spend the summer studying and attending that class. Or…"I just blew it off," said Squires, who also decided not to inform his parents about the situation.

Weeks passed, and in early July, Wilson got word of the matter and phoned Squires. But the track star stubbornly thought it was unfair to be asked to obtain a higher grade than other students, and he defiantly ignored the coach's advice. Squires rationalized that Notre Dame should give him the extra points he needed. In return, he promised to himself, he'd start attending the study groups and other academically related activities come next school year. For the remainder of the summer, Squires spent time at Harvard University in Cambridge—not in a classroom, but on its indoor track to train. And since he was not quite forthcoming with his parents, both of whom were still unaware of his probation status, Squires did not benefit from any homespun counsel. He was naïve to the impending implications; that is, until he returned to Notre Dame in the fall of 1953 for his first sophomore semester.

During his four years at Notre Dame, Squires can recall only two track and field athletes who dropped out of school. By mid-semester of his sophomore year, it quite easily could have been three. "I felt the pressure terribly. I enjoyed racing, but schoolwork was the pressure. But I knew that I could go to these other jock schools like Kentucky, Alabama, Texas, Nebraska, Seton Hall." He thought that way largely due, in part, to his solid performances as a freshman. But his lackadaisical attitude and inexcusable inaction forced the university's hand. There would be consequences. While his grade-point average did maintain the academic standards required to advance to his sophomore year, not so for athletics. He returned to campus at the end of August 1953 and found himself off the team. For the first time since he laced up and committed to the sport, both physically and mentally, Squires was suspended! The 1953 cross-country season would go on without him. He let down the University of Notre Dame, which believed in him enough to pay for his education and athletics; he let down Wilson, his coach who believed in him enough to have traveled all the way to Massachusetts to recruit the newcomer; he let down his teammates, who looked up to him for leadership; and more importantly, but perhaps at the time not yet fully realized, he let down himself and his family.

"I can't run!" he repeated in disbelief. "Coach said, 'You know what cross-country did for you last year! That got your times down [in track] and knocked your [mile] time down, too.' He got my attention quick." On academic shaky ground, his options were limited. He could drop out of Notre Dame. He could transfer to another school. He could leave school altogether. Or he could finish what he started, which would be in adherence to his father's ingrained precept. His first sophomore semester was pivotal. He needed a minimum grade of 81 to continue in athletics; eight points higher than his previous best. But without cross-country, he felt there was plenty of time—and mental energy—available to achieve this goal. He decided to stay in South Bend. For now. "They didn't want to lose you. If you dropped out, after a year you could come back to take classes. You'd call your advisor and he'd tell you what classes to take. But it was tough because you didn't want to go back home in disgrace to your parish and your friends because they usually threw you a going-away party and gave you this and gave you that and so on. There was a lot of pressure."

Squires smartened up and focused on his studies. He took five courses, including one in which he felt didn't require as much attention as the others. And he studied. And he carefully read the work. And he attended study groups. As a freshman, he lacked the motivation to maintain good study habits and grades. With his suspension, there was no longer an incentive problem because he was now immersed in the consequences. Running was taken away as punishment. And he missed it. "I wanted to compete. I'm getting under 4:20 in the mile. I knew that was a helluva thing as a freshman. I knew my time would win open meets in the gardens (Madison Square and Boston). I knew I had a chance to be very good. Not fairly good, but very good—even outstanding. But I needed the tool of academics. You know, you need that for life. This was 1953; I knew nearly every college graduate had a job when they got out. That motivated me. And I did not want to let my mother down. I knew I would stay at Notre Dame for my sophomore year. But if things didn't work out well, I'd transfer out. I'll go to some school that'll roll me through. Not *give* it to me, but roll me through. But I had to get those grades first."

With mental promissory notes of possible alternatives, Squires essentially eliminated the pressure that had previously suffocated him. Without fully grasping this psychological exercise at the time, he paved a new path for himself to succeed. The blessing in disguise, of course, was his suspension. Without cross-country about which to worry, for which to train, in which to compete, he was able to better handle the academic workload and accompanying weight of studying. On the other hand, the suspension also allotted Squires additional free time he felt compelled to fill. Ever the opportunist—as evident from his many jobs during high school and the summer months back home—he entered the world of entrepreneurialism, a place in which he would often dabble while in college, despite strict NCAA rules regarding athlete income.

His first "job" involved delivering cakes baked at a downtown eatery. "One of the football players did it, and he said why don't I bring birthday cakes around campus. So I was a runner for him. The cakes would be delivered to my room on campus, and he told me how it would work. He would ask everyone in the dormitory when their birthday was and their home address, and he'd write it down on a little form and say, 'There'll be a little surprise for you then.' When a birthday came around, we'd go to the roommates and friends and get them to buy a cake for five dollars, and we'd write anything on it they wanted. For two semesters I was bringing them over to people." When the football player left and Squires took over the "service," he saw room for growth. First, he found a fellow student who worked for the university with access to birthdates and accompanying dorm-room numbers and paid that person 10 cents per birthdate provided. He felt this avenue by which to obtain the data far more efficient than that of his predecessor. "When I got the job by myself, we got bigger. I had three people working for me, including two runners, and we got 50 cents a cake. If anyone came in my room, they'd always ask why there were so many cakes in there. I'd say I was just storing them for someone. They'd say, 'I don't want to know about it,' because of NCAA rules."

On the track during his suspension, Squires was on his own. As self-motivation propelled his studies and outside income, so too did it advance his training. Because Wilson could not officially coach him, Squires was forced to run and train himself. He ran on the track, he ran the local golf-course terrain, he ran the trails, the hills. And he ran longer. He was not under the constricts of training for regularly scheduled meets, so he ran for longer periods of time. And since his "plan" included the very real possibility of this being his final year at Notre Dame, he pushed himself even more for the upcoming indoor track season in which he obviously excelled, based on his freshman exploits. "I wasn't going to let it go. And yeah, when the indoor season started, I'm gonna clue ya, I was thinking this might be my last year at ND."

All the studying did pay off. Squires earned an 83. That not only reinstated him athletically for indoors, but also put him in very good academic standing for the required overall 77 as he headed into his second semester. With the possible end in sight—as he promised himself for when he finished his sophomore year—he was back on track *in* track. Practice for the 1953-54 indoors began in December, prior to the holiday break. With the addition of a few new transfers, Notre Dame hosted an open invitational meet. Wilson suggested Squires compete in the 1000-yard run, a distance he previously raced only a handful of times in high school. "I stayed with the leaders and then I kicked like hell." He chuckles when explaining his strategy. "This was my home arena, and I knew where to put my foot down. The sod that was on the track was just so soft. On the last lap I just took off and ran the hell out of the last corners. A lot of guys won't do that—they'll save it for the [very] last corner. But I had the tendency to bang the last two corners and then get myself in place to go in fast." Squires recalled he handily won in 2:12. The time was good enough to catch the attention of the local newspapers and the esteemed *Track & Field News*. In addition, the result garnered Squires an invitation by the Boston Athletic Association (B.A.A.) to later run in its own sponsored meet at the Boston Garden.

The Irish opened their dual-meet schedule on February 6, 1954, with a loss to the University of Missouri. But that date marked the stellar dual-meet debut of Squires, whose winning 4:16.8 mile and victorious 1:55 half-mile set three new records. And 14 days later, versus Indiana University, Squires broke legendary Irish six-time All-American national champion Greg Rice's 1937 indoor mile and Fieldhouse record of 4:16.2, with a time of 4:13.2. Five records in two weeks. "Holy Criminy! That was something! I broke the Notre Dame varsity mile record as a sophomore! And Rice was well-trained. He was America's best three-miler. I wasn't even thinking of a record. It was one of those things that I just went out there and ran hard."

At the B.A.A. meet in Boston, Squires competed in the 1000 against 29-year-old Ohio State University Tuskegee Airman Malvin "Mal" Whitfield, three-time gold medalist at the 1948 London and 1952 Helsinki Olympic Games. "My idol was in the race!" Squires beamed. "You know how you say you like to be like a guy? Well, he was a half-miler, he was the strongest-looking guy, he had the best form of anyone, and he could run!" Whitfield was a legend in his own time, and all eyes turned to the sure-to-be great competition. "We go out at the start of that race, and we're running," Squires describes the moment, "and I knock him into the stands." He chuckles at the recollection of his accidental contact. "We were on the first corner—*the first corner*—and I lifted him with my elbow as I pumped my arms on the turn. I didn't know who it was at the time because you're looking straight ahead. But everyone's booing, and I hear the announcer say, '*And Whitfield's out!*' I go, 'Oh, geez!' They came to see *him* run!" Forced to mentally regroup, Squires continued. "Toward the end of the race, I'm coming around the boards and I'm thinking I'm gonna come off the last corner hard. I'm doing this all off memory from the four times I ran the 1000 in high school on wood. They say some people have an instinct and just do things. That's what I did. I had instinct. I could run the boards."

And run he did. For most of the race, Squires hung around third, where he found himself down the final stretch when he watched the only two runners ahead of him cross the finish line. But right as he approached the finish himself, two-time US national team member William "Billy" Smith appeared from behind and swiftly nipped third. Squires came in fourth. (Whitfield later won the 600.) Among the spectators—who were there to actually watch only Squires—were Murt and Florence. "That was nice having my parents there. It was big for them.

And when you come out to run, they announce your name—'*Notre Dame record-holder who competed in Madison Square Garden, William Squires!*' They liked hearing that."

Notre Dame won the 1954 Central Collegiate Conference Championship, which included a winning 4:16.3 mile from Squires, who often ran multiple events in each meet. Wilson habitually entered him in the half-mile, mile, mile relay, two-mile relay, sprint medley relay (SMR—200 meters, 200 meters, 400 meters, 800 meters), and distance medley relay (DMR—1200, 400, 800, 1600). "I competed nine times in the fall, and in track I had 10 meets, and I tripled most times indoors. Outdoors I'd run five times. I was a tough bastard. There's an odd thing with me—when I have to do something, goddarnit, I'll do it! And guess what? I'll punish ya. You'll frigin' remember me. And that's the thing [later as a coach] that I put into [elite marathon champions such as] Alberto Salazar and Greg Meyer and all those guys," added Squires of what he brought from his running to his coaching. "I don't tell them to do that, but it's part of my coaching. I tell them, 'We don't run against *no* talent. We go against good teams. Are we going to waste our time? No. We're going to get something out of this race.' I think that was instilled in me as a runner. As a coach, I'll control a race at certain spots with code words or gestures. But at the end, we've broken it down and we know what the competitor's tendencies are. And we're not going to give him his race. We're going to break him up. That's all the guys did."

After indoors, Squires was in a rhythm athletically. But he started to pick up on a pattern academically in which he began each semester strong, but faltered toward the end. On the track, as a lone competitor but within a team, it was easy for him. He extended himself, he pushed himself, and he excelled. But in the classroom, he reverted back to that sheltered, lonely boy sequestered in that room as a small child. As a result, he settled back and failed to apply himself enough to succeed. "Racing had no stress for me. But I'd go in there in class and go, 'Please don't call on me.' I dreaded exams. I'd be good at the beginning of the semester, but then I tried coasting. It went back to that two years that I spent in that room at home as a kid. My mother was nice, taking me out for ice cream once in a while, but I'm sitting there at home, looking out, and I knew when it was three o'clock in the afternoon because the kids were out there playing, and I couldn't go. And she'd cry, 'Oh, I know. We'll go down to the candy store and we'll get a Hoodsie.' She was a sweet woman. And I know that there were times I heard whispering, and it was all about me. And I think she always worried that, you know, I was going to…die," he said after a pause. "Really."

There was a struggle between the shy and introverted Billy and the gregarious and extraverted Bill. At times he slipped back to the comfort of silence, which was often accompanied by fear, such as being singled out in class to answer a question in front of everyone. And then at times an inner strength peeked through and surprised even himself, such as when after meets he talked and talked to reporters when asked about his running. "I think because of that—the years of bottling up of that—made me later on become a total chatterbox. It was me wanting to escape, and I got into it and I couldn't even change it. Before this, I would talk internally all the time. I'd want to say things, but I didn't. But there were times that I *was* able to say what I wanted."

Back on the track for his first outdoor season without the restriction of freshman rules, Squires picked up where he left off in regard to running multiple events. Outdoors opened in April 1954 with the Texas Relays in which he looked forward to competing in the Jerry Thompson Mile. But his excitement about being able to run full-out in a key mile was dampened—again—when Wilson—again—included him in the two-mile relay and the SMR. "Tripling again. Well, at least I didn't have to run the mile relay, too," Squires said mockingly. But he nevertheless charged out of the gates in the mile. "The track was solid and I knew this was going to be good. That morning there was a drizzle and it helped the track get hard when the sun came out and baked it. I'm thinking that this is going to be a good race. In those days, you could tell where people were behind you because the announcer would say 62, 63, 64, so you could hear where they were when they passed each quarter. We were going on at a 4:06 pace, which was pretty good."

But then, from across the track, blew the mighty winds of Texas. "Are you kidding me?" Squires laughs. "The wind is coming and it's blowing the stuff that's on the track, the fine pieces of gravel we're running on. The cover layer of the little white stones were getting blown up in our face and bouncing off our legs. The wind's swirling and swirling. It was a dust storm or a windstorm or a squall—something like that they said happens in Texas. And we ran right into it and ran through one of the swirling funnel-things." He maintained his poise, and quickly adjusted. "I have to lead it so I don't get screwed in, and I also don't want to be a shield [against the wind] for someone else. I got away and started pushing the third quarter, which meant I had to run the whole last half by myself. That's a long time. But I wanted to make damn sure if I'm running with someone that I don't get blown into anyone." Toward the latter stages of the race it appeared the winds gravitated primarily onto one side of the track, and even focused its concentration to mimic the spin of a tornado. "The last lap or second-to-last lap I actually saw not just the big winds, but a swirl of wind and papers and leaves and dust. It was dancing around and then went to the infield, and I'm thinking to myself that I was hoping I wouldn't get caught up in it. And everything had gotten quiet—either my ears popped or something—and there were not many people in the stands. A lot of them left—they probably went underneath. It was like when you see people on TV walking against the wind like they're going backwards. So I just put down my head as I ran."

With about a 200 left, Squires made his move. "I knew I wasn't going to be able to do a full lap of a kick-job, but I ran all-out the last 200 and won. It wasn't a fast mile, but the next two guys were about two seconds behind me, so I had to pick it up. And then the wind disappeared and the sun came out. It was a bit overcast, but that was it." His victorious 4:14.2 placed him fourth in the nation and set a new Notre Dame outdoor track mile record. It catapulted Squires into the record books as the fastest miler in Fighting Irish history, as within 42 days he clocked both the indoor (4:13.7) and outdoor (4:14.2) mile records. While Wilson congratulated Squires and reiterated he wouldn't have to run the mile relay, before the sophomore exhaled in relief, the subject of the two-mile relay was broached. Squires shook his head. "Well, I said okay, and asked if I could do the second leg. He said he'd check with the other guys, came back, and said no—they wanted me to anchor. But I figured we wouldn't be doing too many two-mile relays because it was an indoor thing, so I did it. And we lost." An up-close, full-body Associated Press Wirephoto of Squires in the mile appeared in newspapers nationwide; and newsreel footage from the Texas Relays made its way onto the big screen between movies. Back home, people told Florence that her son was featured in the papers, which she had to buy, and that she had to go to the cinema and watch him run. "That was always nice for her. And whenever I went home, people would tell me they saw me at the movies."

At the Kansas Relays against the Bill Easton-coached University of Kansas squad, Squires faced 1952 US Olympic great Wes Santee. The previous week, Santee famously won a triple in the 880 yards, mile, and 440 relay leg. Similarly, Santee also ran multiple events, and Easton wanted to check off another relay record, this time the SMR. At the relay exchange zone, it is based on which team member is closing in next who officials will announce can ready himself to start their leg and take his place in the lane for the exchange. For the final lap between Kansas and Notre Dame, Santee left first, followed by Squires. "I'm looking back, at the [exchange-zone] line, and I don't know how far ahead Wes is. When I got the stick and looked up, he was a good 15 yards ahead. You can't make that up. No way! I'm a rookie in this, really, and I'm going big-league with these guys, so in my head I know I'm dying. I run, probably under 49 seconds in the first quarter. At the end I just wore out. I had nothing left. They had better talent." Notre Dame finished two seconds under the AR. But Kansas won, and *did* set the new national mark. Despite the good showing, Squires was disgruntled. And angry. He was extremely disappointed. "You see, the legs didn't hold up. When you get in the quick races, the iron horse cannot win it," he commented on himself in the third person. "He needs help. He has to have short range to be able to do something. Coach Wilson comes up to me and says that was great. I said, 'It sucked!' I was pissed." By the time of the mile relay, Notre Dame was worn out and subsequently lost. "We only had about half-an-hour between events. Our leadoff guy was tired. I was tired. And Wilson had Aubrey Lewis in the long jump, high hurdles, 200, mile relay—all speed events. We were all tired."

Squires, within a two-week span in May, headed into nationals with impressive and record-setting wins. At Michigan State University, he won the mile (4:17.4) and two-mile (9:41.3); versus Michigan State Normal College, his 4:18.2-winning mile by five seconds set a new meet record; and at the University of Pittsburgh, his 4:14.6 won the mile and set a new meet and Pitt Stadium record. Squires even found time to co-coach the Lyons Hall track team to the inaugural Notre Dame Interhall Track Meet title, a campus-wide league in which current varsity runners are not allowed to compete.

In June at the 1954 NCAA outdoor track championship at the University of Michigan, Squires ran the mile. Race day began sunny, but he toed the line under growing ominous-looking skies. He had knowledge of only a couple of the other milers, one of whom was Bill Dellinger of the University of Oregon, the soon-to-be three-time US Olympian and future coach of Steve Prefontaine. "What you did in the bigger races is you have to run your own race. You go out in 32 seconds, and then run a 61-second quarter, a 62-second quarter. The first lap you can shake them out and get in position." Within the first lap, however, as the runners were in gear and raced the corners, they felt a whirling wind pick up with a mix of dust and dirt, and the world above grew dark. There were sounds of heavy breathing, footfalls, and an angry wind. For Squires, it was deja vu. "We're out half a lap, and the wind—it's a dust storm, literally. You could hardly see. On the last corner, I'm with Dellinger and a guy from the Army named Lou Olive. And I swear on my mother, Florence Trainor, the wind blows me to the side, and I touch a guy, his arm. The wind does this!"

At the wire, amidst the swirling winds and darkening skies, photographers capture the final moment of Dellinger first, Olive second, Squires third. "I knew Dellinger won. I knew," Squires recalled of Dellinger's lunge, the image of which later graced the cover of the official track and field manual of rules and dates for coaches. "Fair is fair." And right after the race, winds picked up, pole-vault pits sailed away, and hurdles toppled. This being the Midwest, a tornado warning sounded for everyone to head into the nearby fieldhouse. As police maintained order, people hurriedly moved to safety, and winds grew, there was another announcement faintly heard regarding a disqualification. Behind the mile runners, on the track steadfastly flapping against the wind, was a red flag held up by an elderly race official. "While all this confusion is going on and the police are moving us inside, as I'm going to the fieldhouse I didn't know the red flag's up. I'm walking off the field and I hear, '*We've got a disqualification in the mile. Squires from Notre Dame has been disqualified.*' The police keep moving us to get inside. But I was furious! The official said I had hit a guy's arm. Coach Wilson went at him, arguing. Back then, officials did not have to even take a [certification] examination. They do now, but not back then. Boy, was I pissed. Wilson wrote a letter [of appeal] later on, but it didn't do anything. I was disqualified." The siren warning was well served. Washtenaw County in Ann Arbor—which included the track meet—experienced on the Fujita Tornado Scale an F0 tornado of 40-72 mph winds; the lowest designation for a tornado, but with dust and winds powerful enough to force the meet to finish indoors.

Squires concluded his sophomore season in the mile at the 1954 National AAU (NAAU) Championships in Missouri, where 50 years earlier was held the combined 1904 St. Louis World's Fair and the Summer Games of the III Olympiad. This was the highest level of talent against whom Squires had competed. And as was his style, he charged out fast and stayed with the front group of about six runners. But he soon, and wisely, backed down. "I had trouble trying to stay up with the top three. At the first half-mile, I eased off because they were *moving*;

they were pressing. Some of these guys had run in the 1952 Olympic Trials two years before, and they were now making a decision to see if they would go two more years for the 1956 Games." It was also an extremely hot evening in which to run, which prompted Squires to employ whatever tricks he remembered from his coaches in regard to hydration. "It was in the 90s—I mean, it was St. Louis in June! An hour before the race is the last time you drink a glass of water. And I knew, from Doc, to wash my mouth out. If your mouth was dry, I remembered that tip of his to find a pebble, move it around your mouth, and moisture would start coming. Don't spit the spit out, but do make sure to get the pebble out. And I did that. It worked."

Squires stayed in third and fourth places, and then moved back to fifth, sixth, and seventh, as the pace continued hard. He turned in a 61-second opening lap. "It felt like in the second lap, after a 61 [by Squires] and a 58 [by the leaders], instead of easing off, the guys in the lead just pressed. And the third quarter is usually where people would kind of run hard. The strength guys would try to burn the speed guys and see who responds. And as I'm running, I pass a guy that's located off the track that I thought was the announcer, but he was the radio guy. The race was on the radio and he was doing the call. He was that close to the track. I could hear him when I ran by." Squires recalled a slowdown 62-second lap for a 2:03 first half-mile. "I was tired. They went out quick and I was tired. And I was running extra distance that first half, trying to get into that top three. But I couldn't get in there with them. I was young—I could have gotten in the top three then. But my race would have been over quick."

His legs felt the effects of that early 61 when he clocked a 63 for the third lap that gave him a 3:06 into the final lap. "They were a different caliber of talent. When they're in that packed zone, you have to shake them out. And you're doing all the work on the corners." His slowest lap was his final one at 64 seconds. He added one second to each lap—61, 62, 63, 64—for a 4:10.8 mile and fifth place. He was not used to such a low result. He had either won every mile in which he competed or was usually no worse than second or a rare third. Fifth was his worst showing to date. But it was also his best. "I ran well. I ran my best time. Fifth was good. I was just running with those guys. I didn't worry about time because Coach kept saying to me, 'The bigger the competition, your time will go down. It'll have to go down.' He said to just run with them because they're more experienced and they're going to *run*."

CHAPTER 4

"I CAN TASTE BLOOD."

Frustrated athletically and with mounting pressure academically, if Squires was going to transfer, this was the time—as a rising junior before he entered year three. It would be a clean cut. A well-established student-athlete and record-setting All-American with two years at Notre Dame? What university or college wouldn't welcome the 21-year-old? This was decision-making time; a major turning point. But he had to ask himself some serious questions: are the academics too difficult; is he running too much; can he handle the pressures? "I am running tired. When I'm running fresh, I'm racing. But I'm running races instead of racing races. You know what the difference is? Focus."

He could *race* the half-mile and mile, but the additional relays exhausted him. His legs felt the increased number of hard-run laps. "I could feel it. And I would taste blood. Really! In the relays at the end of the meets after I had run the other events, I could taste blood. I wouldn't see any blood or cough it up, but I could taste it because I was running so damn hard!" (During instances of consecutive hard runs, his malformed heart valve—the full diagnosis of which was decades away—could not pump blood quickly enough to match the increased demand. This resulted in the occasional backup of blood in his esophagus and throat.)

Then there were his studies. While he finally understood he could not coast, no matter which school he attended, classwork at Notre Dame was the toughest experience of his life. After he struggled for so long, but then surpassed his academic goal, Squires knew he could do it. But was all of this worth the effort—on the track and in the classroom? "I'm working my can off academically, and

I'm thinking, 'I'd like to get direction.' And secondly, my coach was the nicest guy ever, but he's using a system on me and I am actually destroying some of my teammates that weren't as strong as me physically. They're getting leg pulls, they're tired—they can only do one-third of the work. I'm a very team-oriented guy. I never wanted them to hurt. I wanted them to be able to train well and to be able to give me leads in the relays. I knew I had to be a leader, that I had the leadership thing because of the way I said things and did things; coaching ideas." Another wrinkle to his decision-making occurred via a letter he received. "It had a Division I school's name on it, but it wasn't from the school or a coach there. It was from another top athlete at the school. He was expressing an interest in me going there. There was interest outside of Notre Dame!"

All of this compounded his decision. And when he received his grades, his overall average was just above the required 77. He was still in. No options were eliminated. Had he failed, of course, deciding on whether or not to remain would have been moot. "The grades weren't bad, but I knew I had to go to summer school only because I have to catch up from my freshman year. You were always behind because you were only taking 12 hours instead of 15. And for me, one of those semesters I flunked a course, so I'm behind a course. But I don't have to pay for the courses because of my ride, so I didn't have to worry about that." But Squires vacillated. He kept changing his mind. His thoughts were scattered—he should attend summer school; he thought he was ready to leave; a transfer would cause him to lose some college credits; he'd need to attend junior college; perhaps the studying and training weren't that bad; he was prepared to leave. This was the waffling process he experienced. But finally, he decided. "That was it. I had enough. I can transfer."

With his transfer decision set, and just days before the start of summer school, Squires had to make it official. He paid a final visit to Edward "Moose" Krause, the school's athletic director. But he was not in. Nor was Squires's coach, who already departed for his summer camp in Wisconsin. There was no one left for Squires to see before his exit, he surmised, until he thought of the Rev. Edmund P. Joyce, the university's executive vice president. "I go into the office of his assistant and I say, 'I'd like to talk about a transfer.' He says, 'Aren't you an athlete?' I said I was, and he told me he didn't handle that, and I should talk to the AD. I told him he wasn't in, and that it was kind of immediate and I'd like to make this decision before summer school." Squires wanted this to be over as quickly as possible. At the main administration building, under the iconic Golden Dome, Squires for the first time climbed the fabled stairs of the landmark building. His fear was to mistakenly enter the office of the Rev. Theodore M. Hesburgh, 15th president of Notre Dame. Squires was nervous enough to meet the EVP, let alone stumble into the chambers of the president! After a quick elevator ride to the office floor, and an unsure knock on the EVP's door, a voice rang out. "I hear, 'Come in, Squires!'" He was still nervous. "Father Joyce doesn't speak too loud, but when he says something, it hits you. I was scared! And I didn't even know what the guy looked like. I knew all about him from orientation. He went to Notre Dame, he was in business management, he went from there to the stock market after the Depression, and he came right in as vice president. Father Hesburgh knew how to make the money for Notre Dame, and Father Joyce knew how to invest it." He took in a deep breath and entered the majestic office of the second-in-command. "He goes, 'What's this I hear? You want to transfer?'" Before Squires responded, he continued. "He says, 'You've had a phenomenal year. I've never seen you race, but I do read the South Bend paper and both Chicago papers, and even *The New York Times*,'" Squires recalled Father Joyce saying. "He said, 'You've had a very, very good year. What is the problem?'"

Squires felt like he was shrinking into the chair, but he found a silent moment in which to respond. It was time for this once sickly kid from Arlington, this frightened and confused 21-year-old, to be open and honest with *the* executive vice president of *the* University of Notre Dame. "I told him the school was too much for me, that it's way over my head. I told him at the high school I was at, I was only in the College 2 Prep program. We only had College 2, and I should have been in a College 4. And I got a lot of gifted Cs. The few B and A grades I got, I earned. But I said the students at this university are phenomenal. Academically, they are whiz kids." That was it. Short and to the point. He opened up and expressed his vulnerability, his weakness, his failure. With great anticipation, and some trepidation, he awaited Father Joyce's words. He hoped a nice thank you and a handshake would complete the deal. "He said to me, 'I'm not going to keep you if it's really what you want. But I want you to stay.' He goes on. 'What if I made sure you had tutoring aide? I'll give you tutoring aide.' He asked me if I knew how to type, which I didn't. He said he'd get the professors' typing pool to help type my papers, and said, 'What about that? That eases off all that time.' He was doing a selling job!" Father Joyce then addressed athletics. He talked about Wilson and how good he was as a runner and now also a coach—points on which they both agreed. "He says, 'Then why the heck do you want to go?'" Squires recalls him asking. "'And where are you going to go?'" The University of Kansas and the University of Southern California were the answers given by Squires, who was assured by Father Joyce that both institutions would no doubt welcome such a quality student-athlete. But the EVP added if Squires was dead set on transferring, he had to choose one school; and soon, because of what was involved in the transfer process.

After the friendly, yet purposeful, tete-a-tete, Squires was afforded 48 hours. From this very short impromptu meeting, it appeared, Father Joyce felt Squires was still a cause to pursue; a graduate to secure. But he wanted the decision in his office by 10 o'clock in two days. Squires was beside himself. "I'm out of my mind! I was more confused now! So I tried to relax. I go downtown. I go to a movie. I can't even concentrate. I go back to my dorm. I'm praying. I'm thinking. I'm tossing and turning. I don't know what to do. I knew at home I could get a job in Arlington. And I knew I could probably go to Northeastern University or Boston University evenings if I needed courses. But I can't tell anyone because something like this would make it in the papers—top runner to transfer." He needed to decide on his own. By himself. So he turned to a place of refuge where he often found peace and answers: the on-campus Basilica of the Sacred Heart, where he attended Mass and knew he could ponder. "I felt comfortable there. I could think there. I could find peace there. I kept saying, in prayer, 'You've given me a lot of power. [As a kid] You got me to Dr. Carroll [who said] that my heart was good.' And so on. I really did appreciate God's talent. God gave me my life. I'm better in the world because of Him." Squires still grappled that night, but he boiled it down to the nugget of importance that would persuade him whether or not to stay at Notre Dame. It appeared to him as a sudden jolt. "I remember it was about three in the morning the next morning. It came to me. I said to myself that I'm going to lay it right on Wilson that I've got to run more trophy races—the marquee races. That this is it."

Forty-eight hours passed and Squires approached the EVP to present his case. He told Father Joyce about his athletic ultimatum for Wilson, and that group tutoring with four or five fellow student-athletes would also be helpful. They discussed other details as well, such as Squires's thoughts on his difficulty to take proper notes during class while he attempted to simultaneously focus on what the professor said. "He understood. He said okay. And we shook hands." Squires stayed. He decided to remain at Notre Dame. It was admittedly one of the most difficult—and important—decisions he would ever make in his life.

During the summer of 1954, prior to his junior year, he attended classes, and, once again, re-entered the "job market" with another business endeavor. He was "hired" by Notre Dame's ground crew to periodically move the water hoses that were used to water the grass throughout the entire campus (Squires recalls they paid him through their overtime so they wouldn't have to return each night). And that spawned another job when he noticed abandoned furniture inside an on-campus barn that would be discarded before each semester. "For the next two years, what I actually did was sell them. I started bringing over chairs and things to my room, and I'd pay another student a few bucks to help carry some things over. But I'd go around to the rooms and ask how many would need a couch, a lamp, a desk, and so on, and I'd bring over three or four guys—only three or four at a time—to the barn and I'd sell them stuff."

In addition to his summer jobs and studies, Squires maintained a steady training schedule, which included on a regular basis running five-plus miles on the nine-hole Notre Dame Golf Course, which covered over 3,000 yards of real estate. He also continued this kind of workout when he spent the last few weeks of the summer back home, with more mileage on the nearby Winchester Country Club, including a hilly five-mile course that was in addition to the three-mile round trip. "It's funny, but I would always see Dick Bradley working at Winchester when I'd run by the caddie shack," Squires said of the father of eventual World Golf Hall of Fame member Pat Bradley, whose neighbors always knew when she won an LPGA event because her mother, Kathleen, rang a cowbell on their backyard porch. "He had to wait until the last caddy came in, so he was there until seven o'clock at night, and I would be running there after work at around quarter after. He said that when I was running, when I get to about the 16th hole, I could cut over on the other side so I don't see any of the golfers that might complain. So I'd run the first nine, when I knew no one was out there, and then I'd know where the last foursome was and cut over so they wouldn't see me."

In August 1954, a renewed Squires returned to Notre Dame for his junior year, and both Krause and Wilson gave him an earful. Each felt they could have provided some assistance without him having met with the EVP. Squires pointed out that he even left Wilson a note that said he'd explain everything upon his return, and that he did not ask Father Joyce to bother him or Krause. But none of that seemed to matter. "Father Joyce had called Moose, who then told Wilson; and they both weren't happy with me. Wilson gets me in his office and he said, 'Why didn't you tell me? I could have done some of those things for you.' I needed the tutoring and the typing, and the trophy races—I don't know what he could have really done about most of that. But I respected him. We talked it over. Wilson joked, 'I'm out of town for two weeks and you do this!' But we talked it out."

Cross-country prep included training in the heat on the university's golf course with fast miles, half-miles, and quarter-miles. This proved easy for Squires due to his previous mileage over the same area. The five-mile route included the undulating terrain of the golf course, from the fairway flats to the hills of the rough. And it was all by design. "For years they stayed off golf courses because they kept thinking someone could get hit by a ball or something. But Wilson got smart and knew we should run the golf course and not along the lake—which was too flat—since most of the races are on golf courses. And he came up with this novel idea; he would measure distances of every half-mile and put a marker up, like a flag. We didn't know about this. And then after we began running, he'd fire a gun from the start at certain intervals to see where you were each time in relation to a marker. Sometimes I was ahead of the gun. And then at the end, he'd fire it again, and sometimes I'd be over the line when he did, so I'd tell him how far I was."

Academically, Squires found courses that interested him. And a man who inspired him. Rev. Thomas J. Brennan, professor of philosophy, taught a logic course and a reasoning course, in that order, per semester. He was so respected and revered that he delivered the commencement address to the wartime class of 1944; and in 1972 received the seventh annual Sorin Award, named in honor of Notre Dame's first president, in recognition of distinguished service. "He was a fan-priest. There weren't many fan-priests. You'd see him watching football, and practices, and games. He'd be off to the side, but he'd say nothing to draw attention to himself. But you'd see him there at games and meets. And it was tough to get into his class because people loved him. I loved him. And I was intrigued by these courses. In the logic class, he'd get into it right away. He'd say, 'Why does man wear clothes?' And he'd go after us, and you had to be ready with quick answers, like, clothes keep you warm, clothes for morality, clothes because you're shy, and so on. You have to think quick. And then you had to tie it all together with a summation within minutes. And who was picked on the worst? Me. No one wanted to sit near me. They'd ask where was I going to sit. I always thought, no matter what, that I was street smart. My father kind of made me able to think this way and think that way." After he received an A- in the logic course, Squires followed with the second-part reasoning course. "Boy, was I picked on in that logic course. And I thanked him for the mark, and he said, 'You earned it, Bill. You earned it. I don't give gifts.' He was funny like that. But you see, the reasoning course was built on the logic course by introducing more sensitivity of how you use reasoning with different nationalities, different religions, and how you attach things to that. And he'd apply a lot of this to business because he knew all of us were going out to be professionals. It was like a courtroom with four people, and then the rest of the class throwing in answers and things. And to get our attention sometimes, he'd have a rock in his pocket and he'd throw it in the metal garbage can. That'd get us."

Father Brennan also took an interest in the students outside the classroom. He knew something about his students, whether they were athletes, musicians, artists. Regarding Squires, he was aware of his honesty, sense of humor, faith; and with genuine interest he talked with the junior about many subjects. "He'd see me and come over, and he'd say, 'I see you had a good race last week. That's good.' And I'd listen. He'd say, 'I asked Coach about you, and he said you're coming out of your shell. You were kind of quiet. You're not quiet in my class!' I laughed because if I was quiet in his class, he'd pull the answers out of my tongue if I didn't say anything. But he'd use me in his class. He'd walk around and if there were new guys there who came in within the first two weeks when some guys would drop the course, he'd loosen it up and say, 'Hey, it's Bill Squires. He runs around in circles.' I'd laugh." Father Brennan evolved as a mentor for Squires, who had no intention of seeking out a member of the Jesuits for such a role. But they got along well and conversations continued before and after Mass to the point where Father Brennan solicited Squires's opinion. "He'd ask me what would I think sermons should be. I went to daily Mass and I read ahead to what was going to be on Sunday because I knew he might be out at track practice during the week and he'd come by and say about the sermon, 'What do you think it should be?' Say it was about moneylenders. I'd say, 'The moneylenders—like the people, in this day and age, credit card companies, pawn shops—that's usury; that's a sin, asking way more than you should.' He wanted a perspective from someone, not talking about the year 1000 that would bore people, but one relatable to nowadays."

Others took notice of Squires's sincerity, faith, devotion, and he was asked about more ideas and was invited to accompany priests to missions around the South Bend area. "We'd go to these little churches where it'd be the only one for 20 miles around, and we'd do everything—baptisms, Masses—and I could help serve Mass. There'd be a lot of people at these churches. There were seven or eight priests doing these state missions, but I'd be with two or three at a time and we'd go to two churches a day. I'd serve Mass as an altar boy. And on the way to the churches, we'd talk about the sermons and the message. Then later, in the sermons, I'd hear what I was talking to the priests about. What they wanted was a young person's view on things. And the food we got there from the people—oh, boy! It was great." Squires traveled on other journeys in addition to church missions. One in particular was a private visit to a 37-year-old woman at the St. Coletta School for Exceptional Children in nearby Wisconsin. The eldest daughter of nine of a wealthy political family in Boston, Mass., Rose Marie "Rosemary" Kennedy was institutionalized at the facility ever since she was subjected to a horrifically damaging lobotomy 14 years earlier. "She was in a hospital, but the place looked like a regular house. Father Brennan went in with the holy oils and his bag for about an hour. I didn't go in. I was doing my schoolwork or something while he was with her. At the time, her brother, John, was a congressman and known for the PT-109 boat when he helped his crew get rescued during the war."

After two rocky years at Notre Dame, when at times he felt lost and adrift, Squires found someone with whom he could commiserate, share ideas, chat carefree, and discuss his struggles. He felt some comfort as a student-athlete. There was even an assignment in a sociology class that interested him: spending no more than $25, students had to produce a project related to social work—that was the broad limited restriction. With that in mind, and focused on an education degree, Squires started a junior high school fitness program. At the time, there was only one track in town for everyone to use. Squires designed a seven-sport program. "Hey, I was way ahead of the Presidential Physical Fitness thing." He laughed. "It cost me under $25. And the professor gave me an A grade." But this was no one-shot deal. What began as a simple class assignment grew into a continual athletic program. He was asked to write up a program that could be used. "I called it the South Bend Indiana Junior High Feeder Program."

As he headed into his junior year of cross-country in the fall of 1954, Squires was near his peak in terms of fitness. All the golf-course miles, plus his outdoor and indoor track experience, provided him with a tremendous advantage, despite it being his least favorite competition. The short regular season, which included less than a half-dozen meets, lasted from September to November. His sophomore suspension denied him the access to keep tabs on his competition. To get back into the competitive cross-country groove after 22 months, instead of charging out of the blocks, so to speak, he started out slow and turned it on closer to the finish to tap into his reserves without the prospect of coming up short. "Around that time, I was named as a top runner in track magazines. And because of my status, I learned that when you got those red shoes from that company in Germany—adidas—you were a stud. They saw that I ran well. I got two pairs of size 11 shoes—one pair of spikes and one pair of flats. They were free as a 'congratulations' and 'have a good year.'" But he still favored used ones because of his tender ankle from his childhood ax incident. Despite his injury-induced unorthodox running that produced a pronounced stride supination, "No one ever joked about or said anything about my running style. No one said anything about my foot going way out when I ran. Because when I'd land, I'd have to correct myself and my foot would go back. I'd come down pretty solid, but I was wasting energy." Squires was even part of an on-campus experiment to determine in a quantitative measure how much his extra running motions cost him timewise. "Someone on the team that was a mechanical engineer used me as a project on how I ran. He analyzed how I ran, how my legs and feet moved, and all of that. They said I was losing seven-tenths of a second per lap or something; about three to four seconds a mile. To help, they tried to tape me up or use an elastic band, which I stretched real bad. They just gave up. But I couldn't help it."

Notre Dame finished 3-2 and was second at the 1954 Central Collegiate Conference Championship, where Squires won the four-miler. "I worked my way through that one. This had something like 20 clubs in it and a lot of individuals. It was like a tune-up to go to the NCAAs two weeks later at Michigan State that was also four miles."

His first foray in nationals was the NCAA Men's Cross-Country Championship. Nearly 120 harriers competed, including Canadian Rich Ferguson, who three months earlier at the British Empire and Commonwealth Games—in the "Mile of the Century"—was third behind Roger Bannister and John Landy; and University of North Carolina at Chapel Hill's Jim Beatty, future US Olympian and world record-holder. "When I saw Ferguson, I knew he went out hard and I wanted to hang onto this guy. We were back a ways, and we didn't know where we were. I kept saying, 'C'mon, c'mon! Stay with me. Stay with me.' We held for a while. I was good for about three miles. And then the real distance guys really started jockeying and moving for the last mile. I got out well, but they were really, really fit. I got myself back and kept thinking that I'd catch them when we got back to the field again. But these guys were probably doing 50-mile weeks, which was a lot back then. I was only doing 32 miles a week for cross-country, and in track, 28 miles a week." Behind Ferguson (8th) and Beatty (13th), Squires earned All-American honors in 14th as the first finisher from Notre Dame, which was sixth. But it is worth to note that without Squires the previous year, Notre Dame failed to even place as a team and the first Irish runner was 47th. With Squires, Notre Dame's sixth place was its best finish since 1950, and he turned in the fastest school time since 1942 (and third fastest since 1938) and was the best individual placing for Notre Dame in four years.

Several weeks separated cross-country from indoors, which began after Christmas. Wilson, in mid-December, used some of his Loyola University Chicago connections for a scrimmage. And Squires ran the half-mile instead of the mile, which pleased the junior. At home during the break, Squires continued to train in earnest. He frequented Harvard's elevated, 12-lap-to-a-mile, three-lane board track situated high above a five-lane, teacup, ground-floor dirt track. The upper-floor track was used mostly by university runners to familiarize themselves with the harder surface. On those boards, Squires noticed reigning 1500-meter world champion and two-time Olympian Joseph "Josy" Barthel of Luxembourg, who ran a record-setting 3:45.2 for 1500 gold at the 1952 Helsinki Games. While at Harvard for his master's degree, Barthel also competed indoors and sought out runners with whom he could train. Enter Squires. "I was used to short rests with Wilson and I knew we were going to run quick. But, oh boy! First, we must have done five circuits around the grass area around Harvard Stadium and some buildings. It was probably a 35-minute warm-up. I'm used to a 25-minute warm-up. Then he said we were going indoors to do half-miles at a two-minute pace." Workouts were intense. Barthel was coached by Frank Stampfl, legendary Austrian coach into whose arms seven months earlier pupil Bannister fell when he broke the elusive four-minute-mile on the Iffley Road track at Oxford. Stampfl incorporated short rests in practice, which Barthel embraced. While on the Harvard track, Squires recalled heavy dust from runners on the dirt track below billowed up to the wood track and found its way into their lungs. It was dense enough that when they stopped for a drink, they'd often cough up dirt into the water bubbler. "Oh, I swear, you had to spit it up. And in the shower you could see the dirt. And they had these windows, like sunroofs, and you could see the dust coming up through the sunbeams. You're just sucking it in." For the next two half-miles, Barthel ordered Squires to lead. "As I was leading, I told him if I was going a little bit slower, just tell me 'Quicker.' So we're going along and he goes, 'Good, good. Good, good. Little faster! Good, good.' Each half-mile we were doing 60 seconds. We did about six of them and I was pretty tired. The corners are overly tight, so you had to back off and then catch up. You can't be on someone's shoulder there. But I felt good."

Squires learned techniques he would later use as a coach, which included the pivotal equation of a workload. He vividly recalled the price his fellow Irish paid when it came to matching his workouts, a lesson he would never forget. "They didn't have the leg strength to take the work that Coach was giving us. I could do it, but it was all I could do to take this stuff. They had to struggle. And they were on scholarship! They were darn good high-school kids. I think the speed Wilson was doing, the number of repetitions, was almost too much. You needed more rest and you didn't need to do as many. And we should have been doing six-mile runs probably three days a week; one day doing an 11-mile run; and two days of that speedwork—one short speed and one longer speed. That would have been ideal."

All this work paid off. To start the 1954-55 indoors, Squires set new meet, Fieldhouse, and Irish indoor mile records in the season opener versus Purdue University. His 4:10.7-winning mile shattered the 1949 meet-record 4:21, and also Squires's own indoor Fieldhouse record of 4:13.7 he set the previous year. To put that in perspective, it took 20 years for American and world-record-setting Rice's mile record to be broken—by Squires—whereas it took but one season for Squires to best his own mark. All told up to this point, Squires impressively held several meet and Fieldhouse records; both indoor and outdoor Notre Dame mile records; two-mile relay record (with baton-mates Dick O'Keefe, Al Schoenig, Al Porter); and back-to-back conference mile titles.

But Wilson soon returned Squires to his multi-event schedule, with predictable results. At Indiana University, he tripled with the mile, half-mile, and mile relay. He came in second in the mile, and 40 minutes later won the half. But only 10 minutes separated the half from the relay, the latter of which featured Milt Campbell, 1953 US national decathlon champion and decathlon silver medalist at the 1954 Helsinki Olympics who at the 1956 Melbourne Olympics would win decathlon gold! In the relay, Notre Dame was in second when Squires began the two-and-a-half-lap leg behind Campbell. "We're back from first about four yards when I got the stick. I wanted to go out fast, catch him, and use him. I went with him for about one lap. I knew he was so powerful and strong and quick. I tried working both quarters almost all out—usually you rest on the corners. But I could not recover at all. He was baiting me—I could tell—on one of the straightaways, so I came hard at him on the corners." Within a few strides of each other, Campbell and Squires rounded the final corner and headed for home. The win came down to the best final push. "I remember seeing the tape, and then all of a sudden the lights went out and I saw stars. I blanked out over the last yards. I don't know how I got across the line, but I did. I must have fallen over the finish line into the dirt. I remember the ol' trainer picked me up and gave me smelling salts, and I asked him if we won. He said, 'No. But you did good, kid.' Campbell ran me unconscious! He had more innate speed than most people. I can't think of a miler that can hold him. And this was a big, big meet. I did all of that in an hour and 40 minutes—the half, the mile, the relay. Tripling in these meets killed me. But this *was* a big meet."

Notre Dame defended its title at the 1955 Central Collegiate Conference Championship, where Squires did likewise in the mile. And in the 34th Bankers Mile at the Chicago Daily News Relays three weeks later, Squires once again battled top talent in US All-Army steeplechase champion and 4:11.2-miler Phil Coleman; Art Dalzell, University of Kansas outdoor mile conference champion; Charles "Deacon" Jones, University of Iowa freshman with a 4:11.4 mile; and Wes Santee, who nine months earlier clocked an AR 4:00.6 mile at the 1954 Compton Invitational. But Squires recalls receiving an odd request from his coach on behalf of Santee by way of Easton. Santee wanted to break the American indoor mile record, and "Wilson asked if I could bring Wes through in the mile in 3:02 for three-quarters. And he said I had to do an honest effort, I have to keep running. By honest effort he meant I had to finish. You could pace-set, but you had to finish the race and you couldn't do a jog-athon. Later on you could pace and then run off the track. Not then. He wants me to go 61, 61, 61—a little bit less—for 3:02. I said okay. I was running 62s all the time, so just taking off a second, and having the crowd there, I knew I could do that. And I was used to tripling events anyway."

To accommodate this attempt—without officially accommodating this attempt—the placement order of the two-mile relay and mile relay events was moved, which allowed Squires (some) rest time to compete in his events and then run with Santee. Thirty minutes after the Irish two-mile relay team of O'Keefe, Schoenig, Porter, Squires finished in second, the mile commenced. "At the start, we just nodded at each other," said Squires of Santee, who was accompanied by Dalzell for a 62-second quarter and Squires for an approximate 2:04 half. "I talked to him with about 200 yards to go for the three-quarters, and I said, 'How're you doing?' He goes, 'Good. Good.' I picked it up and paced him through and let him pass me just at three-quarters. Then I went along and did 4:13 in sixth or seventh place. And he broke the meet record with 4:04.2. He was America's premier miler. I didn't mind giving up my mile." In the mile relay, a late addition for Squires, he knew he'd be pushed to the limit; his legs would be taxed; and his resources tapped. That was what he expected. But there was much that he didn't expect. "I'm running and I was coming down to the finish and I'm leaning over to win, and this woman comes out of the stands and starts beating me over the head with what I thought was a baton. I mean, holy geez! Bang, bang, bang on the head! Turns out it was a program. One of my teammates was there and was yelling at her. She runs away, and she's screaming. We end up winning it in a photo finish. It was a bitch of a race." And that's not all. "Yeah, well, we were disqualified. They said one of my teammates was cheering us on along the fence that lines the track, and he somehow hit the stick and knocked it out of the hands of one of the teams. It was a freak thing to happen, something crazy. We had to give the awards back."

With numerous relays, Squires was "bogged down," which, he felt, sapped his energy to really shine in the marquee miles. He figured the earlier assurances that he'd see more showcase miles as an enticement to remain at Notre Dame was a fete de compli. But he soon realized it would most likely not materialize; that for the sake of the *team*, he'd be put in various relays to earn *team* points. While the academic promises of tutors, typists, and so on, came to be, Squires was still nevertheless frustrated regarding his races. But he thought against rocking the boat. "I'm into schoolwork. I started going over to the tutor bureau and I'd get grad students as tutors, and my grades were going up. Not running the good miles didn't bother me—well, to a point. But I didn't say anything. My parents brought me up to respect authority. I have a year-and-a-half to go—the countdown! And also I read that while the Korean War was over—this was 1955, a couple of years after the war—they still need people to take the troops home from Korea and all those people drafted will go right to Korea. And they did. So I shut up."

During outdoors, Squires was looked upon by the team to talk to Wilson about the workload. The point which he attempted to make during the previous season began to adversely affect the team. They felt it during indoors, so the thought of another three months of harmful training outdoors started to infest the team. Wilson's training method was based in large part on research by renowned exercise physiologist Dr. Sidney "Sid" Robinson—with a Harvard University doctorate, Cornell University master's—who thrice coached the cross-country Indiana Hoosiers to league championship titles and two NAAU titles. As an athlete himself, Robinson was second in the 1928 US Olympic Trials NAAU 1500 and competed in the Amsterdam Olympic Games. Wilson, who anchored the bronze-medal-winning Canadians in the 4x400 relay at those 1928 Olympics, had every reason to buy into anything Robinson offered. Short runs was what Wilson drove into his Fighting Irish, but to the absence of balancing it with distance training. What he missed, and in later years acknowledged, according to Squires, was to adjust and incorporate the various training elements for his own teams. "Wilson was a nice guy, a smart guy, but he's believing Sid's giving him scientific stuff. You've gotta have both [speed and distance], but you have to *blend* both. If I had done distance work in those workouts [had it been included], it would have worked. It really would have because I was strong enough to do them without the legs under me. I was doing it on natural legs from my caddying days and running up and down those hills. But I'd lose it all running all those relays two seasons in a row. If it was a short race, I could kick great. But if you look at my quarter-mile, half-mile, and mile times, they're off because you need a staying power."

Wilson continued to utilize Squires in multiple events, but the junior was older now and felt more comfortable taking a stand. He tried to take more of a stance during outdoors. "I would run the mile and the half-mile, and if they needed me in the relay, fine. But if not, I said no. And I was emphatic. I told Wilson I didn't want to run more than twice in the little meets. But when we went to the big ones, he'd say, 'Billy, the team needs you.' When he started calling me Billy instead of Bill, I knew he was playing chummy—kind of working me. I knew I was the leader, and I demonstrated that and I cared about winning and I cared about the team. But they kept on me to get through to him to forget about the crazy system he was using. But I never did. I didn't know how to approach him. I mean, I was just coming out of my shyness." While there were times when Wilson reduced the number of events for Squires and the relay teams in smaller meets, the junior was run down. He was still tired, slept less, and was generally miserable. This adverse combination, which began as a freshman and continued as a sophomore, was still apparent enough in his appearance as an upperclassman that he was again given by the school extra food voucher booklets to encourage him to eat more at the cafeteria. Relay and meet losses continued, although Squires still won the mile and two-mile. But it was a struggle. He was unable to run each mile at full speed, knowing he had to save energy for relays. So he adapted. "I had to run hard miles. I wouldn't take the pace. But it got to a point where I knew there were real, real good guys there. I don't mind taking the pace for the first half-mile. That never bothered me. I'd keep it honest. I could run 2:05, 2:06 in my sleep, which was a pair of 63s, and then I'd put the hammer down." He'd run hard if it was close; slow it down if he gained a healthy lead; or maintain pace. "I couldn't run every event all-out. I had to conserve."

Squires entered the mile at the 1955 NCAA Outdoor Track and Field Championships in Los Angeles after a season with three one-mile wins and a pair of two-mile victories. Unlike the previous year when he battled Dellinger and the soulless tornado winds of Michigan, he looked forward to calmer conditions on the West Coast, especially since Dellinger switched to the two-mile. He was confident, and at the gun charged out successfully. The NAAU championship was scheduled for the following week, and he wanted to finish strong leading up to that event. With about 500 yards remaining, near a corner, just before the bell lap, Squires prepared himself to turn it on for the final push. "I was in third place. I wanted to be on the leader. But the leaders changed, and as they changed, one guy moved over and another guy got on him. So I was right in there. I was running a little longer, but I could see the move. My plan was, right at the bell when they listen for their times, go fast at that distraction. That's the time to catch people. I would have got it going at the corner. But a guy spikes me from behind! I'm running along—and I can't believe this—but I get spiked from behind in my calf on my outside leg! He rips me down, and I tumble and fall. And as I go down, another guy goes by—and over—and tears apart my shin to the bone." Upon impact with the track and stomping spiked shoes, on the ground in lane two he rolled with the fall and eventually picked himself up. By this time, he's in lane four and attempted to regain his stride. Spectators saw blood streaming down his leg and shin. "I get up and I have to get going in rhythm. And they're moving like hell, but I get up near the back of the field. I hear people yelling, 'Stop! Stop!' And officials are waving the white flag to get my attention—not the red flag, which means a violation—and saying, 'Stop! Stop!' And I go, 'Frig that! No way!' I pass the three or four runners in the back, catch a breather, and then I gave everything I could on that last straightaway to get down to the final curve. But I was out of it."

He was unaware of the damage. "All of a sudden, people were grabbing me when I finished. I looked down at my leg, and the whole leg was covered in blood. My red adidas shoe was completely covered because I kept slamming my foot down when I was running and it just filled with blood. It wasn't squirting, but it was coming down from the gashes that were ripped open." Squires was carried off the track and taken to the medical area. They took off his shoe and there was a pool of blood inside, which soaked the bag in which the shoe was placed. A nurse scrubbed the wounds to clean them out before she dressed them with 28 stitches. "I'll clue ya, that hurt more than the fall! I put a rolled-up towel in my mouth and clenched down on it when she did that. Then I told them I can't lose those shoes. You only get two a year, so I made sure I got them back." Due to his injury, Squires did not compete in nationals. The conclusion of outdoors marked the end of 10 consecutive months of hard running—cross-country (September to November), indoors (December to March), outdoors (April to June). Even the short breaks between the seasons were full of training and maintaining. But the individual results were stunning. Among the many meet and facility records, Squires simultaneously held the Notre Dame indoor (4:10.7) and outdoor (4:14.2) mile records, as well as the anchor of the two-mile relay record (7:40.3) with O'Keefe, Schoenig, and Porter.

With the end of his junior year of high-intensity running on a regular basis at his elevated caliber, the added stress and pressure of academics continued with two exams remaining. He was concerned about his grades. Not necessarily grades for the semester, but in particular grades from these last two finals. "I really felt I was in a bind. My grades the first semester were good and I was doing okay. But I was hoping I would do well because you know how a professor has a ton of exams to do at the same time? Well, now all he has to do is grade *my* exam!" But Squires was afforded extra time to study with a tutor. His grades averaged 84. He was relieved.

For the summer while he attended classes, he once again became a lifeguard, which he had done back home as a kid; this time at the university's St. Joseph's

Lake. It was an easy job because of his background in that position, and because the majority of those on the beach were elder clergy who didn't require much. "I'd talk to them a lot. A real old, skinny priest would come up to me every so often and we'd talk. I didn't know who he was, and he asks me, 'What's your name?' When I said Billy Squires, he said, 'Oh, I think I've seen your picture in a magazine. You're an athletics boy.' I said, 'Yes, Father. I'm a runner.' And we talked about summer school and that I was a lifeguard before. He kept coming around and we'd talk." Around this time, while on duty, Squires noticed a mother and her young children playing in the shallow end of the water, where the beach face mostly contained slippery seaweed. There was no inherent danger, but the kids thought it felt gross. As did the mother. Squires said he'd try to find a fix, but he realized the difficulty. Shortly thereafter, while on duty another day, Squires watched that old, skinny priest come by for another visit. As he approached, he overheard other priests greet him as Your Eminence. "I'm thinking, 'Who is this guy?' He comes over to me and I say, 'Father, excuse me. I thought you were a priest.' He says, 'Of course I'm a priest.' I said, 'Oh. I know. But what level?' He said, 'I'm a cardinal.' And I say, 'A cardinal? Well, you're the first cardinal I've met.' I'm really flabbergasted." He was Father J. Hugh O'Donnell, Notre Dame president from 1940 to 1946. When Squires finally collected himself enough to continue, he thought a former president could solve the seaweed dilemma. The next day, it looked as if all the attention of the entire maintenance department was directed toward the beach. "When I saw that! The grounds-crew guys were all there, yelling at me. They had machines, but they didn't work. Then they're out there with their pants rolled up and they're pulling the seaweed. Then they're shoveling sand on it with snow shovels. And they're still yelling at me," Squires recalled with a laugh.

Also located nearby is St. Mary's Lake and a sacred place in proximity to the lakes, known as the Notre Dame Grotto. The grotto is a manmade cave of large rocks built in 1896 in the shape of the original grotto shrine to Our Lady of Lourdes, in France. It is where respectful visitors—under the statue of the Blessed Virgin Mary, as Bernadette Soubirous said she had appeared to her—light candles and present offerings in the hopes their prayers are answered. "I don't know how many times I went down there and lit a candle if I had half a buck or something to offer. And I'd always be praying; not to win an event, but to just get me through this school! There were times I hated this place. I kept saying I was in over my head."

CHAPTER 5

FINALLY!

With three weeks of summer remaining before the start of his final year at Notre Dame, Squires returned home. The only long-term thoughts he's had were on the following meet, the following season, the following year, let alone a relationship. Regarding a social life, Squires did find time to date while at South Bend. Despite his shyness, a nice, fit, handsome All-American athlete did not suffer from meeting women. But with the demand of high academic standards, and as one of the nation's top three-sport runners, nothing took root in terms of a personal commitment or plans for a family. In fact, the thought was never on his mind. At home, he filled his days with light training to maintain fitness, and working in a garage to recondition cars—a skill he learned from his self-taught, mechanically-inclined father. To break up the boredom one time, he was talked into going ice skating, an activity from which he often shied away due to potential injury to his bread-and-butter, and the obvious expected pain from the tightness of lacing up skates around his sensitive ankle.

With appearances on the radio, big-screen newsreels, and in magazines and newspapers throughout the country, Squires was a nationally recognized, well-known hometown figure especially in and around Arlington. Such attention often attracted fans and hangers-on, especially in public. But on this particular evening of ice skating, a face familiar to *him* appeared amidst the crowd at the rink. It was, he thought, a woman he remembered from high school. "I look over and said to myself, 'That looks like that pretty girl from Arlington.' She lived on the flatlands of East Arlington, about two streets down from me. Around that time, I'd see her walking around and I thought she was a very attractive woman, a very good looker. She was on the pep squad and she played field hockey." Turned out it *was* that good-looking girl—Sally Ann Kuhn—who was studying at Mount Auburn Hospital in Cambridge to become an operating-room nurse. Right on the spot, some time that night, for some unavoidable reason, he asked her out. She said yes, and suggested he pick her up after a shift at the hospital. Which he did. But something about the date, on their very first time out together, didn't…smell right. "Oh, boy! We're on the date and I'm suffering. I don't know what to do. She asks me what's wrong, and I said, 'I don't know how to say this…but I'm smelling your ether.' I can't stand ether—it makes me nauseous. When I split my nose with that two-by-four when I was a kid, they had a hard time giving ether to me. I must have been allergic to it or something. But it just gets to me! So she goes, 'Are we going to go out again?' I said, 'I hope so!' I think she just wanted to make sure. So she'd always shampoo it out of her hair or have some kind of spray if I met her at the hospital."

The romance continued when he returned to Notre Dame. Via letters and conversations, they grew closer. Their relationship was building. But as he headed into his last cross-country season, Squires realized during practice with the team that he was not as fit as he could—and should—have been. Due to a number of circumstances, which ranged from his outdoor track injury, dating, and arduous summer work, he had lost a step. But by the time he faced off against Wes Santee in a tri-meet against the Quantico Marines and the Chicago Track Club, the Irish were 4-0 and Squires—with two wins—had shed his bandages and regained some speed. "Not Santee! Again! When I saw him years later, I said, 'You know, you beat me down. I'm doing 27 miles a week, and you're doing 65-70, and I have to run against you! I can run up your backside, but I have no lift in the last part of the race.' We laughed at that."

They led the field throughout the majority of the two-loop route along the course, whose golfers held up their games and with interest watched the race. Squires was steadily ahead of Santee, but never by more than five to six yards. "I said to him, 'Santee, you're gonna get a hard run. You're not gonna just walk away with this one. I'm gonna push.' And I did. And at about 65, 70 yards from the finish line—*woosh!*—he went right by me. He was using me. That was a hard effort. I pushed like hell. But it was a helluva race. And other than a couple of relays, this was one of only a few times that I lost an individual race at Notre Dame—may have been only three times." But Notre Dame won.

And behind wins by Squires, the undefeated Fighting Irish also defended their state and conference titles. But having the 1955 Central Collegiate Conference Championship in Chicago held on the same day as the Big Ten Conference Championship that followed—with nearly 300 runners in the four-miler—presented problems. Within the first three miles of the race in Grant Park, which included the only portion Squires thought required any attention—a small incline over a little bridge—the lead pack dwindled down to three, with Squires among them. With just under one mile remaining, he decided to make an assertive move, the result of which afforded him an apparent comfortable 80-yard edge. "As I'm coming down toward the finish, I thought the start and finish were at the same spot. The year before, it was out and back. But they [must have] needed to extend it, and the finish wasn't where I thought it was. My coach comes across the field and yells, 'Go directly back, follow the same way, and then it's over here!' I was all set to cut across the field to the finish because I was following the powdered lines on the grass. But there were all kinds of lines because the Big Ten was starting from some other place. He saved me from doing that, from cutting across and getting disqualified."

By that time, however, Squires already had deviated from the course. He now had to retrace his steps to that point before he could continue. Meanwhile, his 80-yard lead was eaten up by the runners behind him. The amount of time and distance he wasted proved extremely costly. "I go all the way back to where I originally was before I got off the course, hooked a left back onto the correct way to the finish, and I look up and see this guy about 25 yards *in front of me!* Either he knew the course or maybe they got an official down there to direct. I don't remember seeing anyone there when I got there—maybe I saw an official there and ran right by him, thinking I-don't-know-what. But now I am going like a madman. I am so pissed at myself that I screwed up."

He was in second. "I go after this guy and I'm thinking I am running, believe it or not, the quarter-mile in one of my meets," he explains of his mental mind trick. "With about 15 to 20 yards to go, I went by him like a freight train. I knew enough to go right by him and not slow up at all. I only beat him by a second or two. Boy, did I feel that! And I fell right over. I don't think the guy knew I was coming because of the grass muffling my run. Actually, he deserved to win. He worked together with another guy. But up to that point, it was the hardest race that I ever remember running. And I almost lost the race." Squires turned in a sub-20:00 win in 19:45. A press photo that was taken of the moment of the finish showed the painful-looking contorted expression on Squires's face as he fought for every bit of energy to win just before he collapsed. And it was that wire-service photograph which was used in newspapers across the nation, which included back home. "The next day, the picture that went to Boston showed the worst grimace on my face. My mother said to me, 'Oh, Billy. Someone brought me a picture of you. Oh, Billy. That was...why are you making that face?' I didn't know what to say," he says, laughing.

Notre Dame concluded its cross-country season at the NCAAs four days after Thanksgiving, at Michigan State University. In the snow. "Looked like a blizzard. We get there the day before we're supposed to run, and to do a warm-up we go out on the course, which is the same one as the year before. And there's a big, big stretch of grass for about 150 yards. And that's it—the rest is snow, about an inch and a half so far." Then Squires thought of something he later as a coach shared with his athletes. "Bring an old pair of warm-up shoes, bring your spikes, and bring another pair of warm-up shoes. All of us just had our regular warm-up shoes and our spikes, but we saved our spikes for the race. It's still snowing, and it's slushy on the grass and we're slipping and sliding. I don't wear socks, so my feet are freezing." After a warm-up over parts of the course, and some direction from Squires to teammates Dick DiCamillo, John Michno, Ed Monnelly, Dale Vandenberg, and Neil Wallace, the Irish finished with a basic idea of the course without having traversed the entire route. The next morning revealed more snow. Cars were stranded en route, and an emergency meeting was held to discuss if the meet should be canceled (it was not). Snow continued to accumulate. And despite the fact the course was cleared by seven o'clock, it was still a mess by the time teams arrived. "They used a big street-sweeper machine to clear off the grass. I remember I told everyone to use the dagger spikes, the long ones. And between the spikes, I put gunks of petroleum jelly that I hoped the snow wouldn't stick to. I even wore socks."

But nothing seemed to work—long sleeve shirts, gloves, watch caps, full sweats, socks, warming cream. Eighty-four runners from 13 schools faced 4 miles of cold, snow, sleet, slush, and 20 mph winds in a reported chilly 12 degrees Fahrenheit. Flat, slippery conditions worsened with every footfall, and athletes bumped and elbowed each other for position and stability. "We ran a fast first mile of about 4:27, 4:28. The ground at the start was bare; you could see the dirt from the plows. Then we actually had to run around the plow because it couldn't push any farther because of all the slush-snow. We were then going into about five inches of unplowed snow the rest of the way. Our feet were covered! The slush numbed my feet, and my face was also numb. And then we're running under trees, and the snow on the branches would fall on us. That was a pisser!" With the plow truck stranded, runners made tracks on their own and tried to follow the officials who were positioned along the course and waved flags to draw attention as to where to run. All the while doing this at sub-five-minute pace! "The thing was, you're running on snow and then into slush. And you didn't know who the heck was ahead of you or around you. Everyone looked the same covered in snow." As runners passed by dormitories, they benefited from the cheers of students who leaned out the windows. This was welcome support, especially since the coaches who usually station themselves at various approved points along the course, were nowhere to be seen.

Still among the first few groupings of runners, Squires increasingly felt the harshness of the weather, as his face and feet grew dangerously numb. And he was not alone. "I had that heating cream on my hands, and the heat was melting the snow and ice on my gloves. Slush was coming up into my gloves from being kicked up from other runners. They say when you get a tingling sensation and you feel heat, then that could be frostbite. Well, tingling was common at about the two-mile mark, and the next mile it was the feet. But I kept thinking it's the heating cream that was working. Was I wrong. And then a friggin' log was across the course—a big branch that fell right down in the path. We had to jump over it like in a steeplechase. This is nuts! But we kept going." The surface of the final mile was that of the first, so the ground was a bit easier on which to maneuver due to it having been partially plowed before the truck stalled. "I was still back a ways, but then I started picking off people. The grass was really, really bad. We were slipping and sliding." The grass grew extremely unsettled, and runners by this time were exhausted, wet, and mostly frozen. Even a teammate, with about 70 yards to go and in 20th position, fell victim to the newly created puddles when during a battle with two other runners was tripped up and found himself off his feet and *in* that body of water. Officials rushed to his side, and after several moments of no movement, picked him up and brought him to the medical area. He was okay, but DNF'd (Did Not Finish).

Finishers were swiftly directed inside to the nearby gymnasium, where their change of clothes was stored, and they could begin to warm up and get dry.

Problem was that they were soaked, shivering, cold, and drained of energy. The main concern was, of course, frostbite. The most common areas were the extremities, private and otherwise. With 81 runners finishing within a span of less than five minutes, the gym quickly took on the look of a casualty triage with dozens of volunteers carrying in athletes, pans of warm water, blankets, and other emergency items. "Right away, my hands are numb. I pull off my gloves and my skin's coming off, and I go, 'You've gotta be kidding me!' I can't believe it. A lot of us had frostbite. They had pans of lukewarm water that they used. It hurt like a bastard taking off the gloves." Squires finished 12th at 20:32.5, and Notre Dame tied for third.

It was evident that the Irish put together some of the university's top distance teams over the past few years. "We're starting to become a good distance outfit. And I kind of think there were two of us that really were pulling more than ourselves. I think we were helping to develop the team that came after me in 1957 that did win the NCAAs. I would run pretty hard, but I would encourage the guys. I was used to being on winning teams from all the sports that I played on. I wasn't into that *individual* stuff. In cross-country, it's a *team*. In the relays, it's a *team*. When you get out there, it's *you*. I've always believed in the *we*, but when you are out there, it's the *me*. You're on the line and you've got no one to answer to but yourself and your mirror if you didn't commit the way you should have. Anyone that runs a hard race, no matter what place you are, can look in the mirror and say, 'Hey, I gave my best. And I'll give a little bit more.' I've felt that and I have told that to people all the time."

Some of the Irish—including Squires—spent the short Thanksgiving break at the nearby home of their coach, who welcomed out-of-state athletes. For indoors, Squires once again discussed those elusive trophy races. "I wanted in my senior year to make darn sure to get some decent races in the mile. Wilson said, 'Yeah, you paid your dues, your studies are good, you're okay.'"

During the Christmas break at home, Squires enjoyed another round of indoor track work at Harvard with Josy Barthel. But love was in the air for the senior. After a year of courtship, and impending duty in the service after graduation, Squires and Kuhn (who was a year out of nursing school and working as a nurse at Mount Auburn Hospital) were engaged. "She was the one. So I asked Sally, 'How would you like to be engaged?' That's what I said." He chuckled. At the age of 23, he was set to marry. "Well, I knew I was going to the military and I'd be away two to three years. I was going to be drafted. The only thing that kept me out now was that I was taking science courses. And she was very attractive and she had the qualities of being a good mother. She was going up the big-league ladder—she'd be in charge of the operating room. She'd be massaging the heart before the machine would kick over. She'd have a menu, she called it, of all the surgical instruments and in what order they were to be used. She also made sure everyone was doing their job around the operating table and she'd keep track of all the instruments." Powered in part by his insecurities, Squires also feared in his absence that someone would certainly take his place.

With the engagement secure and a wedding date pending, he returned to Notre Dame for his last semester and learned Wilson's emphasis was still the same—relays, relays, relays. He hoped the talk of an American record was the start of a stretch of high-end races on which he could build his indoor and, finally, outdoor miles.

It was a stellar 1955-56 indoor season for both Notre Dame and Squires. The Irish, 2-1 in dual meets, won four relays and their third straight conference title, and tied for fifth in the NAAUs. Squires, who won three one-mile races and two half-miles, was also a leg on the four victorious relay wins. In addition, he set a meet record against the University of Missouri in the mile (4:13.6); a dual meet record against Indiana University in the half-mile (1:54.2); a conference meet record and Michigan State Normal College Fieldhouse record in the mile (4:14.9); and a Michigan State Normal College Fieldhouse record in the mile relay with Bill Keegan, Joe Foreman, and Porter (3:24.1). And despite a fifth-place showing at the 1956 NAAU Indoor Track Championship in Madison Square Garden, among those in the crowd was Squires's fiancée, to whom he suggested a wedding date of July 6, 1956—a mere five months away. "I knew by then it would be about a month after graduation and time enough before I'd be leaving for the service. Then I started to think, what if I had to go to summer school? Well, if I had to, we'd have them out to Notre Dame and get married on the campus. And she said, 'What? No!' You see," he said with a chuckle, "she did all the big arrangements—she and her sister and aunt—and getting married at Notre Dame wasn't part of the planning."

Also at nationals, Squires in the mile was pitted against pre-race favorite Ron Delany, an Ireland-born miler with a 4:04 in high school and 4:05 in 1955. Squires stayed back with him and a few others, even when at the midway point one runner accelerated. With a quarter-mile remaining, Squires adopted a new mindset to take himself through to the finish. "I'm going to stay with this guy as long as I can. But we went out slow. No one would take the bait to move. It threw me off a bit for the first half, which was about 2:06 or 2:08. I wanted to get going, but I didn't want to lead the whole thing with good national-caliber people and foreign athletes. At the last quarter, I said to myself to think of this as the mile relay and *run*! And I ran! And when I took off, I had a few yards on Delany, but I could hear him near me, I could hear the light clip-clop of his shoes on the wood track. So I run hard to the last corner, and over the last 30 yards he gets by me and I finish in second."

Afterward, about half a dozen athletes, including Squires, regaled themselves at the famous Jack Dempsey's Broadway Restaurant, across from Madison Square Garden. Dempsey, the former National Boxing Association World Heavyweight Champion, at six-feet, one-inch, was still imposing at the age of 60, nearly 30 years after he retired from the ring. "Just as we got seated, this big guy comes over and says hello. It was the champ! He comes over and makes a big deal about us. I mean, he's the *champ*! So I had him sit down and I ask him if he's here every night. He said, 'Oh, no, no. I'm here about three nights a week. Always gotta come in. All you guys are college guys, right, and you're gonna get jobs, right?' Then he says, 'You've gotta watch what you own. You've gotta be on the premises and never have it always be the same time you're there. You'll find out. And watch your bartenders!' We laughed at that. And then I asked him about his early career, if it was true that he had about 38 fights in the beginning. He said that a lot of them were what they called amateur fights, and that some were in bars and they were called fights by a manager or agent to give a fighter a record. There were very few that had rings. That's how a guy got a record. He was very nice. And he took care of us that night."

At Notre Dame, Squires co-coached Lyons Hall to the inaugural on-campus Interhall Track Meet indoor title. Wilson followed up with Squires about the AR for the three-quarter-mile (also listed as 1200 meters or 1320 yards). The record was 3:01.2 by US Air Force Airman and Georgetown University Hoya Joe Deady at the 1955 Metropolitan AAU Championships. "Based on my times then, before I got into Wilson's schemes of cross-country and all those indoor and outdoor events, I could have broken the American record," he surmised of his 3:06 average. "Back when I did run three quarters, I'd finish [slower] because my legs would give out [from multiple events]. I didn't have enough leg strength. I could, at that time, pull. But I'd need more strength."

Engineers re-measured the Notre Dame Fieldhouse track at 200 yards plus one. It was a soft track, so they rolled it firm. Wilson notified newspapers from South Bend, Chicago, and environs to witness the record attempt. Squires planned to use his fellow competitors until the final three laps, and then take over to the finish. And if this plan did not work, he would adapt. Turned out no one followed his plan. "I had to take over before three laps to go. I thought I'd have a little bit of help, so it threw me off a bit." He ran two consecutive 60-second quarters and received help from the track announcer. "I could hear him saying things like, 'All he has to do is run 61 seconds.' And, 'Now he has to do 30,' and so on. What he was doing was the mathematics, which was good. Wilson was giving the splits to the guy and he was announcing it to everyone. And I was feeling good. I was full of life. I didn't have to do the mile and the relay and come back and do the quarter-mile. I came through in two minutes flat, and ran the last quarter in 58.2 seconds. I pushed the last 200." Officials conferred over their watches, as did Wilson and his extra timepieces, and the unofficial (due to its track configuration) three-quarter-mile world record for Squires was indeed 2:58.2. "I felt good, and all the students there were screaming and yelling." He smiled, and then added under his breath, "and it would have been a 4:02 mile." Squires recalled legendary Fighting Irish alum and sportswriter Richard "Red" Smith there as well. "Red Smith called me the Fifth Horse." It was in reference to the Four Horsemen of Notre Dame 1924 gridiron nickname for quarterback Harry Stuhldreher and backs Jim Crowley, Elmer Layden, and Don Miller. "I said to Red, 'Naw, I was the plow horse.' He said, 'No, Bill. I'm going to call you the Fifth Horse.' That was nice. And the race became a big thing. Officials and students were coming up to me and saying, 'Great job!' It was big."

On the heels of the unofficial world record, Squires was invited to run the mile as part of a few track events staged during halftime of the 1956 Sugar Bowl college football game in New Orleans between the Georgia Institute of Technology and the University of Pittsburgh. The game was slated for just after the new year in front of 80,000 people at Tulane Stadium. "Wilson asked me about it, and I said I'd love to run. He also said he was going to see if Aubrey Lewis could run, too. Wilson said he didn't think they knew how good Aubrey is. He could run the quarter at the game. And Wilson said me and Aubrey could room together, which we always did." But neither athlete competed.

Wilson's request concerning Squires's teammate was denied. Lewis in high school won two football state titles; in one meet set three state records; and was a two-time All-American world record-holder in track who two years earlier at the 1954 nationals came in second to US Olympian Bob Richards. And he was African American. It was that last fact which prevented Lewis from his participation because around the time of the January 2, 1956, game, several indirectly related events occurred in the Deep South which began to shatter the lines of perception and tradition, independence and equality, and obtainable rights. On December 1, African-American seamstress Rosa Parks was arrested in Montgomery, Alabama, when she did not give up her bus seat to a white passenger; on December 2, in the bordering state of Georgia, segregationist Democratic Gov. Marvin Griffin in public remarks regarding the upcoming Sugar Bowl, stated he did not want Georgia Tech, a team from his own state, to play Pitt, whose roster included Bob Grier, an African American. In response to the building outcry, specifically in relation to the game, Pittsburgh remained steadfast that the entire team play, which it did. Squires, likewise, stood behind his fellow teammate. "When Wilson got the telegram about a week before the game, he said he was told something like, 'We're sorry, we don't take colored fellows.' He told me Aubrey couldn't go because they just don't take blacks down there. So I said to him, 'Well, then I'm not going, Alex.' He said, 'That's the Christian thing.' He said I could still go, but I'd be without my roommate. But I didn't want to. That stuff bothered me."

Notre Dame continued its relay dominance to open the 1956 outdoors with the DMR team of Keegan, Vandenberg, DiCamillo, Squires; and the SMR team of Foreman, Vandenberg, DiCamillo, and Squires. Including the tail end of indoors and the start of outdoors, Irish relay teams in six events did no worse than third, with four wins, one second, and one third. In addition to the relays, of course, Squires still yearned for marquee miles. The US Olympic Trials were coming up for the Melbourne Olympic Games (held during the Australian summer months of November and December). Squires still wanted—and felt he needed—to run additional highly-competitive miles as prep. He got another chance when Notre Dame met the University of Pittsburgh and Arnie Sowell—1955 Pan American Games 800-meter gold medalist—who tripled in the mile, half-mile, and mile relay. "I started kicking to try and get the kick out of him, and when I got down to about 50 yards to go, before the curb, I was running a 160-yard kick. When I got down to about 25 yards, I'm not hearing anyone near me and I'm thinking I've got it now." With other events to run, Squires conserved. Just then, Sowell breezed past for the win. "I had him! But you know something? Every meet, I always knew I had to try and put my brakes on because I knew I had to run another race or two," a known point which was actually mentioned in the newspaper coverage.

A rematch of sorts soon followed, as both Squires and Sowell faced off in the latter's specialty. Squires was still boiling. He felt he had the mile won, and lost it, rather than being beat. So he vowed, on determination alone, that he was not going to repeat that same mistake in the half. "There was no way. I'm thinking to myself that I had him with 160 left, and I got around the corner and then I let up. I am not going to let up. I am going to run hard the whole race, and maybe *I'll* get the Pitt record. So I let him take the lead. I'm breathing heavy and doing all sorts of tricks so he'd bite. After about 200, I just *go*! I pushed like there was no tomorrow. That's a long kick. Usually it's a buildup kick. But I ran the friggin' balls off this race." But Sowell won the half, as well as the mile relay as anchor. At the 1956 Indiana State Meet, held at Notre Dame, Squires doubled again with wins in the mile and two-mile. By 40 points, Notre Dame won the state title for the first time since 1950. The Fighting Irish later also claimed the 1956 conference championship, which complemented its indoor track conference title three months earlier. That was a special feat for the Irish—to win consecutive season titles. "That was something. That was a goal of ours, to win the conference in indoors and outdoors. We had five of us that could run three events each. Some of them were in sprint events, some were in the jumps, hurdles—we put together a team that, conference-wise, should be able to win."

June, which included exams and graduation, closed out the season. But there was a date conflict between the NCAA Track & Field Championships at the University of California at Berkeley, and Notre Dame's commencement ceremonies. "And you didn't know until the Wednesday before graduation if you were going to walk through the graduation on Sunday and then go to summer school. In most cases, you get a pigskin cylinder for the ol' photo op if you had to go to summer school." Wilson gave the seniors a choice in regard to participating in graduation, the NCAAs, or the AAUs. "I had such bad luck in the past at the NCAAs that I wanted to redeem myself. But my parents had never been to Notre Dame, and this was their big, big to-do. I wanted to show my parents the campus, so I didn't go to the nationals." Squires told Father Brennan of his family's impending visit to campus, and in a telling moment of brutal honesty, that he wasn't sure what his path would entail after graduation. "He says to me, 'You know, I have a feeling about you. And I've had it for a while. I don't know what you're going to do or where you're going to be, but you know how to think on your feet. You're going to be so successful in life…'" recalled Squires, still emotional after all these years as he retells Father Brennan's words, "'it's going to be beyond your comprehension. I know you won't lose your head because you're a good Christian kid. It was a pleasure having you in class.' That man made me able to go through school. He was it. He doesn't know how much he did. He made me perform. And he was on me. He didn't want me to fail."

CHAPTER 6

ONE THING AFTER
THE OTHER

In June 1956—after four long and formative years of tutors, labs, study halls, captaincies, monogram letters, All-American honors, six championship teams, nearly two dozen records—Squires, at 23-and-a-half years old, graduated with an 81.22 grade-point-average (4.22 above the required 77 GPA) and a bachelor of science degree. And according to the newly minted Fighting Irish alumnus, he could not leave soon enough. "I remember as a kid back then that I hated it! It was a horror show. Four years of my life—horrors!" But he grew to realize it was those very same years in which he was pushed to grow that helped shape and form his life. "Boy, did I need Notre Dame. I'll clue ya, I didn't know it then, really, how much I did, but obviously it was a godsend. I look back with great fondness. To this day, I still use things I learned there. They made me."

For his graduation, Squires's parents, the future Mrs. Bill Squires, and his future mother-in-law, took on the 900-mile drive from Massachusetts to Indiana. Murt and Florence stayed at The Morris Inn, an on-campus hotel. "It was a very nice place. I got reservations early for my parents to get in. I showed them where I ran. I brought them over to the fields, the buildings. But they cared so little about sports. What they cared about—the biggest thing in the world—was they were going to have a college graduate. And my father kept saying, 'Oh, everybody talks about Notre Dame. We have to take a lot of pictures.' My mother had a little old Brownie camera from, I think, the 1930s, and they took pictures of all of us, and we got copies for everyone. I remember for one picture I had Dad stand over by the stadium because his friends that like sports will really get a kick out of it." Commencement was held at Notre Dame Stadium and featured as speaker World War II and Korean War veteran, Admiral Arleigh A. Burke, United States Navy Chief of Navel Operations. Presiding were university president Hesburgh and AVP Joyce. "Up to that time, we were the largest graduating class, with 920. That was a helluva class. And as I come up there [for the diploma], Father Joyce moves over and says to me, 'Come over here.' I walk over and he goes, 'Here's that running guy. Did a good job for us. Worked hard. Had a hard time freshman year. Good job, Bill.' Then Father Hesburgh says, 'Good job. I've heard about you. Good job, Bill.' And my parents said afterwards, 'What happened? What were you talking about? No one else stopped and talked to them.' Which was true. The only ones who stopped were the ones who got an award. Everyone else just walked through. My father goes, 'Was it good, Billy, or bad?' And my mother said, 'Murt, be quiet.'" Squires laughs.

With the pomp and ceremony behind him, Squires returned his focus to the US Olympic Trials. There were three meets in which to qualify: the NCAA Track and Field Championships that Squires skipped in favor of graduation; the Interservice Championships for military athletes; the NAAU Track and Field Championships in California. To prepare for nationals, Squires rested his legs and slept. "No exaggeration, I slept 12-hour days. I rested the whole week. And I felt I could beat the world." He arrived two days before the mile event in order to acclimate himself to the time difference, weather, and the Bakersfield Stadium track. As he often did since his childhood accidents, he tested his leg with a light jog in a park. But he did walk a lot to keep it loose. While Wilson was occupied elsewhere on the field, Squires came across Ike Matza, New York University 3000-meter steeplechaser. "I'm watching Matza, and we talk about the steeplechase, and I end up doing two steeplechase water jumps. Ike did about six in front of me, talking me through it, and I did a few more. I said that someday I'd like to run the steeplechase." Weather-wise, Squires does recall brutally hot Southern California temperatures. "It was 82 degrees [Fahrenheit] at seven o'clock at night! I remember that. And it didn't get cool till around nine, which was after I had run. As I was going into the stadium to run my event, coming out of the stadium on a stretcher was a guy from the six-mile run. He had collapsed—I don't know how far into the race he did. He looked bad. They were taking him to the hospital as I was going in. He was dehydrated."

For the mile, Squires had his leg wrapped, which made it feel secure. He felt fresh and energized, but could also feel the oppressive heat. He was among about a dozen men, all of whom had run at least a sub-4:10 in order to compete. He was familiar with most of them, but not so much with the military and California entrants. "I didn't really realize the military people—who were very good and had up to nine months to train—had their own race," he said of the Interservice meet at Fort MacArthur the previous week. "They wanted to go to the 1956 Olympics with a good team because it was us against the Russians. The Cold War was on! Someone had come up to me and asked if I had seen the results of the military trials. I'm like, 'Military trials? You mean the Fort MacArthur guys?' They had put them under Fort MacArthur. That's when I first heard about them."

On medium spikes and a solid track, at the last minute Squires changed his strategy against the heat and the highly-rated field. His calculated decision was to stay close to the army's Fred Dwyer, the Villanova University four-minute miler. "Because it was so hot there, when I was warming up, I could feel the dampness on my legs from the thickness in the air. It was like water in the air. Very thick," Squires observed. "They take off fairly good for the first quarter, in about 62 seconds—not blazing. Looked like we were going to be in a strategic race. I'm in seventh or eighth place and there was a tight group ahead, and we're in the second group, about five guys back. And I could hear the splits—61, 62—so we were within a second or so back. And then they'd announce us as we ran, which I wish they never did. They'd say something like, 'And the great miler from Notre Dame at the quarter, Billy Squires,' and I'm like, 'Don't say that. Don't announce me!' It's like sticking a big needle in the other runners to wake them up."

A few seconds behind the lead group, Squires recalled the words of his high school coach. "Doc would say, 'You've gotta be in the hunt.' That's what he'd say. If you're running fourth, you have to own third place, but you're right there—you're not back. At the half, they pick it up and they threw a 58 at me. I'm looking at Dwyer's legs in front of me and they don't look like they're that far away from me, but they were. From the half, he starts picking it up and I'm with him and I'm drifting, which is fine. But we're not gaining, we're holding." At three-quarters, Squires ran 3:03. "That stunk! And they ran about a 3:01 ahead of us at three-quarters, and then they take off. They just took off!" Squires could not catch up. As the top six spots qualified for the US Olympic Trials, Squires missed out with a seventh-place 4:08. Just ahead of him in sixth was Dwyer, whose innocent post-race revelation infuriated and forever haunted Squires. "I said to him, 'What happened today?' He said, 'Oh, nothing. I'm qualified. Four of us [military runners] qualified. One of the guys in there qualified already.' I was shocked," said Squires, still second-guessing himself decades later. "He was using this as a tune-up, not a qualifier! He was just using it to see how he would go the last half of the race."

Squires's changed strategy failed him. It was an enormous error in judgment. Yet, many years later as a coach, he used this example as a useful teaching tool. "Wilson asked me what happened, and I told him I did something that I would never do again. I said to him, 'Have you ever seen me not go to the front and be right in there in short races where I didn't belong?' He said, 'No, you're a master at that. You have the sense about that.' Well, this was the biggest race of my life, and I changed my strategy! As a coach, that has been one of the things that I've talked to all my athletes about—my failure. *You don't change your strategy!* You stay with your training system. When you're in the race, as a coach I can't go in and say 'Switch this, switch that. I just found out such-and-such'. If you're in it, you're in it. Changing my strategy was the stupidest thing."

To add insult to injury, due to the technicality that athletes ahead of Squires had previously qualified, the top five spots sans the previous qualifiers advanced. "If I ran normally, I could have made it. Since it went to sixth place, I missed by one place by a technicality. I didn't respect some of their abilities. The thing was, they—about four guys—got away at two seconds on the first quarter, and kicked the second and the fourth quarters. That's the race I would have loved to have run. But we got into no-man's land trying to do a half-mile kick. Very seldom did I get back that far. And to be truthful, I didn't run the good mile enough in college to really sense this." Tasting bitter regret and the error of his decision, and still surrounded by the competitive atmosphere of potential Olympic participation, Squires requested Wilson petition him to compete in the 3000-meter steeplechase. "I had the time to get in the steeplechase. All you had to run then, I think, was a mile in 4:12, to get in the steeplechase. I had to do it."

The next morning, Squires was in the steeplechase; and with no more than two jumps and one water jump worth of training that week with Matza! As in the adage to be careful what you wish for, it was for the first time he would cover one-and-three-quarter miles full of 25 barriers and six water jumps over seven laps. Also in the race was 1952 Helsinki Olympic champion and world record-holder Horace

"Nip" Ashenfelter of Penn State University. But all that consumed Squires was personal vindication. "I knew nothing of how to run this. But I had to. I wasted away six years of my life breaking my back for the mile, and I screwed that up the day before. So I was ready for this." The problem for Squires wasn't the distance, but the demanding and intricate technique of approaching, handling, and exiting the jumps. Runners either jumped on or over the solid three-foot barriers. Unlike regular hurdles that bend forward when hit by a runner, steeplechase barriers are not forgiving. They do not move.

"When we start, I'm with about five guys, including Matza. And I'm winging it. I'm going to do for each lap a 72-yard baby acceleration so I can get enough momentum to go over the hurdles. I hurdled for the first four laps, but then I stepped on them if I knew I was coming up with the wrong leg. Either way is okay." Squires, who keyed on Matza, felt remarkably fresh and speedy. Halfway through the 3000, he took the lead. The announcers, once again, delivered a litany of superlatives as they ran. "This time, it was good. Keep it going! Scare the crap out of them," he says, laughing. On the fifth lap, however, whatever freshness his legs possessed, was gone. Because of the constant demand of hurdling and jumping while pushing hard for more than a mile, Squires was reduced to a hard labor just to clear the barriers. He struggled. His legs failed him. "I am so tired. My quads! I can't hurdle anymore. All that landing. I kept telling myself I have to get up for the water jumps. So I step up on them and run hard between them. It hurt."

During the latter stages, though, Squires heard some words of encouragement from Matza. But he couldn't see where he was. "I hear him say, 'You're running great, Billy.' I look around, and then I finally look down and he's on the ground at the edge of a water jump and he's looking for his glasses that snapped off during the lap before. He's looking for the pieces in the water! Seeing him digging in the water with his hands while looking up at me, that was funny to see." With two laps to go and two more water jumps, Squires faltered and quickly lost ground. The more experienced steeplechasers sensed his weakness, and systematically began to overpower him. "I hear the announcer say that Ashenfelter is moving right up. Well, that wasn't bad—I didn't hear anyone else. But then I hear name after name after name." Squires led into the sixth lap, but Ashenfelter passed by with confidence. "My quads! I can't pick my legs up. Even if I have to walk, I know I'm going to finish this race. I make the water jump, but it was a killer. And that last water jump—oh, boy!" The first spot behind a legend is not a bad place, he thought, when Ashenfelter blew by him. But for Squires, that was not where he finished. All those other names he heard who were gaining? They gained. "Within the last 600 yards to go, nine people pass me. Nine! I was dead tired." Out of the 13 entrants, Squires was 10th. "When I finished, I went over to the infield and I laid down. I was dead tired. And Ashenfelter comes over and he goes, 'Good effort.' Which was nice of him. But I was so tired. My calf muscles were blown up, like after a marathon when they swell up. So I got a bag of ice for them. And they gave me a cane!"

Once he finally collected himself, Squires joined Lewis to watch teammate Bernie Allard in the high jump. At one point, three top athletes, who did not compete that day, walked over and began a conversation that was sparked by their amazement at Squires's steeplechase run. "One of them was a sprinter, I think, and the others were high-jumpers. I didn't really know them then, but, boy I sure would later on." They were University of San Francisco teammates Bill Russell (1956 Central California AAU and Pacific AAU high-jump champion) and K.C. Jones (1955 Los Angeles Rams 30th-round NFL draft pick) who both in six months shared basketball gold at the 1956 Melbourne Olympics, and subsequently embarked on stellar NBA Hall of Fame careers with the Boston Celtics; and John Mathis of San Francisco State College, who was on schedule to make the US Olympic team with a record-setting high-jump career but was instead drafted by Columbia Records. "Someone who was with Johnny gave us free tickets to see him sing later on at a club. So I went with Aubrey. And K.C. was there. Johnny sounded real good. And then, when I'm in the service later, all I hear is 'Chances Are' on the radio." He laughs about the number-one Mathis hit. "That's all you heard—'Chances Are.'"

On the flight back to Notre Dame, Squires sat next to a man in his mid-30s, a fellow New Englander from Connecticut. An obvious athlete by his appearance, despite being only five-feet, five-inches tall. He looked rugged, battle-tested, and he sat next to his manager. While Squires didn't want to stare at him, there was still something familiar about the man. "He had glasses on and he looks over at me and my cane and he says, 'What happened to ya?' I told him I strained my knee in a race and that I was a runner and my career's over now and so on. He says, 'Oh, yah? Good. You went to school, right?' I said I did. He said, 'That's good. You went to school. You graduate?' I told him I did and that Uncle Sam's got me now. He says, 'Good. You're a smart guy. You got through school. Don't be like me. You married?' I told him not yet, but I might be soon. And he goes, 'I've been married five times and I have to keep fighting.' I said, 'Fighting? What's your name?' He tells me he's Willie Pep. I say, 'Willie Pep? The featherweight champ? Oh, my god. It's a pleasure.' He takes his glasses off, and he says to me, 'See these mouses and cuts all over my face? This is what you get for not having an education, for not being smart. And I'd have money, but paying five alimonies is a helluva thing. I hope she's worth it.' He was a nice guy. I think at the time he had over 200 wins (Pep's record was 202-7-1)."

Regarding his own track results in the meet, Squires called his mother and informed her that he missed out on qualifying for the US Olympic Trials. "And I had to lie again to my mother. I told her I finished seventh in the mile and I did things wrong. She said, 'Oh, was Coach Wilson mad at you?' I said no, but that I didn't run the race the way I should have. But what I lied about was not telling her about my legs; how much they hurt. I never tell her about my injuries or anything." But at home, Florence did notice his limp. "She says, 'Billy, I can't figure this. One year, they rip your leg apart [with spikes], and you didn't tell me about it. Then your first year you were supposed to go to summer school, and you didn't go.' I used to call them gray lies—they weren't totally black. But you see, she fed all my friends when they visited, so they were all coming to the house and talking to her about how I did. I kept forgetting about that. So she knew."

A month after graduation—July 6, 1956—was Squires's wedding, at Saint Agnes Parish in Arlington. His younger brother, John, was best man. With six years between the brothers, it was sometimes a hit-or-miss connection when Bill was briefly home during the summers as often John was working or with friends, and Bill was training. "We always had fun together. I remember one time when our mother had a birthday party or something and he cut a square off the cake before she put on the name and candles. That was funny."

The wedding with a top track star was also big news! "Yeah, there was even a big thing in the newspaper about me getting married. The sports pages!" About three weeks later, after a honeymoon in Canada, Squires was drafted into the US Army. In the interim, though, he struggled. It was a difficult four years, capped by a disappointing last meet. When he finally caught his breath and began to process everything, he sat alone one day in his old Arlington bedroom and leafed through the scrapbooks and yearbooks his mother created over the years. Instead of a reinforcement of the good and positive from Notre Dame, in his mind it highlighted his failures and pain. Impetuously, he collected the photos, clippings, scrapbooks, and memorabilia, and exorcised those demons. "I burned it all. I didn't destroy the scrapbooks themselves because I knew she bought those herself. But I burned all the contents. My mother went crazy. I lied to her for about four months, and then she asked again, 'Where are all the scrapbooks I made?' I finally said, 'Ma, I got mad and I went down and burned them over the sewer down the street.' She said, 'What? What?' Then she asked me about all my medals, and I said, 'Oh, I didn't think about those. I would have thrown those away, too.' And she said, 'Nooo!' I didn't. But I did tell her how I felt about Notre Dame and everything that I went through. It all came out. And she said she thought I liked it there. It was a good talk."

In August, Squires reported for duty at Fort Dix in New Jersey. About six weeks in, he was assigned to the air wing. "I should have put down advanced infantry because I would have been in the running for Special Services. But with the army air wing, there were helicopters and fixed-wing and prop planes, which I later found out turned out to be spy planes. I thought they were going to be cargo planes or something." Squires also knew enough not to boast about his athletic prowess; that is, until about two weeks to go in basic when they administered a physical fitness competition for a three-day pass. His performance caught the attention of a major, who subsequently questioned if he had been an athlete. "They said I ran the second-fastest all-time result at Fort Dix. But I didn't want to say too much about being an athlete because the next thing I know, I'll be in Korea running messages from foxhole to foxhole. I can't remember exactly what I said when they asked me, but I'm a good improviser. I can make fairly good 1000th-of-a-second decisions. I can think that way and I can actually react that way. One time, some guy had a hand grenade and the friggin' thing dropped and came to me. I kicked the thing and jumped back. It was a good thing I did. The guy said, 'You could have blown your foot up!' I didn't want to tell him about my foot, that it's already been done in with the ax." Squires won a three-day pass, which he used to celebrate with his newlywed bride at the New Yorker Hotel in Manhattan.

With competitive athletic fire still burning while at Fort Dix, Private First Class (PFC) Squires wanted to run. Assigned to the army air wing at Fort Eustis in Virginia, he would also compete in military track meets and competitions for the 29th TC TAAM Company (Transportation Corps Theater Army Aviation Maintenance). Once again, though, doubt crept in when it came to studies. "I'm in a separate school and I show up and there are these guys that had these thick books—four of them—that were their own company books that described the engines and everything. And I'm thinking, 'What the hell did I get myself into?' I don't know anything about helicopters. I'm in the warrant officer's class and I raise my hand and I say, 'Sir.' And he says, 'Don't address me as sir. I'm a warrant officer. I've flown helicopters for eight years...' Fine. I asked him about the class, and he said he could look around and see at least six guys that could build a plane. Great."

Squires's specialty was engines and rotor blades, and he quickly learned about flight hours in relation to every related part. An army private first class, he was ordered to a newly formed, 10-year-old clandestine government organization located at the United States Bureau of Medicine and Surgery, in D.C. So new and secretive was this department that for a number of years there was no sign posted outside as to the group to which Squires reported inside 2430 E Street NW (a fitting headquarters in nearby Langley was finally built nearly six years after his initial visit). "It was the CIA," Squires noted of the original Central Intelligence Agency HQ, spawned from the wartime Office of Strategic Services. "I went there with three or four other guys to get cleared. For what, I still did not know. This was only about seven months in! And they went through my history and everything. And I later learned that the CIA or FBI had been to houses on my street where I had just moved to and also where I used to live, and they interviewed everyone about me—my neighbors, schoolteachers, priests. So somewhere there must be a file on me. Anyway, I took some tests, and one was a psychological test about a bunch of different situations, and how would I react to them. And with about 20 other guys there, I raised my right hand and we took an oath, a pledge, to our country and to secrecy and this and that. In my head, I'm like, am I a spy or in some kind of espionage?" Later that day, during a break at CIA HQ, Squires recalled, he noticed a display of crosses and Stars of David clustered together on a wall. "I didn't know what that was, but I found out. Each cross and Star of David was for a guy that died in the line of duty. And Atheists had a little line as a symbol. There were no names and no year, just those signs. I remember that very clearly."

Squires endeavored to return to competitive shape, and he wasn't too far off with close to a 5:05 mile. "I wasn't too rusty. There were no real hills around, but it didn't matter. I didn't analyze the hill-thing yet until later—the Americans weren't into hills yet. We'd hear about these European guys that were running up a hill, along the flats, and make a big move then, and so on. But I'll give ol' Doc

McCarthy credit—he knew the great Finnish guys from way back were doing that with the hills." One day, Squires visited the nearby College of William & Mary and inquired about training on campus. Under Tribe coach Harry Groves, cross-country had won the Virginia Intercollegiate and the Southern Conference titles, and both indoor and outdoor track won the Southern Conference championship. Grove suggested he run with the freshmen, to whom Squires would soon guide. They respected the "older" Notre Dame All-American, and he eventually was offered an on-campus locker, new running shoes, and to coach the freshmen team. "The varsity coach doesn't really have the time to coach them, so he asked me if I wanted to be his freshmen cross-country coach—with no pay, of course, because I was in the service. I couldn't go with the team on the road because I was in school at Eustis, but I could use all their facilities; I could eat there, coach the freshmen, and so on."

His plate was full again with his Fort Eustis commitment; specialty school; living with his wife, who found a job at Bell Hospital in Williamsburg, near the couple's off-base residence; running on his own; and coaching at William & Mary. The Tribe benefited from how he incorporated coaching techniques he learned, plus treating each athlete by his own ability rather than lump an entire team into one scheme. They came in second to Duke University at the freshmen Atlantic Coast Conference Cross-Country Championship. Squires enjoyed his first real taste—and subsequent success—of college-level coaching. He found it an easy transition to formulate and deliver instruction. He recalled how as a high school and collegiate athlete he effortlessly digested his coach's direction and even dispensed it succinctly as a captain. In this new role as a coach, it seemed like a natural progression of that ability. Squires also advanced his skills in the service; ran regularly; and enjoyed being a new husband.

As is often the case in the army, servicemen are told what they need to know when they need to know it. When Squires was told to board a bus and then a ship, he did just that with many of his fellow soldiers. They were then (partially) notified of their (partial) orders. Deutschland! "It took five-and-a-half days by ship to get from the Brooklyn Navy Yard to Germany. We were there with a whole bunch of other companies that had to go to bases in different parts of Germany. There were about 2,000 of us on board. And guys were sick on the ship all the time. I couldn't take the people vomiting all day and night. I mean, it was bad. When you're out in the middle of the ocean, the ship's going up and down, and you had ropes that were tied to the sides that you had to hang onto when you walked around. And I could feel the spray of the water even when I was up top [on the deck]." He was aboard the USNS *Upshur*, a Military Sea Transportation Service (MSTS) troop transport formerly known as the SS *President Hayes* when launched in 1951. They arrived at Bremerhaven Port, in the northern German town of Bremen, and Squires was assigned to the US Seventh Army in Stuttgart, Germany. When he finally made it to the US European Command (EUCOM) in Stuttgart, he learned they were the first to occupy the base since the departure of the Nazis. "You could still see where the swastikas were all painted over. People in the town were all looking at us, and a lot of them were all walking about the base like it was an open field. We had to get rid of them when we got there. We had bombed this whole area during the war, so the hangers had already been rebuilt by us."

Squires learned the purpose for his CIA clearance and secretive assignment was because one of the main reasons there was such a strong American force in Stuttgart was due to the reported presence of possible espionage and infiltration against US choppers and planes. His main job was to investigate aircraft accidents. "They didn't know what or how these things were going down. There was a group of five of us, and we were all cleared. We'd get to accidents and I'd know if the reason it went down was maintenance or not. I was told by a colonel that there was [possible suspected] inferior work being done on our helicopters, and they had accident after accident. He said they didn't know if they were accidents or espionage. And within the previous year, he said they had 12 wrecks, and there were captains and majors in those helicopters and planes each time." It was further explained that during his investigations, he may come across "rings" and "outer components" not found on most other craft. He was informed of this, in part, because these specific items were nowhere to be located in his materials and instruction manuals. "They were cameras. These were espionage helicopters and planes. Spy planes! The pilot would pull a ring when he was going down, and all the cameras and film—the outer components—would burn up so no one else could get their hands on whatever was being photographed."

Due to the obvious sensitive nature of his work, Squires was ordered to not discuss it with anyone—family, friends, bunkmates. So serious was this responsibility that he was also *reminded* that his mail would be censored if necessary. He even had to be inventive to his captain upon his return. He described his new duties along the lines that he would be "working with the inventory." With no time to waste, his first job-related trip was to a US base in Frankfurt, Germany, where in an MP-guarded hanger was stored the engines of the 12 wrecks. "We found defective ones, we found some brand-new engines that shouldn't have gone down, and so on. And if we could track a good engine to a crew chief that was still here; boy, he'd lose a stripe or two and he'd end up cleaning the practice guns." At the report of a downed helicopter, Squires was either immediately flown to the crash site, or the engine et al. was brought to a hanger in Stuttgart for him to search. If it involved a trip, once onsite they sifted through the wreckage and, at times, carnage. "I could go out at any time. There'd be a few of us with a couple of sergeants. When we'd get there—and we'd be dropped off and the pilot would fly off right away and leave us—you'd walk to the engine and often pass by other parts of the fuselage and things. There can be all kinds of gore. Once in a while there'd be these…burnt…objects. Some sites were bad. Most of the time it'd be cleared by the time we got there."

To offset the nature of this work, Squires found time and places to run. It wasn't always easy. On one particular trip to a major US base in Munich, he met army officer Paul Robert Giel of the US Seventh Army. A two-sport All-American in football and baseball at the University of Minnesota, Giel by this time had played two seasons as a major-league pitcher for the New York Giants. "He told me about a big meet with all the service teams, and that they were actually coaching guys in different sports, like football and baseball. He said they were also trying to coach the guys in running, too. And he asked me about my background," said Squires, who informed him of his Notre Dame and William & Mary experiences. "He asked if I could give the Special Services guys some tips and coach them for military meets that are run against other branches and teams in Europe." Squires organized a running schedule for himself and the others. "I measured distances in a Jeep so I knew what I was running. Without a track, of course, I had to improvise. I incorporated surges and pickups and things like that. I told Giel that I didn't want any special treatment, but the only thing that I might need is, on base, I might have to practice on a track. I always had my running gear with me because I knew I'd be running, but the surfaces on the base were tough." Again, Squires approached the athletes as individuals in regard to their discipline—sprinters had speed-related workouts; long-distance runners worked on endurance. He made sure of this. He knew the uselessness of grouping everyone together by way of specialty. He learned about specialization. While he did lend some coaching knowledge to the sprinters, hurdlers, and jumpers, it was the small group of distance athletes in particular on which Squires mainly focused.

Doubling up as an athlete and a coach, Squires maintained focus on his own races. There were various team and individual outdoor track meets throughout the European theater for which he was training and coaching. There was a progression of meets that began in May, with biweekly contests against other bases; followed in June by qualifying finals versus athletes from other countries; and finally, international competitions in July. Squires ran the mile between 4:12 and 4:14 without expending what he considered an all-out effort. "To be truthful, I made sure that I *just* won. I knew I'd be going against these guys again and I didn't want to show anyone what I could really do." His first marquee international meet was in July 1957 at Denmark's national stadium in Copenhagen, which Squires had to visit. "We went downtown and saw all the, ah, ladies, hanging out on the streets. It was different. And the women—from Denmark, Sweden, Norway—are all beautiful people." The meet featured a higher-caliber level of talent. He was serious about this. "I was intense. I was adapting because these guys were doing more distance than I had ever done. I heard they were doing 60 miles a week! I was getting up to about 40, 45, 50 miles a week. I was picking up my mileage. That averages to about seven miles a day! That was the most I had done. I went slower because of it. I used to run everything under five-minute miles, from my warm-ups on. I kept doing my speedwork, too. For the week or two before Denmark, I increased my intensity and built up my mileage on the base or on the track in Stuttgart three days a week with repeat half-miles, repeat quarters, repeat 600s, and I'd play mental games. I did this by myself. And it was very boring. But I was wondering about these guys doing 60 miles a week and what were they doing that I couldn't do. If they're doing that many miles, it must strengthen the legs, and therefore you'll get tired later instead of sooner. So I upped everything. I could see that running on dirt and grass was better, but I couldn't run on the grass on the base because the grass was between the two airports, so I ran on the roads, which was tar. My calf muscles tightened because I wasn't used to it. And I'd alternate between two pairs of shoes. This was my first foray into running distance."

For the Denmark event's metric mile of 4,921 feet, which is 359 feet shy of a statute mile, Squires did not recognize any of the names of the competing servicemen. But he did know some of the foreign athletes. "But they didn't worry me because I know with my mentality I can go 90 percent of any race with anyone—except marathons—because I have that focus and I have natural genes of speed in my body. From there, it's up to the training. It was a very strategic race. I wanted to hang as long as I could in second or third place, but I wanted to be with the leader. If it was in second place, fine. If it was in third, fine. But just draft. And I knew with these guys I'd have to long-kick, meaning I'd have to kick probably 150 yards to the finish instead of 90 yards. These were the pros of their countries. These were their Olympians. It worked out well, but the leader got away on me with about 200 meters to go on a little move he did. I moved with him, but he was just testing, and he finally moved away off the corner and there was no way I could stay with him. I came in second place about two or three seconds behind. I think I ran a 3:49 (metric mile), which is about a 4:11 mile."

During the summer months of 1957, Squires took part in twice-weekly evening open races. Clad in a T-shirt with either his 29th TC TAAM insignia or the ubiquitous USA shield, he competed in what were called the B series of meets. "The A series were the ones you'd read about in the papers and magazines that were run in Stockholm or Bislett—the big, big ones. To get into them you had to run at least a 4:02 mile, which I hadn't done. I knew I had to go to the B races." One day, just prior to cross-country, while at Stuttgart, Squires was summoned to report to the company office, the notice of which caused him some consternation. "I had a phone call. And then I knew that it must be about my wife because we were expecting around this time. And it was. It was my mother-in-law on the phone." Squires smiled. He became a first-time father when their daughter was born at Mount Auburn Hospital in Cambridge, Mass., on August 27, 1957. "It's a startling thing. It hits you when you hear it. Here I am, I'm a father at 24 years old! Well, the first sergeant was with another guy there, and he says, 'You know what people do now, they buy cigars, buddy!' So I did. And for a name, my wife wanted Mary, and I liked Susan, so we went with Mary Susan. I still call her Susan. And it was a year before I even saw her—when I got home in August of 1958."

It was in late 1956 when Sally had briefly spent time with her husband in Germany. With her nursing experience and education, she easily found a job nearby. "Right away they needed nurses. It was nice having her there, but [eventually] we agreed that she had to go home because it was not a good environment still. The [German] people there were still very hostile; they knew they were in the wrong [and] it was only about 10 years later [after the war ended]."

In the fall of 1957, Squires competed in cross-country, the top meets of which primarily fell under the International Military Sports Council organizing body CISM (Conseil International de Sport Militaire). He was in a regular schedule now as far as running, and his weight leveled off at a healthy 160 to just under 170 pounds. "That was good. I had strength. I could run with that weight. At Notre Dame, I had lost so much weight, they were scared. But in the service, I was relaxed and I had pretty good workouts and I put on good weight." There was one aspect of international cross-country that was foreign to Squires: the distance. European courses ranged from 10 kilometers (6.2 miles) to 12 kilometers (7.5 miles). "They stop running track around the third week in September, take it easy for a week or two, and then go into cross-country until late November. Then they have the world championships, but that was way above my level. But they also have around that time their own country's championships, like we do. And they were running 10K and 12K races all the time." The problem he experienced was he never ran that long at one time, despite having increased his regular mileage to 50-mile weeks. To advance to the season-ending US/European military cross-country 12K championship in mid-November, Squires competed in several "regular season" meets to qualify. While not as prestigious as international cross-country championships, which featured Olympians and other top harriers, he nevertheless wanted to represent the US in the military 12K.

"The military meet was held before the international championship, which was big-time in Europe—like Wimbledon in tennis. For the military meet, I thought we, the US troops, could train for something shorter and not get burned out. We measured out about an 8K, which is about five miles. That would build us up. So I started running long runs of seven miles every week. I'd take a day off and then for the seven miles I'd run quick for about two miles, run moderately for about four miles, and then try to run the last mile a little quicker. I just felt if I did sevens, I'd feel comfortable at it. I didn't know that racing sevens I should be doing 'twelves.' I didn't know that yet. But I had a feeling about what I was doing would help." To prepare for the final meet, Squires ran in a couple of the six-mile cross-country races and also trained with some of the German athletes to maintain his high level of fitness. "These 50-mile weeks are the most I could get up to. And within those 50 miles, I wanted honest miles. I didn't want to get myself into a slower trot or a five-minute-mile pace. I wanted to keep at a faster range. I didn't want to get into a different running gage by doing more. The other US guys were doing more mileage than me, so I would bluff them about what I was doing. I'd still coach them about their own running and what they did in college before the service, and to keep doing that. But here I am, a cross-country All-American, and I'm the only one with less distance but more speed and more ultra-confidence."

Darmstadt, north of Stuttgart, was the site for his last cross-country meet before the military international championship. For competitors, Squires recognized one who outshone the others. At one time unflatteringly known as "Zatopek's Shadow," he was Alain Mimoun, three-time French Olympian who collected three silver medals in two Games behind the legendary Emil Zatopek. "I couldn't believe it. Mimoun was going to run! Zatopek beat him every time. But Mimoun finally won a gold medal in the marathon at the 1956 Olympics in Melbourne, and that was just a couple years before this meet." The race featured familiar golf-course terrain. And since times were not announced, Squires adjusted his wristwatch for all hands—minute, hour, second—at 12 (in the days before electronic digital running watches). "In Europe, on cross-country courses, they'd have red and white flags to guide you, and they also had black flags along the way that would mark kilometers. I was excited about this race. But I wanted to make sure I didn't blow up. I had to hang with these people and then bust away a little bit and then let them catch up, and then go strong at the end. If it's done correctly, you can waste a person. And this is something I kept as a coach years later." He hoped what skills he lacked in "long" distance he could compensate for with his mile speed. He figured if he boiled it down to the last mile, and still maintained some speed and could be among the leaders around that point, that would afford him a better chance at success.

As it turned out, the race unfolded the way Squires had hoped. "I did my first burst after four miles, and after I did another one after four-and-a-half, I kept it going for about two minutes, which I thought was a long time. In training I was doing intervals. But for the other US guys, I would tell them to do a certain amount of one-minute and two-minute intervals. But when you're not there as a coach, athletes tend to not do them. And if they do, they don't do it correctly—they'll do the easy ones. Anyway, I felt comfortable in my execution in the race. And sure enough, there were only two other guys with me in the last mile, and my speed took over and I won. And I was tired. It was a very challenging course. It was a good thing that I had run on golf courses before and was used to it, because it was tough trying to find grass around my base to train on." Led by Squires in first, the Special Services team out of Munich won (Giel signed up Squires as part of his Munich team, not the US Army team out of Stuttgart). "I should have been listed on the army team. When the results came out in the papers and I was listed under the Special Services team, my captain said nothing. I don't even know if it occurred to him. But one of the guys on my army team said to me, 'Hey, Bill. You in Special Services? You getting Special Services money as well as your TDY (Temporary Duty) money?' I said no. He told me he saw the race in the paper, and I told him that it was a mistake I was listed in Special Services." But it was semi-true. "I *was* getting the extra money, about $75 a month, as TDY because of my specialty. I could have gone one of two ways with my specialty work: either get more money from the TDY pay or get a higher rank as a specialist. I just wanted to do my two years and leave. And since I just got married, I needed the money more than a stripe. So I took the TDY instead of the rank. As a PFC, I was doing pretty well. Anyway, when I ran again, I made darn sure I ran with the 29th TAAM shirt."

Three weeks later was the CISM-run international meet. Squires took it easy the first few days after his win, but then added a longer workout to his routine. "I did 70-minute runs. It got boring, so what I did was every time my watch hit five minutes, I would go hard for 30 seconds and then run steady for a four-and-a-half-minute rest period. I knew I was going to go against guys that were going to kill me. I'd love to be fifth in the race—I knew some of the guys were former *distance* Olympians. So I knew I had to stretch my legs out and give me another cadence. And time passed in the workouts. I still do something like that to this day. That was my idea. It was all games. That's what I always did. I'd play games when I ran. And it worked." The day before the event, Squires took part in a jog-through of the course, although not the entire route. The athletes were presented with a festive pre-race meal, which also included the presence of previous champions who were recognized. At 10 o'clock the next morning, on a cold Saturday in November, about 10 dozen or so runners gathered at the start on a large open field. "There were military people everywhere on the course to guide us along the way, and there were spectators watching it, too. By this time, I just wanted it to start—get it over with. I hate waiting at a big, big race. It's cold, you warm up, you take your warm-up clothes off, they have announcements, this guy talks, that guys talk. You just want it to go. I was up on the start line so I didn't have to fight through all those people. But it went off like a shot. I wore flats, not spikes, because we went on grass, roads, and gravel. You couldn't wear spikes the whole way. If you did, you'd have to jump on the side of the roads to get on the grass. And you didn't want to do that."

Squires kept up the steady pace and maintained a backend connection to the lead pack. The distance between first and last of that pack was only about 30 or 40 yards, he recalled, but the leader pulled away and created an insurmountable separation. Squires passed several runners, and when he settled down from pushing, prepared his next move. "I knew I had to do a real full one-minute push. I kept going, and then my pickups began to kick in and I was now in fourth place. I could see the second-place guy, and he was fading. I knew he was coming back to us. And I saw a hill coming up, so I knew I could use it. I kept telling myself to rest on the hill. Just like back in Arlington when I was eight and 10 years old— rest on the hill. I'd tell myself, 'The hill's not going to beat me!' I knew first and second were gone, so I wondered if I could get third. I ran hard and broke my ass, but I ended up fourth. I was pleased with what I did. I was the first American, and I even beat the French Olympian, Alain Mimoun! But I was dead tired. This was the longest race of my life!" As athlete and coach, this was a golden learning experience. As an athlete, he learned firsthand some of the intricacies involved on how to compete at a top level against an international field. As a coach, he gained great insight into some of the mechanics involved. "I did learn a lot. I found out what I would need to do for the next time I ran. They had so much speed at the end. And as a coach years later, I always had my track guys train and run cross-country. I kept saying that if they run cross-country, they'll hurt guys in the track [seasons] because they'd be that much better. And with the track guys, I'd have them run 10K races because that'd give them an edge. I'll clue ya, I was out of my comfort area with that race. Those are the things that later in life helped me put things together as a coach. Because I did things like that, it made me a better coach."

Instead of following up with an indoor track season, Squires spent the winter months maintaining his conditioning. He picked up a few new tricks from his outdoor track and cross-country seasons, and having settled in with his work schedule, was able to plan more workouts. He got to know more people on the base, which included several pilots who'd often take him to various meets around Europe. One flier in particular was a former college football player from

Oklahoma who used to kid Squires about the Notre Dame gridiron team. They'd tease each other back and forth about their respective schools. After more than a year in the service, Squires established a routine at Stuttgart. He had competed in a number of meets and races, so his comfort level in that capacity had grown. He had also by this time investigated enough accidents to become an on-scene expert. "Most of the accidents during the winter months, we went to the site. This one wreck I go to, there was still blood inside. I mean, blood is blood. But I go to this wreck, and guess what. It was his wreck—my Oklahoma buddy. I got weak. Before that, as I say, blood is blood. But when you know the guy, it was…" Squires pauses at the memory, "…he didn't make it. That was bad. And it was an accident, too. Most helicopters are no more than a half-mile up, and when you come down, you come down hard. Hopefully, you can come down into something soft like a soft field or even trees, where I've heard and seen you can make it then. But if you come down on cement or rocks or a mountain, it's different."

In addition to the occasional somber assignment, there were enjoyable non-military moments as well. One in particular came from a Notre Dame Jesuit who surprised him in Stuttgart. After they caught up, he informed Squires they were going to visit Therese Neumann in the Bavarian municipality of Konnersreuth, Germany. She was said to have experienced many religious phenomena, which included stigmata—bleeding from points on her body which resembled the points from where Jesus Christ bled from the crucifixion. She was 59 years old at the time, four years from her death. Rightful permission had been received from Joseph Kardinal Wendel, Archbishop of Munich-Freising, and Squires was "volunteered" as the driver. "We pull up to her place and she's working on her garden. She's out on this little garden in front of her house. There she was! I was fascinated. I'm looking at her, and he's talking with her. You could see the gaping holes [in her hands], but during the bleeding times the only ones that are with her are some nuns and the bishop, for protection. It was something I'll never forget."

Based on his top athletic performances, Squires was selected to compete in the historic and venerable Panathinaiko Stadium amidst the ancient echoes of Athens, Greece. For an athlete, especially a runner, this open-air cathedral is the ultimate venue in which to compete. And Squires understood the history. He realized he would step foot on the very same ground where centuries of athletes before him battled in the quadrennial Panathenaic Games that honored Greek Goddess Pallas Athena for nearly a thousand years, from about 600 BC to 300

AD. It was also the hallowed site of the rebirth of the Modern Olympic Games in 1896, and the Intercalated (Olympic) Games of 1906. "Now, a stadium's a stadium, but there's only one original. And this was it! Athens! This is a thousand times better than running in Italy or Spain or wherever." With his biggest race coming up in Athens, and after a year of running track and cross-country in the service, Squires yearned for some advanced training techniques. The best place for this, he thought, was England. He realized that based on international and Olympic history, British athletes knew far more than the Americans when it came to proper workouts in direct relation to specific disciplines. He felt he had to get to London. Specifically, his focus was the famed Paddington Recreation Grounds. Built in 1888, among the many activities offered on its two-dozen-acre parcel of open space, is a track on which some of the greatest local athletes trained, which included sub-four-minute-mile legend Roger Bannister. The location of the green is in Westminster, and where Squires believed he could meet up with some of the top English athletes. "This is when I found out I have to do more distance. I was faking my distance. I was doing about 15 more miles per week, but I was always tired. I didn't know if I was doing things right or wrong. I was just adapting a little of what I've done, but I didn't really know."

Via a one-week pass, Squires arrived at Paddington, and, like with most athletic clubs, paid a nominal fee that afforded him access to the grounds, along with a towel and a small bar of soap for his post-workout shower. Under his US Army sweatsuit he wore shorts and a plain blue singlet. He noticed that the packed dirt outdoor track was in very good shape, as he expected. When he approached the perimeter of the track, he came across a proper older gentleman sitting on a small fold-up stool. "I say hello to him, and he says, 'Can I tim' yer?' And he points to a stopwatch. I said 'Oh, ah, okay—maybe later.' I get on the track and do my warm-up strides. I go by him again, and he goes, 'Oh, you're a Yank!' I said I was. He says, 'Overhea' ta race?' I said I didn't have a race; that I'm over here to learn, to talk to some of the runners. He says, 'You a tour'st?' I told him I wasn't; that I'm in the army in Germany. He told me that they won't be here until later in the day, around six o'clock. They, being the good runners. This was about noontime, and I was putting on my spikes when I was talking to the guy. So I started doing some light running because I knew I had to come back later. I think I did two halves and some more strides. And the old guy goes, 'Hey, Yank, you pretty good.' I told him I'll be back in the evening." Squires instantly learned new things, such as when he began his shower in the locker room and quickly found out hot water was at a premium! After a few minutes of frigid cold, he was informed he had to pay extra for heat.

When he returned to the Grounds later in the day, he noticed the older gentleman was still in the same place as before, but this time talking with a group of runners. When Squires looked up, they turned his way. "When they were pointing over to me, I figured I'd better go over there now. They asked me about my running and what I just did last year in the military races. They also told me their training schedule for the week; this being Monday, they said I was welcome to join, which was very nice of them. We did about a two-mile warm-up. We did two big laps on the track and then we went outside of the Grounds and did some backstreets and then came back in. They were going like 5:15 to 5:25 miles, and they were chatting away." The leader of the group, who took charge and also helped Squires, was Royal Air Force British Olympian Derek Ibbotson, who two years earlier at the 1956 Melbourne Olympic Games, won 5000-meter bronze, and in July 1957 at the International Invitation Mile in London, clocked a record-setting 3:57.2 mile that stood for nearly a year. Squires knew of the Olympian.

After the warm-up, they put on their spikes, ran another short round of warm-ups, stretched, added a few loose strides, and then included some straightaways on the track. "I was familiar with all of that stuff. Then Ibbotson said we were going to do five or six 600s and go through them at 61 [seconds], which was fine with me. We do them all, and the intervals were good—I had shorter intervals before, so this was good. I loved it. And that was that. They said they were coming back in three days, on Thursday." The following two days—Tuesday and Wednesday—Squires relaxed at London's 350-acre Hyde Park, where he ran about 40 minutes with some strides to stay loose. "It reminded me of Central Park in New York, but not as big. It had paths of cement or something that was too hard to run on, so I ran on the grass. I'm running and I get a few looks from people as I'm running—mostly from women—so I smile back. I'm thinking it's because I'm an athlete or because I look like a military guy with my crew cut. But as I finish up my running, I see a sign on the park that says to stay off the grass." He laughs. His "off-days" were also filled with the usual sightseeing, as the young American wanted to see the world. Part of his exploration included the legendary London Palladium, where he saw popular English entertainer Vera Lynn. "Wow! She was famous. And what a voice. She sang those World War II songs, 'We'll Meet Again' and 'The White Cliffs of Dover.' She was great. And you talk about respect; the soldiers loved her. And the Palladium was gigantic. The place was huge, and they had this big ballroom and a huge mirror ball that would spin around. I could just watch the ball and the lights all night. And there was a big, big dance floor. What a night!"

On Thursday, Squires met up again with the group at Paddington. This time, however, part of the warm-up conversation turned to surnames. "We're all running, and Derek says to me, 'Squires. That's an English name.' I explained that my grandfather on my father's side married an Irish woman, and that she came from Ireland and then they lived somewhere over here [in England]. And he goes, 'Well, you've gotta find out where they lived, man!' I laughed and said I was going to do that. Which I wanted to do." Squires also learned that in the two previous days, between their track workouts when he trotted around Hyde Park for 40 minutes, they ran eight to nine miles on Tuesday and another five miles on Wednesday. Squires was flabbergasted. That meant Monday was track work; Tuesday—eight, nine miles; Wednesday—five miles; Thursday—track work. "When I heard that! This is just in the last four days, from Monday to Thursday. I know it's normal with them, but for me? For four miles, I'd warm up at 4:15, 4:16 to 4:20. They would have croaked me if I went with them for eight miles. I don't have those slow-twitch fibers that are effective."

After the conversational warm-up, the Thursday track workout featured 1200s, which was a great increase from Monday's 600s. That also surprised Squires. He marveled at the succession of commitment, but at the same time began to witness how they built upon layers of workouts. It wasn't just miles upon miles. There was a method to the addition of mileage. And this was the very reason he was in London. To learn. "We did a few 1200s next at about three minutes, and went faster as we went, with normal short rests. And this was after the eight to nine miles and five miles they did the days in between! If these guys warm up at 5:20 to 5:30 miles, they're going to hold that for the longer miles. I can't do that. But you see, they went through the winter when that's all they were doing." The three-mile warm-up—which included stretches, laps around the track, neighborhood miles, and a return to the Paddington Grounds where they ran on the grass around the athletic field—was interesting on its own. Squires took note that the pace had quickened and the sets were cumulative. They were definitely building. And a friendship was also forming. "They certainly knew what they were doing. And I was glad they brought me along with them. They told me I should run a race that was coming up, but I said I only had a one-week pass and was leaving in a few days. They asked me what I was doing all week, and when I told them I saw Vera Lynn at the Palladium, they loved that. They said, 'Vera Lynn! She's like our Statue of Liberty!' I think they liked the fact that a Yank liked her."

The runners liked Squires, too. They were impressed with the All-American, especially since he made the effort to travel to their backyard to honestly learn about running. They realized he had talent, but it was also his interest they noticed. And they let him know that. "Based on our workouts, Derek told me he could understand I could run the half-mile well, but that my half-mile time didn't register with my mile time, in that I should be running about four seconds faster in the mile, based on what he saw and what I had told him about my collegiate running. I told him that in college, I'd run three to five times in a meet and twice fast (speedwork) during the week from September to May, and I only had five weeks off. I told them even when I was on vacation or back home, my coach encouraged me to run. He didn't believe in an off-season." Ibbotson and the others disagreed with that approach. "They couldn't believe that. He told me I should be pointing toward specific things and building myself up for that. He said, 'I'll tell you, young guy, you said you do speedwork two days a week and you said it's harder than we ran the other day, which I think was pretty hard. That's too much.' And he said that's not enough time off between seasons, either; and that must be why the Americans always seem to disintegrate. He used that word—disintegrate. And he was right. They have two seasons a year—half a year of racing and the other half a year building up. And he said you have to run more distance to get your legs to be able to carry you. At that time, fast-twitch and slow-twitch fibers [the difference between leg muscle types] were just being talked about, which we got out of the Russians. He also said that I should be able to run six to eight miles at a moderate pace on the in-between days, which they did. For me, a moderate pace would be 5:20 to 5:30. And it has to be comfortable, and as long as you can talk while you run. All of that made sense."

Friday, Squires ran on his own; Saturday, the group had its long-run day of 12 miles in the country. "I wasn't ready for 12 miles. They asked me to go, but there was no way I could do that. And besides, I had to get ready to leave. The end of my one-week pass was coming up. But it was good talking with Ibbotson. I remember what he said to me about American coaches, that he always wondered what they do to their athletes. I explained to him that the main thing with the collegiate coaches is that they want to win their division or conference, which I told him I knew they don't have in England."

Back at Stuttgart, Squires prepared for the upcoming international meet in Athens. He had about six weeks to incorporate his newfound knowledge and workouts. He refocused his attention on the buildups about which Ibbotson discussed, on the basis that the Brit had estimated Squires should be in the mile neighborhood of 4:04 to 4:05, based on his half-mile times. "I remember him saying that. You know, real good athletes don't throw bouquets at other athletes. They say it the way it is, and I respect that. Even me. As a coach, I never talk about what you're going to do for a time. I will say you'll be in this place or the top 10 or something, but not a time [which he would only put on paper as a predictor to be read after a race]."

Part of his prep work included half-mile races at a few German biweekly all-comers meets. While tough competition lacked in these weekend events, he nevertheless benefited from the "workout," which he treated as time trials. He was coaching himself. "These were held every other Saturday. And I did have one good match with a real good German guy that showed up and gave me fits. He went out like a bullet, and at around 600 meters—about a lap and a half—I'm sucking wind, and I ran about a 1:52, which isn't a good time. But the tracks there weren't really that good. The officials were volunteers and these meets weren't the big ones like I've been in, but they were okay. But I really did screw up. What I should have done was get a couple of the Special Services guys up in Munich that I was still coaching, and have them pace-set me in these races. And I should have alternated between the mile and the half-mile in these meets. The way I run the half-mile is for the first 200, you're getting your body into a rhythm and you're trying to hold your speed as you go. There's no rest in the half. You're going 90 percent of your body speed. And the monkey doesn't jump on your back—you can get through it. In the mile, you're going at 85 percent, and for longer. And the monkey can get at you because you get into an oxygen debt when you get past 1000 yards, like two-and-a-half laps. You've used up a lot of your glycogen, so you're training's got to be able to get you through it."

For the CISM meet inside Panathinaiko Stadium, ceremony preceded competition. Squires recalled the possible presence of the entire immediate Greek royal family at what he recollects was the Balkan Games, an annual championship meet in alternating sites that began with an unofficial competition in 1929. "I think the king and queen were in the stands, not on the field. And when we came in behind our flag bearer, and the sun hit the white stone of the stadium, it was all bright and beautiful. The whole city was wonderful. We had a chance the couple days before to sightsee. It was lovely. Walking into this place was something. I'd gone to the NCAA and AAU championships and you don't march in to them. This was different. You're representing your country and you're wearing the blue uniform with USA on it, and there was a high with that. There was. And I even stole a royal kiss. When we were in line to meet the royal family, I leaned in and kissed the Queen on the cheek. You're not supposed to do that, and their people— some guards or whoever behind them—looked over at me and nodded me away." He laughs at the impulsive maneuver. "I was young," he says, laughing again.

In the event program, the hometown of Squires was listed as Boston instead of Arlington, a common practice in such materials to use the closest major city. As he learned when he competed away from home, the Massachusetts state capital is often associated with running, especially with the revered formation of the well-known Boston Athletic Association in 1887 and the Boston Marathon 10 years later. It always drew attention to Squires. "One of the officials comes over to me the day of the meet after he saw Boston in the program. He was a fit, skinny, tan-looking guy, and he says to me, 'Boston. Please to meet you.' I didn't recognize him until he came right up to me. It was the great Greek runner, Stylianos Kyriakides," noted Squires of "Stelios," the Greek Olympian who won the 1946 Boston Marathon. "Years later, many years later, I met his son, Dimitri. He told me that he was about 12 years old at the time of that meeting, and his father could have brought him down, but his father didn't want him to miss too much school, so he didn't. But Dimitri did say that when his father got home after the meet, he did say there was a Boston man that ran. And I told Dimitri that after the meet, Stelios and I had a good conversation about the marathon and running, and that it was nice to meet his father."

Unlike the majority of track ovals commonly found in the US, the track layout inside Panathinaiko was oblong with extremely narrow corners. Runners were forced to take into account the sharp edges of the short corners and carefully negotiate each turn after the long straightaway. "It was brutal. We didn't know what it was like. We'd seen it the day before, but when we were doing our strides, we were kind of doing baby-jogs around the corners. Trying to run a 51-second corner, which you had to do, was like someone had thrown us all into a small space at the same time. It was so narrow and long, and there were poles at each end. They kept it the way it was for the ancient athletes, when they basically ran up and down a long straightaway, stuck their hand out, grabbed the pole, and swung around and went back."

In the first heat of the metric mile, Squires came in fourth and advanced to the final. "I ended up passing one guy in that race, and I think it was only smart because to get third I would have had to go suicidal on that last corner. It was tough. Instead of a normal 120-yard straightaway, it was probably 140 yards, and we lost at least 25 yards on each corner. You just ran hard." He hoped to take with him into the final that experience from the qualifying heat, and strategize to a top-three podium finish. He now had a feel for the long straightwy and short corners. "On the first lap, we were all piled up. And on the second one, these guys figured if they could go three turns up front, no one could pass them. And they were right. It was the only way. That's called suicide. It's called front door, meaning you're going all out. You can do it, but you can also get injured. But I think they had quicker acceleration than I did. I wasn't the way I used to be when I was doing relays because I'd been away from doing 300s and 200s. I had run 21.7 in the 200, which is pretty quick, and my quarter-mile time was at about 1:47, 1:48 at one point. But not now." Squires was among the group in front, but he was still too far behind to make up any ground. With such a compact cluster of runners, he was unable to ignite any charges to infiltrate the top three. In an approximate time of 3:51.9, Squires came in fourth in the 1500, about two seconds behind the winner. "Two seconds was a good margin. And I was tired. You had a qualifying trial and then the final with only about an hour in between. During that time, I walked, jogged, and stayed warmed up, and drank water. I didn't want to sit down, so I kept moving along. Thing is, I didn't simulate that in my training. But I don't know if I could have anyway."

Back at Stuttgart, with about a month left in his hitch, Squires trained a newcomer his duties in order for him to complete his two-year service. In addition, he still wanted to turn in a top mile time before he departed. This was his last chance to shine in Europe. So he barnstormed the mile. "Every 10 days, I found a mile race somewhere. I was going out and I was headhunting for races. Even the pilots helped me. If they needed flight time, I'd tell them to just drop me off here or there for a race. I had to wear army fatigues and then have a bag with civilian clothes in it to change into because you didn't want to walk around these little towns with your fatigues on. You could, but they'd just gone through the war and they didn't want to see it anymore. But the quality was up and down, and I only found one good race. And I ran a 3:49 metric mile, which is a 4:07 mile, which was very good. I could feel the leg strength coming. The training was helping."

Since the time he had been in the service, Squires improved his mile from around 4:12 to 4:07. He looked forward to dropping that even further when he once again qualified for the season-ending international track meet. But unlike the previous year in Denmark, the 1958 edition was in Belgium. "I hadn't been to Belgium before, so I was excited about that. This is one of the things I wanted to do while I was here—to visit all these different countries and run in them." The only drawback he faced was training, where he lacked running partners who could properly push him. As an accomplished runner, he understood what it took. And as a beginner coach, he also realized what *else* it took: he couldn't do it alone. He knew to reach that next level would require assistance. "It was two years from college and I was doing pretty well. I'm doing all this by myself. I've added mileage on, I've learned a lot, but I have no one to train with, except when I go up to Munich and help coach the Special Services guys. But no one has the speed I have to really train with. But lo and behold, Munich gets a kid that I had at William & Mary. This kid gets drafted as a sophomore! He's over there in Munich and he remembers me when they brought my name up. They were telling him all about what I was doing with them as a coach, and he was telling them what I did with him at William & Mary. What are the odds?"

Squires grabbed a weekend in Munich and met up with the former Tribe and current army private. Two weeks separated the qualifying meet and the Belgium final, so there was no time to waste. "In those two weeks, I sharpened up. I did a lot of 600s and 300s, which were sharpening things for me. I'd run a 300, rest 200, run a 300, rest 200, and so on—*boom, boom, boom*! Three straightaways! I'd run the straightaway, rest the corner, run the straightaway, and so on. And then I'd jog a lap after each one I did, and with each one I'd go a little faster. I'd do circuits like that, rest, and do it again. Four sets. And with the 600s, I'd double the 300 circuit. I'd do the 300s at half-mile pace, and the 600s at mile pace. All with short rests. And then I'd do my old bread-and-butter workout of a four-minute mile in five minutes, where I'd do a lap, rest 20 seconds, do a lap, rest 20 seconds, and continue it for five minutes. You never stop moving. It was tough, but very good. I'd also do ladders of 200, 300, 500, 600, 1000—you could play around with that."

According to Squires, the international track meet was held at the Stade Maurice Dufrasne, a soccer stadium in Liege. The metric mile field was about 10 runners strong. Standing shoulder to shoulder along the start line, Squires focused on surviving the first turn, where oftentimes aggression could result in a spill. Once safely past that first corner, there were no lane distinctions and everyone beelined it to the inside position. In his final international competition, Squires from the middle lane shot out fast for the opening 300 yards. He successfully reached the first corner, turned with the field, and continued on unabated. "For me, this was *balls to the wall!* The races were scheduled so that you could run more than one event, like I always did in college. But *no way!* I wanted a good mile time. This was it. This was my focus. Nothing else." Along the first straightaway, he feigned early exhaustion as a lure in the hopes of a bite. He was fishing. And some bit. "I'm breathing heavy—getting an Academy Award—and all of a sudden here comes a couple of guppies thinking I'm out. I stay behind them. I stay close so going around the corner I could stay tight so I wouldn't lose any yards. You don't lose anything on the straightaway, it's only on the corners."

The pace settled, then slowed up a bit, which forced Squires to huff and puff another trick. This time, it dropped a runner. It was working. "The lead group was getting smaller. And I could feel that someone's going to take this with about a half-mile to go. I could tell. They were trained guys and they were waiting for that. They were going to go! After about a 60-second first lap, we hit the half at about 62 for a 2:02 half-mile time. We were slow. I wanted a 1:59. So I knew I had to run my ass off the next quarter, which I did. I ran hard and we did a 3:02. That was good—a 60! But I was getting tired. I was doing bull work, I was working hard and pushing it. So, now, I wanted to see what we could do. And then it was finesse city!" The key was the final kick. "With 200 to go, I decided to go suicidal to race the corner, to really race it. I'm pumping my arms and I'm just touching the track with my feet because I'm trying to spend no time on the ground. I can hear their heavy breathing, and I know they're going to kick off the corner, but I have to get them to accelerate to try to catch up but then decelerate toward the finish line." Once on that last straightaway, Squires locked his sights on the officials at the finish line, as three runners joined him on his outside lane. "We're rolling down and I'm starting to feel it. I look at the tape at the finish, and two guys go by me. They're gone, so I focus on this other guy for third. He's up on me, and I'm not about to look at him, and the next thing I know, he's about four or five feet ahead of me. And that's how we finished. He got me by a few seconds. When he accelerated, I couldn't react to it."

In fourth place in a metric-mile time of 3:47.6, Squires posted his mile PR with a 4:05.6. "That was very, very good for me. And I was tired. I walked for about 200 yards before I jogged a bit. I felt it in my calf muscles because I was pushing off so much, and plus the track was a soft track. But I really feel that having run that 12K [earlier], and the 300s and 600s, really did help my head. And if I didn't do those moves in the race—and thank god I did them—I wouldn't have got that time. All those guys wanted was wins, but I was happy with my time." Afterward, Squires with his teammates celebrated. It was a time to enjoy and reflect. "I think I even had a few beers, which I never cared about doing after a race. But it was happiness. I was happy because I think I was closing the mile down. Back in the east, back in New England, no one was going to be able to run with me. I won't be able to get that mile time down because I'd need help to do that."

In August 1958, Squires was honorably discharged. He traveled back to Fort Dix, from where he phoned his wife, "to let her know I was all right and that I didn't drown in the ocean or anything," and he decided to surprise her with an unannounced connection home. "I hadn't seen Sally in a long while. I think she only spent about 10 days in Germany with me the whole time. She had come over on a vacation, thinking she may stay, but that didn't happen. The officers with me took good care of her. They were nice. And I was dying to see my little baby. I hadn't seen her at all. She was about a year old by now." On August 16, Squires arrived home. He was a new father, and as he soon found out, an unemployed one. There was no promised sales job waiting for him. And despite the completion of his military service, for a dozen years thereafter—largely due to his CIA clearance, and despite having only a single arc chevron on the shoulder of his uniform—Squires was still "on call," so to speak. As such, he was expected to respond at a moment's notice, whether or not a drill. "I was an army wing technical parts specialist, but because I was also cleared, they didn't want to lose me. When you're in and you wonder what you were about or not about, they were very vague to me. But they did say I may be needed someday again. I remember during the Vietnam War years when I was coaching and teaching at Boston State College, they said, 'We may need you again.' And I had a military guy come to the school and ask me if I had my alert bag, which was supposed to include my helmet liner, field uniform, boots, and things like that. Which I did. I always needed that in my car at all times. He said, 'What's your license plate number? Give me your keys.' He wanted to see it. They would periodically check. If I had to go right to the field, I was set to go with that bag." (In 1970, at the age of 38, Squires was finally "totally" discharged from the United States Army.)

CHAPTER 7

WARRIOR

In the spring of 1959, the formation of the coaching philosophies, approaches, styles, and results, for which Squires would become known worldwide, began to take shape in earnest. He had not made such a concerted attempt before. In Wakefield, Mass., and his hometown of Arlington, all his collected experiences as an athlete and a coach began to jell into the early foundation of his successful program. While not necessarily in the forefront of his thought process—he primarily focused on providing for his family and newborn daughter rather than beginning a six-decade-long illustrious coaching career—this moment in time was a tremendously prophetic turning point in his life. The magnitude of accepting seemingly pedestrian high school teaching and coaching positions would reverberate not only throughout his own life, but that of countless others too numerous to count.

Instead of working in sales, or even as a Notre Dame coach—which at one time was offered to him—he looked to teach and coach in his home state. He went to school to teach and was certified in 12 states, but Massachusetts required one more class, in psychology. He eventually began teaching biology at Wakefield High School for the 1958-59 school year, and pursued his master's in health science at Salem State College, the University of Lowell, and Boston University. In the fall, fellow Wakefield teacher John "Deke" DiComandrea reintroduced Squires to road races. A runner himself (12th in the 1955 Boston Marathon), he and Squires mostly ran five-milers and the occasional 10-miler. This, in turn, reignited Squires's competitive love of the sport. In their first races, Squires won a five-miler; and at the New England 15K championship in Wakefield, turned in a top-10 performance. To improve his time and endurance, Squires increased his mileage and ran to school, where he showered and changed before class. Unbeknownst to him, teachers and students watched him on the streets as he ran in his official USA or AAU singlets, and red, white, and blue sweats. Soon, athletic director Frank Charbonneau approached Squires to coach track and cross-country. "What I didn't know was that the kids went to the AD and I guess they said they wanted a different coach. I didn't know anything about it. I didn't even have any of those kids in my class. Apparently, the kids would see me running around the town and they also had read about me in the papers. What could I tell this guy now? So I told him that I'll coach in the fall."

After a full school year of teaching biology, 26-year-old Squires began his coaching career in the spring of 1959 in a preseason cross-country meeting with the Wakefield Warriors, who, it was pointed out to him, had not recorded a winning season under the coach he replaced. "I wasn't worried about winning at this point. In May, a few months before the season began, I just wanted to meet them and to get them running. Most of them were also in track, which was good. So I said I wanted them to take three weeks off after track, and then I'll give them a program for the summer."

He also continued to compete under the B.A.A. At the 1959 NEAAU Cross-Country Championship 15K, he came in sixth in 55:39. It was this kind of competitiveness, and results, that Squires brought to his coaching. He figured he could spend a month or two and coach the team through the summer so by the time cross-country began in September, he and his athletes would have learned much about each other, and head into the first meet prepared. But he soon realized he was unfamiliar with the National Federation of State High School Associations rules. Coaches were not allowed to hold summer practices. But captains could. After captains were chosen by the team, the newly elected leaders brought Squires to their home cross-country course at Breakheart Reservation, where the large protected wooded area featured an interior running trail of approximately two miles and an exterior course of about three. "The cross-country courses in high schools then were from 2.3-2.5 miles, which was the length of the state championship course at [Boston's] Franklin Park at the time," noted Squires, who made sure it was 2.5 miles. He then incorporated an early version of his simulation technique. "That was my own idea. I didn't get this from England or anywhere. This was the first time. I wanted to create a simulation course because I thought why don't I make our course like the state championship course. And for the summer, I can have the kids run over that so they'll be used to it for the season and in the state championship."

A natural drawback of not being present at summer practices was, of course, the lack of attendance. In cross-country, where teams are small, the absence of even a few runners makes a great impact. And sure enough, Squires found only about a third of the 13 Warriors at the first few sessions. Practices were not mandatory, but the large number of no-shows indicated a pattern of apathy. Squires addressed this quickly. "During some of the practices, I'd go down to the course and I'd start jogging the opposite direction of the team. And as I come across the team, I'd say hi to the captains as I ran. I'd tell them not to tell anyone I was there, but that we were going to work through this [low-turnout issue]. I think they liked that support. So I'd get back into my car and I'd drive to the other side of Breakheart because I knew they were going to run to a point there where they were going to turn around and then go back at a quicker pace. So I start to jog there, and I come across the kids, and I say hi, and I count out loud—'Oh, one, two, three, four, five. Okay, five. Where are the other eight?' And I keep going." Later, Squires called the captains to maintain a list of participants so he knew who'd be in shape and who he'd focus on if they missed practices due to vacations or other legitimate reasons. He did this because he wanted to introduce weekly runoffs to determine who would compete. "And I said I'd run it with them. I didn't want to scare anyone away. I didn't want to lose anyone. We only had 13 kids, and you need seven in a meet. And that's with injuries and getting sick and so on. And I didn't want any of the kids to get discouraged." Another incentive to do well in the runoffs, in addition to making the top seven spots to compete, was the chance to receive a free pair of new running shoes, which Squires obtained via personal connections. This also rewarded those who put the time in during the summer.

Squires depended on a solid top three, but the remaining potential point-getters fluctuated. Thinking ahead long-term, he developed a program where younger students in seventh and eighth grades—not yet allowed to compete with the high school runners—ran and maintained a fitness level and approach that benefited both team and coach when they competed as freshmen. He formed a farm system of sorts—similar to his junior-high program in South Bend; a common practice in team sports, but not yet fully utilized in running. "I knew how to do it because it worked well back then. And I knew I needed a feed-up system at Wakefield because I gave myself at least three years teaching so I knew I'd need talent down the road. If I at least set up a foundation for these kids, it would work."

Less than two weeks separated the first day of school and the first meet. But Wakefield entered the 1959 cross-country season fit and confident. In varsity meets, 10 ran but only the top seven scored. In JV meets, at least five participated because the top five scored. "I told the kids we were going to do all kinds of new training. These kids were slow, so I knew this was going to be a task. The top two kids were pretty good, and there was this other kid that trained like a bear when he went away during the summer. He, I think, became the top third kid. And it was a long day for the meets. You'd go over the course first. After that, the JV team would run their meet, and then the varsity meet would go." Squires surmised that the first three meets would be "shakeout" meets to evaluate the team status. He told the kids that by the end of the season, he wanted a secured varsity seven for the state championship, even though 10 could enter. In regard to junior varsity, the term of which he did not favor (Squires in front of the kids said "second squad"), he also wanted a solid core because at the time, both the conference and state championship meets were held the same week.

During his first season, Wakefield lost two dual meets, but was still competitive, according to Squires, who acknowledged that the Warriors lacked a strong fifth point-getter. But as the team began to take shape, so too did the coaching. "As time went on, I had four kids that got better. Then I started seeing this young kid, a sophomore, and I talked to him about running with our fourth kid. Then I thought about working them in groups. The first two kids ran together, the third and fourth kids ran together, and the other two or three kids were together. I told them they have to work together. Then, in meets, when they see me at wherever I was along the course, to push real, real hard. And I made sure they'd see me about three times in the race, and always around the last quarter-mile." Wakefield entered the 1959 Massachusetts State Cross-Country Championship at Franklin Park with a winning record. They performed well under the tutelage of the first-time high school coach. In his pep talk to the nervous harriers on the bus to the meet, he combined a boost of confidence and a bit of strategy. "I said, 'Just do your best. These are memories you'll always have, so make them fun. There're coaches here with only two guys. They won't score enough to win. Their teams are terrible, but they have a good kid or two and that's all they bring. But as long as I coach, my *teams* will come. And I'll guarantee—I will guarantee—you will not be last! And I think you can be in the top 10.' That got them. They look at me and then they look around at each other. And I said, 'I really feel that when we went against those teams in the Essex County meet, I was impressed. You see, you have to go against the iron. And you lose to the iron, but guess what? The iron becomes steel, and you can't break steel.' It was something along those lines to get their heads into the race." Since coaching during the meet was prohibited, Squires instructed his kids that he would position himself on the sidelines somewhere about midway through the course, and when they approached him, would utter either "pick up" or "hold." He would say only one of those two commands. "I knew you couldn't coach, but to me, that isn't coaching," he said with a wink and a smile.

At the state meet, Squires ensured his kids stayed focused because there were so many teams to compete and races scheduled—four separate races for each division. "When our race goes off, I watch them run, they go by me; and later, I see our kids coming in around 28th, 30th, 40th, and so on. The officials add up the points afterward, but it takes so long for them to get the overall results from all the races and teams. I knew that with the points we got, we should be in the top 10, and maybe even in fifth. But by the time we were ready to leave—I mean, we were done and the kids were hungry and so on—we didn't know the results yet. But I knew we did well." As the Warriors began to depart, Squires was called back. "When I get there, the official goes, 'Billy Squires, what are you doing? Your kids ran great!' I thanked him and said that the kids haven't eaten all day and that we were leaving. We got to Franklin Park around seven in the morning, didn't run until around 11, and we're ready to get back. So I thanked them again and was about to leave when he stopped me and hands me a trophy and he says to me, 'You won the championship!' I was stunned. Here I am thinking fifth place, maybe. But we won! We win the state championship! Great!"

In his first outing as a high school coach, the state cross-country championship was his. Wakefield scored a record 190 points to finish atop the Class B division. While lowest score wins, the record was the highest because the average winning score is consistently in the range of 30 to 40 points. Winning the title with nearly 200 points was unheard of to the point of implausible. "That's the most points, I think, to ever win the high school state meet. To this day, I don't know how 190 points won a championship. But what I think happened was that none of the teams had any depth. They had a few teams with one or two good kids up front, but they wouldn't have anyone behind them to get more low-point totals. I can remember only one other time something like this happened. When I was in the army, I read in the paper that Notre Dame—it figures, without me—won the national cross-country championship with the highest total ever with 200 points. I thought it was a misprint. This was after I graduated! And the first guy to cross was, I think, in 31st place. How does that happen on that level?" When the team returned to Wakefield High, with trophy in hand, Squires instructed the captains to hand-deliver it to the athletic director, who was at the home football game that was in progress. The AD was equally thrilled. And during halftime, just hours after they won, the champs were recognized in front of their hometown crowd. "That was nice. They made an announcement that the kids won the state championship, and everyone applauded. The cheerleaders did a cheer for them, and the captains went on the field with the trophy. And I told the rest of the team to go run out there, so they were all on the field. I didn't go on the field because that's not the time for a coach to be a hotdog. I've always felt that's the time for the athletes to be honored."

The culmination of running and coaching experiences that Squires pooled together for the first time in an organized arena empowered him as a coach. He was onto something. And when his wife later reminded him that he initially thought these kids were at least two years away from such success, it gave him pause. "That made me think. What did I do different in practice? What made the difference? And it was running together in pairs; it was repeat hills; and it was group running, with Group 1 and Group 2. That was it. I later added pickups and more group running, but I could see the benefits of what was started here. This is where it began. And it was all what I envisioned. With the groups, I wanted the first to the fourth guy to be able to know they could be able to stay with each guy and be able to lead. Because in a race, it'll give everyone a feeling that they could do a sustained run, which is what happens in a race when you pass someone or you get passed. They have to be prepared for that." At the high-school level, for repeat hill work, Squires directed his kids to warm up for 20 minutes and then run up the hill for 90 yards, run down, jog a three-minute rest, and repeat. In the beginning, this was done twice. During the season, however, distance increased to 100 yards and then 125 yards. The entire team finished with one hill-run in about 75 percent effort. "This was for cross-country. Track was different, but for cross-country this would be part of the workout. And as far as doing any tempo or speedwork, not in my first year. In my first year, they learned how to 'run strong,' I called it. You can't do too much too soon with kids. I had to visualize, analytically, what was taking place in training. This was the first time for these workouts."

Squires taught and coached at Wakefield, traveled with his team to meets, attended classes for his master's, and worked various construction and landscaping side jobs. He also became a father once again when on May 16, 1959, William Joseph Squires Jr., expanded the family. With such a workload, Squires particularly looked forward to Sundays, when he took his family on mystery adventures. "I wouldn't tell them where we were going, and Sally would be like, 'Will you tell me where the heck we're going?' We'd laugh because I wouldn't tell her; but I'd say, 'Isn't it better you don't know in case the kids hate it?' I'd look up places and I'd read about places to go, like farms and ships, museums and old historical sites, zoos and parks. It was great fun."

Squires inevitably was asked to coach track, which began with the 1960 spring outdoor season. To attract fresh talent, he approached the football, basketball, and ice hockey teams. He also wanted their coaches present at the meetings when he'd make his pitch. "I told the coaches to talk it up, to talk about track, and that I'll need them there when I meet with their kids. And they *were* there. I told the kids that I played basketball, I played hockey, and I played football. So right away I got their attention and, I hope, I got their respect because now they know I know what it takes because I played their sport. And I told them I can guarantee I'll make them quicker and stronger for their sport." He speculated to the kids that it would take at least two years before Wakefield track would be competitive in terms of wins and championships. That was his expectation. "I wanted to be honest with them. I also talked about the cross-country team that just won the state title. I told the kids, 'If you ask them, they'll tell you I didn't kill them in practice, but they worked hard. And guess what? They believed! And I believe in myself. And in this sport, it's an individual thing, even in the relay, so you've gotta be mentally tough. You can't blame the guard, you can't blame the forward, you can't blame the defenseman.' I wanted to make a point with each of their sports. And I said, 'But I know you'll be better in your given sport. I know what it takes.' I wanted to make it attractive for them."

He also recruited in the lunchrooms during school and talked up the sport when he attended various Warrior games. And it worked. Between 45 and 50 kids came out for track and field. He even spread the word with radio giveaways and raffles, which resulted in the attendance of several hundred spectators at any given meet. But he forgot about Wakefield's track. "It was awful. It was a clay track, and when we started in March, it was flooded. Flooded! It was all water. It wouldn't drain, so they were doing everything they could with squeegees, lime. It was an old track—five laps to the mile. We were the only track in the league that couldn't have the league meet! But we needed to practice. My speed guys needed speedwork, so I thought about using telephone poles as markers for pickups. I asked a repair guy once that was working on them about what the distance was between the poles. He said it was 30 yards, depending on the ground layout and such. That was great. Four poles—30, 60, 90, 120 yards—that's a straightaway on a track. Perfect! So I came up with pickups on the road for the kids. With a five-minute rest period, we'd go to every fourth pole, five-minute rest, four poles, five minutes, and so on. They did sets of eight poles of rest, four poles of a pickup, eight poles of rest, four poles."

In Squires's first track season, Wakefield finished the regular season in second place, and third in the state meet. "We were strong in all of our running events. And I had introduced simulations—in cross-country it was simulating the course; in track it was the events—so the athlete feels at home in the race." It was also not uncommon to see Squires on his hands and knees on the streets of Wakefield, as he crawled around with his measuring tape and bright paint. He measured and marked various distances up a hill, along flats—anywhere he would work his kids. "I'd get some people coming out of their houses, yelling at me, 'What are you doing out there?' And I'd say, 'I'm just making sure we've got the street measured.' I'd only paint a dot or a small line of orange paint or something like that. But they'd yell, 'Are you with the public works department?' I'd say, 'No. I'm just doing it as a survey.' I had to make something up to say, then measure and paint it quick, and get out. But I wanted my kids to be able to see it when I had them train on the roads."

In the five years from 1958 to 1963 at Wakefield, Squires's teams won two cross-country state titles, an indoor state and conference title, and an outdoor state championship. He compiled a 71-6 record in track. And as a competitor himself, on his own, he was third in the 1961 National 30K Championships, and as a 28-year-old was 20th in the 1961 Boston Marathon with a time of 2:47:46 as the seventh B.A.A. member. But it was bittersweet. At the time, it was his first—and last—chance to run the venerable race because the AAU notified him that due to his acceptance of a salary as a Wakefield High coach, he lost his amateur status and could no longer compete. It was only out of his pleading, and the kindness of AAU officials he knew, that he was allowed to run this one time. "That hurt. It really did. And not long after that, the rules changed. But I don't embitter that. I did break a rule. I knew what the rule was. It turned out to be the best thing that ever happened to me. When I got declared as a pro, that made me run the Marathon and get a taste of the training and the distance. I know I would have run at least one, because I lived in Boston, but I would have run it when I was about 35 years old. Just think of how many lousy marathoners we would have had [in that time], because I helped a helluva lot of runners get out of the 100-mile weeks of only running miles and miles. I got them doing speedwork and improving times."

For his 1961 Boston training, Squires put together the most miles he had ever run. So dense was his workout that he was determined to not only just run it, but do well. "The farthest [back on the course] I had ever gone in my runs was Ashland High School. I had never been to Hopkinton before, but I knew that the first few miles were all pitched downhill. So I really went easy early. But what I didn't know cost me a place against a real good runner." Squires miscalculated the finish. In 1961, the Boston finish line was located near the B.A.A. Clubhouse on Exeter Street. Running against cold and chilly winds, temperatures in the high 30s, and the occasional reported snow squall, Squires made a mistake as a runner he swore he would never repeat as a coach: *he did not research the entire course*; specifically, the finish and its approach. In the last mile, the course proceeds through Kenmore Square onto Commonwealth Avenue and over Massachusetts Avenue. From there, it passes by on the right-hand side a set of short alternating one-way streets that bisect parallel roadways Commonwealth Avenue, Newbury Street, and Boylston Street, to form a rectangular grid. After passing Hereford Street, Gloucester Street, and Fairfield Street, the course turned right onto Exeter to finish near the clubhouse. As a way to remember the bisecting street names, starting with the letter H as runners head east toward the finish, the names are in reverse alphabetical order—Hereford, Gloucester, Fairfield, Exeter, followed by Dartmouth, Clarendon, Berkeley, Arlington. "I never knew those streets went alphabetically! I didn't know Exeter Street was coming, and I didn't know the finish. When I was going toward Exeter, from about 70 yards away I saw a barrier they put there. I got confused and thought I was somewhere I wasn't [the finish line]. It cost me." Lesson learned.

To balance his hectic life of coaching, and teaching, Squires continued to run. He even hooked up with fellow Arlington native Thomas "Tom" McNeeley, Jr., who was in preparation to fight National Boxing Association World Heavyweight Champion Floyd Patterson in Canada for the title. McNeeley even appeared on the cover of the November 13, 1961, issue of *Sports Illustrated* during his training. "He did some heavy training for that fight, and I would do some roadwork with him in Arlington." (With former World Heavyweight Champion "Jersey" Joe Walcott as the referee, McNeeley hit the canvas 11 times in a fourth-round knockout to Patterson, who retained the title.)

CHAPTER 8

"CHAMPIONS OF YOUR ABILITY."

Out of the blue in 1963, Squires received a call from James "Gus" Sullivan, director of athletics of State College at Boston. Located near Wentworth Institute of Technology and Northeastern University, it was commonly known as Boston State College or its shorter nickname of BoState, and its athletes were also the Warriors. It was about a coaching job. "Gus also said they were getting a new gym and that the plans were right in his office. He told me about that because he said he didn't want to embarrass me with the gym they had." Good thing, too, because as Squires entered the gymnasium on his way to see Sullivan, overhead—*inside*—he noticed birds flying around. "Pigeons! The gym was a million years old! In my interview, I keep seeing these pigeons flying there."

Sullivan saw in Squires the new direction he wanted to take Boston State. In 1948 when Sullivan started as the AD, the only varsity sport was basketball. By the time of Squires's interview, baseball, track, golf, ice hockey, and wrestling had been added. One of the coaches Sullivan hired was basketball coach James "Loscy" Loscutoff Jr., former pro basketball player who the year before being hired won the last of his seven NBA World Championship titles with the Boston Celtics. "Loscy comes into the office and he shakes my hand, and his hand wraps around mine. And he says, 'You like to join us?' I could see he was a happy-go-lucky guy. And I said, 'I like what you have here.' Then Gus and I talked about a new track, and I said if you're going to get one, it has to be a 10-lap-to-a-mile track so the relay passing zones and everything are even. I said it'd be great if it was eight laps, but that would take up too much room. He asked about having it around the basketball court, and I said what about the roof!" A novel idea at the time, for obvious reasons—cost and structural integrity as the main ones—Squires thought it was something that could be achieved. And he wanted to be a part of it. "I told Gus he can make it a four-lane track, and as long as you can put up a seven-foot barrier around it so there wouldn't be any wind, and within three to five years we could just dome it, it could work. He loved it. And I said that in the wintertime, after it's domed, let the kids use it. And Loscy's looking at me like I'm nuts."

Inevitably, Squires joined Boston State as associate professor and coach for the 1964-65 school year. Having arrived partway through indoors, he primarily focused on the upcoming spring outdoor track season. With enough similarity between indoors and outdoors, he was confident in planning his new training system, which he discussed with his team. "I told them it was too late for this indoor season, but next year I'd like to have them go to the big track meet at the Boston Garden. They're looking at me like I'm crazy, but I told them I have a few ideas that will help. I would have them do long runs on Sundays, medium runs on Mondays, track on Tuesdays, medium runs on Wednesdays, medium runs or hills or short-track work on Thursdays, and medium runs on Fridays and Saturdays. I remember the first kids in, they wondered why we didn't run more; that in high school, they ran for mileage twice a week and now they're only running every third week. I told them when we run, we race! I said, 'There's a difference. When we race, you're going to have happy feet.' I told them that in the early season, we're going to watch some of these teams stay with us and some will kill us—not bury us, but get to us. And at the end of the year, those kids that have better ability than us—the dormitory-school kids that get that work-study aid and dorms—well, we'll get them!"

Boston State had no on-campus home track; the Warriors rented the indoor oval at the nearby YMCA, which was near the Fenway Park home of the Boston Red Sox. "It was a very old wood track with steep corners and a lot of dust. When you ran, the dust would come up from the track. When you blew your nose afterwards, it'd be all the dust in there." For two hours, three days a week, they used the Y's 12-laps-to-a-mile track. And as often happened to Squires, he met some interesting people. "There was a priest there, a running priest, who was nice. He was from the church on Arch Street—St. Anthony Shrine—in Boston. He'd bless the kids. And he'd tell me, 'These kids are good.' He could tell. And so did Arthur Fiedler," Squires noted of the legendary Boston Pops Orchestra conductor. "He'd be there because there was a club he liked that had a few weights, a massage therapist, the gym. He liked that. And he'd say to me, 'You know, they're pretty quick.' And I'd say, 'Maestro, they are.' He knew. And then one of my guys later on almost knocked him over! Running the straightway on the track was fine, but on the corners, it was like a cliff and you couldn't always see people there. Half of the kids I had to tell them who he was, but I told them all to watch out for him."

Squires continued to recruit. Unlike when he received bags full of recruitment letters as a high-school athlete, Boston State was in Division III and provided no Division I cachet, no athletic scholarships, no home-field track, no dorms, no frills. He was forced to be creative to spread the word and attract new talent. "The first year or two I tried to recruit the top athletes, but I gave up because they'd always go to the dormitory state schools like Westfield State or Framingham State. Then I decided I would pick kids that were around seventh to tenth in their conference. When I would see a kid like that, I made sure he and his coach would know I was interested the whole way through his senior year. And I'd talk to them at their meets. I'd also send postcards from our road trips. I'd have some of my guys write things like, 'We're on the road at the whatever invitational or the wherever relays. Hope you're here next year.' I'd have the cards with me and they'd write them out. I had nothing to give them at BoState, so I had to do things like that." One of the first indoor tests was the 1965 Boston YMCA Invitational Track and Field Meet in February, about a month after Squires joined the squad. An open all-comers meet, he took advantage of this baptism by fire and made sure everyone competed so he could evaluate the talent.

The 1965 outdoors was not only the first one for Squires, it was also the first for Boston State, which previously featured it as a club sport. So new were the Warriors to the sport at the varsity level that Squires had to search for an outdoor track on which to practice. He found one down the street at Boston English High School; a decades-old dirt track that cut through the outfield grass of the baseball field. (A year or two later, the track was mysteriously filled in with grass to dissuade further use.) By the time of their first big meet—the 1965 New England Small College Outdoor Track Championship—Boston State placed an impressive fifth in the 4x100 relay. "We got points! Top six get points. That's great! We had about 15, 16 kids—not a full slate of kids, which would be about 30-35. You have about

14 events to fill with two kids each, so some of the kids said they could double up. And that was fine." In the half-mile later in the meet, two Warriors finished within the top five. And Boston State won the mile. "I'm looking at this now, and I'm starting to add the points up. There's a fifth place, a win, a couple in the top five—it's adding up. Then I'm thinking, if we can get some points in the discus, the shot, and if we win the mile relay at the end…but then I tell myself to stop it. I tell myself, 'Don't do it. Don't think this is going to happen like at Wakefield.' But I'm getting wrapped up in it!" By the time of the last event—the mile relay—Boston State had failed to earn the field-event points required to win outright. But they did collect enough to be in the hunt. And the pre-meet favorite to beat was no longer the team to beat. If Boston State finished within the top three, they'd win!

The Warriors came in second. "We won!" cheered Squires of the school's first New England championship title in track. "Wow! And the kids were really excited. What a freak thing, winning that, though. How do you start like that? But then when I thought about it—the training, my system, my program—it was working, just like at Wakefield High."

His reputation began to precede him. An example of this occurred one day in the spring of 1965 when he trained his track team at Franklin Park. While he ran with his Warriors along the cross-country course, Squires heard his name called out from a group of men near the trail. He broke off from his team and told them to continue on with another loop while he checked who was there. A small group of African-American men—three in identical black suits, white shirt, black tie, dark sunglasses; a fourth in an old-looking gray sweat suit, army boots, and a towel wrapped around his neck—stood waiting. "Right away, when I saw the towel around the guy's neck, I knew he must be a boxer. That's what all boxers did when they were working out or running. One of the other guys says, 'Hi, my name is Louis Farrakhan.' I didn't know him, and he says, 'You know me as Louis Walcott.' I say, 'The 200-meter guy! Boston English! The guy that played the hum-and-strum! The great orator!' They all start smiling, and he goes, 'Billy, you really do know a lot about me.' I said, 'Oh, I remember.' He was a good runner at Boston English High School and got a track scholarship for college. And he played the violin, too. But back then, he wasn't Farrakhan. So, he introduces me to the boxer next to him as Muhammad Ali."

The fighter was closing in on his rescheduled rematch against former heavy-weight champion Sonny Liston, in Lewiston, Maine. "I didn't know a Muhammad

Ali. And then Louis said, 'You may know him as Cassius Clay.' I said, 'Cassius Clay! Of course. You were great in the Olympics," noted Squires of the gold medalist who was 15 months removed from being known as Cassius Marcellus Clay Jr., before he joined Farrakhan's Nation of Islam. "What a nice man, Ali. And the most handsome man I have ever seen. He was like a movie actor. No facial cuts or anything. And I kept referring to him as Cassius. And Farrakhan'd go, 'Muhammad! It's Muhammad.' He was good about that. So, Louis says, 'I told Muhammad that you'd know everything about what you should do in running. I heard you're a big guy in this area in running. I know you were a good runner when we were there at the New Englands years ago.' He was good back then." Ali asked Squires about running tips, including footwear. He wondered about using high-top tennis sneakers, which were becoming common for ankle support. "I said, 'No. You're wearing the best things in the world right now. I lived in army boots because I had a bad foot, and the support you get is perfect. When you box, you have high-laced shoes on to make sure you don't turn an ankle or something, right? With tennis sneakers, you could step on a rock or a twig when you're running and turn your ankle.' He leans in to me, and goes, 'Good.' Then he asks about running more on grass than roads. He's asking good questions back then. This is the mid-Sixties! No one's asking things like this. So I told him about the risks of each; that grass could be uneven, roads could have potholes, dirt could be soft. But with the high boots, I told him to get two pairs and he could run on all the surfaces well. This went on for a little while. He was very nice and he thanked me."

As the group left, Ali pointed to Squires and delivered verse. "He said something like, 'The coach does know, 'bout the shoes and the surface; Coach done told me, the means and the purpose.'" Squires laughed at the recollection. "I wish I could remember it all. But everyone was laughing. And they asked if I wanted to go to the fight, but I couldn't with the track events I had to attend." (On May 25, 1965, Ali knocked out Liston in the first round.)

As he did for track, Squires tweaked his system for the inaugural 1965 cross-country season, which had also previously only been a club sport at Boston State. He once again incorporated groups, a staple in the Squires repertoire. "I'd put the freshmen and sophomores together in Group 2, and the juniors and seniors together in Group 1. And everyone would warm up together. Group 1 would go off and then the Group 2 kids would go off much slower. On distance days, everyone goes together for the first mile-and-a-half. After a mile-and-a-half, Group 1 pulls away and the freshmen and sophomores in Group 2 stay at a steady pace because the Group 1 guys are going under six minutes and the Group 2 guys are going 6:40 to 6:50. The freshmen and sophomores wanted to do what Group 1 was doing, and I told them they could eventually. Not the freshmen, but the sophomores could at some time." Boston State was led by Alan Siegal, who one time set a record in four consecutive meets, and Frank McCarthy as captain. Behind Siegal, ranked in the top 10 in New England among open amateur meets and races, and McCarthy, who consistently turned in top-five points in eight meets, the Warriors won the 1965 NESC Championship title. For Squires, right out of the gate it was two titles in two sports. Success was begetting success.

The final meet of the season was the 1966 B.A.A. Invitational at Boston Garden. For the relay, strategically, most teams are built with the fastest runner in the first leg to open up a lead, followed by the second leg who can at least maintain a (hopeful) lead; the third leg can be the slowest of the four; and the anchor is another fast runner who can either increase or obtain a lead. "Universally, that's about right. But I wanted my second-fastest guy to lead off. I would have a real 600-yard guy go out like hell and get a lead, and as he fades, to just hang on. The second leg will hold it, and then I'd put my third and fourth legs together—the fast ones. It's a strategy based on who are you going to go against and how will one guy work off the other. There's a lot involved." Squires before the race gave one last talk to his team of Bryan Jones, Louis Dittami, Don Murphy, and Frank McCarthy. "They were all kind of new to this, so I told them to not get nervous. And I see that Frank's eyeballs are wide open. Anyway, there were six teams in our heat, and we were the last one that was announced to line up."

Jones got out fast and settled down in third; Dittami stepped it up as the second leg, and by a few feet overtook second; Murphy maintained that position for Boston State, but kept the gap close for McCarthy's anchor. "I'm thinking we'll get second. I'm yelling out to Murphy to keep it up, keep it close, and then I get yelled at to shut up because you can't coach during the event. Then I'm thinking, the way Frank's going, I don't know how he'll run that last quarter. When he passes me—he's got two-and-three-quarter laps; it's 11 laps to the mile—I keep saying to him, 'Work up gradually. Work up gradually.' I try to say it softly to him. He had won the 600, so I don't know what he has left." What McCarthy had left—in front of a packed Garden of nearly 14,000, which included a Boston State contingent of its president, VP, AD, athletic committee members, and students and spectators—was an estimated 50.6 quarter that propelled the Warriors to victory, which stunned many observers. "Frank had caught up to the leader at the gun lap, and he had 160 yards left. When he ran by me, I said, 'All out! All out!' And he did. He overtook the guy at the last corner, and he won it. Can you believe that? What a run! Before the race, I knew we could get at least fourth because we had been doing enough work. Afterwards, when they got their B.A.A. medals, I told them, 'That baby there, that medal, that's balls-to-the-wall! That's a good one to have. Gus was ecstatic! Ecstatic! And Loscy was there and he goes, 'I got you that guy. It was me!' Which was right. That's where Frank came from. Loscy cut him. And that's true. I always say that about Frank. I owe it to Loscy."

Squires successfully adjusted his system from high-school-age kids to college-age kids. In their second spring season, Boston State dominated the 1966 outdoors when it won the Brandeis Invitational, Southern New England Championship, National Association of Intercollegiate Athletics District I Championship, NESC Championship, and the NESC-Athletic Conference Championship. The quick success provided Squires with some cachet when it came to recruiting. "I knew I had to hustle. I knew I'd have to blitz these newspapers with how well we did at all those meets. I also wanted to make sure they mention the hometowns of these kids and get that in the papers. And I wanted to get to each kid's local paper, too, because some of them covered more than one town. And I made sure to always say, when I was interviewed, the name of the kid's high school coach. That always went over big. And when I'd walk around at all the meets, wearing my BoState jacket, I could talk to the coaches and kids. They'd approach me, too."

In addition to the usual regular season meets, Squires brought his team to several meets at the 169th Street Armory in Manhattan. Known simply as The Armory, "It was *the* place to run. I wanted to get my kids competing in New York because I was going to get them into the Boston Garden. They were excited about that. I made sure the kids had all their classes done by around three o'clock on Fridays so we could get there on time. The professors at BoState were very serious about giving their best to the kids, which they should, and they also understood that as a coach I was on the same wavelength. If there was any problem, it could be worked out, like taking another lab on a different day or whatnot. But some of these meets at The Armory lasted forever. We'd drive four-and-a-half hours each way without staying overnight. And sometimes the last event would start just before midnight, and we'd get back to Boston at four or five in the morning!" But the late-night drive meant a favorite stopover at the Green Comet Diner on King's Highway in Connecticut. Visited so often by Squires and his teams that even the waitstaff welcomed them inside when they approached the early-morning cleanup hour when the diner closed before the breakfast crowd. "If we ran late and got there just as they were going to close, they'd throw us down one end of the place and then they'd lock up and vacuum the other end. And they'd do the dishes and get the place ready for the next group."

Squires refined and improved his system each year. He possessed the unique ability to at first sight of an athlete, observe and rattle off a litany of physical faults, ticks, correctable elements, potential, strengths; and with further examination, produce deeper insight and foresight. "With my training, it would take me a year-and-a-half with an athlete to get to where the system—the steps—would work. And then all of a sudden he's at a different level. He thinks he's at one point of his limit, but in reality, he's up higher, beyond what he thinks. I'm trying to rebuild his heart engine, his legs, his physiological engine; and if I rebuild those, I won't have to do anything with his head. His head will know what he can do. Let the system work. And they'll understand."

Boston State in 1967 joined the Eastern College Athletic Conference (ECAC). In that year's outdoors, the freshmen Warriors won the DMR at the BC Outdoor Track Relays, which paved the way for the Penn Relays at the University of Pennsylvania. "These kids were absorbing my training and they liked it. I knew they weren't like the kids at Wakefield High that were two-year projects. We were second in the freshmen division, I think. We ran pretty well. And that told me something. That told me that my system was totally right. My kids were running against scholarship kids and top talent, and they were doing well." In early July, with an influx of freshmen talent, Squires prepared his cross-country team with moderate three-mile runs at Franklin Park. They ran *with* their coach, who gradually increased the mileage. He even invited former Warriors to join, so the group ranged anywhere between 15-20 runners. And he'd literally coach on the run! He'd maintain the group at a pace of 7:00-7:30 per mile, and also dispense tips, stories, aid, humor, and whatever else he deemed necessary to push and teach. "I can slow down, speed up, see if a kid has to slow down, keep his arms up. I wanted to make sure they were staying within themselves and stay with what I wanted them to do. Then, when we got close to the finish, I'd say, 'Okay, it's from here to the finish.' I'd pick it up a bit, and I'd say, 'No one's to pass me, but you can be right on my arm.' And if there were three or four or five with me, that'd be good. That'd let me know what I had. And I'd do that a lot because that's how it could be at the end of a race. And I had enough kids for an A and a B team in cross-country. And later on in track, I had enough in some events for two kids."

While under freshmen rules the rookie underclassmen were only allowed to compete in a tournament meet or two, Squires worked them in training for a promising 1968 season. "The only thing I could let them run in against the varsity was like a Boston YMCA meet or something, but not the New Englands or a big meet. But I was building for the next year. These kids were super freshmen."

By this time, he had several seasons under his belt and felt comfortable enough to embark on an eventual long-term tradition. In October 1967, the first annual Codfish Bowl Cross-Country 5-Miler was held at Franklin Park. The brainchild of Squires, who carried over the moniker from Boston State's ice hockey tournament, it did not even have a chance to start out small. Nearly 100 runners competed in the inaugural event. (By the time Squires retired, the Codfish Bowl grew to include an average of nearly 20 teams and 100 runners in a men's 8K; more than 20 teams and over 150 runners in a women's 5K; and an occasional prep boys 5K.) "I wanted to have an invitational meet in cross-country, but I also wanted to have it as an open meet so freshmen could be eligible. No one had a meet like this. No one! Gus Sullivan made the Codfish Bowl a hockey tournament based on the Beanpot Tournament in Boston (between BC, BU, Harvard, NU). They're the two oldest invitational hockey tournaments in the country," noted Squires of the Beanpot (1952) and Codfish (1966). "That summer I sent race information everywhere I could think of. I wasn't sure who would come because most schools already have commitments for two or three seasons in advance. At BoState, I was doing each season one at a time because we were just starting. But I got eight teams for the first Codfish Bowl. We had Division I teams, Division II teams—everyone. I didn't care who came because it was an open meet. And I had originally said that teams could only run up to 10 kids, not knowing how many I would get. But with eight teams, everyone could run."

Boston State won the inaugural Codfish Bowl. And success continued to the 1967-68 indoors, where behind the two-mile relay team, the Warriors won the second-tier division at the B.A.A. Invitational in Boston Garden. "Boy, were they great ones! We did the same thing this time that we did two years before. We won! And my freshmen kids finished within the top three—I think third—in the freshmen division." In an attempt to recruit athletes and also design more open competitions, Squires started meets at an old haunt of his, the George Robert White Schoolboy Stadium in Franklin Park. He came across local sprinter George Carter, who would in his collegiate career set six school records and earn numerous track honors. "I had decided to go into the inner-city to put on some open meets at White Stadium and look for kids for BoState. And I ended up picking up three sprinters—two bona fide sprinters and a phenomenal quarter-miler. And George was one of them."

While at White Stadium one year, Squires brought along his eldest son, Bill Squires Jr., who was in elementary school. The eight-year-old ran the 100 and qualified for the East Coast Regionals of the Jesse Owens National Youth Games in Washington, D.C. Named after the legendary African-American Olympian who won four gold medals at the 1936 Berlin Olympics in Nazi Germany, only regional winners age 11 and older advanced to the nationals. With his parents in the stands, Squires's son ran hard in the 100. Toward the end of the race, however, while in about fourth place with approximately 30 yards to go, he fell to the ground. "That happens all the time, but when it's your own kid, you feel different when it happens. But he gets up and keeps going and actually beat, I think, two kids." After the race, Squires was approaching his son, who was talking to an adult near the stands. He was Jesse Owens. "Jesse's saying to my son, 'That was great, sonny. Getting up. Finishing the race. That's tremendous.' Bill had tears in his eyes. He's younger than everyone else in the race, and he's got some bumps and bruises from falling. And he says, 'Thank you. Thank you.' I'm there by the doorway and I'm just listening, and Jesse turns around and he doesn't know if I'm his coach or whatever, and says, 'The boy's all right.' And he left." (About a dozen years later at a US Olympic Committee meeting, where Squires and Owens were members in separate capacities, the two met again. Squires refreshed Owens's memory of that day. He told him about the positive impression he made, and thanked him again for his kindness and generosity.)

As the Warriors began to prove themselves worthy season after season, invitations to higher-level meets arrived. One in particular, of which Squires took note, was for the 1968 Dartmouth Relays. But before that meet, Boston State turned in a top-10 finish in the ECAC Eastern championships. And on a personal note for Squires, about two weeks before the 1969 Boston Marathon, he became a father for the third time, with the birth of Gerard "Gerry" Squires, on April 6. "Like all our kids, he was born at Mount Auburn Hospital. It went pretty normal, not like me when I had the umbilical cord all twisted around and it took my mother over 70 hours of labor. But I was there. I babysat the two other kids. And we named him after Saint Gerard, who's the Patron Saint of Motherhood."

Squires still pinched pennies for Boston State. For example, as they often did for their Penn Relay trips, as a money-saver he and his Warriors found accommodations in cheaper New Jersey instead of the more expensive Pennsylvania. Specifically, they stayed at the downtown YMCA. But they still enjoyed themselves. After they competed in the Penn Relays one year, in which the Boston State mile relay team came in second in their heat, on their return trip home they stopped for dinner at a fine restaurant/nightclub in Cherry Hill, New Jersey. Squires noticed as he entered the eatery that top-name entertainment was also featured in the adjoining club. During dinner, he left his table of athletes for the restroom, and recognized that evening's headliner—award-winning actress/singer Diahann Carroll of "Julia" fame—sitting a few tables away. Once again, the coach did not let an opportunity pass. "I saw her picture there as we came in to the place to eat, and she was gorgeous. And then there she was! Right there! When I had gone over to her table, I'd told her who I was and that I had my team over there, and if she could just wave to them or something that'd be great. But she got up and said she'd love to meet them all. So we walk over—very classy. Everyone had their medals on, and I introduced her to them. She was very nice, and she congratulated everybody. The kids were just beside themselves. After she left, one of the kids goes to me, 'How the heck did you do that?' They loved things like that. It made the trips fun."

The end of the 60s also marked the departure of several more All-New England and All-Eastern athletes, including Ed O'Donoghue, the school's first track and field All-American. But Squires and Boston State did not rest in the new decade. The 70s featured a stellar collection of athletes that included Warriors who set dozens of school records in cross-country, track and field;

competed in US Olympic Trials; and earned multiple all-athletic honors as well. "The 1970s, particularly the early part, I consider the golden age for BoState. In the previous seven years, we won seven New England state championships, and we were coming off of cross-country seasons in 1968 and 1969 when we were sixth in the IC4As. In 1971, we came in ninth at the NAIA Indoor Championships. It got to a point where kids were seeing our athletes tear apart people in the Boston Garden. That's worth a thousand recruiting letters that I'd send. Also, when I would send something to a kid, I'd also mention where we were going to go because so many of these guys had already cleared the way to these championships."

Squires expanded the athletic horizon with extra non-New England competitions down south and in the Midwest. And with still a minimal budget, the ever-frugal Squires excelled at financial improvisation, especially when it came to road trips that usually involved a car instead of a plane. One journey in particular, to the Kansas Relays, Sullivan after the fact read about the trip and wondered how Squires accomplished the 1,500 miles halfway across the country. "I told Gus it was school vacation week, so we stopped at Ohio State, Notre Dame, the University of Chicago—about six colleges. I would ask them at each school if they could find rooms for us, that we'd be there for a day or two. And if not, we could sleep on the high-jump pits. All my guys brought their own pillows with them just in case. And then we'd go into the school cafeterias, which were pretty good. I also did this for a trip to Chicago." After he detailed the logistics to the AD—and they both shared a few (nervous) laughs—it was finally agreed upon that in the future, the team had to fly to long-distance meets and that additional funds would be available. "But you know something, the kids would always talk about these trips. It was about eight or 10 days each time, and we were all together and we had fun. And Gus would read about it in the paper because I'd always call the papers with the results. And he'd say to me later, 'I wish I'd gone.' First of all he's criticizing me," says Squires laughing, "then he wished he went."

In addition to road-trip tales, the kids also enjoyed the many side-visits Squires took at away meets. Ever the teacher, he found many non-athletic educational excursions. One such time, in Castine, Maine, he led his team to a teaching ship on the campus of the Maine Maritime Academy. Docked there was the decommissioned vessel TS *State of Maine*. An informational plaque, which presented its history, notified visitors that the ship was originally commissioned in 1949 as the SS *President Hayes*, and launched two years later. In 1952 it was reassigned to the United States Navy, then utilized as a Military Sea Transportation Service troop transport as the renamed USNS *Upshur* through the 1950s, 60s, and into the early 70s. After it received an out-of-service designation in 1973, the ship was loaned by the United States Department of Transportation's Maritime Administration to the Maine Maritime Academy and renamed the TS *State of Maine*. As Squires read this, some details seemed familiar, despite having never previously visited the academy. He again read the plaque. And then it clicked when he focused on its history as a troop transport ship during the 1950s. "I said aloud, 'Holy, cripes!' I said to my guys, 'Hey! This is my ship!' They were, like, what the heck is he saying now. 'This is my ship. This is, or was, the *Upshur*. This is the ship that brought me from Fort Eustis to Germany in '57 when I was in the service.' They all moaned because they thought they were going to have to hear all my old stories about it. Which was true. But they liked it. They still talk about all the things we'd seen. But I never thought I'd see that ship again."

In addition to his Boston State duties, Squires presided over lectures, seminars, clinics, and even an early website called Coach on the Road. "I had a woman help me and we'd do things like getting three running clubs together, charge $10 a head, and that'd pay for my expenses. I tried to get two or three cities or states close together, and I'd go out for two weeks at a time." With his rich background and history, Squires knew what was working and what was missing in his sport, be it on the athletic level or with training, coaching, administering. He was prepared. While his talks took on a certain direction, he also allowed room for deviations, whether from him or the audience. "At these clinics, I'd have people fill out little cards so I could answer as many questions as I could. A lot of people'd be embarrassed to raise their hands, so I'd end up talking to everyone afterward. But with these cards, I could address everything *during* the clinic, and that'd help everyone there. And I started to see a pattern, especially with questions about injuries. I ended up studying those things so I'd know what the heck I was talking about with podiatry, knees, hips, feet, ankles, muscles—everything! This was before orthotics, pads, special lifts, and things like that. Now you can get special laces, pads, individualized supports. But back then, nothing! I even had one of those early phone recorders, and it cost me about $125!" he said about his answering machine. "I was told to get one so I could answer people that called for advice. It ended up costing me about $200 before I finally got rid of it. I'm calling people back on my dime! I'm longwinded, so you know these calls took a while. Anyway, that was the last time I had one of those damn answering machines."

With not enough time in the day, it was family who he missed. "I was trying to make money for my family and do a lot. Maybe too much. Sally had her job at the hospital, and she did great with the kids. And I made sure to see them as much as I could – dinners, sports, trips."

Interspersed between college, clubs, and clinics, Squires through various national and international organizations in the 1970s and 80s found himself with unique opportunities to travel the country and the world to coach athletes and coaches of all levels. In Portugal, he addressed the 1983 European Congress of the IAAF as the first US coach to do so. There were also development programs by the United States Olympic Committee (USOC) and trips via the International Olympic Committee (IOC), when he trained track and field coaches in such locales as Belgium, England, Japan, and Puerto Rico. In 1971, while at Boston State, through the United States Department of State a group of Americans was sent to India to aid its top athletes and coaches in time for the 1972 Munich Olympics and also the 1976 Montreal Olympics. Squires was the coach and a consultant. With this chance of a lifetime—and thanks to Boston State's approval; and coaches Gordon "Gordie" Webb and Greg Olson in place during his absence—Squires reported to the US State Department in Washington, D.C., where he was briefed.

In India for three months—mid-August to mid-November—he would serve in the capacity as athletic coach, lecturer, educator, consultant; and with his health sciences background, an advisory role regarding such issues that involved health, water filtration, and the like, for whenever he visited smaller, less-developed villages. Payment for his time and service was $15,000, all of which he contributed back to Boston State. At the state department, Squires explains, "They even re-fingerprinted me and did some voice-recognition thing where I had to speak into this machine to make sure it was me. Then they told me to get cleaned up, and they took me to my residence. Residence?" Squires was escorted to the Blair House, where US presidents live during White House renovations; heads of state and visitors of the president stay; and also the site of an assassination attempt of President Harry Truman in 1950. Squires marveled at the history and the official guest book which featured the stunning array of visitors' signatures that included Truman; French General Charles de Gaulle; President of the Republic of the Philippines Ferdinand Marcos, and First Lady Imelda Marcos; and Prime Minister of India Jawaharlal Nehru, and his daughter, Indira Gandhi, the latter of whom was the prime minister of India during Squires's overseas visit. "I'm reading the history of all the kings and queens and dignitaries that have stayed there, and then there's me—a scrawny little kid from the hills of Arlington. It was something. Anyway, I had to get ready to go to the Capitol building with a big delegation of people and meet the secretary of state. It was all very nice."

Squires flew from Washington to England to New Delhi, India. "It didn't start out too good. As we're rushing to the airport in D.C. and we know the gates of my plane are closing, the guy with me in the car says on his phone or whatever, 'This is a State Department envoy. Hold the plane!' It wasn't even my fault that we're late! So we pull up to the airport and another guy gets my bag and we're going to the ticket counter and the guy goes, 'This is an emergency from the State Department. Hold the plane!' I look through the windows to the tarmac, and the plane's already pulled away from the gate. They finally stop the plane and open the door for me. I finally get on and I'm hearing people whispering as I get to my seat. They're all thinking I'm someone important."

Finally at the Oberoi Intercontinental Hotel in New Delhi, to combat jetlag, Squires went for a walk on the streets around the hotel. "I'm in India less than an hour, and I'm at a traffic light with a bunch of people. With that traffic, you don't cross the street without the light! So, I'm waiting there at a red light with everyone else, and this woman's in front of me and she has a little baby on her shoulder and it's looking back at me. It reaches out and touches my neck, so I make some silly faces and googly-eyes, just to be nice. I reach into my pocket and take out some rupee bills I just got as change, and I stick it in her collar, and the mother smiles at me." Prior to his arrival, Squires was provided 1969 US Department of State Publication materials on India. He read there were 17 states, 14 different languages, three seasons. "And I knew about the British outpost in India in 1619; that the Parliament in England voted Queen Victoria as Empress of India in 1877. I knew about Mahatma Gandhi; and in 1947, India got its independence and their national flag, and a few years later they got their constitution." But what he *did not* absorb about the Indian rupee exchange rate and certain cultural class differences swiftly cascaded into a set of calamitous chain reactions at that intersection.

"The light changes and everyone's walking across the street. The next thing I know, I get a baby thrown into my arms! The baby! People are jumping away from me. I look at the baby, I look at the mother and she's taking off! So I run after her with the baby in my arms, and I'm holding her head carefully— fortunately, I had kids, so I knew how to hold a baby. People are looking at me; you know, a white man running with an Indian baby. She goes into some kind of an open marketplace, and I'm running after her, in between fruit stands and stalls, bouncing off people, and yelling like a madman, 'Stop her! Stop her!' I'm catching up. Finally, I see a cop about 20 yards ahead of me, and I yell again, 'Stop her! Wearing white! Stop her!' He blows a whistle." After about 150 yards of this, the Delhi Police officer stopped the woman, and Squires finally caught up and handed back the baby. The officer, unaware of what transpired, brought everyone to the nearby New Delhi District Police Station.

"As we walk into the station, the cop says something very quick, not in English, and another cop points me to the superintendent's office, which is like our captain in the states. I get in there, and the superintendent had his hat off, and he puts it back on, and looks at me. The first cop, in English, says to the superintendent, 'This girl, giving this man a baby. He's running. He yells to stop her. I caught them in the marketplace. And I did stop her.' The superintendent looks at me, and says, 'Is that true?' I say it is. And I said, 'At the corner, I made some funny faces at the baby, I gave the woman some money, as a nice gesture. I didn't want a baby! I don't know why she gave me her baby and ran. Then I ran after her. And this good officer stopped her.' The superintendent asks the cop for the money I gave her, and when he looks at it, he says it's worth about a thousand rupees or whatever. I didn't know. He said, 'She thought you wanted the baby. This is an unclean woman.' I found out that meant the baby was out of wedlock. He says, 'They come here all the time. I never heard of anyone giving a baby to a person and running away, but I know they do sell them. We'll press charges.' I said 'No, no, no. That's okay. I want the woman to use the money for the baby.' He said it's a lot of money. I said, 'That's all right.' He goes to her and lashes out at her, and then he tells me he told her that if she does anything else like this, she'll go to prison." The superintendent returned the money to Squires, who handed it back to the woman. And in her grateful appreciation, she kissed Squires's feet and thanked him profusely. "I'm in India less than an hour from the time I landed! It took me about half an hour to get from the airport to the hotel, 15 minutes to wash my face, and then I walk across the street and this happens. I knew that I had to read up more."

The three-month schedule for Squires included clinics, programs, and training sessions in South India (Madras, Bangalore, Trivandrum, Hyderabad) and North India (New Delhi, Chandigarh, Patiala). His arrival was anticipated with such reverence and excitement that his picture appeared on billboards, the sides of buses and trains, and in sports magazines. His presence was an event! "I had photographers and reporters around me all the time. They were taking my picture every day and asking me questions about everything. It was crazy." While some were kind and welcoming, others were unsure of this American visitor. He successfully conveyed his training techniques and programs, but it was not until *he* competed in one of India's national 15K races did he prove himself worthy and earn their respect. "They had grass tracks to run on, and when the grass wore away, it was dirt. It would keep wearing away in lane one and then lane two and so on. That was tough to train on, but that's what they used so I used it. And it was so hot! But I ran the 15K and I was the first white person to finish. I came in 12th. And I died! The heat! It was like being on a golf course in the summer heat, with no shade or anything. I died! But they liked that I did it. I think it helped."

He spent 13 days in Madras, which included visits and instruction at a coaching camp at the YMCA College of Physical Education in Royapettah; Stella Maris College in Chennai; Loyola College in Chennai; and Madras Christian College, where he also attended a scheduled Inter-Collegiate Athletic Meet. In Bangalore for a week, at Sree Kanteerava Stadium, he demonstrated and explained his training techniques to the assembled, with the assistance of local specialty coaches; and coaches, in advance, received mimeographed copies of the programs and exercises so they were prepared. "I would basically show them more or less how to train. They always wanted to train in the cool weather, at 6:30 in the morning. I said that was fine, but I said they also have to practice what's going to happen in the race—to train in the afternoon if the race is in the afternoon—because they'd go to the Asian Games and they'd get their butts kicked. There were times during the day they couldn't train—I think the hottest part of the day was noon to 3:00 p.m.—but we worked it out."

In addition to a different mindset and schedule, there were other unexpected elements of India to which he had to get accustomed. At one lecture over which he presided inside a hall, Squires's attention was distracted by an unsettling noise from the back of the room. "I hear this screaming and yelling in the corridor out back. All of a sudden I hear people talking—not in English—and then I hear this banging, like someone's hitting something over and over. A cobra had come into the building to get cool, and they were killing it with sticks. They always have a person at the door, and it's always open for a breeze. And snakes and things always come in from the heat. I saw it. The snake was about 10 feet long! They said that cobras and vipers are everywhere." One night, around twilight, Squires ran on a nearby grass track. He was filled with good feelings about the trip thus far. "I'm feeling pretty good. I'm running along the track, in lane two, all alone. I've got my flats on, and I step on something and roll my ankle over. I thought I stepped on a snake! I panicked and just ran back to the hotel as quick as I could. It was about a mile or two away. I left my gym bag at the track with all my stuff. It scared the hell out of me! It made my ankle roll to the side, and it didn't feel like a branch or something hard. I was shaking! I'm thinking either cobra or viper. I didn't want to wait to find out which one. I had someone else go get my bag. I'm not kidding!" At the end of his stay in Bangalore, a competition was held where certificates were awarded by Squires and Mysore State Sports Council Secretary S.R. Vijay. Time Trial Certificates were presented in connection with the Mysore State Sports Council and the United States Information Service. This enabled the athletes to apply in competition some of what Squires taught. For the week he spent in Hyderabad, a typical day consisted of an average of 12 hours of instruction. Teamed with Rudolf Ruegember, a West German athletic coach, morning sessions featured work for Indian coaches and physical education teachers (PETs) for running and field events. In afternoon sessions, Squires was the main speaker for track events for coaches, PETs, and athletes. The number of athletes in attendance averaged around 30, with 50 to 60 coaches and PETs.

In North India, the schedule included several days in New Delhi and Chandigarh, and over a month in the city of Patiala, at the National Institute of Sports (the NIS was renamed Netaji Subhas National Institute of Sports two years later). The nearly 270 acres of land and buildings were handed over to the government upon India's independence, and in 1961 the NIS was created to better develop its own athletes and coaches, where a decade later Squires was part of that mandate. "I stayed there, in the mansion—or palace—and the place was huge. It was a phenomenal estate with several fields and a track for all kinds of athletics. And I think there were over 300 rooms in that place. I stayed in a special suite.

For the bathroom, they had rainwater and some kind of filter above to use, with a heater. And the bathtub had gold in marble. All these queens and prime ministers and people stayed in these rooms. I read all the names. And I added my name to the list. Me!" In the nearby city of Amritsar, during the time of another clinic and lecture, Squires was accompanied to visit The Harmandir Sahib in the state of Punjab. Known as The Golden Temple for its glittering gold exterior, the 1604 Sikh gurdwara—a holy temple of worship for the Sikh followers—is the holiest of shrines. Three stories tall at just under 27 feet, it occupies an approximate 41-foot square shape. Located at the end of a footbridge of 202 feet, it is surrounded by a large body of holy water. "It's a beautiful temple. It really is. You have to step down to get into it. And to dress appropriately, I had to wear a sheet and go bare-chested and remove my medal that I won in a race we just had. I also had to go in with bare feet, and put holy salt on my head so the gods would not be offended. The place is gorgeous. And it looks like it's all made out of gold. It glistens, there's so much. And there's a moat, well, like a lake, that surrounds the whole temple that always shows the reflection of the temple."

At the NIS, clinics and lectures included topics such as Aerobic Endurance, and Speed and Strength. Squires discussed the history and development of aerobic training methods, and then showed some examples. For speed and strength, he presented how the relation of both attribute to middle-distance running and long-distance running. "Other than having to run more in the heat to get used to that for races, they weren't doing enough of what I call quick-work. I showed them my system of pickups, and they loved it. They bought into that."

Some days were 12 to 14 hours long for Squires. He was exhausted by the time he returned to his room. And when in his room, he wrote down the very programs and training he just presented because it was requested of him to create several books of the materials he taught. But on occasion, he was rewarded from time to time with a day off. "That's when I could call or write home. These trips were killers, but I was able to send them lots of things. They [in India] would give me some kind of present – wood carvings, handmade crafts – and I sent them home to Sally and the kids. I also picked up trinkets and things. They loved getting things like that. I liked doing that."

Squires also stumbled into some difficult circumstances during his days off. "I tried to get some full days off, usually on a Saturday or a Sunday, and spend it by myself so I could travel around. One time, I went to a war area by mistake and I could hear the gunfire and cannons. What an idiot I was. And the monkeys! I'd fight with the monkeys because I forgot the guy told me to always carry a stick to shoo them away. They're everywhere. Then one time I was camping on some cliff at about 6,500-7,000 feet, and I'm freezing at eight o'clock at night. Freezing! It's India! Where's the heat?' It was cold. And I also learned to not lay down on beaches there. I almost got eaten by a vulture. They were all circling overhead. You don't lay on beaches, unless there's a lot going on that'll scare them away. But if you're just lying there, the vultures will come down and take a bite out of you." Another animal with which Squires learned to deal was the cow. Like monkeys, cows are everywhere. But unlike monkeys, cows are sacred animals and commanded the same kind of respect as mothers due to their capacity for milk. "Right, the cows. They're sacred, so *you* get out of *their* way. One time we were on a 12-mile run and we come across them a lot on the roads. The guys taught me how to clap my hands in such a way that the cows would move; you cup your hands a certain way when you see the cows ahead, and then you clap when you're far enough away, and they usually move. Now, I never noticed it before, but their tails are tied up in a knot. There's a knot near the end of their tail. So we're running through a town, and we're clapping, but we'd have to run around them once in a while if they didn't move. Well, I did that, and we run around a couple of cows, and one of the tails swings up and hits me right in the crotch. Oh, I cried. I actually had tears in my eyes," He laughs, now. "Then the guys tell me to run wider around the cows. Oh, boy!"

In the three months throughout India, Squires was well received. He coached, taught, informed, and instructed several hundred athletes and coaches, many of whom continued his teachings for years after his departure. Two athletes in particular—Sri Ram Singh Shekhawat (aka Sriram Singh) of Badnagar; and Shivnath Singh of Manjaria—benefited greatly from Squires. Coached by Ilyas Babar, Sriram Singh possessed talent, as evidenced at the 1970 Asian Games in Thailand, where he was second in the 800. At the 1972 Munich Games, 10 months after Squires's visit, he ran 1:47.7 in his 800 heat, and by just two-tenths of a second missed a qualifying time to advance. However, at the 1974 Asian Games in Iran, he won the 800; and repeated at the 1978 Asian Games. And in his second consecutive Olympics, at the 1976 Montreal Games, he advanced in the 800 with a second-place 1:45.86 in his heat, which was .14 seconds behind eventual bronze medalist Rick Wohlhuter of the US; fourth in the semifinals in 1:46.42, just .28

behind eventual fifth-place Steve Ovett of Great Britain, for the final qualifying spot in his heat; and a seventh-place 1:45.77 in the medal round, at the age of 26. Shivnath Singh ran well in the 5000 and 10,000 at the 1973 Asian Athletics Championships in the Philippines and the 1975 Asian Athletics Championships in Korea for second place each time. In the 1974 Asian Games, he finally won the 5000 and came in second in the 10,000. Then, with direction from coaches Joginder Saini and Ilyas Babar, he moved up to the marathon, where he debuted at the national trials for the 1976 Olympics with an impressive 2:15:58. Nursing an injury at the Montreal Games, he came in 11th at 2:16:22. He also started the Olympic Marathon at the 1980 Moscow Summer Games in the Soviet Union, but did not finish.

"Because I wasn't an Indian national, I couldn't go to the Olympic Games with them. But both of them achieved great success on the national and international level, which was pretty damn good for India. Their nature is a lot different—it's hot there, it's lousy. They needed motivation. I think they could be ideal marathoners. I found that they listened well and they were very eager to learn." For his efforts in India, Squires received from the country many expressions of appreciation, which included trophies, awards, honors, certificates, and an honorary degree Diploma of Merit Lecturing Technology from the University of Bangalore. "I also got a package, a rolled-up package, that they wanted me to open before I left. I opened it, and believe it or not they had taken that cobra they had killed during my lecture and they had gutted it out, cut its head off, and salted it. And they presented it to me so I could bring it home!"

Shortly after his return to the US was the passage of Title IX of the Education Amendments of 1972—which stated, in part, equality for male and female sports in federally-funded programs. Even before its passing, Squires was fully aware of the growing interest of women running and knew it was only a matter of time before women would be "allowed" to run. And he welcomed it. "There were articles after articles, with guys making a big deal out of the women that fell down in races. In the 1928 Olympics, some of the women in the 800 meters fell at the finish line and some of them looked like they were going to die," he recites the apocryphal tale. "But so did the men all the time! They also fell and looked like they were going to die. No one died! But that story was used against women until 1972. That was crap! They should have been able to run all those years. They weren't allowed to run over 200 meters in the Games until 1960!"

At Boston State, Squires was approached to help coach women. He understood the differences between coaching the sexes, and he immediately incorporated his expertise to not only provide workouts and programs, but also goals and championships. "Some women runners came over to me and asked for some guidance on running. They asked about how to get around in the meets and things. I told them I'll set something up and I'll talk to the school about it. They got Boston State shirts, which were different from the men, and I coached them. They were a club then. There were probably no more than five in outdoor track, and maybe the same number in indoor track. And I told them if they did the work for indoors, I would get them in the B.A.A. meet. They only had a women's relay then. But they did their work and I got them in. We beat one team and finished third. That was good. And something that most people may not remember, for them to run up and down the streets in the beginning was bad. It was tough. Guys were whistling and yelling at them when they were running on the streets. It was tough," noted Squires, who also created the Codfish Bowl Women's Track Championship.

Under the B.A.A., Squires continued to compete as an athlete. At the 1970 State of Maine Mini Marathon of 13.1 miles, he was 16th (1:16:58). At a Masters Mile race in New Hampshire, the 40-year-old ran 4:38.2. And at the 1973 NEAAU Masters Cross-Country Championship, he was second (34:12). While this sated his competitiveness, it also enabled him to keep up with his athletes during training runs. But it also took time away from his family, even though he did make time to watch his daughter become a champion amateur figure skater and his boys excel in running. In addition to teaching and coaching at Boston State, within a span of about nine years—from 1969 to 1978—Squires spoke at clinics, conventions, running camps, road races; represented the US State Department overseas; wrote and co-wrote several training books; coached clubs, programs, teams; earned his Certificate of Advanced Graduate Studies from California Western University; and trained for and ran the 1978 Boston Marathon (2:48:29). With the substantial increase of club competitions and road races, and the onset of the running boom, his time grew more valuable and was in shorter supply. He spent more time on the track and on the road, and less time at home with his family. And he was increasingly tired and overworked. Around this time, in 1978, he retired from college coaching; and a few years later, gave up his race directorship of the Codfish Bowl Cross-Country Championship. But the toll had already been taken. By 1979, and after more than 20 years of marriage—and three children—the couple grew apart and the marriage ended in divorce. "It was just one of those things. As I've said before, it was probably me. I was doing too much. She was a wonderful woman. It just wasn't to be. We were just on two different wavelengths. We were totally, really, in a way, different. I say it was my fault. It wasn't running that destroyed our marriage. I don't know, maybe it was her career and my career together—we both had careers that took a lot of time and maybe we just weren't around a lot together. We both appreciated each other's jobs, and they did take a lot of time. She was very talented in her area. There were times we'd each wonder why we did things in our own jobs, but we did respect what each other did. I think we just weren't around a lot. But we've stayed friends. That's good."

As the 1980s dawned, big changes came to Boston State. About 20 years earlier arose a new campus for the three-institute University of Massachusetts school system. Located in the heart of the city, the Park Square campus ironically opened about the same time Squires began his college coaching career. In 1982, UMass moved to a newly built campus on a former landfill at Columbia Point in South Boston in the shadow of BC High School, from which the land was taken. On January 25, the 130-year-old Boston State College lost its identity when it merged with the 18-year-old University of Massachusetts at Boston. "I remember when there was nothing there. It was the city of Boston's landfill and they had an outer barrier there to contain the trash. And when they would burn the trash, if you were downwind there, you'd see this island of trash with smoke and you could smell it. It was awful."

UMB was established in 1964, and 10 years later the first classes were held at the Dorchester Bay campus in South Boston. Surprisingly, both schools existed until the official merge. And like most of the Boston State professors and coaches who were extended an offer to move to UMB, Squires joined the state university. "People knew I had offers to other places because of whatever coaching knowledge I had between my ears. And I was always asked why don't I go to a Division I school. And I always answered that I was waiting for a pension. I needed seven more years to get 30 years in for a full pension, or at least four more years for 80 percent. But I knew I needed my security of my retirement. Later on, I realized that, you see, I was a Depression-era kid, when you didn't have a great amount of money. And my father always talked about having a roof over your head, money in your pocket, and money put away for a rainy day—like a pension. Even back then, he knew. With a roof over your head, you wouldn't need too much. But as renters, which we were, you needed more." The instilment of those values drove Squires to earn and save. But it also laid the groundwork for him to give; as an adult he regularly donated 15 to 20 percent of his income to those less fortunate. "My father made me frugal, and I'm glad he did. I'm very glad. And I'm glad the charities benefit. I am! And I don't miss anything—that's the thing. I have people say to me, 'What's wrong with you? Why do you give away so much?' But I'm happy. And thank God I don't have all those computers and things because I couldn't do this if I had a computer at home. My head would be spinning. I'd be home, fighting with these idiots when I read about what they say on the Internet."

Squires's parents were proud to see their son as a respected educator and well-known coach. They were especially delighted that their eldest boy helped people earn an education and expand their athletic horizons. By the time of UMB, his parents were aging. In 1984, Murt suffered a heart attack at the age of 84. "He was lying in bed. I remember there was a big storm outside and this huge tree in front of our house fell over at three in the morning. I don't know if that precipitated him having the heart attack or not. But he's in bed and I come up the stairs and I can hear him talking to my mother…" Squires pauses. "I'm getting there, to the room, and he says, 'Oh, Billy. I'm glad you're here. Be good to your mother, now.' And he died. As soon as I got in the damn door, he died." The Squires family was a strong one, which was evident from the parents. And Florence maintained that matriarchal strength when she assured her boys when Murt died that she would be okay. "When Dad passed away, Mom says, 'Oh, I can take care of myself. I'm okay.'" After a decade as a widow, Florence suffered a stroke and passed away 10 days shy of her 97th birthday. Squires did find comfort in having his brother around for support, as well as Sally and the kids. They all stayed close.

During his years of retirement from collegiate coaching, associate professor Squires maintained a heavy presence in running at UMB, with physical education courses in track and field and a program for conditioning. He also responded favorably to the many requests for athletic advice and assistance. After he spent his collegiate retirement years coaching the esteemed trailblazing Greater Boston Track Club and the New Balance running teams, Squires returned to college coaching just in time for the 1986 men's cross-country season at UMB. "I felt it was time. It was time to get back into college coaching, and it was time to get back the Codfish [as director]. And when I came back, we had about two dozen men's teams and about the same number of women's teams. Much different from the first year it started." He returned to his proven means of success, which differed from other coaches at the time. "Most of the college coaches I knew just dictated to their kids. They'd send them mimeographed things and tell them to do this and do that. If I had kids all over the country, what I would do is I'd have them call me at least one certain evening a week and tell me what they've done—on their mother's honor—so we could adjust. I didn't care how good they'd be, but they turned out to be pretty good. If you can't give me six hours a week, forget it. I need six hours of your body. For a marathoner, I need 12 hours. You do what I say and I can make you the champion of your ability. I will improve it, but you've got to do what I say."

Squires finally completely retired from UMB—as coach and associate professor—in 1991 at age 58. In 18 cross-country, indoor and outdoor track seasons at Boston State (1964 to 1978), he accumulated a combined record of 274-84. In addition to that .765 winning percentage, he was named National Association of Intercollegiate Athletes Coach of the Year three times, won 49 team championship titles, and coached four NCAA champions, six New England champions, and 16 collegiate All-Americans. In the five years at UMB (1986 to 1991), in men's cross-country and men's indoor and outdoor track, he coached several team championships, top rankings, school records, and numerous All-NCAA, All-IC4A, All-NENAIA, All-NESCAC, All-NEAAU, All-MSAC, All-Eastern, and All-New England athletes. He also bore witness to, with the occasional push, Boston State's inclusion into the ECAC, and later, NCAA. And he helped pave the way to Division II and eventual Division I status. But the statistic of which he is most proud does not come from the wins and losses, the championships and titles. He recognized as his most enduring legacy the athletes he coached who themselves became coaches and teachers. "I had about 50 kids in total [as coaches/teachers], and at one time there were about five college coaches. That was something! Also, at one point, 19 of the guys I was coaching were in the Massachusetts State Athletic Hall of Fame! I'm very proud of that. I did not want a kid to flunk out. In all my years of college coaching, five guys did not get their degree. I had four transfers because after their sophomore year they had majors that we didn't have; and one of the kids was a two-time All-American that I shipped to another school. How many coaches would do that? But if that kid was my son or daughter, I'd want it done because I'd want my kid to get that major."

Squires also experienced the privilege of having one of his own kids excel at UMB. Gerry Squires, who earned six letters (three in cross-country, three in track) graduated in May 1991, after his father had fully retired. "It's funny, but I was not encouraging my own kids to go running. There were times when they were small that I'd take them to my meets, but I never pushed them to run. I'll clue ya, to be honest, I thought that this sport, in this part of America, was not recognized as it should be. The athletes weren't here. And any of the good athletes got the heck out of here. It's tough in the East."

In 2007, 17 years after the elder Squires retired, the "Boston State College Wall of Fame: 1963-1982" to honor outstanding performances in track and field was unveiled. It featured their coach, who was also later inducted into the Boston State College/UMB Hall of Fame.

CHAPTER 9

GBTC IN THE BEGINNING

Decades before his retirement, and in the midst of his stellar coaching career, history was created on August 16, 1973, with a track-club birth in the downstairs locker room at Boston College. Squires, at the age of 40, met a group of college track athletes who yearned to further their running ability to compete post-collegiately. This was a time of great talent and expanse in the sport of running. It was one year after the 1972 Munich Olympics, where the US won 22 medals by athletes such as Frank Shorter (marathon gold) and Dave Wottle (800 gold), and Steve Prefontaine was just edged out of 5000-meter bronze. The year 1973 also marked the beginning of long-lasting marquee events named Cherry Blossom 10-Mile, Falmouth Marathon (the seven-plus-mile Falmouth Road Race), and Honolulu Marathon. The running boom was about to take hold of the nation, but there were no Rock 'n' Roll races of any kind; New Balance Arch Support Company was bought one year earlier and became New Balance Athletic Shoe; Blue Ribbon Sports was five years away from being known as Nike; and Jim Fixx's *The Complete Book of Running* was four years in the future.

Squires possessed a lifetime of experience and had already been twice named college Coach of the Year. "I put very high goals on my own standard. When you run for me, I'm running in your damn legs! And you've gotta have a mad leader who believes in you but he believes more in himself." Along with the confluence of availability and talent, that unique approach was precisely what connected with recent BC grad and club founder Jack McDonald, and athletes Charlie Diehl, Dave Elliott, Dick Mahoney, Kirk Pfrangle, Don Ricciato, Bob Sevene; track official

Chris Lane; and coaches John Pistone and William "Billy" Smith. They wanted—and got—Squires. He was in his 9th year as the successful cross-country and track coach at Boston State, and a number of his Warriors knew and competed against these runners. Thus was born the Greater Boston Track Club, named in part from the well-known multi-collegiate Greater Boston Championships.

Since the start of cross-country was about to commence, there was no time to waste. "For mileage, I already had it figured out: half-milers between 50 to 55 miles a week, and milers maybe 62 miles a week—no more, because of recovery days." For workouts, Squires committed Tuesdays, Thursdays, Sundays: experienced quarter-milers on Tuesdays and Thursdays, with hills every 10 days, and, if they wanted to, on Sundays, run one-third the distance of the half-milers and milers. Short-distance runners (100, 200, new quarter-milers) received a handout of pickups and hill work, about which Squires was adamant they did to be prepared for when he started with them in earnest in September. And there would be runoffs for the mile relay and two-mile relay.

Among those athletes who gathered at the first practice session that following Tuesday evening were seven distance runners who ranged between two to six miles, and about a half-dozen half-milers. They stood on Commonwealth Avenue, near the Parish of St. Ignatius of Loyola, between miles 21 and 22 of the Boston Marathon course at BC. Warm-up was at 6:15 p.m., with the workout at 6:30 p.m. Day one? Hills. And almost instantly, secrets were revealed. Squires told them about the benefits of running Heartbreak Hill. "I ran with the guys and I said, 'Get used to them.' And they said, 'Oh, yeah. We run down and we run back [on their own before].' I said, 'Oh, we don't do that. I'm lazy. We just go down to Heartbreak Hill and we play games on Heartbreak Hill.' They said, 'Is that what you guys do?'" To warm up first, he had them run a familiar route on and around the Boston Marathon course that included Newton Center and then back to Newton City Hall on Commonwealth Avenue. They had all done this before on their own, before this club, and informed him that they usually then ran Heartbreak hard and finished with strides on the school track. Squires acknowledged that that was indeed good, but then informed them of his plan. "I said, 'See the traffic light? We're going to start hill training there. I'll run with you, but don't run all out…because you're going to do *nine* of these.' I said, 'This hill has been here for a reason. Maybe geologists put it here [for training].'" One of the runners attempted to respond about the true origin of the hill being glacier formations, to wit Squires jokingly retorted, "'Hey, I didn't go to Bozo U like you did up the street. Cut it out!'" Squires laughed. "So right away I keep them on their feet. And I was challenging them with humor."

Games were also incorporated toward the end of workouts when runners are most tired and fatigued. Light to Light was one of those exercises, where they ran hard from traffic light to traffic light. "To keep in form, I'd tell them they're not going to race it, but this is going to give them [that push in a race] when they are tired. I said, 'I'm going to tell you all the time—I'm a teacher, and a coach is supposedly a teacher. Now, why did you do this? Everyone runs on sand dunes— one sand dune and they rest—and they run another one. Or they run for eight miles, the Swedish system, and all this and all that. It didn't do what I wanted.'" They responded that it was for road running. "I said, 'No. This is to make you quick, buddy, not for road running. You can't beat a hill. How did you get up over a hill? Didn't I teach you to shorten your stride and use more? To do that [well], you shorten your stride. Didn't you lift your knees? At the end of the race—any race, from a marathon to 100 meters—your legs are tired. But you have to lift. Those that can lift quicker, turn—they call it—turn the wheel quicker, win the race or part of the race. Those that can't, they're not doing anything to enhance their speed, and they're tired.'"

While they were good collegiate runners who enjoyed success, a lot of Squires's insights sounded foreign. He blended together successful elements from what he was coached in high school, college, overseas, and as a coach himself of high school, collegiate, and international athletes. From firsthand experience, he knew what worked and what did not, whether psychological or physical. "I'd never tell them what they were going to do. I'd never say we're going to do seven or eight reps. I could see sometimes people had enough or they were struggling at five or six, and I'd say, 'All right. That's it. Good.' And they'd say they could do more. And I'd say, 'That's great. We can leave it there, and you could do more. Good, I haven't burned the body. We want to build strength. We don't want to shred it and then go back fatigued.' You've got to have a person that believes that the vehicle getting them there definitely will. And it will! But it's patience. It has to be patience of the coach, and it's got to be patience of the athlete. And the coach has to control it. If not—and we've got some fine coaches that were too easy and let athletes dictate 'I can do more'—it doesn't work. Do it in competition. Show me more then. But I think what they want to do is they like to perform in front of you. You're there, and they want to show you what they can do." Squires regulated workouts to maximize the best effort out of his runners. He recognized who required more attention and who could work on his own. "There are kids that are practice runners; they'll run like ball bearings, but it doesn't teach them how they're going to have to race. You've got to contain, move, contain, move. You just can't go out *bang, bang, bang*, because that'll drain you. It'll come back at you and it'll tire you. And I never put pressure on anyone. I never will. I saw some of my college teammates that wilted under pressure, and it wasn't a happy thing."

In addition to the training on the roads and around the nearby 1.7-mile Chestnut Hill Reservoir, workouts were also held on the BC outdoor track that encircled the football field in Alumni Stadium. Since GBTC had no official home—and no base, no address, no clubhouse, no facility, no track—entry to the stadium track was improvised. Despite the fact permission was granted due to Squires's friendship with BC athletic director Bill Flynn, the AD had one time good-naturedly commented to Squires that his workouts seemed to include the exercise of high-jumping over the stadium fence. "Yeah, he saw that and came up to me about it." Squires laughed. "He told me to just call him whenever we needed the track. He said he lived right down the street, and he'd come over to unlock the track. Initially, I didn't know how it would be. I didn't know if we could go over there to BC. But Bill was good about that. We were able to come over there and train outdoors. We reported at 6:15 p.m. at the stadium, warmed up with two laps around the reservoir, and then came over to the track and stretched. Then I'd have a 50-minute workout, and that could include quarters if the track guys needed early-season work; and I'd alternate where we'd do something on the track, cut through the campus, go up the downhill of Heartbreak Hill, come back to the track, and go at it again to work that hill."

Squires employed his proven system of groups—fastest runners in Group 1; slowest runners in Group 3; and those in Group 2 could move up or down, dependent upon talent and speed. With the outward appearance of mass chaos when all his athletes were simultaneously running, it was with three stopwatches around his neck that he orchestrated the symphony. "I had the three groups, but they were all doing the same thing. I would start one group, and when they were 200 meters away, the second group would go, and when they were 200 out, the third group would go. Or, for example, I'd have Group 1 doing five times half-miles at 68[-second] pace for a 2:16 [marathon]; Group 2 would be going at 72 pace for a 2:32; and Group 3 would be going at probably 75 or 76 for a 2:48. And there is always a guy in each group for a rest watch [to monitor] how much rest they have before we start up again. And I'd have three stopwatches with three different colors, so I'd know which one was for each group." Squires incorporated the opposite approach on the roads on Sunday runs. "Group 3 would start and they'll get a seven-minute handicap, and when the next group catches up to them, they are to stay with them for two minutes, and then *go!* I didn't want them to run right by them because they had to surge to catch up to that group. That's a surge-and-rest. Everything that I do actually functions for a race. It's not wasting. That could be 12 pickups with baby surges in an easy 20-mile run, 16-mile run, and 14-mile run. And they've done these things so many times, I don't have any head cases. None! But the key is the period of rest—it has to be the same rest period. It's not too much. You're learning to recycle, just like in a race. Your heart's pumping, but not at a fast rate. Eventually, I'll get the heart to actually respond to the training. The mechanisms right from your feet all the way to your heart and your chamber, you're learning to work off fumes. Recycling."

Another day, within set time splits in accordance to each group, and without stopping, runners began with a specific workout on the Alumni Field track. That was followed by a moderate run through the lower campus of BC to the Boston Marathon course on Commonwealth Avenue, where they ran hard up the downhill portion of the Newton hills, returned to the track by way of the campus, and continued to the starting line where they kicked it in when they heard the start command. And repeat. Squires knew personally of the benefits of these workouts because they were similar to what he ran and also what he coached at Wakefield High School. "It was hills, it was surges, and they never knew how many they were going to do. But they had to adhere to the split time. I thought of all kinds of things they could do. And if someone did well, I'd recognize them for that. It was good for motivation. I didn't care how many guys I had in each group, but I did want to make sure they could handle it in whatever group they were in."

One of the local runners who showed up on a regular basis and became a noted GBTC member was a young 15-year-old Cuban-born high school sophomore from Wayland, Mass., who knew Pfrangle. And despite the obvious talent the kid possessed, the skill was not obvious to the average observer. He was Alberto Salazar, affectionately tagged Rookie. "He was all skin and bones, and he had the lousiest form in the history of mankind," Squires half-jokingly stated. "He had a bad back. He had tremendous strength, but his back would be a negative factor. He had great leg turnover, even though it was low—not as high—because of his bad back. He had good form up above with his arms, but his legs were very low to the ground—it was like a shuffle. When the press would comment that he had odd form, I would say, 'He's going to be a great distance runner because he's got what we call the marathon shuffle.' Because they thought I knew everything about running and marathoning, they put that in." Even at a young age, Salazar felt there was a level of talent in him which required extra attention to properly flourish in high school, college, and beyond. To supplement his high school running, he turned to the new club and its coach, who *did* recognize the potential. As a result, he trained under Squires and ran with the older athletes. "Rookie would come down on just Tuesdays. And I would also tell him what to do on Sundays, and his [high school] coach understood that he was going to do good runs on Tuesdays. And if there was a big, big race in high school on a Tuesday, I'd make sure he'd go to that. I had to put him in Group 1, and I was giving him half of what my guys in Group 1 were doing. In Group 2 he could have been beating them, but in Group 1, going halfway, fed his head."

Squires did not want to ruin Salazar, so he pared down his workouts and gave him age-appropriate training—more than he would for the average high school sophomore, yet less than that for an older veteran—and encouraged him to run in *some* races, but not a lot. "When his season went on, I'd train him, but he would not race. In between seasons, I could race him, but not that much. I wanted him to be successful, but I also understood the Massachusetts state [high school] rules for athletes and I didn't want to start anything. But I told his coach that against the hard teams he had, I wanted Al to be there and run hard. And he won't even come down to practice that day if he has a Thursday meet. If he has a Friday meet, he can come down on Tuesday like he does. But Al's got to tell me! And he did, he told me. He was honest with me [about the high school meets], but he wasn't honest with me about the weekends. Al'd lie. He'd go out and do 12-mile runs and then he'd say to me, 'You always said, 'When you're doing nothing, there's a kid out there training and he's going to kick your ass.' Geez, they remember these things I'd say. Al told me that every other week he probably ran 73 miles. I was like, 'What!!' A high school kid! Oh, geez! But that was Al."

Also training on Tuesdays were Squires's Boston State athletes. He included his Warriors among the GBTC runners to bolster workouts, and also to duly combine his multiple coaching duties. Despite the fact GBTC was his first club to coach, he benefited from a wide range of coaching experiences. "When I was starting out as a coach, I couldn't find written material. I had to go and read Czechoslovakian stuff—at least I could read the numbers; the numbers don't change. And I would even analyze Emil Zatopek's programs. That's why I ended up printing all these little books and pamphlets because I wanted to get this stuff out because I couldn't find anything." That was fortunate because the inaugural GBTC class possessed great talent, and he quickly understood he had to train it to be continually successful. And while most of the athletes either already had good coaches in school or were good enough to guide themselves, they all recognized the need for improvement required coaching to reach the next level. "Everything in my program is adapting you to race. Everything! So when you go to a race, you've had so many dress rehearsals it's like the movies. If you get beaten, you get beaten—but you're in the race. If you're not there halfway in, I know you're sick because we know everyone can run 80 percent of any damn race you're in. And when you step into a race, you've got 15 percent more than you'll ever get in a practice if you want to use it. That's the adrenaline."

Squires often baffled his athletes with such nuggets of wisdom, as well as a healthy dose of humor. One thing he always made sure he did was keep workouts fun and light. He learned first-hand there was no need to lead with a heavy hand. He found that athletes responded better with encouragement and support than abuse and fault, at least that was what he gleaned from his own experience. "You don't get results unless you're good and know what the heck you're doing. I know it's better to have a person that's humorous. I am teaching a sport that is actually very, very hard. You know, most sports are fun—kicking a ball around, hitting a ball—that's fun. And the fans are there, cheering you on. Well, I'm there [coaching], and there's hardly anyone there, and there's hardly anyone that understands the sport. It's very difficult. You can laugh at me and you can laugh with me. I have used this cliché many times when asked how do I do this and be wacky and kid around: you know that guy, Billy Shakespeare, that said the jester stole the crown from the king? Well, I steal the crown from the kings. Those that think they know coaching—well, guess what? They're gonna have a big, big headache because they're going to find that the guys I have, we make it fun. And it's not fun. It's hard, hard work. And we're going to beat the daylights out of a lot of people. And those other coaches will be sitting there with their guys and they'll have frozen faces [of disbelief]."

Squires also benefited from the natural progression of the graduated levels of those he coached. It was serendipity that he went from high school teens to college kids to post-collegiate adults and eventually to professionals. To achieve success in each instance, he adapted his understanding to the point of view of whatever group he coached. For top results at each level, he had to. High school kids are there because they either want to be (for fun) or they have to be (for scholarship); college athletes are there because they are paying for it (or are having it paid for them); and post-collegiate adults are there on their own accord (to either make a living or fulfill a dream). Those are uniquely and vastly different attitudes and approaches to which Squires had to adjust. "What I watched were coaches that ran their people out. When I got to high school coaching, I said I'm never going to abuse anyone to win. The winning record is for the coach—whoopee! They won, the coach gets the recognition, even the assistants get nothing. It's the coach! Give him more money!" he said with sarcasm. "My thing is development. How many kids did you get into college? How good did you have assistant coaches that could make those kids great to earn full rides? That makes you a great coach."

His benevolence did have boundaries. While his heart was always in the right place in terms of the best interest of his athletes, Squires at the same time did not want to tip his hand to anyone who could possibly learn something from his teachings and use it against him. Championships were at stake! There was no need to give another coach, team, or competitor, any of his own insight or advantage. As a result, he kept his instruction close to the vest. "A lot of this stuff I didn't want to give away. I never knew when these guys would go off, and who knows, come back and beat my system to the ground. I was very nebulous how I did things and what I gave away. I kept all the workouts on pieces of paper; in a big pile at home; in my pocket. I'd never show the guys their workouts; I'd leave it in my pockets. I had a bag at home with workouts on all kinds of scraps of paper because that would make it tougher for someone to copy my workouts or make sense of them. On napkins, too."

He was skillful in the art of workouts. He possessed a unique talent where he could, based on only a few questions or observances, craft successful goal-specific training that if adhered to could produce results. And it was proven. "I'd make them up on Monday, Wednesday, and Saturday—that's when I'd make my training schemes up. I had to change every week because of all the different races and different guys. And sometimes I'd say, 'Okay, where did we leave off with the average quarter pace last time?' And they'd say 67. And I'd know. I'd know where I'd left off last time. My short-distance guys would do five miles worth of work on a Tuesday, and my distance guys would do about seven—quick. I called it tempo-quick. The Thursday guys were doing real faster stuff because this was it for them. On Tuesday, for a while I didn't even bother with them. I'd give them starts to do. I'd be over there before the guys were warming up and we'd do start drills. They didn't need timing with the drills, they needed the explosiveness with the starts. In about an hour I could sit down and look at what I'd done the past week and I'd take that out and I'd upgrade it. And with any of the guys that'd race on the weekend, I'd move them to Group 2 so they wouldn't get burned out. I had to be flexible. And they had to open their mouths and tell me if they were tired or struggling. I'd say, 'Now, don't be dumbos! Don't be a nerdling! It's for you, so tell me.' But sometimes they didn't. And later on they'd say [the reason] was because they didn't want to miss the workout. But they didn't even know what it was going to be because I wouldn't even tell them!"

CHAPTER 10

GBTC YEAR ONE

Squires didn't have much time to get GBTC in the game. Their first cross-country season was upon them when they began. But there was an air of focus and determination with this group. Despite its novice status as a newborn club, these athletes carried with them a different sense of purpose. No one forced them to join a club or jump on board an established clique of teammates. This was their doing, by their own volition; at stake was their personal commitment. And Squires understood that. He knew what was on the line. He foresaw a long-term vision of greatness. If GBTC approached it the right way, he felt, history could be made. But it was vitally important—from the very first day—to do one thing consistently, and that was to think big. That meant both in training and competing. Simply put, when the athletes thought locally, Squires thought nationally. "We had guys that'd run races and win against the nerdlings in these little dandelion races. I told them when we go run, we go to the big ones." Local races were not the goal. Local races were a *means* to a goal. And those goals were lofty. "We're working regionally to see who goes nationally. We'll use them as runoffs for the nationals."

In front of him was a blank canvas of adults with no academic high school restrictions or Massachusetts Interscholastic Athletic Council rules; no four-year collegiate limitations or NCAA laws. Squires was able to fully incorporate, execute, and enforce—from soup to nuts—all his designs and systems. Some elements he kept, some he tweaked, some he skipped. Runoffs, he liked. On a regular basis, athletes competed against each other for certain spots. For example, if two runners were needed for an event, the top two in a runoff earned those positions. "There were no favorites. That's how it was. If you're injured, and I said you're injured and you're not going to run, that was it. Someone else was going to take your spot. The one thing was, I made it as fair as it can be so that I didn't want to have a kid say there was favoritism. When we went on the road, you *deserved* to go on the road. I knew some coaches that would take an athlete 'because he's good, so we have to take him.' Frig that! He's got to earn his way!"

Heading into the 1973 NAAU 20K Cross-Country Championship, Squires subjected his athletes to a 10-mile warm-up in the form of a five-mile run leading into an 8K race. He split up his team into two groups and two workouts because they were not competing in a 10K race, but rather a five-mile run right before the 8K. "I told them to wear their numbers because they're coming right in [to the race]. They're not going to go back to the car, so if they have to pee, go pee in your pants or find the woods. Hey, they'll learn." The NAAU 20K was held over a formidable 12.43-mile course in Massachusetts. Despite its difficulty, Squires felt his guys were prepared. "It's a bitchy course. It's a killer. About five hills. But they learned how to pull and push. In cross-country, they really didn't run because they just sat in the back and ran like sheep. But now they were going to be like wolves—they were going to stay in a pack. I said, 'When you see me at a mile-and-a-quarter away [from the finish], you're going to go balls to the wall! Remember that hill that you did nine times at BC when you're on the flat. You're going to fly.'"

Initial signs of how remarkable GBTC was to become arose immediately. After just two months in existence, the club won the NAAU 20K title. The upset occurred with half-milers and milers, and one three-miler. Squires's goal was met. And as he looked over his team at the finish, he noticed off in the distance a 25-year-old former smoker from Wesleyan University who did not even run his senior year. He walked over to Squires in a chance meeting that would forever change the landscape of competitive running, and both their lives. Bill Rodgers, the gangly blonde-haired kid from Connecticut, said, "'You're the coach?'" recalled Squires of the exchange. "'Who are these guys? I know two or three of them, I don't know the others. How long have they been training?'" He responded that the club's been training for only a couple of months, which surprised and impressed Rodgers. And when asked what GBTC was training for, Squires replied, "And I said it loud enough for my guys to hear, 'They're training to get into Madison Square Garden…without buying a ticket.'" Rodgers's eyes widened at the confidence, and the GBTC runners, who obviously overheard their new coach, began to realize the potential and magnitude of their club. "They were shell-shocked. I said to them, 'You won. I thought you would be in second place. But you won. Things worked.' And they go, 'Don't tell me we're going to become a road-running club.' I said, 'No way, Jose! I'm a track coach. I like track. Distance running? I know a little about that.'"

Rodgers was interested in the training. He saw results unfold before him. His sights, however, unbeknownst to Squires at the time, *was* on distance running—the marathon! He told Squires he was running between 100 and 120 miles a week, and that he also liked to run a good number of road races on weekends. But he still wondered about training with GBTC. "I told him he could. I said they'll be controlled because I do it that way. And I'm sure he'd be able to do it with them because he had some strength. But I told him to go easy on them. And we'll talk about [the races] later." The timing was right, too. Squires promised his guys would begin some track workouts, so Rodgers started from the beginning. The first workout after the national 20K was a road workout, but the week following that was on the track. "I told him I would start with the track, the basics, and it was good that he would be involved right from the beginning with the basic." After the first workout, Rodgers approached Squires and asked if he knew much about the marathon. At the time, Squires only dabbled, and said his best was a 2:47:46 for 20th place overall in 1961. Rodgers asked which marathon. "I said Boston!" That resonated with the youngster. *The Boston Marathon! Twentieth place!* And Squires followed that with a few more seeds. "I told him I had two kids that made the Olympic Trials. And I said, 'Maybe you will someday.'" Rodgers was intrigued. "I told him they were just college kids. Those kids were little over 10 minutes in high school for the two-mile run. They weren't good enough for the athlete aid."

Along with Rodgers, Wesleyan featured future US Olympian Jeff Galloway and 1968 Boston Marathon champion Ambrose "Amby" Burfoot. "I said, 'I saw ya. You had the big three and I had the little five, and we beat your team,'" said Squires in reference to his Boston State squad. "I said to him, 'I remember you.'" Rodgers was impressed, and asked Squires for a training program. It was tricky in that while both of them were B.A.A. members, Squires—although he coached GBTC—also had a loyal friendship with longtime B.A.A. member and official John "Jock" Semple. Squires never wanted to take away runners from Semple, so he advised Rodgers to stay a B.A.A. member, but that he could come join GBTC training sessions on his own. "I said, 'First of all, Bill, I don't want to start [anyone] thinking I'm going to raid the B.A.A. [starting] with you. Train with us. I like these guys. I'm part of a team.' But I'm not robbing clubs. I told him he could do what he wanted for distance. I never stop that [in a] person. But when you get in and you can't do the real workouts to give you speed, I'm the guy to give you speed. And you're the person that can give you strength. I said, 'You give yourself too much strength. I don't think you should be doing 100-mile weeks all the time, particularly when you're a young person. I think you've got to hang onto those speed fibers because you want to utilize them and you have to do it with the special training that you need two days a week, and then the other four days you can do your work.'"

Rodgers did just that; he remained with the B.A.A. and trained with GBTC. But by late fall of 1973, he departed the 86-year-old club and joined the months-old club, of which he formally became a member after he ran during the mandatory unattached waiting period between club affiliations. And Rodgers had developed a unique running style. His form was unorthodox—each stride compensated for the imbalance of uneven legs. And Squires initially tried to fix it. "I did try to correct it. It's a balancing act. Rodgers goes over on the side of his foot and with his arms he washes the windows, I call it. They move all around. On the corners on the track, I wanted him to straighten out. He worked at it. You could see the anguish on his face from the effort. He doesn't know it, but he had such good form he could have been a helluva runner indoors. But on the corners he had to straighten out his arms so he wouldn't cause a collision. On his right foot he wears out the outside edge of his shoes. When he was done with them because of the worn-out sides, he'd give away perfect shoes because the heels were not worn out. Anyone could wear them."

A pair of New England Association of the AAU Cross-Country championships in 1973 offered a unique presentation of what was in store for the running landscape. Competing in those NEAAAU meets were various club members who on their own soon joined GBTC—Pat Doherty, Tom Doherty, Mark Duggan, Rodgers of the B.A.A.; Chuck Riley of Cambridge Sports Union; Vinnie Fleming, Bob Hodge of Johnson & Wales College; Brad Hurst of Lowell Tech Athletic Club; Tom Derderian, David McGillivray, Earl McGilvery of North Medford Club; and Scott Graham (unattached). "I told them to bring guys in. I said I'd gladly take anyone on, say, up to December. We'll help them get their AAU card. They can stay with their club and I'll train them, but after December, I won't train them unless they're a member of our club. I wasn't trying to have them be a member of our club or stealing members from other clubs, but I knew we were going to be a damn successful club—I'm putting my heart and soul into this!—and I didn't want the negatives of guys saying I robbed this club and that club. And I wouldn't even have to because I can go after the guys coming out of college." Runners on their own would also switch clubs.

The 1973-74 indoors began almost immediately after cross-country. While the track and relay guys came off their training and were ready, Squires told his harriers to take two easy weeks to recover. But some of them also ran the indoor mile, 5000, or the relay. "They'd be in the runoffs to make the relay team, but they wanted to structure themselves into road racing and they wanted to structure themselves into individual activities, which I thought was smart. And I had two levels. My Group 1 guys would be on the national level; and on the national level, qualifying times had to be met in a national race. And I would have my Group 2 and 3 guys in regional races; regionally, we had one race around here, at Harvard University. They put on a big invitational track meet, and eventually we took it over and called it the Greater Boston Invitational. Anyway, we looked at two meets around us that were big-league: the Dartmouth Invitational and the Harvard Invitational, both about three weeks apart in January. And the indoor nationals were in February. I wanted each group to have things to shoot for." While Group 1 focused on nationals, one of the goals Squires set for Group 2 and 3 on the regional level was the NEAAU Men's Indoor Track Championship. "I'd get their times so they could get in there to Dartmouth and Harvard. But they weren't ready for the nationals. It would take two years before I could really get half of my Group 2 guys to be considered to be able to go to the nationals. That meant there were kids that were right on the cusp. These kids would develop. They came out of colleges where they were just worn to shreds or they did little to nothing as far as direction. The college coach just cared about how well he did in his conference. They didn't have goals to go to nationals or Olympic Trials."

The track guys began to grumble about when they were going to train indoors. They wanted to get on the track. And they let their coach know about it. Constantly. But unbeknownst to them at the time, there was no track. GBTC still had no home. Squires continued to search, of course, but he also had to stall. "I said to my guys, 'You're kidding me! If you're good enough—if you are good enough—I will get a place.' But, I told them I've done *41 quarters* on a track without stopping!

Zatopek's [program]! 'Now, you want to do this? Then I'll pick you up with your silver spoons. They said, 'Oh! No! No.' You see, whatever they did, I had tried it. I'd experiment." But while he sounded confident, he was still uncertain. With such a large number of colleges and universities clustered together in and around the Boston area, Squires banked on the simple law of averages that he could, in time, acquire the use of an indoor track. But his experience at Boston State, which also did not have a track of its own, was not promising. "I really didn't know what we were going to do. MIT was a dustbowl—12 laps to a mile. I knew Northeastern University wouldn't give me anything. For BoState they didn't—we had to go to the Y. And the indoor track at Boston College was too tight. You could get injured in there."

For the time being, he settled on the local YMCA. But in addition to the dependable use of the Y track, accommodations were found via Clarence "Ding" Dussault at Tufts University. For its use, it was only requested of Squires to keep the arrangement to himself so word would not spread to other trackless clubs. With an inherent time limit for each workout, Squires with his three different-colored watches, was precise when it came to training. "They put the lights out at seven o'clock, supposedly. I mean, who's going to rob them then—the rats and the dust? Anyway, we'd go inside at Tufts one day a week. We'd work at Tufts for about 45 minutes, but we'd warm up outside until 6:15 p.m. I'd have them run about two or three miles outside and then go inside and run an easy mile to get acclimated indoors. Then I'd have my workouts of repeat half-miles or repeat three-quarter miles; ladders—all kinds. I'd have Group 1 at a 72-second pace per quarter, Group 2 at 75 pace, and Group 3 at 78 pace. They knew the pace pattern. And we'd have what they call a rest pattern of 2:40 rest, which everyone would have. It was a circuit. And it was about 50 minutes. If you can't get it in and done quick, I mean, this thought of keeping them all day is fool's anonymous."

As for immediate competitive goals for their inaugural indoor track season, they suggested the open meets at Brown University in Rhode Island. But GBTC instead sent Mahoney, McDonald, and Sevene to the closer five-mile NU Indoor Track Club Invitational. Squires still had his other, loftier, plans in mind. "Those meets last for hours. It's an all-night affair. It would start with the 50, 1000, and every Tom, Dick and Harry high school kid and post-project kid were there. They'd run on a big track [at Brown as a perk] because for indoors in high school they had run in corridors and on outdoor tracks. I told them some coaches went to New York City on Friday nights at the 168th Street Armory. It was a flat, wood, eight-lap track with cones on it, and the meet was held by the AAU of New York City. It was open, but some of the best that were going to run the indoor season came." Upstate New York was a short-term focus for Squires, with perhaps in a year Quebec City and Montreal. And after that, maybe even the Toronto Games and Highland Games the following year, and eventually, down the road, *the* Millrose Games. "Well, they thought I was cracked!" Whereas the guys still had their sights aimed locally—and as a result, limited—Squires opened it up wider than they had ever imagined. "That was the goal for Group 1—the national championship. But we needed the times. And I knew the times we needed. I'd throw these times out to them, like 2:13 for the 1000, and of course came the faces [of disbelief]. They all gasped. I said, 'Hey, I've been there. I've done it. You can do it!' I was working them so that they weren't just going to be a relay guy. I went through that! They were going to get in their event. I knew my Group 1 guys weren't that far off from the times. And I told Group 2 and Group 3 that I wanted to win the New England AAUs with them."

After several weeks of training and an addictive taste of competition, they wanted to see more of Squires's training schedule. They were increasingly curious as to its long-term layout. The more he broadened their horizons, the more they wanted to see. But careful not to scare them off with too much information too soon, Squires doled it out piecemeal as he saw fit. "I told them, 'Basic training.' I said to them, 'I'll see you Sundays at about 11:30 a.m.—you don't want it Saturdays. And we're going to run a little longer, so keep your beers to two or three [the night before].' So, the next weekend I said, 'Every other Sunday, I own you. Every Tuesday, I own you. And eventually, it'll be Tuesdays, Thursdays, Sundays. Lucky you have me?!" Workouts increased proportionately in a manner in which his goal was for them to improve three to five minutes over the same runs within a few weeks. Training still featured hills—much to their chagrin—because they had yet to make that connection between hill work and race performance. "I told them they were going to do hills weekly. And then we started doing the surge-and-pickups—30 seconds, one minute, 30 seconds—with groups. Like a train— first two go, then two more rest, and then every time you see five minutes on your watch—*bang!*—you move. And you alternate." What they did not see at first was that Squires was meticulous in his building. Each workout was a layer for the next; building blocks of workouts. To knock the guys out of their comfort zone, there were times when he exposed the narrow vision and poked a little fun at it. "I said, 'I'm going to intensify [training]. If anyone asks when we're going to go on the track, you'll go on the track but you're now going to go to little dinky road races, not the big ones. Falmouth? You're not ready for Falmouth.' I said, 'You're all going to pick different ones, and then you can tell war stories when we're warming up.' I said, 'Look, you were beating these poor little guys that are untrained. They've got no direction, it's all hit or miss, and most of them don't have any coach. And you were the elite high school athletes. Remember that.'"

The Millrose Games was their first real dip in a major indoor track pool. The main objective for Squires was to get them prepared—mentally and physically. It was easier to forge their bodies because more thought went into forging their minds, and that left too much of a chance for their minds to wander and doubt to sneak in. "When I said they were going to Millrose, they said, 'Coach, you can't get us into Millrose.' I said, 'Oh, yeah? You're friggin' in! We're in the Demolition Derby. Because you're a club, the open guys have a Demolition Derby—that's all invited running clubs. At 6:30 at night they put them all together, five deep, like a road race. It's survival of the fittest.'" As they absorbed this, digesting the fact they will compete against numerous clubs on the famed track, Squires continued: "I told them they better be [at least] third, because if they did that, I think I can get them into the Olympic Invitational." He always lifted the spirit of his runners. As a new team, he constantly raised the bar. Whenever they wondered if they were good enough or if they belonged at a certain meet, he not only reassured them they were, but he also handed them another goal down the road, as if to say when they succeed here, they will succeed there. "I said to them, 'You're not going to let yourself down. *If you do lousy, that means I do lousy. And I don't do lousy!*' When I put a person on the starting line, that's me there. And guess what? Me turns to We, and we're in this together. I'm putting my workouts on the line. Results count for you and your team. That's what I believe. And that means *me, you, him,* the *wes.* Never worry about the *theys.* The theys are aliens. The theys don't even know how to run. They talk about it. 'What are *they* going to think?'"

His reputation as a successful coach was built upon the fact the athletes he put out there gave their best, win or lose. And that is all he asked of them. "That's all I want. And we'll talk about how we could have done better later, 'You and I.' But that's all I ask. Each one is an individual. I do not coach them as groups. I work in groups, that's how I've been successful in high school, college, clubs." During the winter months en route to the Derby, he continued to train them at Tufts; and to stay sharp, they competed at select New York armory meets. "Right away they're running good times. I had them do one event in a meet. They wanted to run more, but I said, 'No, no, no! That's lollypop. That's why you had the silver spoon—that's foolishness. You're going to run one, and you're going to run balls to the wall.'" After one such armory meet, where they finished around 12:30 in the morning, on the way home they stopped at the Green Comet Diner, the favorite Connecticut truck-stop diner to which Squires brought his college kids. "They could eat a horse by then. They'd snack [at the meet], but from about 7:00 p.m. on, different guys would run, and if I saw any of the group go up there to get a hot dog and a drink, I'd kick them in the butt. So, at the Green Comet, I can hear them talk [at the tables] behind my back, saying things like, 'He's still talking about going to the Millrose Games. And he keeps saying Demolition Derby.' See, it's in their heads. Good." The early focus for Squires was the relay because he realized with the small number of runners, he didn't want to spread the wealth too thin. He wanted to find something in which the club could dominate across the board, and that was to create a juggernaut in the two-mile relay. "I had five good half-milers, and I knew I wasn't going to get them in as individuals. Not even one. But I could get them into the relay. I knew this from the beginning, even before Greater Boston. I knew these guys had ability."

At the 1974 NAAU Indoor Track Championship in Madison Square Garden, Squires gathered his troops for the open two-mile relay—the Demolition Derby! After talking it up for so many weeks, they were actually in the Garden! Ready to go. But they still did not fully get it. The Derby was still foreign to them in a way that Squires felt compelled to explain. Again. "The Derby is run first, and most people that get there to watch the events usually only catch the last few laps of it. They never knew what was going on with all these guys running around. And my guys didn't even know that kind of a relay was there. When they got there before, when they were on their college teams, they arrived after it was over. I told them it was a special relay. I said, 'Why do you think I have Don Ricciato out in lane four at Tufts and he's looking back at you guys?' For the first 75 yards, my leadoff guy runs like it was a quarter-mile. He'd get out and *then* he'd turn." With such a large number of runners crammed within the six-lane Derby, Squires positioned his leadoff guy—Ricciato—far outside in or near lane four. This undoubtedly forced GBTC to run more yardage than the others, and lose about five seconds, since the majority of the clubs sought the inside lane for better logistics. But Squires had that figured out, too. "I told Donny he had to stay out there until the second leg when you could move in for the exchange. And the passing zones were on the tilted corner. It was so congested that I didn't want my guys banging into everyone. There would be people dropping relay sticks, lapping guys—it was a mess. But I told Donny that once we get out of these and into the real relays, you won't have to do this outside-lane stuff. In fact, if you went out there, I'll kick your ass. But this was a means to an end."

Ricciato—with the extra distance in lane four for all his laps—passed off the baton to Sevene. "Donny was a quick guy, and I gave him strength, so I wanted him to lead off with his speed. Sevene was slower, but he could take it to Dave Elliott." From Sevene to Elliott, the anchor leg was handed to McDonald. "I felt my last two guys were the fastest guys, and as it turned out, that was right. We had made up something like 300 yards, about two laps. Elliott was fast and I knew he would improve where we were. And I knew Jack could at least maintain our place. That was about it." GBTC did not win, but they did place. Squires felt they still succeeded, especially in such a confined, hectic, chaotic event. It was a very good test of mettle. "I put them in the Derby to get their nose bled a bit. It was good for them. My goal was to get a fast time, not necessarily a win. I was running to get the fastest time that they (the officials) could see to get us out of the Derby and get us on the circuit. You had to do something spectacular to get noticed, and we did. That's how Greater Boston started."

The first few bricks of that powerhouse were laid rather swiftly in 1974 when later the same two-mile relay team won the New York Knights of Columbus Indoor Track Meet at Madison Square Garden, and the New England Men's Indoor Track Championship at Tufts. In addition, the foursome also came in second at the Olympic Invitational Indoor Track Meet at the Meadowlands in New Jersey, and third at the NAAU Indoor Track Meet at the Garden in New York. GBTC found itself at meets alongside such well-established groups as the Capital Athletic Club of Washington, D.C.; New York clubs like the New York Athletic Club, Pioneer Athletic Club, Westchester Club, Syracuse Striders; clubs from New Jersey and Maryland; and, of course, the B.A.A. "This was good. Meets were open if you had your AAU card. And some teams had three vans of people, A and B teams, and they all had one or two good studs that were good in the three miles—before the 5K—and milers."

As GBTC entered each season for the first time, there was always a period of adjustment. The 1973 cross-country season, their first-ever competition, was a blur. The 1973-74 indoors, while a bit more settled, was still nevertheless frenzied. They basically knew what to do—and Squires likewise as the coach—but the overall blending of all the components was still a work in progress. And the first outdoors in 1974 was no exception. "Greater Boston was following my college system. It takes my system two years. In two years you'll see phenomenal growth because you're doing a step system and your body responds. I'm building your engine up, and as time goes on, you're a total different body. After a while you understand and it's your turn to lead. And you look forward to racing."

In the spring of 1974, Squires experienced difficulty locating outdoor track meets. It was a struggle for him to maintain a competitive schedule that best put to use his buildup training. "There weren't too many championships around here— you really had to go looking for them. Most post-collegiate athletes wouldn't go beyond college. California had them, but it was so hard to go to the finals of the championships because you had five meets before you'd go to the finals. Five meets! So, around here, the colleges would put something on, and that was about it. And I had to figure out who was going to run what. We didn't have enough guys for every event." Around this time, the longest distance event offered in outdoors was switched to three miles/5000 meters. Squires could nurture his athletes for that distance, but an ideal match would be something longer—the 10K/10,000. But with America's resistance to metric, the closest he found was the occasional six-miler. "You didn't have the two-miler anymore; it finally went up to the three. But no one wanted to put the six-mile run on."

Squires had vision. He understood there was a gap, a missing distance, that could easily be filled by a wanting group. "For the majority of cross-country kids that were very, very good—the third, fourth, and fifth guys—track was a loss for them because in indoors they only went to the two-mile run. The stars—the first two guys on the team—could keep going. And what most coaches brought were more milers, and a lot of the milers were negatives. I wasn't one of them because I kept saying if they ran five miles they should be able to run six." After some coaxing, he finally persuaded BC, and later, the nation's most well-known and oldest track and field competition—the Penn Relay Carnival in Philadelphia— to add the longer distances. It was several years in the making, but this was a gateway, he felt, to the nationals where the six-mile run was routinely held. "It took some time, but I'm glad I did it. It helped, not just my own club, but the whole of distance racing to be able to take care of the real road runners."

Prior to the longer distances and the inclusion of open athletes, however, GBTC battled the younger, more fine-tuned college and university teams. And as it was still in its infancy, GBTC experienced its own growing pains. "We did well at BC and at Penn. We got points in the field events. In the relays, we were in the hunt. But at Penn, we were up against the collegiate studleys. We're talking about the best of the best. But we did okay." Word-of-mouth from indoors resulted in a couple dozen newcomers to GBTC, which gave Squires more to work with in terms of personnel and talent. And all along, the club's relay teams continued to flourish and build upon their indoor success. "I knew my distance guys from cross-country and indoors talked to other guys about joining. I told them to tell anyone that if they wanted to come down, they better be in shape. I'm not getting anyone new in shape."

Outdoors consisted of at least four meets, with the goal of ending the season at the NAAU meet; that is, if GBTC qualified. The first level of any real outdoor competition for the club was found at BC's relatively new two-day track meet. Modeled after the Penn Relays, BC included the mile, sprints, hurdles, and relays such as the DMR, SMR, mile relay. But prior to the formation of GBTC, the BC Relays was a spring school-only competition that featured several events, which included a variety of obscure relays, such as the hurdle shuttle and the discus relay. "The hurdle shuttle was held in the middle of the field with a set of hurdles set up across from each other, and guys would run back and forth between the [opposite] hurdles and each guy had to wait until his teammate slapped his hand before he could begin his leg. The discus relay had three guys to a team and they'd add up the total amount of distances, or record the longest toss. They had all kinds of different relays, and some of them actually made it into the Penn Relays." By the time GBTC formed in 1973, the BC event blossomed to include clubs, thanks in no small part to Squires. Prior to any inkling of ever coaching a club, it was as the Boston State coach that he spoke to BC organizers about expanding the event to include more than just schools. He saw the advantages of the addition of clubs. "I'd told them that with clubs, they're going to make money out of it from them, and that some of those guys are big stars and people will want to come and see them. I said if they wanted to give prizes and they wanted to separate awards [between club and non-club runners], fine. But for most kids it isn't the medal, it's to get ink in the newspaper. The medal is hidden—who's going to see it other than mom and dad and sis and their girlfriend. But their name in the paper was big."

At one of those early BC meets, Squires recalled the time he met future United States Speaker of the House, Thomas "Tip" O'Neill Jr., a 1936 BC alum and at the time US House Majority Whip; and his son, future Massachusetts lieutenant governor Thomas O'Neill III. "Someone said to Tip, 'This guy here knows all about everything.' So he asked me if I could explain to him what was going on at the meet with all the different relays, like the distance medley. He asked if they were all running a long distance, which was smart. And I told him that 'distance' means about 2.5 miles collectively over the run, and in it you involve everyone—your milers, half-milers, and quarter-milers. He asked how that was done, and I told him you start off with the three-quarter-mile run, and right from that into a quarter-mile sprint, and then to a half, and then the strategy of the mile. I told him it opened and closed with distance, and had two speed guys in the middle." Tip, who was involved in sports as a youngster and held that love as an adult, understood. He then followed with an observation that the SMR must therefore include only sprinters. "And I said, 'Right.' Then he said he always remembered the mile relay. And I said that was when each guy did a quarter-mile. And I told him we used to also have the half-mile relay where everyone would run 200 meters."

Never one who failed to recognize an opportunity in the form of a person of possible means, Squires continued to explain the events and answer Tip's questions and also slipped in personal views about the event itself. "The BC Relays were, well, you know, not that good. But I remember explaining the whole thing to him and what I thought they should do with the clubs. I said that whoever told [AD] Bill Flynn to do the track the way they did it, it was too long. Bill was a nice guy, but because they wanted to save money and not dismantle the football stands, they put the track *around* the stands. Runners had to run around the stands! And then they had the field events behind it, so for people to see it they had to come around and they'd be standing on the track to watch the field events. Are you kidding me?" The standard track setup of four laps to a mile is based on each lap being 440 yards, which adds up to 1760 yards—one mile. At BC, however, the elongated track equaled 469 yards per lap. For some distances, that eliminated a turn. One benefit of the long track for Squires was the steeplechase. The standard 3000-meter event begins with a portion of no jumps, and then features seven water jumps and 28 barriers—one water jump and four barriers per lap. "People were always wondering how was I getting all these qualifying times in the steeplechase to go to the nationals. When you do the steeplechase at BC, you have one less barrier and you have one less turn for the timing thing. Does that mean a lot? Sure does—four to six seconds. So my guys'd get times and we'd go down to the Penn Relays with them." (Squires never knew if Tip ever forwarded these views when a new track was built.)

While the BC track was not ideal, GBTC was still more familiar with the confines of the configuration. For other meets, they simply had to adjust. "For practice it was good, but not for events. In training, if, say, I was having my guys do 200s, I had cones set up at 200 meters and when they went by the cones they'd raise their hands and I'd be standing where they started and I'd yell out their times. Good thing I have a voice that carried." GBTC was well represented at the BC meets because Squires brought everyone. And he once again expanded the limited thinking of his athletes. Instead of entering his strong two-mile relay team, which would have been the logical plan of attack, he had his guys compete in nearly every relay *but* the two-mile. "I wanted to try something new. And they liked that. It was healthy. I wanted to expand my track guys and I wanted to get some of my field guys in. That was my goal to open the season with. I didn't look at it as anything but that. And we did well. We won some events." Sometimes that decision was taken out of his hands. Outdoors favored the mile relay over the two-mile relay, which was more prevalent indoors. But since Squires had oftentimes changed up the events, his athletes were better prepared if and when their event was not held. "It was a built-in thing. The two-mile relay was quick enough to keep the people interested indoors. Outdoors, the mile relay was enough. And my guys were always ready."

While staying local provided easier access to tracks and competition, it was not an ideal ingredient Squires saw for greater success. For that, he surmised, GBTC had to travel to face better competition. The main hurdle was not the lack of talent, but the lack of funds. "If someone had a van—not a little two-seater, but a van— what we did was everyone threw five bucks in and that paid for the gas. And if there are tolls, it'll cost everyone six or seven bucks. At the end, it's wear and tear on his car, so he ends up with a few bucks for that." There were relays in New England, but the road trip that was always worth the gas money was to the Penn Relays. With some of these top events, athletes needed a little extra help to aid their admittance. Because there were so few qualifying events in which to compete, having a notable coach such as Squires was pivotal to fill in any requirement gaps. "I knew enough people in track to help get guys in. As an open [competition] guy, you really needed some pull. You'd have an athlete that ran or threw well or something, but not that recently, and they'd say, 'What has he done since?' And it was up to me to get them in. Most college kids were run into the ground; or with the field guys, they didn't have coaches that knew what they were doing."

Penn Relay competition featured a healthy mix of schools, colleges, universities, clubs. Thousands of athletes competed before thousands more spectators in the stands. At times it took on the look of mass chaos. But at the 1974 Penn Relays, GBTC managed a hard-earned third place in the DMR. "From what we had done indoors, I felt we were justified in getting in. I just didn't know where we'd be because we hadn't run that event more than twice. But I did think we could come in the top five, which we did. We got beaten fairly well, but we were close to second."

Several weeks separated the Penn and Dartmouth relays from the season-ending championships, so most clubs found local meets in which to compete. Squires still favored putting his guys up against tougher competition, but with a limited budget he was forced to spend sparingly. At the NEAAU Track and Field Championship, the steadfast two-mile relay team of Ricciato, Sevene, Elliott, McDonald, extended its dominance with another win. In addition, GBTC won the NAAU 20K Championship in Connecticut. "The first time we went to the New Englands we won by something like 35 points. I told my big boys in Group 1 that I've gotta get my second group in there and be successful, so that's what I did after that year. I knew we were too much for our region. I had people running off for my relay team that ran, like, 1:52 in the half-mile. And after the first few years, I'd have three to four people who'd qualify for the nationals."

The conclusion of the first competitive year for GBTC—a full season each of cross-country, indoors, outdoors—led to the "off-season" of road races. GBTC went through the three-season cycle relatively unscathed. There was plenty of room for a tremendous amount of improvement, both coach and athletes admitted, yet the direction was positive. One thing that was learned early and often was who the boss was from August to June. It was made crystal clear that was Squires. But during the "off" weeks between the end of outdoors and the start of cross-country, he did let up. But not too much. "I said they could run a bit hard in the guppy races if they wanted to run in one or two. I'd tell them they could run in these little nerdling road races if they wanted, like the town July 4th races, which is fine. This will keep them in shape because I don't want to start from scratch in August. The two months of August and September will be their base for the half-milers and up; and the track guys I'd see then. I still wanted them to maintain their running, and that included a nerd race or two."

During the summer, some athletes experimented and tested themselves at various local races and distances, which Squires encouraged. One such odd-distance race that began in August 1973, in Cape Cod, Mass., was the Falmouth Road Race. At seven miles—give or take extra yardage in the beginning—the point-to-point course went from the village of Woods Hole to the beaches at Falmouth Heights. GBTC contributed to the early (and ongoing) success when each year many of the winners and top-echelon finishers were from the club. "I remember my college kids told me about a new race in Falmouth. I'm like, 'Falmouth? Where the hell is Falmouth? Falmouth, Maine?' No one knew where it was." At the second running, in 1974, Rodgers won in a CR 34:16. As for Squires, who at Boston State was named 1974 Coach of the Year, he spent part of his "off-season" at Stonehill College in Easton, Mass., where he helmed the Coach Squires Summer Camp. Among those in attendance was Rodgers.

CHAPTER 11

GBTC IDENTITY CRISIS

Squires began GBTC's 1974 cross-country preseason as they all did, on the second Tuesday in August. This date allowed him a solo month with his Boston State athletes, who began their cross-country preseason on the second Wednesday in July. "They needed more work," he said of his collegiate Warriors. "I have new kids every year. And you talk about green kids, they didn't even know enough about double knotting their shoes! I needed at least a month with my BoState kids under my belt because their season started early in September, and the Greater Boston guys started at the end of September. So I had enough leeway with that kind of schedule. And the preseason is the most important thing to get right."

Heading into its second full cross-country season, GBTC had already won a team title at the 1973 NAAU 20K Championship. The club added to that the 1974 NU and 1974 New England 15K cross-country championship titles. "I started this cross-country season off with a funny thing—a quarter-mile—to prove they had not lost their speed. It was a first test to see if they did their summer work. I'd do that every year. I know some coaches that would have had them do a hard mile instead. Frig that—no! I didn't want to break their heads. They've been doing endurance work, and I'd know if they've lost speed or not. Then there'd be little pickups on the road—not measured—and they wouldn't know in a minute if they'd gone 310 yards or 430 yards. Then I'd say, 'Group 1, we're going to work 74 seconds. Group 2, we're going to do 76 seconds. Group 3, we're going to look at 79 seconds. With two-minute rests.' And someone would say, 'How many are we gonna do?' And I'd say, 'Hey, talk to the friggin' rookies! Shut your mouth!'" He laughs. "I wouldn't tell them, but I'd know. I could tell with their legs when it was enough. Probably eight. But I didn't let on." That was one of the keys for Squires: he never announced the number of reps in a workout. This point was lost on the new members, but veterans understood.

The Squires program continued GBTC's successful ways with stalwarts like Rodgers (NAAU 20K winner), Randy Thomas (second at the IC4As), and high school junior Salazar (USA-USSR Junior Meet 5000 meters winner). The big meet to end cross-country was the 1974 NEAAU six-miler at Franklin Park, where GBTC failed to place the previous year. But behind a final 5:08 mile, Rodgers won in 29:18 and the club earned the team title.

As it entered its second indoor track season, GBTC numbers nearly doubled with close to 20 members. They were getting stronger, as individuals and as a team. And Squires prepared them for the Millrose Games. "They started seeing the work coming out in these meets. And then at the end of the season, the Group 2 and 3 guys killed at the New Englands. We never used the big boys from Group 1 [because they would always win, so this gave other runners a chance], but they always congratulated the Group 2 and 3 guys. We were all still one team. There were no prima donnas. Now, to make the Demolition Derby at Madison Square Garden, we had runoffs on times. The fastest four times would hold. Whatever these people do on Saturdays, in the big meets, if someone can beat that time [in training] on Tuesdays, they can go. The original Derby guys are absolved—they don't have to do this time trial [due to experience]. That's an open spot. But they can come back the following week [and try] because I had another big meet in mind. So I had the competition going. Every year I'd find a new guy that would take someone's spot on that original Derby team. I told them they only bring in 12 people, and then six go to the final. Same thing with the hurdles. And with the quarter, it's eight to 10 people—five in each heat, with five in the final. The stopwatch doesn't deny you, you deny it."

As spectators found their seats at the 1975 Millrose Games, 14 club teams congregated for the two-mile relay, which featured four pass-off exchange zones. It was massive. Runners drew sticks for their placement up front. Squires instructed his runners as to where to start and when to push. He advised his first runner, Don Ricciato, who drew the second row on the inside, to start over on the outside and stay in his lane while everyone else bunched up together for the inside. After the usual hectic start, Ricciato more-than survived his "extra" leg of the relay, and safely handed off the stick to Sevene, who pushed the pace to Elliott, who passed the baton on to anchor McDonald for a top-10 finish. "For two laps, my guys were going to run a long half, but we went out like a bullet and took off. When it all ended, we got our medals, and I said, 'Boys, you're in Millrose. Good race.'"

GBTC flourished. Money came in from various raffles, victories, and other avenues. Because of their successful performance at the Olympic Invitational in the Meadowlands, the club was put in the final among only 12 teams to compete in the two-mile relay at the 1975 NAAU Indoor Track Championship, also in Madison Square Garden. Three spots behind the Chicago Track Club, GBTC was fourth. "Chicago was an all-star team of the Midwest Big Ten. They were big-league." Also during indoors, Squires heard about an old track meet in Hamilton, Ontario, Canada. Organized by the venerable 91st Highlanders Athletic Association—a committee of the original 91st Regiment Canadian Highlanders from 1904, and the 91st Highlanders from 1903—he regaled his guys about the history of the indoor games and that in 1925 a new wood indoor track was dedicated, in part, to directly entice Paavo Nurmi, who eight months earlier at the VIII Olympiad in France had won four gold medals. "They built this track for Nurmi to run—and he eventually did—and they built seats for about 4- or 5,000 people, with some standing room," noted Squires.

This anniversary sendoff was its final meet before it moved to the new Copps Coliseum in Hamilton. Only three from GBTC made the trip to Canada—Sevene, who won the mile in 4:12; future Massachusetts State Track Coaches Association Hall of Fame member Bill Martin, who ran the 880-yard in 1:56; and Squires, who talked his way into the mile B heat because his 4:38 was not under the qualifying 4:30 standard. "The official tells me everyone's supposed to be under 4:30. I said, 'I'll guarantee I won't be last.' So he put me in as a provisional, which means I'd be lined up in the back. Which is where I was going to go anyway." At the age of 41, Squires beat three other milers in the B heat with a 4:29, which nearly broke the *outdoor* record *indoors* on a 12-lap track. "That's very difficult to do, to beat an outdoor record on an indoor track. And I was, I think, about one second off." The track for decades was too-often disassembled and reassembled, Squires recalled, and was for the last time dismantled after the meet. "I remember they were going to cut the track up sometime after the meet and later on you could take pieces home. I remember they had an announcement that you can take away what you can carry. I didn't take any pieces, but as I look back, I guess I should have."

Meanwhile, away from track events, GBTC's most recognizable member strung together a steady collection of high-profile finishes. Rodgers in 1973 won the Bay State Marathon and the NAAU 20K; in 1974 won the Philadelphia Marathon, NEAAU Cross-Country Championship, New England 15K, Falmouth Road Race, was 14th at the Boston Marathon, fifth at the New York City Marathon; and in 1975 was fourth at the US Men's Cross-Country 15,000-Meter Trials. Rodgers was making a name for himself on the roads, specifically, in longer distances and the marathon. And his sights were set on the 1975 Boston Marathon. With such a superb running resume, he garnered full-page attention in the February 14, 1975, edition of the *Boston Globe* newspaper, in which Squires was quoted as saying he felt Rodgers would run in the Olympic Marathon in Montreal the following year. But the Rodgers name was still unfamiliar to some. Case in point was a half-page spread in the city newspaper in which he was repeatedly referred to as Will Rogers (thanks in part to Squires's impish pre-race downplayed hype with the media).

Name recognition notwithstanding, at the behest of Squires to prepare for Boston, Rodgers trained for the 1975 IAAF World Cross-Country 12K championship. Held in Rabat, Morocco, the 7.45-miler was scheduled for about a month before Boston. As part of the training, Squires in December brought Rodgers to Maine to use the all-weather track at Colby College. "I told him he was a pretty good cross-country runner at 10K, but the international distance is 12K. At Colby, I wanted him to do some track work because we had done so much cross-country work. I knew he had a distaste for it. He wasn't coached right [for track work]. A good athlete can understand what a coach is doing when they can see the movements of the training. I'm not going to say, 'We're doing all quarters, miles, and halves, repeats.' They're scatterbrained—they don't understand there's a step system. As they go, you give them things they can do. You don't have them do 62-second quarters when you know they can do one and die. What you do is you have them do seven or eight 67s, and then move on to the half-mile."

While Squires worked with and trained everyone at GBTC, Rodgers was one of those talents who required extra attention. Several Group 1 runners were clearly on their way to world-class status, and as such, needed more fine-tuned programs and workouts. For Rodgers, Squires was concerned that his 2:21:57 win at Philadelphia was over two minutes slower than his 14th-place 2:19:34 at Boston eight months earlier. Both men realized that Rodgers lacked speed over

26.2 miles. At the 1974 Boston, Rodgers contended as late as Heartbreak Hill and was in fourth with nearly 10K to go. But he lost 10 spots and finished about six minutes behind Neil Cusack's winning 2:13:39. As a result, Squires focused on those weaknesses. He knew Rodgers possessed great endurance and distance, but it was that speed and the ability to surge in a race upon which he needed to improve. And that is exactly what they did with the track work. And Rabat.

On March 16, at the 1975 IAAF 12K in Morocco, Rodgers turned in an AR 35:27 and became only the second US male to win bronze at the oldest international cross-country race in the world. Rodgers was just eight seconds behind winner Ian Stewart of Scotland and seven behind Mariano Haro of Spain. This was monumental for the local runner because his competition included Olympic champions from one mile to 10K. It was a tremendous confidence boost. Also as part of training, within one month before the 1975 Boston, Rodgers competed in the Bankathon 30K in New York for its hill finish, despite the fact he was still recovering from dysentery he picked up from fruit he ingested in Morocco (Squires pointed out that Rodgers had discovered too late that a certain type of human fertilizer was often used). "He was doing between 110 to 120 miles a week, but he was doing the speedwork and he was racing almost three weekends a month, which I didn't like. I think every other weekend would have been good. But he used the races for surges and to see what he had. And he knew he had to have easy Mondays because my Tuesdays were a valve cleaner. At that time, he could get away with that. He was like a nobody, so he could sneak away. He didn't have the X on his back, you know!"

With GBTC's Rodgers as a former B.A.A. athlete about to run their Boston Marathon, it was the respect and admiration between Squires and B.A.A. official Jock Semple that ensured the club switch was never considered by either of them as underhanded. "I remember Jock said to me, 'I shouldn't be talking to you, but you were one of my boys and you ran for me all these years. And Rodgers—it would have been great for the B.A.A.' And Jock said to me, 'He (Rodgers) wrote me. And I said if you're gonna run with him (Squires), I told him you were a good coach. But you did that to me?'" Squires recalled Semple saying half-jokingly in his jabbing Scottish accent. "I said to Jock, 'I told him, and he'll tell ya, I told him not to come, to stay there at the B.A.A. I swear on my mother's...' And Jock says to me, 'Oh, you swear on your mother's honor? Okay.' That was good enough for him." When Rodgers won Boston in 1975 under GBTC, it stung a bit for Semple, who would have had his first B.A.A. champion in nearly 20 years, since Johnny "The Younger" Kelley's 1957 victory. In fact, the GBTC team (Rodgers, Scott Graham, Vinnie Fleming) came in third; the B.A.A. team did not place. And there was also another Squires-coached GBTC athlete who made an impact in the 1975 race when Bob Hall became the first official push-rim wheelchair finisher. Hall, who as a child contracted polio, was very active in sports and was a student of Squires at Boston State.

"I had him in class and one day when I was talking about disabilities, and I forgot he was in the class in a wheelchair, I said something like, 'If you put your mind to it, you can do anything.' I think as an example I even told them about when I put the ax through my foot as a kid and then later on had a career in running. I used that as an example of doing anything you want, especially after an accident." Hall asked Squires about track work and training, and subsequently joined GBTC. "He was worried a bit, but I said, 'Track is track. But the traction will be different.' And the training just came to me. I told him he had to glide the corners. I said that with runners, runners are afraid people are going to cut in. But with him, he didn't have to worry about that, so I told him to use [imaginary] lane one-and-a-half. With a runner, you can't do that because someone'll just cut in. I had him doing 200s, quarters—just like a regular track workout. I wanted him to do some sprints, and I taught him about his endurance and that he can go on the road just like roadwork."

But Hall wanted to *race* the Boston Marathon. "He was good on the track. I didn't know what he was eventually planning. I said, 'Huh? You're kidding me.' Then I told him I didn't know how I could get his arms ready for that, but I'll do it." Squires built up Hall to handle in a 43-pound wheelchair the rigorously challenging course. "Five hours is what I thought. And I'll clue ya, this was uncharted territory. I wanted to give him a time trial of 21 miles because I thought when he got there, he'd be so tired that he wouldn't want to do it. But if he wanted to after that, we'll do it."

On his own, Hall lifted weights, repeated pull-ups, and increased his mileage. "We talked about hills. I asked him how does he stop the slippage when he goes up a hill, and he said you have to grip the tire and then open up. So I told him we'd have to do drills for that. We didn't do any races. They would have barred him anyway, and because I did have second thoughts because of the hills of Boston. I didn't want him to start something on hills and run into someone."

Squires incorporated the same training techniques for the wheelchair as he did for feet, and that included simulation and replication of the course. One March day in particular that was specifically scheduled for Hall on which to train the Boston Marathon course, they were greeted by cold rain and sleet, an unfortunate element of New England training. Squires suggested the next day, but Hall convinced him it would be worse by then, so Squires cut the workout short by having it start in Ashland instead of Hopkinton, which eliminated the downhill start. Squires and his eldest son, Bill Squires Jr., accompanied Hall to Ashland High School, from where the workout began. "Bobby went ahead of us on the road and we're behind him with the blinking lights on the car. You could see him slipping and sliding on the roads. At certain points I'd sound the horn and Bill would jump out of the car and run ahead and give Bobby a plastic water bottle and get back in the car. The sleet was coming down pretty steady, and it'd get in your face and your eyes—it was a raw and bitchy day. I had Bill wipe Bobby's face off each time because Bobby had those big gloves on with duct tape. On the downhills, he was flying. He was in control, but I'm yelling, 'Go slower! Go slower!' Then he had to climb. That was a bitch. And when he gets to certain mile markers, I'm yelling out to him where he is because he can't see them on the road. But then my son says to me that we didn't start at the starting line, so we're off a mile or two. We didn't say anything to Bobby. We just left it to him that he's doing those miles anyway."

The 18-mile workout ended near St. Ignatius Church at BC, just after the 21-mile mark. With the bad weather and it being a Sunday, roads were relatively free of cars, which was extremely beneficial to Hall. "When it was over, I looked at his gloves and the duct tape was cut right through and all that was left of the leather gloves was the inner lining." Squires next had to convince Will Cloney, the race director, to include a wheelchair athlete into his Boston Marathon. "He was a tough sell. Will only had about three weeks to get ready for the Marathon. Cloney hated marathons, really. He liked the track aspect. Anyway, I told him that I had this boy from Belmont—and Cloney was also local, so I knew to use that—and I said this boy had polio as a kid and he did this and he did that on the national level. I went through it all to build him up. And I said he wants to do the Marathon. Cloney said he'd have to go to the committee, which he ran, actually. But he did say, 'You're that sure.' And he said, 'Let me think this over.' And he did." In addition to Squires's plea, Hall also wrote to Cloney. The B.A.A. had a well-known aversion to change (prize money, sponsors, water stations, mile markers, earlier start time). It was only three years since the official inclusion of women in the 1972 Boston Marathon—by way of AAU acquiescence—and the addition of wheelchair athletes would be yet another big change. "I finally met back with Will, and he said to me, 'You really feel strongly about this.' I think he trusted me a lot. And he said, 'Okay. It'd be a wonderful thing for the boy.' I said that he'd be an inspiration."

Hall was granted special permission to compete. And only if he managed a sub-three-hour result would he be declared an official finisher and receive an official finisher's certificate. Hall realized that if he failed, not only would his name not appear as an official finisher, but it would inevitably set back any progress wheelchair athletes may have achieved up to that point. There was more at stake than just his own personal accomplishment. To add to the pressure, the immediate future of wheelchair competition laid in his hands. "I told him that in the Marathon, if he could come off Boston College and go easy to Cleveland Circle, and then from there to just work it and think 'three miles' to the finish, the cheerleading people will carry him home the last mile. And I told him that when he goes across that finish line, that will be the biggest thing he will ever have in racing." With exactly two minutes to spare, Hall finished the 1975 Boston Marathon as the first official wheelchair entrant and finisher, which began the official era of wheelchair competition. His 2:58:00 was cut by nearly 18 minutes the next time he raced Boston two years later when he won again in 2:40:10 in what also served as the 1977 National Wheelchair Marathon Championship (no wheelchair entrants were fielded in 1976). "After the race in 1975, Will Cloney joked with me and said, 'You've got me in a helluva thing now. Everyone wants to do it! And you're going to be training them all!'"

The 1975 Boston Marathon was a watershed moment for Squires, Rodgers, Hall, and GBTC. Hall found himself looked upon as the ambassador of wheelchair competitors, which led to directing his fellow athletes at Boston, and eventually his own wheelchair company. Rodgers was in great demand from road-race directors and track organizers, who all wanted him to run in their events to attract larger fields; and by athletic companies, which sought him to help promote their brands. Squires showed he could train marathoners to greatness in addition to track and relay stars. And GBTC became *the* place to work out, train, and earn success. More athletes—track, field, distance—came to GBTC. Squires continued to preach them to think big. He continued to subject his athletes to challenging competitions in which they had little chance of winning—Millrose, Penn, Dartmouth, etc.—but would learn as much in defeat as in victory. "They said again, 'How are you going to get us in there?' I said, '*You get yourself in there! You train. Already you're second best. Can you believe? Remember the up-and-down on those hills? Remember all that? Remember running in the snow? What were those other people doing? They were *thinking* about it. They took their silver spoons and they put it in their mouths.'" Squires laughs as he is reminded of the time his runners actually presented him with a real silver spoon for all the references he mentioned to make a point. "You see, that's how you improve—you go against better."

Sure enough, GBTC got their "noses bled" at the early Penn and Dartmouth relays. It stung. But it also proved beneficial because in 1975, the club won the NAAU 30K Outdoor Track Championship, NAAU 20K Outdoor Track Championship, New England Men's Outdoor Track Championship; and came in third at the NAAU Relays. By spring, the relays, particularly the two-mile team of Ricciato, Sevene, Elliott, McDonald, collected more than a dozen top-three finishes on the track. In indoors, they won the New York Knights of Columbus (1974), New England Men's Championship (1974, 1975), Olympic Invitational (1975); were second at the Olympic Invitational (1974); and third at the NAAU (1974). And in outdoors, they won the NEAAU (1974), NAAU 20K (1974, 1975), New England Men's Championship (1974, 1975), NAAU 20K Championship (1975); and were third at the Penn Relays in the DMR (1974) and the NAAU Relays (1974, 1975). Squires felt by GBTC's third cross-country season in 1975 that they were ready for the heralded NAAU 10K Cross-Country Championship. He once again utilized various competitions as preparation for nationals, and even more of his athletes benefited from his system. GBTC defended its New England 15K Cross-Country Championship title, and Bob Hodge's winning 45:29 broke the CR that was set the previous year by Rodgers (although the 1974 result of 46:28 was thought to be over a distance shorter than 15K). Two-and-a-half weeks later, GBTC won the 1975 NAAU 20K Cross-Country Championship. As a final tune-up, GBTC won a pair of five-mile team titles at the NU Invitational and the NEAAUs. And two weeks before nationals, Alberto Salazar in his senior year at Wayland High won the 2.5-mile high school Massachusetts State Cross-Country Championship in 14:11, which redeemed his second place the previous year.

Several hundred runners from nearly two dozen clubs from around the nation competed at the 1975 NAAU 10K Cross-Country Championship in Maryland. While there were no heats to accommodate the numbers, there were separate 10,000-meter runs for the men and women. Among the throngs of teams and athletes, GBTC attracted its own measure of attention due to its impressive widespread rate of success. People took notice, among them the noted global athletics writer and *Track & Field News* editor James Dunaway, a future Track and Field Writers of America president. "He said, 'You told me about that Rodgers kid. Anyone else like that?' He wanted to know. I told him about a few of my guys that I thought would do well, like Rookie. I ran him in the open with the big boys. He was doing half of what they were doing. I knew the kid was very serious and had the ability—good turnover. I knew he could hold his own." GBTC came in seventh with point-getters "Rookie" Salazar, Thomas, Mark Duggan, Hodge, and Graham. "Top 10! That was a big thing. And my kids were going, 'Hey, we beat Marty Liquori!' I told them that he hurt, too. It hurts everyone a little bit. The winner got a motorcycle, and the guys said, 'Wow! We didn't know this cross-country was that big.' I said, 'You're in New England, for crissakes! You've got the little ones. This *is* big-time!' I'd say things like that to get them going."

By the 1975-76 indoors, GBTC membership grew to about three dozen. This afforded Squires room to expand his groups, his training, and his scope for the club. The result was the immergence of a new class who continued the tradition of the inaugural group. Familiar prominent names still shone. Rodgers, who by *Track & Field News* was ranked the number-one marathoner in the US and the world in 1975, was third at the prestigious Fukuoka International Open Marathon in Japan; the club's two-mile relay team was third at the NAAU Indoor Track Championship; and McDonald at the 1976 Dartmouth Relays set the New England and GBTC indoor mile record in 4:00.9. "That mile was a helluva run. This was an invitational meet, which meant it was open to anyone. There were Olympians there. And the Canadians were coming down then. Helluva run," noted Squires, who in 1976 was named NEAAU Men's Track & Field chairman.

In regard to Salazar, the 1976 outdoors was the last one in which he competed as a high school runner. As a springboard to the University of Oregon, the senior made a few final impressions on the pre-collegiate athletic books. One was in the relays at the BC Invitational. "Rookie's senior year, his [high school] coach petitioned for him to run more. I told his coach that he could petition to bring him over [to BC], but anything he does will go under high school records. If it happens, it happens. I said I'd like to have him there. I had told [the coach earlier] that he'll never get his mile time down. I had said I wanted to see him break 4:20 in the mile, and he did at BC." GBTC records continued. At the Penn Relays, the DMR team of Ricciato, Jim O'Brien, Manny Rivera, McDonald, set a club-record 9:51.2. And at the "only one hill" 7.6-mile Mount Washington Road Race—which features an average grade of 12 percent, with one portion at 18 percent, and a torturous last 50 yards at 30 percent—Hodge won in 1:05:31 for the first of a record seven wins to the summit (the first four of which were under GBTC).

True to Squires's words that it would take about two years for his system to fully bear fruit, GBTC's early athletes in 1975-76 enjoyed that harvest; and just in time for national competitions and the 1976 Montreal Olympics. As the focus of outdoors turned to the XXI Olympiad, Rodgers twice made the team at the US Olympic Trials in Oregon. He was second in the marathon (2:11:58) and one month later fourth in the 10,000 (28:04.42) three days after he won his heat (28:32.79). He was on target to fulfill Squires's prophecy. Several weeks prior to the Games, Rodgers traveled to upstate New York as part of a training program for the US Olympic athletes to prepare for their events. On a routine run, he stopped by a lake and scooped up some water to drink. As he glanced to his side, he noticed sewage flowing out of a pipe and into the water. "Very quickly, he got dysentery, headaches, and he gets sick and everything. He dropped a pound or two. He didn't want to tell anyone because he was afraid he'd get kicked off the team and replaced by someone else—he's always been like that—so he's suffering through it and not telling anyone. Now, I wasn't there yet. I was teaching in school and was going to meet up with him in Montreal in a week or so."

Rodgers later traveled to Montreal for final preparations and taper. While there, he ran through Maisonneuve Park, adjacent to the Olympic Stadium, and stumbled on the trails and injured his calf. "I get a call from his wife at the time, Ellen, and she tells me Bill's in bad shape. She said his calf muscle, if you touch it, it kills him. I asked her what did the trainer say, and she said he won't go to him because he thinks he'll get thrown off the team. I said, 'No he won't. I'll make sure of it. I'll get a doctor for him.' I told her that I'll come up to Montreal now." Squires first instructed them to ice his calf. "Then I wanted him to sit in a chair and move the leg back and forth for about five or six minutes, and then get on the floor and do some bicycle movements with his legs for the same amount of time. I froze it, and then right away he's doing the motion he's going to do. It's to get the circulation going. And then I wanted him to go outside and walk regular." Squires rearranged his Boston State and GBTC schedules and arrived eight days before the Marathon. The directions were faithfully followed, so they were able to hit the ground running, so to speak. "Ellen did a real good job. So I told Bill the more ice and light massage will get the blood circulating. And no heat! We want the cold to freeze the muscle and shrink the cover of it, which will then let the blood to flow the little blood tears and clots away. Heat won't do that." Rodgers was concerned that if this news became known, he would be put on the team's internal daily injury list, which he wanted to avoid. Squires met with officials and explained the importance of not having Rodgers's name on the list. "I think it cost Billy his USA shirt [as a gift]." Squires laughs. "I didn't have my coaches' credentials yet because I was early, but I talked my way in there and explained who I was and who Billy was. The US trainer knew who Rodgers was, and he wasn't even a track guy. So, he iced the calf and massaged it. He did well."

Squires knew Rodgers faced a top Olympic Marathon field that included fellow Americans Frank Shorter and Don Kardong; Lasse Viren of Finland; Kevin Ryan of New Zealand; and German-born Canadian Jerome Drayton. "Bill felt great that morning, but the thing was, he lost three-and-a-half weeks of real training. And then add to that the dysentery, and he had about seven weeks. But he led with the group at the 18.5-mile mark, then he was in the lead crowd at 21 miles." Throughout the race, Squires and a small group from Boston attempted to travel along the course to see Rodgers at certain points. They rode the underground subway Metro to avoid delays on the roads. But it didn't always work smoothly. "The train stalled on the tracks! We're trying to see him at two or three spots on the course, and the train's either slow or stopped. I was out of my mind! I'm pounding on the doors to get going! He was with the leaders at 18 miles; around ninth at 21 miles or so; and then he's fading. That's when the action should really be starting. But Bill's then in the second row of runners in about eighth, ninth, or 10th place. Eventually, we got a couple of cabs and we made our way to about a mile and a half from the stadium, and then we don't see him. We finally see him about 35th or so, and he was slowing. He said later that he didn't want to come into the stadium creeping in like an old man, so he paced himself to get there." In 2:25:14, Rodgers finished 40th.

Squires still regrets not having learned more about the course beforehand, a practice to which he faithfully adhered. "That was one of my biggest mistakes. I didn't go over the course the way I wanted to with my guys. But you give a fighting man that has balls, a chance, at least he can say—and I know he'll finish—that he did it. And Rodgers did it." Montreal was bittersweet for Rodgers. He was filled with great American pride to represent his country in the Olympic Games, but was extremely disappointed at his showing. He was eager for redemption. And the bigger the stage the better. He could not wait another year for Boston to come around in 1977, so he notified his intentions to Squires.

"He told me after Montreal that he was sorry he didn't call me earlier, and that he'd do anything. He said he knew he'd get better, and he told me he was planning to run New York. I said, 'All right, we'll go at it.' The New York press jumped on this. I'd never seen so many media." The 1976 New York City Marathon was scheduled for October—three months after the Olympic Marathon—and was the first time in its young seven-year history to travel through all five boroughs. "It was a big deal after they had you run laps around Central Park all the other years. And I ended up helping to put the finish-line chute system in. There was one long chute and then there was a backup chute. It went down to where the baggage was. They just did not have that many runners before this—usually only a few hundred each year." The first year had 127 entrants; 1976 fielded 2,090. "They thought it'd go through quick. I just remember one long chute, and one backup of ropes. I got down there by train and helped two of my pals from the New York Road Runners Club. They didn't have a clubhouse or anything back then, so everyone helped. Fred Lebow, who started the Marathon, got the money, he got the streets, the police, the commissioner, the mayor—but it wasn't for another few years until the club finally got their own place."

As Rodgers's coach, and a friend of the NYRRC, Squires watched the race on television from inside the Tavern on the Green, the famed Central Park West restaurant near the finish, where coaches, media, and VIPs were housed. "The press were asking me how I thought Rodgers would do, and I said, 'He's going to do well.' They kept asking me about what happened at the Olympics, and what did I think he'd do against all this international competition. I'd step out to go to the bathroom, and to take a break, and when I went back in I'd hear it again from another group. They thought he'd be in the mix, top two or three. They were relentless." The interest was warranted. Rodgers was in a field that included Frank

Shorter, two-time New York winner and defending champion Tom Fleming, Ron Hill, and several other Olympians and world champs. "The TV coverage wasn't great in those days, but you had guys on bicycles cruising along the course and doing their filming and reports that we could see live, and then they had the big TV presence on the press truck. I followed it and then I went outside and I saw the finish. It was a good finish," noted Squires of Rodgers's CR-winning 2:10:09. "Rodgers with his New York win, after his Boston win, didn't look like a fluke. The fluke thing came about when he ended up 40th in the Marathon in the Olympics when he did that jog-athon over the last few miles," said Squires, who also credits these kinds of high-profile successes from GBTC athletes as great advertising for club recruitment. "I really feel that because of this, the following spring and winter Greater Boston started picking up a lot of kids that hadn't run the year or two they were out of college. They saw these runners finishing marathons and figured if those guys can do the marathon, they can run the 10K. So the 10K became the new long distance. We started the little baby program with the 3000 meters. And it didn't bother me because I was already training everyone on a 10K program."

Another stellar cross-country season unfolded in 1976. GBTC defended its NAAU 20K with its fourth consecutive title, and won the five-mile NU Invitational. Also, at the 1976 NEAAU Cross-Country Championship 10,000, GBTC won with point-getters Duggan, Thomas, Fred Doyle, Dick Mahoney. And at the NAAU Cross-Country Championship in Philadelphia, GBTC was ninth out of 32 teams. "I had enough guys that I could send a cross-country team down to a big cross-country meet in New York by car, or two cars, and I could have another team up in Boston at Franklin Park. I could spread it out. They'd all get in the papers and it was a big deal for them." And individual success continued under Squires's coaching. Once again, Rodgers was named by *Track & Field News* in 1976 as a top marathoner in the US (third) and the world (sixth). In addition, Salazar, who was named a First-Team High School All-American in the three-mile, excelled as a freshman at the University of Oregon when in the PAC-8 he came in fourth (and the first Oregon runner). And at Bentley College, Sevene—as coach—was named District I Division III Cross-Country Coach of the Year.

By the mid-1970s, the US running boom was soaring in its early stages, and GBTC was among its nascent emergence. There were obviously many factors involved in the running boom's formation, but two of the main forces were Shorter's gold-medal Olympic Marathon in 1972 and Rodgers's emergence at Boston and New York in 1975. These feats were not only achieved by two Americans, but more serendipitously important was the fact their events were broadcast via radio and television, and not to mention in countless post-event accounts in newspapers and magazines. For the mass marketing of running, Shorter and Rodgers blanketed the world *while* accomplishing this. "Road racing was kind of in its infancy. In the year after Rodgers wins Boston, the big thing was all the magazines played up his win. What transpired then was how will Rodgers do against Shorter. So it was the Shorter-Rodgers thing that caused the boom. Everyone wanted to get in on that. Shorter was more into running. He even got fifth in the Munich Olympics in the 10,000—not a lot of people knew that. And he was going to make his 'money' doing 10Ks because they're not going to wear you out. That fall, road racing went crazy."

And for Squires and GBTC, the floodgates opened. After several successful seasons, the 1975 Boston drew a tremendous amount of attention to the club. With those 10 handwritten letters—GBTC BOSTON—on Rodgers's shirt out in front most of the race for all the world to see, it became apparent an epicenter was the Greater Boston Track Club. And the source was Squires. Their blip showed on the running radar, and as a result, GBTC garnered increased focus from competing clubs. Additionally, the widely-televised success and subsequent media exposure of the victorious "Boston" Billy Rodgers also attracted differing interest in the club, which presented other matters with which Squires was forced to handle. Rodgers never hid the fact where he was training and with whom. And while the advertising was most welcome and the recognition warmly appreciated, it was on the *road* during an *endurance event* where it was viewed by the masses, not on the track, for which GBTC was initially created. "I had said to the guys in the club before he won in 1975, 'You run the team. There're eight of you. This guy's going to come down and train with us.' I told them he was with the B.A.A. [before he switched]. Okay, now, Rodgers mentions to different people and in the press that he trains with us, so guys start to show up. And I never denied them. Jack McDonald tells them about the dues and whatever. We needed their $20, and I would give them $520 worth of training in a year—no kidding; I mean I was giving them things they never even knew about. So, after Rodgers won Boston in 1975, guys who were out of college one or two years—and had not joined a club— start to show up. Also, my big, epic thing was I still didn't know if we were a track club or a road-running club now. Some of them were road runners—they went to college and they were fair or so-so—and they eat up running these road races, which is all well and good. All we had around here were road-running clubs. We didn't really have any track clubs."

Squires held close to the fact the original impetus to form a track club grew from post-collegiate track athletes whose desire to further themselves on the track required a track club. The key here was, of course, *track*! "The big thing with a track club, at the time, was that track was to road running what baseball is compared to softball, in terms of the popularity and respect. Track versus road running was like a joke. Road runners over-race; they do it all on their own. They enjoy the camaraderie, but they have no worries about not getting into a race because there are no qualifying standards. Outside the Boston Marathon and the Olympic Trials and Games, everyone can get into a race, and you can step on the same ground and have a chance to beat an Olympic champion. Now, for you to beat an Olympic champion on the track, you won't even see him, unless you're sitting in the stands! Because track is the epitome of being a pro—you were chosen [by invite or qualification] to be on the track. The minute a track guy starts screwing up in a meet, they don't get invited back and their season could be over."

A track club, by extension, is the vehicle by which an athlete can achieve qualifying times to advance to a higher level of competition. It is an incredibly serious endeavor that involves stringent training programs and an oftentimes rigid schedule of meets. At the time of GBTC, there were only a handful of genuine track clubs, including the Florida Track Club at the University of Florida, New York Athletic Club, New York Pioneer Club; and smaller clubs such as the North Carolina Track Club, Twin Cities Track Club in Minnesota, West Valley Track Club in California, that were not structured quite like the others, but still involved interested runners. Some road-running clubs, by contrast, but by no means inferior in terms of its own purpose, are in some instances more of a social gathering, while still maintaining a schedule of training runs and road races. A higher level of training and commitment by most members is not necessarily warranted in this line of exercise. "And unlike us, most of those track clubs had money behind them. And for the Florida Track Club, unless you were a national champion or an Olympian, that's all that they wanted. It was like 12 teams and they all lived together down in Gainesville. They were that organized back then. I didn't have any ideas of ever growing like them, because they were all taken care of. The Florida Track Club guys were really the first pros. They were going out to road racing and they were killing everyone—until I began taking charge, and we beat them up." Squires half-chuckles. "There were more road-running clubs, but nothing really for the track guys coming out of college."

In the ensuing months after the 1975 Boston, GBTC singlets were seen everywhere—on the roads. "We were a track club, but people kept wondering how did we get so many national championships? What they didn't realize was that we have a seven-day week, and I work four days, and of those four days there'd be a swing of distance training and speed training. The distance guys, I'd give them speed; the speed guys, I'd give them distance." The training Squires employed for the track also benefited the road, which he always knew and his athletes soon learned. Whatever identity crisis the club had, it was obvious GBTC would eventually no longer be solely a track club. For all intents and purposes, they could have called themselves the GBTRRC (Greater Boston Track and Road Running Club). "We called ourselves Greater Boston TC—track club—not Greater Boston RR—road running. I didn't know where we were going to go. We wondered what the complexion of the club was going to be. In the winter, we had all short-distance guys, but now we've got guys joining the club that wanted to run distance. And I had to figure that out. But to be truthful, we never got a heavy identity. We were the best regional club, from New York up to Boston. No one had a big, big post-collegiate club. The best would have been Florida TC, with all their Olympians. And when I came around, New York AC was fading. Their ol' coach had retired."

Squires was the key element. The lure of joining GBTC, *because* of its coach, was expanding. Serious track athletes who wanted to improve their times would look to him, wherever he was. They sought him out. The majority of members who joined the club were recent grads, and they had seen firsthand the success of his Boston State teams. "They saw I had this green and gold uniform of unknowns [at Boston State]—nothings—that became the horror show to a lot of college teams. They didn't even want my kids around. We kicked the hell out of them. And I only had five kids not graduate in 28 years. Five kids! So I didn't bring tramps in; because I couldn't, and because I didn't want any. The school would wonder if we should go around with pamphlets, and I said no. I'm going to have the dregs of the world if they want to commit. And there was a local running magazine that just started up, and I made sure we got in there all the time. Our results were the advertising." With a few track seasons in the books, the top results simply illustrated the success that could be achieved. "They saw that on my relay team I had three guys that came in running about 1:50 [in the half-mile], and they got down to 1:49 to 1:47. One of them ran under four minutes and one ran 4:02. They saw that development. They saw it because they were trackies at New England schools, so they knew what these people came in at and what they were doing now. The sportswriters didn't do a good job writing about it because they didn't understand what the damn effort was needed to get that speed up. But the runners knew." Squires also acknowledged that Massachusetts back then lacked a great history of track runners. "We just don't. I don't know why. Maybe some of it's coaching. Most of the coaches here ran weekly, and they went back to their schools and they became their coach's assistant and learned from him. And those programs came all the way from the 1930s through the 1960s. Then they started adding some distance running by doing some of Lydiard's distance."

Arthur Lydiard, the great New Zealand athlete and coach, and friend of Squires, was credited with what was to become known as the Lydiard system; in basic terms his athletes ran long-distance mileage in training, regardless of the distance of the event. It did not matter if his athlete was an 800-meter runner or a marathoner, the training included serious mileage. "Coaches were using his distance training, but they were doing it wrong. The long-distance training was for *pre-season*! Lydiard cut it back from the 100 miles or so to 65 miles and 55 miles a week in season. He said to me, 'Bill, they never understood what I was doing. They don't!' With so much mileage, you can get stale. And you can get injured."

Squires estimated GBTC was comprised of a 70/30 split of distance/speed athletes, the bulk of whom in college ran the 5000 and 10,000, and that included the steeplechase. He had fewer milers than expected, so he kept changing legs on the relay in order to find another miler. And in response to the growing interest of his athletes wanting to run longer races, he expanded and fine-tuned his coaching to include long distance. One of his favorite workouts during Sunday sessions was a game called Car Tag. It involved a group of runners, the road, and his car. At certain set paces per block, they ran various unknown distances determined by wherever Squires decided to park his car ahead of them. They ran at one pace until they reached him, listened to his next command of pace, and continued until they reached his car again. And so on. "They didn't know if they were going to go two miles at that pace? A mile-and-a-half? Whatever! They'd get to my car and I'd say something like, 'Okay, this is your recovery pace coming up. Until you see me again.' And I'd drive ahead and pull over at a half-mile, or a mile, or two miles, and wait until they got to me. There was no stopping. They're probably dropping 6:10 to 6:05. And within the group each time, two guys would take over [the lead] and the other guys would just toe, and others would be in a recovery time [at a pace to be] able to say a few words. Greg Meyer loved it. He said it was like a game trying to find out where I was up ahead. And none of them knew if it was going to be five minutes, seven minutes, five miles. I'd be honest and I'd tell them the longest they were going to go on this tempo in a section is one 10 and probably a pair of fives. And keep it just under five minutes."

During this time of club transition, when it was uncertain how much time would be devoted to the track and to the road, Squires added the inclusion of the 10K/10,000 meters. He felt there was a lack of proper training for that distance. While this approach provided GBTC the added opportunity to qualify and advance in a longer distance than that of the traditional shorter track events, it also enabled them to train longer and harder and be more prepared for the road if and when the club moved more in that direction. "I said to them, 'You know, the club that's going to Madison Square Garden [is the one that] trains as a 10K track club.' We were going to use the roads as part of it. And I was not going to kill the runners who are track people. I said, 'If you know my way—I have sprinters, hurdlers, and distance runners at little Boston State and I get fifth-string to 10th-string people from high schools. I know how to do it.' And I did." However, some of his long-distance guys expressed an interest to deviate from that specific training in order to increase their speed. And Squires was not averse to that. "We would have one day [for that] and it'd be within their sphere. I didn't want to burn them out. If you want to be a true distance guy, you've gotta run 10K workouts and you've gotta also go and be measured truly on a track. That's where your individual speed is measured. It works. And when you see that, you truly know what you have. In my day, you'd never know the distance of a race. And if you know your pace, you'd be running and you'd get the first mile right, the second mile's long, the third mile's fair, and all of a sudden you get a fast time. Then someone says it's certified by a car. Nope. It has to be done by a bike."

Some of the short-distance runners, especially, inquired about weight workouts in regard to building up their legs. At the time, athletes in those disciplines were the only ones actively interested about incorporating weights with regular training. This was the mid- to late-1970s. "It wasn't really that big with the distance guys, but the sprinters, hurdlers, and quarter-milers thought about it for their legs. And

I told them that I'll get their legs strong. But I said that if they wanted to lift weights and go to a gym, then lift light and quick. I wanted to get them strong in their legs and their back and body. I also gave them bent-knee sit-ups to get their quads good and strong; pushups for their shoulders and arms, where they leave their hips on the ground; and the sit-ups where you fold your arms and sit up and go back slow. I told them to start off with 15 and keep building to 30. That's what they'd need to do to move their arms quick, and then their legs will turn—it's part of the pendulum. I wouldn't talk to the distance guys about the weights, but I would tell them to do the pushups and sit-ups." This was also in addition to hill work, which Squires incorporated into training to build up leg lift. He felt multiple hill repeats on the Boston Marathon course was one of the best ways to accomplish this, although he was also careful not to burn out his athletes or cause injuries. "I told them they had to warm up a mile-and-a-half—about 15 minutes—and then go on the track and do the straightaways and jog the corners. Then I explained to them how to run up a hill and run down a hill, and to do that four times. And I told them that it'll work and they'll be amazed at how quick it'll work. In-season, I had them do it every 10 days, at least. Out of season, they can do it two times a week, but they didn't have to do a ton of these."

Heartbreak Hill was essential. "I had them go up to the first fire hydrant and come back down to the light—which is about 110 yards—and show them what to do. It's not a killer hill when you're not going the whole way. I wanted them to just go up and down that portion four times, take a two-minute rest on the flats, and repeat it three times. But eventually I'd get them to go up and down 200 yards, and then the full hill of 600 yards. I wanted them to condition their legs and go down the hill so that when they got down to the bottom of the hill they're not in oxygen debt. They went up the hill in 85 to 90 percent effort. You see, you go up the hill like you're a tank, using more arms so that you can breathe and you're not breathing heavy. The hill is where you can actually rest. It puts you into a relaxed mode, a rest phase. It changes you. You're taking a short stride." One common workout for leg strength Squires avoided was stairs, where an athlete runs up and down the stairway aisle of bleachers. "I'm afraid you'll bruise your Achilles. You're coming down so hard on the wood or cement. It's too much. I'm always pessimistic about hurting athletes. It's not worth it."

The final kick in a race, ever important at any distance, was another area on which Squires focused his athletes. "In the body of the race, you can make your moves to rattle your competitors up, change gears, do whatever. But when it gets to the kick, I'd always ask each guy, 'Where do you feel comfortable?' It could be 300 yards to go, 220, 190 yards—anything. But I'd also tell them that you can't get into a total pattern because after a while, the other guys'd pick up on it. So I'd tell my guys to work on it, do fakes, move and bait, and let them get going." Squires also knew enough to listen to his athletes and not always be the one instructing. He was smart enough to know when to talk and when to listen. And when to learn. "When you have a real fine athlete, you can learn things from him—a few things, not everything, unless you're a doughnut coach. I wanted to know the total athlete. I just didn't say to all of them, 'You're in Group 1 and everything's generic.' I wasn't one of those guys that said everyone does the same workout and the same intensity. That was crazy. And I'll clue ya, I knew coaches that would do that."

For fear the club was losing its track identity with so many long-distance and marathon runners showing up, Squires stressed its grassroots to his athletes. He didn't want to advertise the club and open it up to the masses because he also didn't want to lose that special uniqueness GBTC created. There was something about its ground-floor start that attracted the true athlete, and he was afraid a publicly open-door invite would water that down. "I encouraged people to talk up the track because no one around here did track clubs. They did it with the little kids, but not with the adults. And at that time, they didn't have the masters divisions. And I never advertised. I didn't want a stampede from other clubs, and I didn't want to go to the magazines and say we were 'open.' Then who knows how many we'd have! So it was word of mouth for athletes to find other real athletes."

While the original GBTC mission remained the same, the training, goals, schedule, and events would not. "We were using road races for conditioning—just to see where we were to get ready to train for track. So I asked the guys if they were focusing on road racing because I will get their speed up like I did with Rodgers. And for those half-milers and milers who come in, I'd work them hard to get in to invitational meets." Some newcomers were under the impression that since they were good runners on their own with some degree of success that they would simply swoop in and instantly compete at a high level. Their collegiate career featured good track results and they could place in local races, but Squires had a system. "We got about 10 guys that came out in August, and they were mostly half-milers. They knew we had runoffs, but the silver-spooners thought they'd get in [without that]. But then they realized I wasn't kidding. I told the new guys to run at least four, five days a week, because when they come with me, they're going to find that I work a very, very stringent base that they've never seen before."

Rodgers's road success enabled him to make money on the race circuit, so he often competed in several races a week, much to the ongoing consternation of the coach. But this did allow Squires to continue his progression of other GBTC runners on the track. "We're going to have more distance guys, and I didn't want Rodgers competing in the national track championships because he would get all the publicity. Let him run the money races around the country, which he was doing anyway. I told him to not wear himself down, but he didn't listen. He'd run Saturday *and* Sunday. But you know what he'd do? He'd take off Monday because he knew there was no mercy on him [in the Tuesday workout]. Each person would move up and learn to lead. That's how I ran my workouts." For distance athletes, he had them run cross-country workouts. And instead of roadwork on Sundays, they ran at Franklin Park, which fielded dirt courses of 5K and 10K distances. "We'd do a loop of two miles, another loop of a mile-and-a-half—odd repeats. It's a different training. You can wear spikes, but you're not getting the bounce that you're going to get out of the track. But I wanted them to get real speed because if they can run a 10K on grass, they can run a helluva 10K on the road."

GBTC's range grew organically to include longer distances. The hope was that this would not only enhance GBTC, but also strengthen it.

Wedding photo of Bill Squires's parents; clockwise from top left: his uncle Bill Squires, his father Murt Squires, his cousin Madeline Chase, his mother Florence (née Trainor) Squires.

Photo courtesy of Bill Squires.

Arlington (Mass.) High School coach William "Doc" McCarthy (left) presented the 1952 outstanding athlete award to senior Bill Squires (right), who set the indoor mile (4:22.6) and outdoor mile (4:22.8) records.

Photo courtesy of Bill Squires.

The person who Bill Squires (left) credits the most with getting him into running as childhood friends in Arlington, Massachusetts, was Charlie Leverone (right). Running soon took over football and ice hockey as his sport of choice.

Photo by Paul Clerici.

In the days prior to the use of metal starting blocks, Bill Squires starts a race from divots he dug into the dirt track at an indoor meet in 1955 while competing for the University of Notre Dame.

Photo courtesy of Bill Squires.

The University of Notre Dame sprint medley relay team set an American record 1:19.4 at the Kansas Relays in 1955. From left, Bill Squires, Al Schoenig, Al Porter, and Dick O'Keefe.
Photo courtesy of Bill Squires.

At the 1956 National AAU mile on the boards in Madison Square Garden, Bill Squires (right) finished second to Ireland Olympian Ron Delany of Villanova, who 41 weeks later would win 1500-meter gold at the Melbourne Olympic Games.
Photo courtesy of Bill Rodgers Running Center.

Newspaper cartoon of Bill Squires in 1956 as a University of Notre Dame track and cross-country Fighting Irish senior.
Photo courtesy of Bill Squires.

Bill Squires set nearly two dozen track and cross-country records as a University of Notre Dame Fighting Irish runner, including when he simultaneously held the record in the indoor mile, outdoor mile, indoor half-mile, and anchor of the two-mile relay team.
Photo courtesy of Bill Squires.

The 1964 Boston State College cross-country champion Warriors, from left, coach Bill Squires, Al Marston, John Buxton, Frank McCarthy, John Hickey, Stratos Valakis, Andrew DiPaulo, manager Jerry Blake, and Mike Granfield.

Photo courtesy of Bill Squires.

On behalf of the US State Department, Bill Squires, foreground, shown in India in 1971, was often sent overseas to coach, instruct, and teach athletes and coaches around the world.

United States Information Service India lab R.N. Khanna photo courtesy of Bill Squires.

Boston Athletic Association (B.A.A.) American-record-mile relay team, from left, Dick Packard, Bob MacVeigh, Bill Squires, John Pistone, with the second-place trophy at the National Masters Championship.

Photo courtesy of Bill Squires.

Bill Squires (left) stands outside the famous Eliot Lounge in Boston, Massachusetts, where runners of all kinds regularly migrated and where his own Coach's Corner "office" seat was located at the end of the bar. Housed inside the Eliot Hotel, it featured memorabilia and running photos on the walls; high jump and long jump records painted on the premises; and the display of international flags and the playing of national anthems for visiting foreign athletes.

Photo courtesy of Bill Squires.

As the first coach of the Greater Boston Track Club, Bill Squires amassed 17 national championships, six national champions, seven American record-holders, and numerous major marathon winners and Olympians.

Photo courtesy of Jack McDonald.

At the old Boston College outdoor track inside Alumni Stadium, Bill Squires is shown coaching Charlotte (Lettis) Richardson, as champion wheelchair pioneer Bob Hall looks on at left, near Alberto Salazar.

Photo by Charlie Rodgers.

The Bill Squires-coached Greater Boston Track Club squad won the 1979 National AAU Cross-Country Championship title in Raleigh, North Carolina, on the strength of having four of the top five finishers, including Alberto Salazar (2) in first, Dan Dillon (3) fourth, and Greg Meyer (1) fifth.

New England Runner photo by Paul Sutton.

During the 1980 Boston Marathon, and under a death threat due to his outspoken opinion against the United States-led boycott of the Moscow Olympics, Greater Boston Track Club runner Bill Rodgers (right) receives water – and a public show of support – from his coach, Bill Squires.

Jeff Johnson photo courtesy Bill Squires.

Several of the original Greater Boston Track Club (GBTC) members in 1993 – with that year's president, Karl Hoyt – at the 20th anniversary celebration of GBTC. From left, Dave Elliott, Dick Mahoney, Bob Sevene, Karl Hoyt, coach Bill Squires, and Kirk Pfrangle.

New England Runner photo by Frank Monkiewicz/GBTC.

US Olympian and four-time winner of the Boston Marathon and New York City Marathon Bill Rodgers (right) with his Greater Boston Track Club coach Bill Squires.

Photo by Paul Clerici.

The John Hancock Running and Fitness Program was created in 1996 to aid its employees in training for and running the Boston Marathon. Bill Squires (left), shown in 2007 with John Hancock Financial Services/Manulife Financial CEO John DesPrez III (center) and coach Fred Treseler III, helped design the program and served as its coach and consultant from 1997-2010.

Photo courtesy of Paul Clerici.

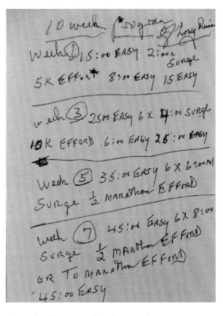

A typical example of a workout scribbled by Bill Squires, who often used bar napkins, scraps of paper, and the back of envelopes, so that his secrets were less likely to fall into the hands of competitors than if written on full sheets of paper or notebooks that could be easily copied.

Photo courtesy of Mark Duggan.

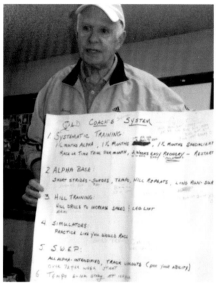

Former Greater Boston Track Club (GBTC) members honored at a Boston Marathon media conference included, from left, 1983 Boston Marathon winner Greg Meyer, 1979 Boston Marathon third-place finisher Bob Hodge, 1979 Boston Marathon 10th-place finisher Dick Mahoney, 1961 Boston Marathon 20th-place finisher and first GBTC coach Bill Squires, 1982 Boston Marathon winner Alberto Salazar, 1982 Scarborough (England) Marathon sixth-place finisher Brad Hurst, and 1977 Boston Marathon fifth-place finisher Vin Fleming.
Photo by Paul Clerici.

At a running clinic, Bill Squires holds a hand-written poster labeled "Old Coach's System" for long-distance runners that includes his steps for Systematic Training, Alpha Base, Hill Training, Simulators, S.W.E.P., and Tempo.
Photo by Jill Beardsley.

Just 31 days before he passed away, legendary New Zealand running coach Arthur Lydiard (center), during his 2004 book tour, sits with his compatriot, Bill Squires. Greater Boston Track Club coach Tom Derderian, standing at left, organized the event at Regis College in Weston, Mass.
Emily Raymond photo courtesy of Tom Derderian/GBTC.

At the 2002 National Distance Running Hall of Fame induction ceremony, those celebrating the presentation of the Bill Bowerman Award included, from left, Tom Ratcliffe, Kirk Pfrangle, John "Jocko" Connolly, Mark Duggan, recipient Bill Squires, Bill Squires Jr., Gerry Squires, and Scott Graham.
Photo courtesy of Bill Squires.

The Squires family, clockwise from top left, Bill Squires, his youngest son Gerry Squires, his eldest son Bill Squires Jr., his daughter Mary Susan Squires, his former wife Sally Squires.
Courtesy Bill Squires

Bill Squires sits atop the Nancy Schon-created Tortoise and the Hare sculpture at Copley Square, located just over a block east from the Boston Marathon finish line.
Photo by Paul Clerici.

At the 2010 Boston Marathon Expo, Bill Squires was part of a panel discussion which featured, from left, 1983 Boston Marathon winner Greg Meyer, Running USA Hall of Champion broadcaster Toni Reavis, four-time Boston Marathon winner Bill Rodgers, Bill Squires, and two-time ESPN National Emmy Award-winner and emcee Larry Rawson, among them.
Photo by Paul Clerici.

At the 30th anniversary of his co-winning the inaugural 1981 London Marathon, Dick Beardsley (far right) looks on as his former coach, Bill Squires, autographs the Dick Beardsley Half-Marathon starting line on the streets of Detroit Lakes, Minnesota, in 2011.
Photo by Jill Beardsley.

Gathered together to celebrate the 40th anniversary of the Greater Boston Track Club in 2013 were, from left, Bill Clark, Don Ricciato, Bill Squires, Bob Hodge, Fred Doyle, Tommy Leonard, Gary Wallace, Randy Thomas, Mike Roche, Mark Duggan, Bob Sevene, and Dick Mahoney.
Photo by Paul Clerici.

Bill Squires "crosses" the finish line of the Boston Marathon on Boylston Street. His involvement with the race dates back decades, as a Boston Athletic Association runner and coach who also often helped race official Jock Semple field applications at the old Boston Garden.
Photo by Paul Clerici.

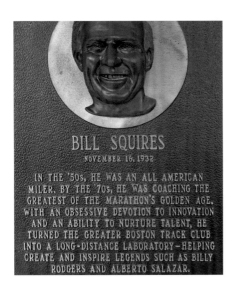

One of Bill Squires's many honors is this 16x22-inch Denali Granholm-created sand-cast bronze plaque with hand-set letters and bas relief face. Fittingly, it adorns The Alberto Salazar Building – named after one of his Greater Boston Track Club athletes – as part of the Walkway of Fame at Nike Headquarters in Beaverton, Oregon.
Photo courtesy of NIKE.

At the Black Tie & Sneaker Gala induction ceremony for the 2017 USATF National Track & Field Hall of Fame class at The Armory in New York City, from left, USATF CEO Max Siegel, Olympic relay world record-holder Leroy Burrell, Olympic gold-medal decathlete Bryan Clay, two-time Olympic hurdler Patty Van Wolvelaere-Weirich, two-time Olympic gold-medal relay and sprinter Lindy Remigino, Greater Boston Track Club champion coach Bill Squires, and USATF President Vin Lananna.
Photo courtesy of USATF.

CHAPTER 12

GBTC TOP OF THE WORLD

Squires was still concerned about money for GBTC. Membership dues, raffles, dances, the occasional Squires-helmed clinic, and any other acquired donations or financial shortcuts kept the club afloat. But road trips required a certain degree of frugalness and ingenuity, qualities Squires generously employed.

"Greater Boston had no money, but the kids didn't care. I'd eat with them at the gin mills and the diners. We knew every diner this side of the Mississippi, and I'd go in and work it a little." Squires would oftentimes turn on the charm and approach the counter with his big blue eyes and a smile. "I'd go to the waitress there and I'd say, 'What's your name? Gladys. Ah, you were Miss Milwaukee in 1972, right?' She'd blush. 'No? The Milwaukee Fair. No? Must be the same name. What's your last name?' She'd give it, and I'd smile. 'Well, I don't know. Looked like you. Brunette.' Then I'd talk about my team, and say, 'These boys are going to run a big, big race.' And the guys are all slouching in their seats. They're used to me. But we'd get more rolls. My coffee was free. She'd be over to our table all the time. And then the next time we'd visit, I'd say I still thought she was Miss Milwaukee. Then I'd say, 'One of the boys has got a birthday.' I'd designate one of the guys and then we'd all sing 'Happy Birthday.' It was a lie, but we'd get a cake and we'd cut it between the team. We'd give a fairly good tip. We'd all chip in. And we'd all say goodbye when we left. It was fun."

Early team travel was in an old Chrysler Town and Country full-size station wagon or Ford Country Squire full-size five-door station wagon, the latter of which was affectionately nicknamed the Squiremobile. Each car uncomfortably fit nine, plus bags. "I'd always get the biggest car I could and we'd run it to the ground. And the springs would always be gone. The guys in the backseat would yell at me to go slower on the roads because they'd be bouncing around. And I had this thing on long trips that every hour and 15 minutes we'd get out and stretch a little bit. We'd alternate who'd get the middle seat, backseat, front."

Similar ingenuity continued for overnight accommodations. Squires made sure not to pull up too close to the hotel/motel lobby front doors so the true number of occupants were hidden from view. He'd enter with only two or three of his athletes while the rest hid in the car or drove around to the back and waited. He registered one or two rooms, met up with the team, and then dismantled the beds to double up sleeping arrangements instead of paying for four or five rooms. "We'd all flip for who was going to get the bedsprings and who was going to get the mattresses. I was the coach, so I never got one. I always took the rug, and I'd tell them it was good for my bad back. Frig that, I think my back became bad because of that! But they were running, so I took the rug. I always had a pillow. And I told everyone to bring one; and if they forgot, I'd show them how to roll up their coat or pants and use that." While not related to savings, another trick up his sleeve involved the manipulation of room temperature. He noticed that people slept better in cool temperatures—which tended to be more cozy and sleep-inducing—than in a warm room, which was more uncomfortable. "In hotel and motel rooms—which are usually stuffy—I would put on the air conditioning. Didn't matter what season. But when you got into bed, you went right to sleep. In a hot, stuffy room, with cigarette and cigar smoke, as it was back then—terrible, especially for athletes—the cold was also refreshing. It took a while for the veterans to figure out it was me, but it worked."

Squires knew that skimping on rooms and finagling for extra food was no way for a club to thrive. He needed a long-term plan to secure funds. At first he solicited top local companies in the Boston area—Raytheon Company, Welch Food, The Gillette Company—and drafted letters for sponsorship assistance of $3,000. He explained that uniform jerseys could be made with their logos on and would be seen wherever they competed—Madison Square Garden, Canada, throughout the Bay State. While GBTC received about a half-dozen replies, there were no takers. He turned to club member Larry Rawson, a 1963 BC business grad with a 4:07 mile. Rawson also tried, but even with a few sit-downs, had no takers. Squires entertained the possibility of approaching competing North

American beer makers when it became apparent companies like Molson Canada of Montreal (which in 1957 bought the Montreal Canadians) and Labatt Brewing Company of Ontario (which in 1976 bought the Toronto Blue Jays) wanted more of a presence in the US and were open to sponsoring sports teams and sporting events. Even within GBTC there was a likely candidate in Scott MacAllister, a Group 3 runner with a job in promotions at Labatt. They discussed matters at the Eliot Lounge with its owner, and the result was a temporary tap of Labatt beer for an occasional Labatt's Night and new Friday night dances. "At the Friday night dances, I remember the first one resembled a seventh-grade dance with Sister Mary with the ruler—no one was dancing! So the ol' coach had to go and start dancing with a lovely lady, and then hand her off to a guy, grab another lovely, and dance again. I had to get things going."

To also promote the sport itself, Squires wrote several informational pamphlets and booklets, among them *World Class Formula for Middle and Long Distance Training*, and with local Converse shoe company *Money-Back Guarantee Formula for Running Improvement*. And he authored the highly successful book *Improved Running*, which for the first time planned out intricate details and workouts that promised to, well, improve your running. Other than the colorful 1970s-era pants he wore in the cover photograph, the book was very well received and had several printings. He also continued to preside over seminars and clinics. "The pamphlets had basic tips on running repeat hills, pickups, speed—things like that. And we put on a lot of coaching clinics for anyone. And the funny thing was that most of the coaches didn't come; it would be the athletes."

In addition to club fundraising and his new chairmanship of NEAAU Men's Track and Field, Squires also was named Coach of the Year in 1977 and an Olympic Development Program advisor. "For the Olympic Development, we had a couple meetings a week with track and field coaches and athletic directors. It was brainstorming on how to improve track and field. They were looking for the long-range, but it was funny—no one offered their track facilities. It was crazy. I had ideas, but I was banging my head against the wall. I was saying things like 'there was no grassroots' and 'we weren't developing.' They said, 'Well, you did up your way [in Boston]!' And I told them that there's me and a few other guys, but what we need is something like 14 coaches in each area of the country and then you bring them in together, and then have some kind of a colossal development meet. And not for the Division I [scholarship] ride guys, which they have, but for the Division II and III unknowns that break their cans and are lost in space without any financial aide. We have to open it up to these kids, and some of these kids'll pop out with this kind of opportunity. Who knows?"

Three years in, with Squires's system further expanding to include long distance, GBTC in the 1976-77 indoors continued to see top results both on the track and the road. For track, Hodge ran a 4:11 mile and 8:52 two-mile at the Dartmouth Relays; and the two-mile relay team took second at the NAAU Indoor Track Championship at Madison Square Garden. On the increasingly popular marathon circuit, at the Boston Marathon Vinnie Fleming led all GBTC runners with a fifth-place showing. And Rodgers, since he joined GBTC in late 1973, had run 13 marathons, which included five in 1976 alone! With the exception of his 14th-place finish at the 1974 Boston and 40th place at the 1976 Olympics, he won six, had five CRs, and an AR; and by *Track & Field News* was listed in the Men's Marathon All-Time US Top 10 Rankings as number one in 1975 and 1977 (and third in 1976), and in the Men's Marathon World Top 10 Rankings as number one in 1975 and 1977 (and sixth in 1976).

Regarding Rodgers, while Squires certainly appreciated the quality, he was still displeased at the quantity. He felt there was too much room for error and injury. But Rodgers always found the races and the energy, two variables with which Squires understood about him. It was one of the reasons Rodgers was always in top shape when he headed into the outdoor track/fall marathon season. "He was working through the winter. He was doing it off his distance training. He was doing it off probably 120 miles a week, at the most, and usually about 100 miles. He'd go to these meets everywhere, like Florida, because their road-racing season starts in February. But he would never miss my Tuesday workouts. He'd sometimes do a double—two 10Ks on a weekend, which is crazy—but he'd look at that and say he'd be doing a 12-mile run anyway, so that was just half of that work. That was his rationale! I would tell him he needed a recuperation period. But his tendons must be the greatest tendons in the world." He long ago realized that Rodgers would—and could—burn the running candle at both ends: maintain great distance work and push himself for the speedwork. They both knew that was his key to success. "I worked him with my 5K and 10K guys. My two-mile relay guys were working on more of what I call quickness—only running a half-mile. I pushed them. They were jumping in with the distance guys on Tuesday, and then on Thursday I would juice them again with leg strengthening, speed, and endurance, because they didn't compete every week. They competed every third week or so. Same thing with Bill, but he would very seldom come in on Thursday. If we had something like a 30K race in two weeks, I would tell him to come in on Thursday. I'd want him to do five miles worth of quick stuff because he'd be running against some real sharp guys. It would depend. But he would be there."

At the 1977 Amsterdam Marathon in The Netherlands, just 33 days after his Boston DNF, Rodgers set a CR with his 2:12:47 win. Overall, including his pre-GBTC marathons, this was his seventh CR, eighth victory, 11th top-five, and 10th top-three marathon performance! With such superior long-distance road-running results—and not just from Rodgers—GBTC grew. Again. "In 1977, there was a big growth. That was because of the marathon, which then got what was called an American flavor. Before that, you never got post-college kids running. But we're getting a lot of college kids, and right away I'm loading them up in Group 2 or Group 3, depending upon their ability. I told them they were going to do the same stuff as the other guys, but at a different timing level. My Group 1 was still composed of my milers and half-milers and Rodgers, because there weren't enough [Group 1-caliber] college kids coming in. We went from 13 athletes to about 23, and when we had 23, those were mostly track guys."

After Hodge ran a 30:14 six-mile at the 1977 NEAAU Outdoor Track & Field Championship, Squires set up a paced time trial at the BC track to qualify Hodge for nationals. It was officially timed; and in accordance to the rules of the day, each pacesetter would finish the race. "I knew Bobby was a real comer and I decided in the time trial that every lap would be listed [ahead of time] up to the last three-quarters of a mile so that he'd be going along with some of our teammates and when he felt strong enough, then he would take over. Hodgie had run pretty well. He had a good mental psyche on being able to run a structured pace pattern. He was good. You'd tell him to run a five-minute pace, and he'd run between 4:59 and 5:01. He was just like a machine." Hodge was paced to a 28:42 six-mile at BC. He also defended his Mount Washington Road Race title in 1:04:44, which was 47 seconds faster than his previous win.

GBTC workouts also continued to benefit Rodgers, whose reign in short-distance contests also went unabated. The running boom's pieces continued to come together. Added to the club's successes and notoriety at the beginning of the 1977 cross-country season was the publication of Jim Fixx's *The Complete Book of Running*, which redefined running and its place in America. In addition to its natural competitive lure and benefits, about which serious runners and racers already knew, running was becoming an accepted activity of fitness in which anyone could engage with any level of success. "Jim said he was a heavy smoker and tipped the bottle and he was overweight. He worked at a newspaper that was killing him. And plus, he had heart problems in his family. But Jim told me he had picked up a *Runner's World* magazine in about 1973, 1974, and he started reading it and he thought that anyone could do this if they put their mind to it. And that's what he did. He started buying up all the old magazines, he read them, and he made his book. At the [publisher's] meeting for his book, he said he saw it written down somewhere that it was a complete a book on running up to that time. And that's where the title came from. And when he got too many speaking gigs, he wanted me to take some of them." Interestingly, Fixx did run the Boston Marathon in 1981.

Squires knew that while those in a club were naturally immersed in it enough to understand and love the sport, non-running observers still did not quite differentiate track runners from road runners. To the "outsider," a runner was a runner. Other than the sporadic education from the Olympic Games, when quadrennially on TV the separation of events was viewed, someone new to running was unaware of its vast levels of speeds, distances, and disciplines. But this world of running was changing. Squires could see it coming. At GBTC, there was a buildup that grew exponentially. "At Greater Boston in 1973 and 1974, it was the relay team, almost totally; in 1974, Rodgers comes aboard; and from 1975 on, we're putting out a track team with some very good results. And guys are seeing these times and these [GBTC] shirts and they're seeing that we're going to Madison Square Garden, the Olympic Invitationals, and we're competing against the top schools. We've always been identified with the hardcore 300 runners that ran around Boston in road racing. We always had that. And nationally, we were *the* road-racing club, but road racing was just a joke. Outside the Boston Marathon, nothing here [in the Boston area] was appreciated. It just wasn't. Our track teams were fair. Our athletes hardly ever made the national championships. Track was tolerated, like one of those things that just dies out. But newspapers around here, with guys like [sportswriter] Jerry Nason, who fell in love with the Boston Marathon, if it wasn't for him, I don't think the Boston Marathon would have made it in the 1940s and 1950s. He got people to really come out and picnic and watch it. Newspapers had a sheet of the runners, and kids would be able to know the numbers and that the low numbers were the big boys."

GBTC dominated its fifth cross-country season in 1977 when it won the NAAU 20K for the fifth consecutive time, and the NEAAU; and was third at the NAAU in Texas, with point-getters Salazar, Thomas, Charlie Duggan, Vinnie Fleming, Mahoney. Individually in third place was Greg Meyer of the New Jersey Athletic Attic. A cross-country and track All-American from the University of Michigan, he found his way to Boston with a little help from Rodgers, his friend who put Meyer to work in his running store while he trained for, ran with, and eventually became a member of, GBTC. Meyer's initial focus was in shorter distances. But Squires thought otherwise. "I knew that Greg had great strength. He started off as a high school miler and he was a halfback in football, so he was a tough-ass. Then they put a four-mile relay together and he ran fairly good. And in his senior year, he tried the steeplechase—which good milers do—and he did very well with that, too. In college, I don't think they knew where to really put Greg. And he was always banging heads with Herb Lindsay of Michigan State University and Craig Virgin of the University of Illinois. That was tough."

Squires recalled it was Matthew Meyer who approached him about his brother. "I was with some of my athletes at the NCAA Division III Championship meet at the long-jump pit, watching the great Edwin Moses. Greg wanted to be part of a team and he knew we were good in cross-country and that my guys were going to the worlds. He wanted cross-country and he wanted to be a 10K road guy up to maybe the half-marathon because he figured since you were doing 14-mile runs, why not. I told him he could do well with that, and I also said I think he'd be able to run a fairly good mile someday under four minutes." (Nearly two months after his third place at the 1977 NAAU Cross-Country Championship, Meyer in January 1978 ran an indoor 3:59.1 mile with the NJAA.)

By the fall of 1977, with American names such as Rodgers, Salazar, Thomas, Hodge of GBTC, and Shorter of FTC, becoming more familiar and noteworthy, long-distance running started to become marketable. Squires saw athletic and shoe companies begin to see there was money in it. With that came more attention to the sport, which boosted numbers, which increased interest. The snowball had begun. "Right then, in 1977, 1978, and 1979, road running was booming. It was the biggest thing in the world. For stories, TV news people were coming to film practice! It mushroomed because of Rodgers and Shorter. But the reason it got really big was that there were these self-promoters that decided they were going to put a race on and they came into town. There were a ton of them."

After GBTC survived into its fourth year with no sponsorship, Labatt finally came through and sponsored the club's first annual self-fundraising road race—the Labatt's Freedom Trail Road Race. "That was big. And I said we should have a committee for the race, and the only thing I suggested was that we could use the Charles River roads as part of the course, which I think up until then only the women's Bonne Bell Mini Marathon used for a race. I also said that in most cases, you don't want to have anything tying up traffic. Well, we certainly did that when we decided on the Freedom Trail [using] the Boston historical walking trail that's about three miles long that the tourists do! That was basically the course." On October 2, 1977, the inaugural race was held on the narrow streets of Boston. Originally scheduled as a 10K, it was closer to eight miles. Festivities included the BC marching band performing at the start, which was located near the historic Faneuil Hall Marketplace. "One of our race committee members, Pat Lynch, talked to the mayor, who at that time was Kevin White. And he thought a race was a good idea. We started on one of the side streets there, went over the bridge where you can look into Charlestown, then we cut over by Bunker Hill Community College, and down to Memorial Drive. Then you went down to Massachusetts Avenue, the bridge, to Beacon Street, up Beacon Hill, by the State House, and a left down to Faneuil Hall right by the marketplace carts, and we finished near the start. John McGrath took care of the logistics," noted Squires, adding with a laugh, "and we really tied up traffic! The worst place was near the Callahan Tunnel for the airport traffic!"

The field comprised of many of the top names in running, which included several former Olympians and marathon champions, and future titleholders. It turned out to be quite a superstar display of running talent, which included Rodgers, Thomas, Hodge, Vinnie Fleming, Dan Dillon from GBTC; US Olympians Shorter, Don Kardong, Garry Bjorklund; former Boston Marathon winners Jack Fultz, Kim Merritt, Drayton; former New York City Marathon winner Tom Fleming; US Pan-American Mike Slack; and local great Lynn Jennings, a future US Olympian, six-time Bonne Bell and three-time World Cross-Country champion. "The papers really played up who was coming in. We had the best of the best. And I think they wanted to come here, and individually, they knew the competition would be good. And these were top guys that actually had good-paying jobs for shoe companies. It was big. And we got a lot of publicity in the magazines, the TV news, and newspapers. I was looking for $4,000 and I think we got about either

$7,000 or $8,000. We were indebted to Labatt's. And to think, it was a foreign company that would come to the aid of an established American track club that was ranked nationally in the top three."

The increase to the treasury provided many benefits, not least of which was travel. With this new infusion, Squires scheduled additional meets against greater competition. "With this money, we'd become within the next two years number one in the world. Not the United States, *the world*! Imagine that! The minute we got the money—we watched where the money went—but I was able to look ahead. That's how we won 17 national championships. Up to that time, I think we won two—they happened to be in our backyard. Before Labatt's, at that time we'd go as far as Maryland, and as far north as Montreal and Toronto. That's a tiring thing in a car. What we were living off of was gas-and-toll money. I'd ask them at the big meets, like Toronto, who enjoyed having Boston come, if they could give us a little extra to get there. There was no appearance money. My kids weren't big, big, big. And they weren't dealing with Rodgers. We were like peasants of the road. The better clubs had money and the better clubs had athletes that were Olympians, so that would automatically get a room and two more teammates to a meet. We didn't have that. But with this money, we decided we could fly from Boston to the Midwest. Anything that was out in California, the flight was too expensive. But it opened up good possibilities."

Squires also saw a surprising upsurge in membership to the tune of more than 350 on the day of the Freedom race alone. All told, GBTC numbers, which reportedly had stood at 37 beforehand, surprisingly grew in an instant to nearly 400 (fortunately, not all of them turned up). He then discovered that the club membership application was printed on the back of the race application, and therefore, filled out. "Oh, yeah." Squires laughs at the unintended printout. "That did happen." Also in 1977, for the first time during the Rodgers era, another GBTC athlete cracked the *Track & Field News* Men's Marathon All-Time US Top 10 Rankings when Thomas was listed at number seven, joining Rodgers, who was again ranked first. "Randy improved so much from college. He was really our first track guy to get an international trip when he got a trip to the USA-USSR meet from his finish at Madison Square Garden. Outside of Rodgers and my other athletes who got trips abroad, as a bona fide track guy Randy was it. He was running against the best and he even moved up to run marathons because he was just a strong guy. He had a job out in Amherst [in western Massachusetts] and he'd travel back and forth all through 1978 for the workouts with the guys every Tuesday and every Sunday—92 miles each way! He was the blood and guts of the team, he really was. He really worked at it. He and Bobby Hodge, without a doubt, were the most improved distance runners that I have ever seen that were national caliber."

After some sprinkled pockets of greatness throughout the previous four indoors, the 1977-78 indoors was the zenith for Squires and GBTC. At the 1977 USCG Relays in Connecticut, an AR 10:56 was set in the family relay with Tom Doherty, Pat Doherty, Mike Doherty, Tim Doherty. There were also several top-five performances at the 1978 Dartmouth Relays, NAAU Indoor Track & Field Championship, and NEAAU Indoor Track Championship, which included wins by Fred Doyle in the mile and Bob McCallum in the triple jump. And for the first time in their fifth consecutive attempt inside Madison Square Garden, the two-mile relay team of Ricciato, Sevene, Elliott, McDonald, finally won the NAAU Indoor Track Championship. After they methodically climbed that ladder from simply competing in the Demolition Derby in 1974, fourth in 1975, third in 1976, and second in 1977, it was in 1978 when they reached the pinnacle and earned the title of being the best in the nation. "When we were second and third, the team that was winning was the all-star team from the Big Ten. They got together and they formed a team of all Big Ten guys, except for their best runner who was the anchor leg. He was from Notre Dame, Rick Wohlhuter, the 1976 Olympic bronze medalist in the 800. But you see, we had been beating some very, very good teams, mostly college teams like Villanova, and clubs like the Chicago TC," noted Squires, who witnessed the victory from a specifically-designated section in the stands because coaches were not allowed on the field nor permitted to coach. "Well, you're not supposed to. I mean, I'd be there with my arms crossed and one hand sort of covering my mouth, and I'd yell out, 'Good!' 'Stay!' 'Red!' Red meant that I wanted my guy to stay on the guy in red shorts. The other coaches'd look over, but most of them knew me. I heard one of them say, 'Oh, that's Squires.' And another one said, and I remember this, he said, 'What the hell are you playing here? You think they're puppets?' Because whenever I'd yell out something, like for one of my guys to stay on another guy, he'd move quickly on command."

Unlike the 1976 nationals when GBTC fought hard right until the very end for third, this win was a bit easier, while still a definite struggle. "That win was huge. We had to get this monkey off our back. We were winning all kinds of national cross-country meets and relays, some they don't even have anymore. But that win was big. In 1978, we were humming. We could truly say we were a bona fide track club. We covered the sprints, the hurdles, and all the running events. Then we started covering the jumps, the javelin, and so on. We had qualifying people to go down to Madison Square Garden, and we're going against really good topnotch guys that are running for running clubs. We knew we could win the New Englands in track and field, which we did by just using my middle-distance guys and distance guys. All we had around then were road-running clubs, so the few track clubs were for little young kids or starter-uppers that would light a flame and then go out within two or three years."

Squires knew the commitment that was required to be good now and in the future. GBTC would not be a flash in the pan. He wanted longevity. And to achieve that ongoing organic growth and progress, he understood the sacrifices. And that was one aspect of coaching he had over his competitors. "It's hard work. I don't think anyone—*anyone!*—knows the amount of work a running coach puts in. And then a running track coach—the combo—*no one!* They found out it was a lot of work. I've been in the game too long and I've never seen anyone do it. They're either one or the other, and they have a lot of help and they're in a mecca area where they get all these great college runners that'll come out. This is not a mecca for running. I'm sorry, but Boston isn't. Wisconsin, Michigan, Illinois, Connecticut—they are. New York City, if they really wanted to work, would have been a mecca. Upper state New York, possibly. But it's hard. You're over there begging to use the high school hurdles, and then you go with your hurdlers to a college to use their high hurdles. There are certain things you have to do. It was work." He also enlisted a field event coach in Bill Clark, one of his GBTC athletes.

Unlike some clubs with only one or two stars, Squires's group system consistently produced nationally and internationally ranked results for numerous standouts. By the young club's fifth anniversary in 1978, Dillon won the US Cross-Country Trials in Georgia; the team of Meyer, Rodgers, Thomas was second at the IAAF World Cross-Country 12K Championship in Scotland; and GBTC won the 1978 Boston Marathon team title with Rodgers (first), Fultz (fourth), Thomas (fifth). In second at the 1978 Boston Marathon was non-GBTC member Jeff Wells, who also benefited from Squires's coaching. Fultz, the 1976 Boston winner, ran in three consecutive US Olympic Trial marathons. At the 1978 NAAU One-Hour Run at BU, GBTC was the Gold Medal Team, led by Rodgers's

AR-victorious 12 miles, 1350 yards, which ranked as the second-best all-time world performance. Eleven days later, versus 4,000 runners that included nine Olympians, 11 sub-4:00 milers, and 16 national champions, GBTC fielded six of the top 10 finishers at the Falmouth Road Race, which Rodgers won with his third CR. Rodgers capped off an amazing year with his third consecutive win at the New York City Marathon and sixth-place finish six weeks later at the Fukuoka International Open Marathon Championship in Japan. In recognition of his second defense of New York, Rodgers made his first solo cover of *Sports Illustrated* with the October 30, 1978, issue that stated "Runaway Marathon—Bill Rodgers Wins New York" (he had previously appeared alongside Bjorklund behind Shorter on the July 5, 1976, cover with the title "Next Stop, Montreal Frank Shorter win the 10,000"). With three top-10 showings in the marathon, which included a pair of wins, Rodgers was once again listed atop the *Track & Field News* 1978 Men's Marathon All-Time US Top 10 Rankings, and as number two in the World list. "He was going to every road race he could find. He did whatever he wanted to do on distance. But I said, 'Bill, I'm going to warn you this way: I am not going to run the program around you.' I'm blunt. The word is *team*. My thing is to have the best *team*. Now, in 1978, we got to a point where even New York running magazines were calling. We were on the move."

Road racing was gaining recognition as a sport unto itself. It was earning respect in the eyes of the non-running public. "In 1978, people started taking heed of road racing because of the boom and because television cameras came out. With television cameras, every news station would have a guy go to a large race. With 2,000, 3,000, 5,000 people in a race, they came out and did the usual and covered the start of all the people coming out and at the end they'd get the winners on the evening news." But around this time of personal struggle for Squires, which included his 1979 divorce, even more was being asked of him. GBTC experienced its biggest growth to date in terms of membership. And with the increase in athletes came the need for more training time, planning, competitions, responsibilities. The club of only eight guys running around Boston was no more. "The big growth was because money came in and because of the running boom. It started in 1977—after Boston in 1975, New York in 1977, and Montreal put a big marathon on in 1978. All of a sudden it started mushrooming in the East Coast, from Philadelphia, New York, and New England—we were like the road-running mecca!"

The 1978 outdoors began with a bang when GBTC won its fifth straight NAAU 20K Championship, won by Thomas, who also came in fourth at the NAAU 10,000-Meter Championship at UCLA. At the NEAAU Outdoor Track & Field Championship, GBTC was second, led by wins from George Reed in the three-mile and Rocco Petitto in the javelin (Doyle's third-place mile time of 4:12.6 was the club's best of the year). Hodge won the BU Track two-mile and was eighth at the Penn Relays 10,000. With more than 60 combined college and open runners, the 10,000 at Penn was made possible thanks in large part to Squires, who had previously approached event director Jim Tuppeny that he felt the Relays were in need of longer distances (some 24 years earlier, legendary Villanova coach James "Jumbo" Elliott and his assistant Tuppeny, had visited the Squires residence on a recruiting trip to Massachusetts). "I asked Tuppeny to put a 5K and a 10K on in the Penn Relays. He said they already had the 5K, but I said it was only for collegians, and there was no 10K. I told him he can run this thing on Friday nights and make a lot of money. The road runners that were former cross-country guys that ran the six-mile and the 10K, they eat up the Penn Relays and they never even got in probably in college. But on Friday nights, you bring them over, charge them the fee, give them medals that cost under two bucks, and I'll guarantee that you'll have, in both events, at least a 100 to 150 people. Well, he got about 400 in the two events and he made a fortune. They even had to have multiple heats. I think it went from eight o'clock Friday night on." The 1978 Penn Relays were the first that featured three days of events.

Over dinner after one of the Penn Relays, among the gathered team coaches, Squires did not let the moment of success pass by without comment. "Tuppeny said that if it was a flop, it'd be a one-year thing. But he was thrilled. And I remember giving him the business afterwards. I said to him, 'The registration fee's, like, what, 15 bucks? And the gosh-darn medals only cost you a buck and a quarter and you don't even give out the little box with it when you hand them out! Did you have to bring the Brink's truck over?' And he goes, 'Don't you start!' Then he said he'd buy two rounds. And I said, 'Forget that, you're buying all the rounds.'"

In its 1978 cross-country season, GBTC once again defended its NAAU 20K title for the sixth straight year. At the NEAAU in Massachusetts, they thoroughly destroyed the field in whatever configuration: first four finishers; eight in the top 10; 10 in the top 15; 12 in the top 20. The dominating A team of Meyer (first), Hodge (second), Bob Hensley (third), Scott Graham (fourth), Paul Oparowski (sixth), was first with 16 points. "If we had them now, they would still kill. People wouldn't even show up. It was like an esprit de corps. If someone was having a tough day, they'd say, 'Not on.' They worked in clusters and they'd know. They knew if they have it or not to say something, because if you're the key man and you're supposed to be pulling the pace and you can't do it, they knew to say it early enough to their teammates so they can plan. And I'd make a big deal about that and say, 'Now there's a smart thing. So-and-so knew it wasn't his day and he told his teammates to take over. That's smart.' And it was. That's a team mentality. Anyone can have a bad day. As a coach, that's planned on. But if you're having a bad day, say you are. And you know what that guy would do when he gets back? He'd be a destroyer. That's what the Kenyans do now." At the 1978 NAAU Senior Men's Cross-Country Championship 10,000 in Washington, GBTC came in third (after a third in 1977 and ninth in 1976). "We finally ran, what I call, at a real championship level. I feel the top four teams in cross-country have usually been well-trained; they actually have much better talent than I would ever have because they include post-collegiate guys in areas that are real running areas, like Texas, Oregon, California; and they've usually been running together for years."

Club expansion continued to widen at a tremendous rate. In the beginning it was all about the relays. In the interim, it was more about short distance and middle distance. Now, longer distances. "Yeah, the minute we got more money, that opened the door for our long-distance runners because the national championships are at 15K, 20K, and 30K. Those are really up the alley of either a half-marathoner or a marathoner. And guys would come in and say they were running 2:29 to 2:40, which is good in the marathon. That meant they were training like a wacko, so I'd put them in Group 2. I knew they would shine on Sundays. Some of them in Group 2 were better milers and 5000-meter and 10K runners, but we would mix it up in training for an 18-mile run, a 22-mile run, and a very fast 14-miler, depending on the weekend. What I'd do is I'd have a succession of long runs of 18 to 22 miles, then I'd start working at 14, 16, 18 miles, and then we'd do a 14, but faster. I try to get to 18, which is just where you start to feel fatigued. At 14, you're halfway in the marathon. But this practice formulates the end of the marathon. This was like we [simulate running] easy, and then all of a sudden we're moving. Then you've got guys doing medium distance, which is about 14 miles a day—maybe 16, or 20 if they're loose, like Rodgers did. You wake up in the morning and you do seven and seven, or eight and eight, or 10 and

10. And then on the track, usually something moderate after doing the long runs. Maybe seven miles worth of some calibrated ladders, either short—300s to 600s—or longer—a mile to a mile-and-a-half—and that's including the jog-downs."

Squires stressed to the newcomers that his goal has not changed since he's been a coach; and that is to get them prepared to race. "These workouts were for big races—a tough race, not an easy one. And if they beat some of those top guys, then the person at the shoe companies that actually hire the help—meaning the runner—they take notice. And I'd explain to the guys that if it happens, you're going to start short. You may get a two-year option at $25,000. Then you may get a four-year contract at $50,000, which means you can pay all your bills and then you're in your glory with whatever you get from under the table." Squires did not burn out his athletes. As an example, for cross-country, GBTC started in August with speedwork for the three months of meets from September until November. Since they worked hard and specialized in cross-country, he sacrificed part of indoors so his guys would be more fit and mentally prepared for the big indoor events. "A lot of clubs and colleges would have three full seasons a year, and I thought it was just too much. You're losing training and your better recovery from a hard season. So after cross-country, they would just go easy to build up some distance and run anywhere from five miles at a slower rate to reduced intensity. I'd never dictate mileage to athletes. I never would! We would lose part of the indoor season, but I didn't care. And it would work because the guys would recover and by February we were able to feel comfortable to do some track work. And even then, they could come to my workouts every other week. And every other week I'd want them to come to the long run so they wouldn't lose that base. When you lose that base, you have to start all over again."

By the 1978-79 indoors, GBTC moved away from its original focus on relays and concentrated more on individual performances. Squires even thought they could host its own invitational. "Billy Okerman got us into Harvard, which had the best track then, and I told him we should get kids from the West Coast or the Midwest to come to the Greater Boston Indoor Meet. All we'll do is tell them they can come in here—it's a fast, fast track—and they can get their times to go to the other big indoor meets. That can be our leverage. The year before, we had the meet in 1978 and we tried to make some money out of it. We did, but it was too low-key. What we should do is set a realistic price for the spectators. The athletes all pay entry fees, but for the people who sit in the stands, we should do $10 for adults and $5 for schoolkids. The place only holds about 1,200, but you have a turnover from the morning to the evening." (After a few low-key years, the first annual New Balance/GBTC Invitational Track and Field Indoor meet was held at Harvard on January 31, 1982, by meet directors Larry Newman, Jim O'Brien, and Okerman; and more than 120 volunteers.)

The 1979 outdoors featured several club highlights on the national and international level, which included their third New England Men's Outdoor Track Championship team title in six years and Hodge's Bay to Breakers 12K win. Squires's program powered a tremendous peak in the marathon at Boston in 1979 with Hodge, Mahoney, McGilvery, Rodgers, and Thomas. GBTC became true "world beaters" in a record field of 7,357 that included marathon winners Tom Fleming (New York twice), Bjorklund (Grandma's), Toshihiko Seko of Japan (Fukuoka), Kevin Ryan of New Zealand (New Zealand Games), Drayton (Fukuoka three times), and 1978 Boston third-place finisher Esa Tikkanen of Finland. In an unprecedented third AR/CR time in five years, Rodgers won in a stunning 2:09:27. Equally significant was the fact that nearly half of the top 10 finishers were from GBTC—Hodge third (2:12:30), Thomas eighth (2:14:12), Mahoney 10th (2:14:36), and McGilvery also with a sub-2:30 time in 2:27:51—for the team title.

"Four guys in the top 10 in the Boston Marathon! That was a freak of nature. Never was done by an organized club before. There may have been some Canadians in the past that came down, but if it was a club it wasn't an organized club, per se. And if Vinnie Fleming wasn't injured, we would have had five. And to think—Rodgers didn't do anything [of note] in college; Hodgie was in Division II—he was good, but in Division II; Randy's peak was coming; and Dickie had the hardest time because of his job as a mailman, so I was glad he did so well. But I actually felt that something like this was very attainable. We were going against these kinds of people in short distance in cross-country, 10K, and we had the money to travel to national road racing, and we were beating these people that were getting $50,000 and $80,000 a year from the running companies! If I were coaching now, I'd beat the Kenyans. They're rhythm runners. It's all built up. They do a lot of fast 30Ks. They warm up in the first two miles, then they haul and do 5:02, 4:58, 4:58, 5:02, 4:58, and so on."

Once again for the Boston Marathon, in 1979 Squires provided the live television commentary from the media stationed atop scaffolding at the Prudential Center Plaza that overlooked the finish line on Ring Road. His access and the elevated view afforded him a unique bird's-eyewitness account. "Well before the race I had to figure out the top three people, male and female, so they could get pictures of them for the broadcast. I did my homework. It was a good show. Of course Rodgers I had to throw in there to win. But I wouldn't have put Hodgie in third because I wouldn't have put that kind of pressure on my guys. When I was doing the commentary, I saw them run as a cluster, which I had told them to do—to work together. At around 16 miles, I could see my four guys in with about another eight guys. You see, the race starts at the Woodland train station, just before 17 miles. I had told my guys that by there, they should be moving into position, and the positions will change no more than three spots. That's all it does—you're either going to lose three or gain three."

The marathon success was a direct result of Squires's design. For Boston, that included surges over the course. "Baby surges of one minute and two minutes, which is where [in a race] they'd be dropping the pack of about 10 guys at usually 10 miles, to about a pack of five around 15 miles. Some of this would be over the hill area on the Boston course, and some would be over the flat, like Ashland to Framingham. How Rodgers through the hills killed them at Boston or on the flats in New York off First Avenue, we'd do a 20-minute at probably 4:50 pace. I'd have him do that anywhere between 16 and 18 miles when you've still got life in your legs. With this, you drop the pack from that five or so to eventually the two of you. That's what Rodgers had. He didn't have great speed, but he had speed from the training in the 10K and that forced him to go on the track [in training]."

From the Newton-Wellesley Hospital to the West Newton Fire Station and up the Commonwealth Avenue hills into Newton is where Squires directed intense focus for his athletes. It was over this stretch of the course where he believed, more often than not, Boston was won or lost. "Anytime I would do those Car Tag runs, I'd purposely put the car about a mile and a quarter from the hospital so they would coast down that hill to the train station, and the minute they hit the station and they see the golf course on the left, they *go*! From there, you go up to the fire station where there'll be a big crowd going crazy—and you relax going up the hill—and then I told them to try and wait for one minute at the top of each hill so they can recover, and then really do a good lift and push it. And in between the hills, I told them to do the quicker movements to gradually pick off other guys. I told my guys that they're going to go by those people that raced the hills, and those guys are going to try and tag onto them. But by the second or third hill, they'll fall off because they won't be able to keep up because they *raced* the hill when my guys *ran* the hill. They'll be too tired. And this is all before Heartbreak Hill!"

In addition to having beat great American talent in the 1979 Boston—Tom Fleming (fourth), Bjorklund (fifth)—Squires was equally impressed with the international class. GBTC bested Seko (second), Ryan (sixth), Drayton (11th), Tikkanen (18th). "In foreign countries, athletes have a doctor, they have a hematologist, they have surgeons—whatever they need. And if the coach feels his athlete should go a thousand miles away to a big race, it's done. And they're not over-raced. To a point, some of the [US] track athletes go crazy because they're run to death between the indoor track circuit from June 1st to September 15th. The rest of the year, the distance guys go to what they call the late season on track, from mid-July to September, because they peaked on wanting to go to the international cross-country championships."

GBTC—with Rodgers, Hodge, Thomas—defended its Boston team title. In 1978 it was won by Rodgers, Fultz, Thomas. And in 1975, when GBTC was third, it was with Rodgers, Graham, Vinnie Fleming. The use of six different runners in three separate top-three Boston Marathon team performances further proved the depth with which Squires had and the successful training he incorporated. "I thought they'd do well in 1979. Well, I always thought my guys would do well. But in 1979, I thought within the top 25 would be 15 to 17 foreigners. The great ones from other countries that did well in the Olympics would always do well at Boston. You had to keep an eye on guys like Seko, Drayton, and Kevin Ryan. They were tough."

Right after the Boston Marathon, on his way to celebrate at the Eliot Lounge, Squires was visited by representatives from the United States Olympic Committee and The Athletics Congress. With the Olympic Games just over a year away, the USOC and TAC decided to include on the US Olympic staff a specialty coach responsible for 10K and marathon runners. In prior Games, that fell upon the mile/5K/steeplechase coach. Squires was recommended. And unbeknownst to him at the time of the 1979 Boston, the representatives watched the race unfold when his club put on quite the show. They met at the Copley Plaza Hotel lobby in downtown Boston. "They came up to me and said they wanted me to submit my name for the US Olympic team as a coach. They said it was time we had a person that knows 10K and marathon people, and they knew I did a mix of both these groups. And they said based on what they just saw at Boston, they knew they wanted me."

As the year continued, the marathon distance became more and more associated with GBTC and Squires. It was not just Rodgers, who still led the way in name recognition, but many other teammates as well who followed in no less than nine other marathons in 1979 alone. At the Foxboro Marathon in Massachusetts, Bob Clifford met the US Olympic Marathon Trials standard with a 2:20:30 win. In the Nike-OTC Marathon in Oregon, with about a half-dozen GBTC runners, Gary Wallace ran 2:18:51 and Fred Doyle 2:20:27. At the New York City Marathon, Rodgers won his historic fourth straight! And at the Cape Cod Marathon in Massachusetts, Tom Joyce, a former Boston State cross-country and track runner under Squires, won his marathon debut in 2:24:20.1; Bob Hall was seventh (and the first wheelchair competitor); and McGillivray was 15th. *Track & Field News* once again listed Rodgers as first in the 1979 Men's Marathon All-Time US Top 10 Rankings and the Men's Marathon All-Time World Top 10 Rankings (with Hodge number eight in the US rankings). "What was happening was we were getting quicker in the fall, we were getting quicker in the wintertime, and we were doing the speed-up and still doing the long runs. You're merging those guys and they stay in that cocoon, which is Group 1. Our second group also finished well, and even Group 3."

For its seventh cross-country season, the ultimate unattainable goal remained the same for Squires—the elusive national 10K title. The 1979 NAAU Senior Men's Cross-Country Championship 10,000 was Thanksgiving weekend in North Carolina. GBTC carried with them the pain from the previous year's third-place showing in Washington, despite Meyer's victorious 29:36. Since Squires had first deemed his guys fit to compete in the nationals back in 1975, GBTC had finished seventh (1975), ninth (1976), and third twice (1977, 1978). "We were really in the hunt for the national championship. You're going against mostly fast 5K and 10K men for a national championship in cross-country."

Leading up to North Carolina, GBTC for the seventh consecutive year won the NAAU 20K Cross-Country Championship. The following month, with 16 points from the one-two-three finish of its A team of Meyer, Dillon, Hodge, the club also won the NEAAU Cross-Country Championship 3000. And two weeks before the national 10K, GBTC "won" the team title at the 1979 Canadian National 12K Cross-Country Championship in Halifax, Nova Scotia. Squires assured race officials they would, of course, pay the registration fee to run, and that they realized and accepted the fact they would not be counted toward any placings or medals. Canadian officials understood, and allowed the foreign club to run in their GBTC singlets. "They were nice about it. To get to Canada, we hit the club treasury because we had to take a plane, even though it's right up the street up north. It was very expensive. I didn't even go! And I had three runoffs—the New Englands; an Eastern regional meet; and my cross-country Codfish Bowl—and that's why we'd win them so big because they went at it in those races. I did put Rookie in without a runoff because he was in college in Oregon, but everyone agreed that he would've made it. They all wanted Salazar in. But my guys would go at it like bandits because they all wanted to go to a big meet."

With the NAAU 10K moment at hand, Squires thought back to his rare preseason pep talk at the beginning of the fall when he gathered his troops together and laid out this cross-country season with the help of an ominous premonition. "I said to them, 'Do me a favor. And I never ask you, I never ask you this, but do me a favor.' They listened because they knew I was serious. 'We've got to get through this [block of not winning] and win the national championship because some of you guys are going to get big contracts and Greater Boston will dissipate. We're starting to have guys get them already, so this is the time.' When you sign a shoe company contract, they'll want you to wear their singlet. You can't wear Greater Boston if you're with, say, adidas, and you just signed a $50,000 or $80,000 contract. With some shoe companies, you could sign with them and also wear the Greater Boston singlet in cross-country because they didn't really care about cross-country. It was the road races they cared about because they were filmed on TV. So you could break it up with some of them. But how could you have a guy under contract with one company and wear a singlet for someone else? But I'll clue ya, I *was* coaching guys that had signed contracts. I was training guys like that, and that was my dilemma. But I didn't care. I was there to develop runners."

Two days after Thanksgiving more than 20 clubs and 400 runners competed in the 1979 NAAU meet. GBTC took full command of the 6.21-mile championship and ran the way they trained; they pushed each other within a group. Squires stood about a half-mile from the finish to observe the closing yardage. First to appear was 21-year-old Salazar, who won in 30:27.8. What made this even more remarkable was that one week earlier, at the NCAA Division I Men's Cross-Country Championship 10,000, Salazar was second (only eight seconds behind 27-year-old legend Henry Rono of Washington State University). Hodge was third, Dillon fourth, and Meyer fifth, for a devastatingly victorious one-three-four-five pounding. "When I saw Al, I thought I'd better start walking back to the finish. The next thing I knew, there was the third- and fourth-place guys—Hodgie and Danny—and they're from Greater Boston! Then the fifth-place guy also from Greater Boston—Meyer. I started laughing to myself. I'm yelling out to my guys that we won it. And as I go along, here comes another Greater Boston guy. We won it!" The stars lined up that day for a who's who in the final standings that led to club domination. "We had the lowest score ever—26 points! That was unheard of! No one had ever done that. It was crazy! That's the lowest ever in American history. That's never been done before. I mean, my *fifth* man was *12th* (Thomas). *Twelfth!* And my sixth (Pete Pfitzinger) and seventh (Bruce Bickford) guys became Olympians. We ran 4:13 to 4:16 [per mile]. That's what we did in my training. I adapted all kinds of things for them, and it paid off. And I'll clue ya, our second team would have won! They added it up. And then I read later that Matti Hannus, the editor of the *Finnish Running News*, had called us the best running club in the world. The world! That's something." GBTC also beat Herb Lindsay (1979 *Runner's World* Road Racer of the Year), Duncan Mcdonald (US Olympian), and Steve Scott (prodigious Sub 4 Track Club miler).

"The first mile was all grass and rolling down. After two miles, there was such a gap. And I knew by five miles that if we did the things we were supposed to do, we could win. And we had Brand X—we had Salazar. We never had him before. I knew if we had him, we could win. Well, I thought we still could have won it if we had gone one-two if I wanted to split the [two GBTC] teams, but then we'd have absolutely no room for error if I did that. And I would have been the biggest jackass if both clubs lost."

With this final elusive national championship under its belt, it was time that night for GBTC to celebrate. Everyone was ready for much merriment; except Squires. He had somehow re-aggravated an old collarbone injury and was in great pain. While his guys went out for their fill of libation, he retreated to his hotel room to rest. "I felt bad. I really did. But I was hurting, so I went to bed. At about four in the morning, I roll over in bed and I feel this metal thing in my bed. I put the light on and there's this big No Trespassing sign in my bed! It had the cement base and everything. It was heavy. How the hell?" The team had somehow overnight picked it up from the hotel parking lot, dragged it inside, through the stairwell, and into bed with their coach. The perfect crime. "They wanted to be one up on me. Anyway, the next morning, after a big laugh, I get the guys together and I tell them they have to bring it back, but I told them not to go down the stairs. We had to at least get it out of our floor. I said if I had my coffee, I'd be thinking better, but I told them to find out where the service elevator is and put it in there and press the button. They go, 'Brilliant!' I remember one of the guys said that word, 'Brilliant!'" He laughs. "So that's what they did. I still don't know whose idea it was."

That was the kind of atmosphere Squires fostered. It was loose, it was fun, it was positive. They worked hard—very hard—but it was always an enjoyable experience. And that was exactly what he wanted. "When they did that with the sign, I loved that. Most runners are vanilla ice cream—no personality, no sense of humor. Not my guys. I'm always jabbing them and having fun, and they loved it. Whenever we were ready to go home from a meet, I was always packed and ready to go before them. And they'd always forget something in their rooms, so when we were all in the lobby and ready to go, I'd go in and out of the rooms while they were waiting. I'd always end up going to the lobby with one guy's hat on, someone else's necktie, a jacket. Always! And they'd go, 'Hey, that's my tie.' 'There's my hat.' I'd say I was selling them."

Regarding the men's relay teams, the 1979-80 indoors featured one of the last great showings under Squires. At the Dartmouth Relays, the DMR team of John Demers, Bill Strang, Doyle, Meyer, was first; the two-mile team of Demers, Rich Nichols, Rich Puckerin, Keith Francis, was second; and the four-mile team of Graham, Doyle, Elliot, Meyer, was second. At the 1980 Millrose Games, the two-mile team of Demers, Nichols, Doyle, Puckerin, was third among 20 teams in the handicap race. And at the Brooks Indoor Track Invitational inside the Astrodome in Texas, the two-mile team of Nichols, Demers, Francis, Puckerin, set a new all-time New England record with its fifth-place 7:26.79. "From 1973 to around 1979 or 1980, the relay was the focus. But what happened was relay guys all got regular jobs in life, got married and everything. After that, we weren't working that specialty as heavy. It was a bygone. Could we have? Yes. But my focus then was on more individuals than the relay. Much more. So I was looking for individuals that would be able to run a good 5K, 10K, marathon, but also a half-mile, mile. The way I looked at it, every two years with the athletes I had, I would change the speed because they got better. If you looked at how I trained the guys in 1978 and 1979, you would see the change."

One of those athletes who greatly benefited was Greg Meyer, the University of Michigan All-American in cross-country and track with a record 8:33.80 in the 3000-meter steeplechase, a 13:41.00 in the 5000, and a 13:11.00 in the three-mile. But Squires saw distance—long distance—in Meyer. "In 1979 when he was training with Greater Boston, he came to me and he said what would I think about if we speed up the work, and instead of having the longer intervals, have shorter rests. I told him there were three of them (George Malley, Meyer, Mike Roche) that came in with good credentials, and I said, 'You know what, I think you're right.' So what I did was I sped it up and we'd see how things would go. He had talked to me about doing the 10K training scheme, which he knew helped the 5K and the 10K and marathons. But he wondered when would we jack it up to get real quick. The concept of the group stayed, but the speed increased. He was used to doing that at Michigan, the quick work. But we did it and it blended very, very well. I've always said to them, if you want to have input, come and talk to me. I'm doing this to make the athletes as good as they can be, and if I can get any input, it's going to make it better, whether we use part of the idea or all of it. And it worked. Meyer proved that." (Meyer won the 1980 Detroit Marathon, 1982 Chicago Marathon, and 1983 Boston Marathon.)

Around the time of the 1979-80 indoors, Squires became conflicted in regard to the increased interest in the club. When it came to more women joining, he was—and always had been—in favor of their additional presence. He incorporated more specialized training that, presided over by Larry Newman and Chuck Riley, closely replicated what he created for the men. And it was working: in the 1979 cross-country season, the women were third at the NEAAU 15K Women's Road Racing Championship in Massachusetts with top-20 finishes by Linda Lecoq, Mary Ann Bray, and Margaret Champion. But regarding the influx of men who had not really run before who decided they wanted to join GBTC, he felt this was not the club for them. They brought with them no experience, no prior high school or collegiate races, and obviously no base. This perplexed Squires, who was used to working with athletes who brought with them an athletic history of some sort; specific goals at a higher level; and the physical means with which he could work. "It got to a point where it got to be rookies that would show up. I mean, really bona fide joggers. They never even raced! And they thought I would teach them to run. I can't do that. So I gave my guys a handout and I told them whenever new people came in, give them the handout. It talked about pickups and baby hills and mileage and so on. It had things like if you're tired, walk and then run. I mean, this was from the beginning! And I had them fill out logs so I could read any progress. They thought because they heard that Rodgers had smoked cigarettes and drank before coming here that they could do it. But they didn't know that he also ran really well. Anyway, I would know that with the ones that came back, they were serious. I didn't want a Group 4. It wasn't that I was looking to be an elitist, but I had about 30 guys—eight to 10 in my Group 1, about seven in my Group 2, and in Group 3 maybe 12. And I wanted them to keep moving up."

Squires was busy focusing on the Olympics. His goal in 1980 was the Olympic Summer Games in Moscow, Russia, set for July and August. Even more so than in the previous Olympics in 1976, when GBTC was no less than three years old, the club now was older, wiser, and stronger. These Games would be *their* international showcase. More and more of the training and workouts and races were in line with that one goal. Everything centered on the Olympic Trials and subsequent Games. However, eight months before the Olympics, in December 1979, military aggression by the Soviet Union when it invaded Afghanistan was met with harsh responses internationally. In the United States, word soon circulated that perhaps the US would boycott the Games if the Soviet Union did not withdraw its troops. "When the rumors started, it was Cold War this, Cold War that, and we can't do this, we can't do that. As a coach, you don't change the training scheme of an athlete. But people were disillusioned. It was a crapshoot. And the running companies were out of their minds. They already spent all their money." Concerned, but undaunted, preparation for the US Olympic Trials for May and June 1980 continued, and began in earnest in February and March. Around the time Squires was named US Olympic 10K/marathon coach, USOC meetings were held in regard to the fate of America's participation. The US set a withdrawal ultimatum and deadline. When it passed unheeded by the Soviet Union, the decision was made official on March 21, when President Jimmy Carter publicly stated that the US will boycott the XXII Olympiad. "That was a shame. I got a letter that said I was certified as the coach, but as of now there would be no coaches meeting because as you've heard about the Games, and so on. I would have had six athletes—the three in the marathon and the three in the 10K. And maybe I would have had the 10K women, too. But I felt for the athletes."

The decision cast a great pall over the still-scheduled US Olympic Trials. For some of the American athletes, the Trials held little more significance than another meet on the road; for others, it was their only chance to compete as an Olympian. One month before the Trials was the Boston Marathon. It drew great attention with a field of nearly 3,500. Rodgers, due to his outspoken public criticism of the US boycott, garnered a death threat for his opinion; one that would reportedly prevent him from living beyond the 24-mile mark in Coolidge Corner. Rodgers defied the threat and ran. Squires, in the face of rules and regulations, and also that potential deadly threat, joined his athlete mid-race in Wellesley. With a cup of water in hand, and the simple presence of his body alongside, the coach for a short spell ran next to the runner. If Rodgers was a target, Squires thought, so would he be a target. It was at once a shared moment of coach and athlete, support and defiance. Rodgers took out his boycott frustration on a hot-weather day with a 2:12:11 victory as the first man since Clarence DeMar (1922-24) to three-peat. There were also nearly 20 GBTC men and women in the field, which included Bob Hall, the first wheelchair competitor at 2:02:21. The heat took its toll on many of the runners at Boston, as temperatures were in the high 70s. It forced Hodge to drop out and Squires to pull several of his runners off the course to run another day. It was so hot that Newman's own estimated four-hour result included a stopover at the GBTC water station, where he helped other runners before he finished the race himself. "There was lots of dehydration," Squires pointed out. "It was hot the whole time and I could tell they were in bad-land. The reason I pulled guys out was because we had the Olympic Trials coming up. And then we didn't have the Trials—they didn't count, I mean."

Squires, as usual, found his way afterward to the Eliot Lounge to cool down. For him, it was a place of refuge and rest, as well as celebration and contemplation. Shortly after the 1980 Boston Marathon, during one of his many trips there, he found he was not alone, which was customary. There was a request for his presence, which was also not unusual. But this time, when from behind the bar his friend—vocational and perennial bartender Tommy Leonard—pointed to the guests in question, it was cause for a raised eyebrow. From his Coach's Corner barstool, Squires noticed British Olympic gold medalist Chris Brasher, who had helped pace Roger Bannister's record sub-4:00 mile. It occurred to Squires that he had yet another opportunity in which he could educate the charmingly loquacious Leonard and the boys, a common activity in which he took great pleasure. He proceeded to regale all about a little race in England some 25 years earlier, in Oxford, to be precise; the mention of which reached the visiting Englishmen. "I said, 'There was this guy, a little guy, that led the way for the first two-and-a-half laps of this race. It was on a cloudy day at that college in England. Oxford! And this guy set the pace for history on the epic date of May 5th, 1954, when he led the way for the first sub-four-minute mile for Roger Bannister." One of the gentlemen had since walked over to Squires, and in an effort to correct a point of fact, gently chimed in. Recalled Squires, "This guy was listening and when he saddled up to me, he says, 'Very good, Coach. But it was May 6.' And I yell out to everyone, 'Hey, this is the guy that led the four-minute-mile for half a mile: Chris Brasher!' And then they all come over and they just swept me away to get to him; even Tommy! I was nobody!" Brasher was on a research mission to learn from Boston and New York how to organize and run a major-city marathon as preparation for the creation of the London Marathon, which in 1981 he and British Olympic bronze medalist John Disley co-founded.

For the 1980 US Olympic Trials Marathon in upstate New York, Squires had seven from GBTC who qualified. But with two months having passed since the boycott notice, interest waned for some. While Bob Hodge, Dick Mahoney, and Bill Rodgers did not compete in the Trials, Randy Thomas, Paul Oparowski, Gary Wallace, and Fred Doyle, participated. In total, of the 225 overall qualifiers, 33 for various reasons did not show. The following month, in June, the US Olympic Qualifying Heats and Trials for track and field were held in Oregon, where Squires sent qualifiers Dan Dillon, Tom Mahan, Greg Meyer, Mike Roche, Alberto Salazar, and Thomas.

The 10K training and track workouts that Squires preached provided wide-ranging benefits, well beyond whatever specific race or meet for which they were originally intended. And they took advantage. Rodgers won the Cherry Blossom 10-Mile Run. At the 1980 National Masters and Sub-Masters Indoor Track and Field Championship at Syracuse University, Rip Dyer with his long jump of 21 feet, 10 1/8 inches, earned national track and field honors when in his age division of 30-35 he beat two dozen other jumpers. Also, GBTC defended its New England Men's Outdoor Track Championship team title for its fourth win in seven years. Doyle ran a 4:09 mile and Bickford an AR three-mile at the NAAU Outdoor Track Meet. At the NTAC Outdoor Track Championship in California, Meyer in the steeplechase was fourth at 8:45.5 for All-American honors (and third in his trial heat to advance), Pfitzinger in the 10,000 was fifth in a 29:24.7 PR (for All-American honors); and at the NEAAU Track 10K at BC, Hodge was first at 29:42. "The workouts worked," noted Squires. "And not just for one distance or one race. You can see how well these guys did all over the place. We were everywhere. It wasn't a fluke."

Squires was especially proud of the GBTC women, whose times and results continually improved. There were several championships and races, some women only, in which they excelled. At the 1980 Women's NAAU 10K Championship in New York, GBTC recorded an impressive 10 PRs, led by Paula Lettis; and prior to the 10K, a 5K was held that featured double-racer Pam Duckworth, who won her division. Squires's structured workouts for women enabled them to compete at a higher level, which included more than half a dozen who ran at the NETAC Outdoor Track Women's 15K Championship. GBTC also co-sponsored with Etonic Shoes the first annual NETAC Women's 25K Road Racing Championship. Affectionately known as "The Wonder Woman 25K," the race director of the three-loop, 15.5-mile course, was GBTC's own Elydia Siegel. Squires noted, "The Greater Boston women really kept improving. They really did. You could tell the ones that were serious. There were some that just came down to the first few workouts and then you'd never see them again. But not the ones that kept competing in the races and the championships. You could see them improve in the workouts, and that translated to when they raced."

In the "off months," Squires allowed his athletes to run more road races that would put their track training to good use. The summer of 1980 featured a remarkable array of races that doubled as championships and track meets which served as major track and field events. At the Boilermaker Road Race 15K in New York, which served as the TAC National 15K Senior Men's Championship, GBTC won the team title with Pfitzinger first, Mark Murray fourth, Gary Wallace 16th, Tom Joyce 18th, Bob Cosman 22nd, Walt Murphy 28th. At the NTAC 20K Championship (formerly the NAAU 20K), Hodge was first. And the GBTC women made their first appearance in a major track event at the 1980 Kendall Women's Classic Track & Field Meet at BU, in which six PRs were recorded.

Just before the start of the next cross-country season, Brandeis University in Massachusetts hosted the New England Track & Field Camp. Among the staff were Randy Thomas and Charlie Leverone, the latter of whom was a school teammate Squires credits as introducing him to running.

CHAPTER 13

GBTC DISMANTLING

Since 1973, and in half a dozen years, Squires and GBTC transformed running from an afterthought, if that, to a respected powerhouse field of endeavor. Stars were born, long-term records made, higher standards set. When the dust settled from the 1970s, the creation of a whole new world had emerged. The new decade, which began with an Olympic year, was full of promise, glory, and celebration. The sport of running was ready to come into its own and reap the rewards of respect. But the new decade began with a schizophrenic entry of amazingly triumphant moments—such as unknowns becoming superstars and the widespread mushrooming popular interest in running—intertwined with depressingly devastating moments—such as the multi-nation Olympic boycott and Rosie Ruiz's first-place cheat at the Boston Marathon.

One particularly devastating moment which directly impacted Squires and GBTC occurred when the 1980 cross-country season began with a giant void via the departure of several of its top runners, some of whom became US Olympians and major-marathon champions. The list of departees included Bruce Bickford, Dan Dillon, Alberto Salazar, to Nike's Athletics West; and Tim Donovan, Mark Duggan, Vinnie Fleming, Scott Graham, Dick Mahoney, Greg Meyer, Bill Okerman, Andy Palmer, Pete Pfitzinger, Mike Roche, Randy Thomas, to Team New Balance. "That was all within about a six-month period when they left. That was a lot. But I knew it was going to happen. And whenever they signed their contracts and told me, I said to them that they were going to finish whichever season they were in—honor the shirt they're running under—and that was it.

They understood. And I didn't care if they told the press about it. That was fine. With New Balance it was different because I had a job with them doing clinics for a stipend. But I didn't want to be their coach. Kevin Ryan of New Zealand, a Greater Boston guy, was also at New Balance. He was recruiting foreign athletes, and he was basically the New Balance coach. That was fine with me. I just stepped back and let him be coach."

However heavy the losses were to the club, Squires was used to athletic turnover. As a high school and college coach, losing athletes on a regular basis—via injuries, transfers, graduation—was an inherent element of his job. But it was a testament to what he did with the mix of new talent and tested veterans that was the key to any of his success. "Also in the fall of 1980, I got five very fast track athletes that came from different places around the country. And they wanted to be part and parcel because they knew there was money—under the table—in road racing to at least get expense money. They knew that our training was allowing a person to run a good mile *and* a good 10,000. We could get guys ready to race various distances. The big thing was you've got to accommodate to the national system if you're going to stay in the ballgame. And I knew I was taking guys that if I was a Division I coach that I would never give a scholarship to. But I was taking these guys and making them faster."

Squires could handle athlete turnover, of course, but this mass exodus was different. It was not only the loss of most of its core founding members in Vinnie Fleming, Graham, Mahoney, and Thomas, but also marquee names in Dillon, Meyer, Roche, Pfitzinger, Salazar (and Rodgers, who departed in 1982 for the PUMA Racing Team). It was ironic that the goal of a club runner was to run well enough to be offered a shoe contract that, in turn, would result in their departure from the club that made them good enough to be offered a shoe contract. The cycle of individual success often led to the dismantling of the club team. Squires realized that was now part of the sport. A shoe contract was the goal. And it usually began innocently enough with a top result in a national competition.

"When an athlete is in the top five of a national championship, all of a sudden it's, 'Who is he?' The kids coming out of college, they have been getting free shoes and all of this all the way through, and the shoe companies are thinking track and field championships and Olympics with them. When the running boom came, then they're thinking they can wait until the NCAAs or the open national championships. Then they say, 'Okay, kid, you're looking promising. We're going to give you a two-year contract at $25,000 to $30,000.' And they're going to call it $30,000 because they're going to give them $5,000 to pay for transportation. It's really $25,000 in your pocket, $5,000 for travel, plus clothing and shoes—that's for beginners," explained Squires of typical deals at that time. "The second tier for a guy or a gal would be a four-year contract for 50 grand. When they got a two-year contract, the thinking was that that person could get to the Olympic Trials in the 5000 or 10,000 meters, and they could also be a good half-marathoner or a good marathoner and even run a good 10K on the road."

Squires also witnessed athletes suffer from the deal. "I hate to say it, but some of these guys were pretty good runners but the runners weren't using their heads on how they—the shoe companies that were now in control—would know how to race these guys properly. I saw more guys that were way more talented than the best in the East—not just my club—that we would beat and we would say, 'What happened to him after three years?' They were ruined because their legs were beat out. They were racing and racing for the contract. And contracts also had clauses, such as if you made the Olympic team you'd get $50,000; and if you're a national champion you'd get $25,000. Now, this is before agents came. All of this was done by a lawyer. Later on, when the agents took over, I don't know, I would think you'd want an agent-lawyer for his wisdom because I've seen some agents that aren't lawyers and I don't think they knew what to do."

Squires recalled contracts were not over calendar years then; they routinely ended in the October after the Olympics, and coincidentally meant an athlete missed the cross-country season. "The next level was $75,000 to $100,000, depending on the shoe company, for the next four years, and more plums of things—more money if you go to the Olympics, the world championships, national records, world records, defending your title. You could get $25,000 or $30,000 for each of those. There were a few contracts that were above that $100,000, but not many. And one of my things I always said to my athletes was to put your money away. I kept telling them to save up for the rainy days, for the bad days."

Squires noted that all of his Group 1 and some of his Group 2 distance runners eventually received free running shoes and made at least the minimum contract. This did not necessarily include relay runners, who were pure track guys. But overall, money talked, whether it was for the individual or the club. And GBTC experienced some difficulty in both areas due to departed talent and a depleted treasury. GBTC did benefit from Rodgers, who provided discounts to club members at his Bill Rodgers Running Centers in Faneuil Hall, Cleveland Circle, and Worcester; and the money raised from its annual Freedom Trail Road Race, which was minimal in 1980 because it had no sponsor that year. Squires dealt with a shrinking club treasury of $4,500 in 1980 to $2,000 in 1981. To stay afloat, it was agreed upon to accept sponsorship from PUMA, which provided shoes and other clothing for about two dozen GBTC runners—chosen by the club—to wear in competition and respond to a PUMA questionnaire about its performance.

For the individual, however, there was money on the roads. And those roads were opening wide with more races, especially the marathon. GBTC routinely fielded (and lost) several long-distance runners. Despite its track-club name, the marathon continued to become *the* thing. In 1980 alone, other than in the Boston Marathon and US Olympic Marathon Trials, more than two dozen GBTC athletes competed in a dozen marathons nationwide. GBTC even found its way into the ultra world via Dave McGillivray in the 1980 Ironman Hawaii Triathlon in Hawaii, where he was 14th overall in 11:33:28 (1:30 in the 2.4-mile Waikiki Roughwater Swim; 6:16 in the 112-mile Around-Oahu Bike Race; 3:47:28 in the Honolulu Marathon). Even Rodgers released *Marathoning*, his autobiographical book with local sportswriter Joe Concannon. As a spectator, fan, participant, champion, and GBTC coach, Squires witnessed the sport's meteoric progression from an oddity to a commodity.

"My marathon awareness was very vague when I was young. I would go down to watch Boston, and I respected the people that were running it, but I didn't truly understand it then. I remember, of course, Johnny Kelley, a local Arlington guy that won it twice in 1935 and 1945; Clarence DeMar, who won Boston seven times, but by then he was at the end of his career; and Abebe Bikila (fifth at Boston in 1963). Johnny and I were very good friends. And I ran against Bikila and Mamo Wolde in a 20K race in Cambridge. They gave me a minute-and-a-half start and both of them beat me! But the thought of marathoning—especially in the Sixties, outside of Patriots' Day being a big thing for the press around here in Boston—was a novelty. There were about 20 guys in the press that would write about the winner and the runner-up for a story to tell their newspaper bosses. That was about it back then. I can only think of four marathons in America then—one in the West Coast; Yonkers in New York, which was one month after Boston; the national championship that was bid on and moved around the country; and Boston."

Squires witnessed the marathon's move from being a novelty in the 1960s to a boom in the 1970s and a moneymaker in the 1980s. And along the way expediently arose running magazines to capture and cover this expansion of distance. "There was only one real running magazine that I recall, and it was called *Distance Running News*. It was by Bob Anderson and it started back in 1966 and eventually became *Runner's World* magazine a few years later. There were other magazines that listed race results of all distances and things, like *The Long Distance Log* by H. Browning Ross out of New Jersey, and locally in the New England area there was the *New England Runners' Magazine* by George Conefrey. But as far as a running magazine, *Distance Running News* and *Runner's World* did it up right. They really did. They delved into distance running. The only other thing in the world, written in English, was a phenomenal thing from England that was called *Athletics Weekly*. It started in 1945 and it was very good. Still is."

A longtime voracious reader of anything running related, Squires recalls reading a telling tidbit circa 1979-1980. The article noted that at the time there were more than 140 marathons in the United States and race fields that averaged 3,000 runners. "I flipped when I read that. I had to look again. And then there were letters to the editor a couple issues later that questioned that. And the magazine said that that was the number they had—141 marathons, and fields that were as low as 25 and some as high as 3,080. And I started to see that [trend] at Greater Boston." With the increase of runners, marathons, and interest, television soon joined magazines and focused more on long-distance events. Marathons became high-profile occurrences and provided great visuals and produced an unlimited amount of untapped human tales. But what was sacrificed to make way for this newfound subject? Track and field. "I'll clue ya, TV made the marathon and killed track and field. TV moved right over track and field. There were more people in marathons than in track and field, so TV said, 'See you later!' to track. And the marathon people had a story to tell. They weren't deemed quick, like the track people. With marathoners, it's like, 'How the heck do you run 26 miles?' There's always a story."

But as television, radio, wire, and print marathon coverage grew, Squires saw ignorance of the sport follow. Very few people—whether the media, whose job it was to cover the sport; or spectators on the streets, who were cheering on the athletes—understood long-distance running. A stunningly clear example of this occurred to Rodgers after one of his Boston Marathon wins when during a radio interview the preface to a question included the insulting declaration, "Well, you're not really an athlete, but…" Marathoning was still an enigma. And that began to bother Squires. "With these local media guys, you had Boston in your backyard. But Boston in your backyard was little kids giving water, parents having a picnic, people watching guys from different countries, and waiting for Clarence DeMar and Johnny Kelley. That was it. Then they're hearing about 100-mile weeks and it was mind-boggling. So I told the newspeople when they're talking about it on the radio and TV, try to break it down for the audience. During the marathon, use a stopwatch for each mile when they run so you can tell people how fast they're running each mile. The leaders then averaged 5:00 to 5:10 per mile. And with 100-mile weeks, and some at 110 miles, that's like almost running a marathon a day. But they're running some slower and some faster. I told them they have to explain what's going on. I did this to educate the public."

There were exceptions, Squires recalls, but very few. One was famed *Wide World of Sports* broadcaster Jim McKay, who early on at one New York City Marathon press conference at the Tavern on the Green, approached Squires for an interview. "He was interested. He was. I kind of think because he covered the Olympics and other international events that he had an appreciation about the sport. He asked me about the training and how many miles a day they run; how fast they'd go; how do I pick my athletes; do I look at what they did in college or do I give them a time trial? Very smart questions."

In addition to the fall marathons, September 1980 also featured several cross-country and shorter-distance highlights for GBTC, for both the team and individuals. The start of its eighth cross-country season was a good example of how the club successfully expanded from being a predominantly dominant *team* to also experiencing the byproduct of continuing to provide top *individual* results, as well as a growing strong contingent of female athletes. But the enjoyment of this new height of recognition and achievement was short-lived. After simmering just under the surface for some time, Squires came to a realization—and decision—with his retirement announcement in the club's October 1, 1980, newsletter. It read, in part, "Now it is time for me to move on. I will now assume the coaching position of the 'new club in town'—the New Balance Track Club. I would be happy to be of any assistance to the GBTC and plan to serve as an associate with weekly coaching sessions to start soon for club members so that I can keep tabs on what is going on."

The full-time all-in Squires Era officially ended. He stayed true to his word in respect to offering assistance as a consultant—which he did until the 1984-85 indoors—but as far as that regular direct connection of his constant daily regimen of advice, training, workouts, and contact, that steady thread ended. But his impact remained. "I think this club lived through my experiences. And I'm gonna clue ya, you're as good as your captain. You go to war, you're as good as the guy that leads you. If he knows what's going on, you follow that man. If you see results, fine. I created *the* running system, but I kind of think I came into this too early. If I came later, I kind of think my system would have been [widely] adopted. We went all over the United States and we won every national championship. If there was one, we go. I mean, there were some lollypops that we didn't go to that were too far away and I knew there'd be no competition. I'd send an individual to win the championship, but I'd never send a team for a gimme where no one's going to show."

Over those final years from 1980 to February 1985 with Squires still onboard, GBTC—under various head coaches—still benefited from his system and assistance. The club won its eighth consecutive NAAU 20K cross-country title in 1980; third straight team title at the 1980 New York City Marathon, with Salazar (first), Rodgers (fifth), Oparowski (39th); third consecutive NEAC men's indoor title in 1981; third straight New England men's outdoor title in 1981; ninth consecutive NAAU 20K cross-country title in 1981; the 1982 NTAC 40K Race Walk Championship, with Troy Engle (fifth), Mark Fenton (sixth), Steve Vaitones (14th); the 1984 National 10-Mile RRCA Championship men's and women's team titles; and the women's teams in 1983 were runners-up at the Women's 25K TAC championships, Bonne Bell Mini Marathon 10K (GBTC A team), and New York City Marathon. And former and current Squires-coached athletes Dick Beardsley, Phil Coppess, Hodge, Meyer, Pfitzinger, Rodgers, and Salazar still graced the top of the *Track and Field News* marathon all-time US and world rankings.

"With all of these times, the guys and the women, you can see the improvement. It was because they all did the same workouts in training. It was adjusted for each group, but they were all doing the same. And the results proved it worked. I've always said that. The workouts work. And the women were doing very well. I can remember a time at BoState and Greater Boston when there were no women teams. But now, you see, they warmed up with the guys, and they also did the same thing in their workouts—sometimes they would run distance, sometimes short runs, long runs, track. They did the same thing, but suited for them. And you could see them getting better in races."

For the 1984 US Olympic Trials Marathon, 201 men and 267 women met their respective standards of 2:19:09 (men) and 2:51:16 (women). Of the 37 from Massachusetts, there were 17 former and current Squires-coached athletes: 12 men (Bob Clifford, Hodge, Bob Johnson, Meyer, Don Norman, Oparowski, Andy Palmer, Pfitzinger, Rodgers, Salazar, Dan Schlesinger, Thomas) and 5 women (Posie Barnett, Bray, Susan Lupica, Patricia Meade, Debbie Mueller). In addition, Squires on some level also coached out-of-staters Coppess, John Lodwick, Gerry Vanasse, and Sue King. Of the athletes with a link to Squires or the Bay State, astonishingly nearly 57 percent—21 of 37—one way or another received some kind of coaching from Squires. The top two finishers were Pfitzinger (first) and Salazar (second), who both advanced to the Olympic Marathon in Los Angeles (Pfitzinger was 11th, Salazar 15th). But Squires did regret not being able to qualify one GBTC athlete in particular—Dave McGillivray, whose benevolence in running included the 3,452-mile Run Across America; 1,520-mile East Coast Run to Benefit the Jimmy Fund; 120-mile Wrentham State School 24-Hour Run; 1,575-step Empire State Building Run-up; and the 1,522-mile run-cycle-swim New England Run. "He missed qualifying by less than a minute. I wanted him to make the Trials badly. I worked with him for seven months. But doing the 40 miles a day just wore him out. He had the strength. I worked on him for speed. But I couldn't put him through what I wanted to because of all those miles he did."

Squires always maintained that the athlete—not the coach—should receive the attention. Other than when he spread the word about his runners in pre-race interviews and press conferences, he shunned the post-race limelight. But his reputation always preceded him. At the Bislett Games in Norway, for example, he joined other coaches on the field to watch the events. Henry Rono—two-time 1978 African Games and Commonwealth Games gold medalist and 1978 world record-holder in the 3000-meter steeplechase, 5000, and 10,000—approached Squires. "He comes up to me, which was really amazing, and he says, 'Coach. Toughest American athlete that I've run against—Salazar. Your man. Toughest. Tiger! That between you and me. Just want to let you know. That's what I think. A tiger!' Rono missed running against Steve Prefontaine, but he ran against Steve Scott, Craig Virgin—good ones. That was something." Also at Bislett, just prior to the Dream Mile and 1000, Squires met Steve Scott and Sebastian "Seb" Coe. Their conversation lasted long enough that the Dream Mile was about to begin and Squires ended up holding their warm-up shoes and sweats. "When I took Coe's warm-up shoes and his sweat suit, he yells up to his father, Peter, who was in the grandstand. I turned around and waved. The next night, the father comes up to me and says, 'Hey, Yank. Thanks for doing that.' And we ended up talking about running. I asked him how Seb trained, and he told me. He said his coach kept him on the track and moved him at a good speed around the corners. You see, when I meet someone like that, I want more than just a paw-job, a handshake. I want to talk about things. And we became friends. I remember watching that mile, as a miler, and thinking about when each guy was going to make his move. [New Zealand Olympic gold medalist John] Walker was playing it cool, and they were all staying close. With the crowd noise, you couldn't hear anything. It was just riveting! When it was over, I had to wait until they did the drug test for them to come back. I congratulated them afterwards and said they were great races. And I told Scott he had set the American record."

In a break from training one day during the week before the 1982 Boston Marathon, while at home one afternoon, Squires received a call from the Eliot Lounge. Which was not unusual. He was informed there was a foreign coach looking for him at the bar. Also not unusual. When Squires arrived, he approached a weathered-looking 65-year-old legendary New Zealand coach. "I looked at him and I said, 'You know, you look like Arthur Lydiard.' He said, 'I am.' I didn't know him from a hole in the wall, but I knew of him, and when he opened his mouth and spoke, I knew. I figured he wanted to look over the course. That's why I thought he was there. But he said to me, 'I want to know what do you do to get guys to run 2:08?' I told him about some of the workouts, and he said, 'I read about you.' He told me he's always looking at *Athletics Weekly* and *Track & Field News* to see what college this guy goes to and that guy. He said, 'One guy's a farmer and he lives way the heck out west (Dick Beardsley); one guy's a steeplechaser (Greg Meyer); one guy has terrible form but runs like hell (Alberto Salazar).' I told him about the rhythm that I use in my training, and about the recovery periods I use; he thought that was smart. He also appreciated what I'd done with introducing speed into marathoning. He liked that. And I told him about the simulations I used, the repeats and surges—all the ingredients I use, really. And he understood, of course. And he said, 'A lot of the runners probably don't know your name, Bill, but they know that club of yours in Boston. They ask what the heck do they have up there?

You win and win. I'd always see Greater Boston listed. They know.' I remember telling him what I'd say to my guys—which is a terrible thing to say as a coach—I'd say, 'There are better guys out there than you. You weren't the chosen ones. If I was a college coach or something, I wouldn't have chosen any of you. But now I'd go to war with you because now you're hard, you're tough, and you're winners. And you're a group.' It was a good talk with him. And this was the first time I ever gave up this much of my training. But it was Lydiard! I respected him. To me, he was an average Joe that nobody really respected. He was a lot like me."

The following day at the Eliot, Squires and Lydiard conspired against Tommy Leonard. Squires learned long ago that his good friend, who often professed great athletic knowledge, was an easy target of gullibility. Squires gathered a crowd around Leonard, who unfortunately for him had failed to recognize Lydiard. "I said, 'We have a guest from New Zealand in here. He's a miler and a half-miler coach, and he wants to coach marathoners. Now, I'm not a real good marathoner, but I was a good miler.' I turn to Lydiard and I say, 'How long have you been coaching?' He says for about 40-something years. I said I had close to 30, so that's good. I then told him he had to have distance runs in training and he has to meet them at least two or three days a week. He said he met with his milers three times a week, which I said was good." Squires turned to Leonard and instructed the barkeep to reassure the visitor that he does indeed know of which he speaks. "Tommy goes, 'Oh, yeah. He really does. He's really good at it.' Then I ask Lydiard what kind of milers and half-milers does he have, and he says he has a few good ones. I ask him, 'Can they double?' He tells me one of his guys ran a 1:44 in the half and also ran the 1500 in 3:32. I yelled, 'A 3:32? That's, that's like a 3:51 mile!' We start to laugh," said Squires, who knew Lydiard was referring to John Walker's 1974 bronze-medal Commonwealth Games 1:44.92 in the 800 and 3:32.4 PR in the 1500 in Oslo in 1975. "Then Tommy looks at him and goes, 'What the hell is your name?' When we said Arthur Lydiard, we got two on the house. Tommy had heard of him and had seen pictures of him, but he didn't know that was Lydiard. That was fun."

Around this time, Squires recalls fielding a phone call from Richard Claxton Gregory, a contemporary track-scholarship middle distance runner who ran for Southern Illinois University Carbondale. Gregory was at SIUC from 1951-53, where he was a two-time letter-winner and voted the school's 1953 Outstanding Student-Athlete. After two years in the US Army, he returned to SIUC from 1955-

57, and despite being a letter-winner for a third time in 1956, began a career in entertainment before graduating. "Out of the blue in the sky, I get, 'Hey, Bill. This is Dick Gregory. Remember me?'" Squires said of the noted comedian and civil rights activist. "I said, 'Sure, sure. The 1:52 half-miler.' He asked me about Salazar and the Greater Boston club, and he said he had this miracle juice he wanted to send me. At the time, he was big on nutrition and he wanted to send me this juice," Squires recalls of what became Dick Gregory's Slim-Safe Bahamian Diet Nutritional Drink Mix powder. "I hemmed and hawed about it and finally told him he could, but that I'll give it to the guys and we'll let them fill out the forms on how they feel with it and so on. And I told him that I don't endorse politicians and I don't endorse any products, but I'll give it to them. He said he understood, and only wanted to send six packages for six people. He said he's using all kinds of fruit and fructose and things, and he wanted this thing to go national."

Within the previous 10 years, Gregory had moved to nearby Plymouth, Mass., and started Health Enterprises, Inc., which among other things distributed products for weight loss. "I'm at a meet one day, sometime way after the juice thing, and sure enough, I see Dick coming over. He thanked me again for helping out with the juice and he said that it did well for a little while but it never really caught on nationally, but that it did work. We also talked about his brother," noted Squires of Ron Gregory, seven-time letter-winner at Notre Dame (1957-1961). "Dick reminded me again and brought up the fact that Ron broke the 880-yard Fieldhouse record and set a world record at the same time. And I said, 'Yeah, yeah. I know. We could have used him when I was there.' Dick also told me how tough it was to do that long walk he did across the country, or part of it. He looked kind of thin when I saw him; kind of gaunt as I recall. But it was good to see him."

In the mid-1980s—and by the time he finally departed GBTC after the 1984-85 indoors—Squires had witnessed over a decade of change and tremendous growth in his sport. He was always able to adjust and grow with it, but he became more concerned. At only 52 years old, with more than 35 years of coaching experience, he noticed that this time there were too many outside influences which he felt were not good for running. He first sensed this back in 1980 when he submitted his initial resignation to GBTC—and when he first discussed his views with the AAU—but he remained involved because he felt there was still enough good in the sport. But, he surmised, it was not getting any better. He felt the sport's governing body—Amateur Athletic Union until 1979; The Athletic Congress from 1979-

1992—repeatedly failed to progress out of its archaic ways, and as a result, stunted the growth of many of America's athletes and its programs. By their inaction, he felt, they got in their own way.

"The AAU/TAC didn't get it. They didn't! Whenever you'd bring up something, they'd be like, 'Well, we're going to have a sealed vote.' Or they'd say, 'Parliamentary rules. Robert's Rules are in force. It has to be brought up in the proper form.' That was it! And I heard from a few of the good coaches that said to me afterwards, 'You're totally right. I could see why you wanted to get out.' It was just getting too much." As examples, Squires pointed to the 10K, steeplechase, and triple jump. He felt that outdated outlooks undoubtedly prevented not only countless athletes the opportunity to reach their national and international goals, but it also stifled the possible ascension of potential United States Olympians. All three events were only offered at the end of the season, which made no sense to Squires. "They only had the 10K in the championships and the only reason a kid would run it in their championship was if you wanted to go to the NCAA. But the NCAA standard was a killer. The African and foreign athletes would load up on the 5K and 10K when we didn't. Our kids only had one shot a year. It was ridiculous. And the steeplechase? For years, only a few colleges had that, but they wouldn't even put it in the conference meets. It was only offered in the Olympic years. And the other Orphan Annie—the triple jump—they could have had easily. All you had to do was put in the markings on the same runway as the long jump. It was that easy! And then the AAU/TAC meet was in June, usually two weeks after the college kids had all gone home or were in summer school, and a lot of them didn't go to the AAU/TAC or their own championship."

The overall attitude and lack of foresight and support truly frustrated Squires. "About adding events to the meets they'd say things like, 'It'll be all day long.' If I had a child that was good in the triple jump or the steeplechase or whatever, and they said that to me, I'd go out of my mind. How many athletes did we miss! There were other things, too. Why did we have the six-mile-run in the AAU/TAC meet in the heat in the second week of June at quarter to 12? We needed it either in the morning or after six at night. I remember them saying things like, 'This is a new venue. Should we change what we've had for the last 48 years of the six-mile run, starting at quarter of, so people can watch them run because it starts the meet?' We're talking about running 24 laps in the heat in June! I had one AAU/TAC coach say to me, 'Then the kids should run the 5K instead.' Are you kidding me?

I said to him, 'Do you have cross-country at your school? Yes you do. What's the distance? Five miles! What do you do with the rest of your kids?' He sank after that. It was things like that you had to deal with."

The final straw for Squires came about when his thought-out, detailed plan to create a nationwide system for athletes—which he broke down into regions and events that also included a systematic measure of teaching, evaluation, and results—was met with resistance, and ultimately, apathy. "I made a proposal to the head of the governing board that I wanted to start a grassroots program, similar to what I did at Greater Boston, in six locations in the US that would be utilizing college tracks. It had to be on a national level. And I said I'm sure that the athletic directors and the coaches and the presidents of the colleges wouldn't mind having athletes utilize their tracks in the evenings. And these athletes would not get paid—they could keep whatever monies they had [via other jobs]. They (AAU/TAC) said we have one [program] at altitude at Colorado Springs, and I said that's an altitude one that's fine for that area. But I included the whole nation!"

Squires mapped the country into six separate regions that covered the four disciplines of running and track and field: sprints, hurdles, jumps; middle distance of the half-mile to 5000 meters, and the steeplechase; long distance of the 5K, 10K, marathon; and jumps and throws, such as the javelin and discus. And some of these events would overlap. "The better the region because of things like weather and facilities would determine where some of these events would be." In addition, each region would include one full-time head coach and two part-time assistant coaches in paid staff positions that required them to search for and nurture post-collegiate talent. One tool would be the administration of exams in the colleges and universities that would begin to locate such athletes. "That's how I did it in the city of Boston. How do you think I got so many great athletes at BoState? No one else was doing it. You've got to do these things! You need to pay three coaches to be able to work this properly. The head coach would be working at it all week long. He'd go to junior high schools, high schools, and with the physical education teachers show them how to do a test for the different events, and they'd also put a test out as well on their own. And you're going to pay this guy $50,000 a year, and anything that he sees that's written about this [in the media] he'll put it in whatever material there'd be for the AAU/TAC Grassroots Program. And the two assistants—either high school coaches, or club coaches if they're that good—will work in the area and stay local. I presume they'll be high school or good club coaches and not college coaches because college coaches wouldn't come over and do this. But what they're looking for are the post-collegiate kids in their region and building that up."

Squires even acknowledged that if such a program was instituted and he was asked to become one of those regional coaches, he would not have accepted because he was still a few years away from attaining a full pension from his teaching. "I didn't want to be the czar of this or anything. I said that up front. If I were free, if I wasn't a 20-plus-year professor in college, I wouldn't have minded it. I would have probably taken the Eastern Regional coach's position. And it wouldn't have been in Boston, it probably would have actually been at UMass Boston. They had tons of room there, and hotels and stuff nearby. It could have been done. And I would have relocated. But that wasn't to be."

In addition, athletes would meet predetermined standards in order to "qualify" for this national program. And as a final step in his proposed system, Squires also devised a competition at the end of the season called the National Development Championship held among the six regions. "This would be held two weeks after the nationals and the top two in each event would go over to Europe to represent the United States. I didn't want the studs doing this because they've already got the national championships. This is total development. And from this, they would get times good enough to go big-league. It would have been great."

Squires estimated the cost would have been $2 million (in the 1980s). It was rejected. "They came back with the fact they have television paying them for meets and they have that under-20 college program and all of this and that. And I told them that those are the studs [being covered by TV] and they get older by the year, they disappear, and that's it. And the other good guys *not on TV* are going over to Europe for two races and they're getting run into the ground. We need some kind of program that helps them get there *and* helps get the other talent that's being missed, because we have faded in track since 1964. They said they'd discuss it. And then I went through another round, a second time, with another new guy at the top and it got nowhere. That was it. I said forget it. And it took 26 years before they did something like that program. Twenty-six years! We went down the friggin' tubes by then. The 1980 Olympic boycott set us back years. And what also happened was the world started catching up. The world decided that they had to meet each other more often instead of just seeing each other every four years at the Olympics. There was money in this, too. And what they did was all these little countries went to where the English, French, Germans, and the Belgians, competed every summer. And these guys were getting money under the table," he alleges, "and some of the countries controlled them, so they made money. And all of this made them catch up to us while we just used our college resources. And post-college we had nothing."

In hindsight in regard to leaving GBTC in 1985, "I had wondered then how distance running was going to be without Greater Boston and without me there with that kind of grassroots program I had. It dropped off. Significantly. And I caused it. I could have kept at it at the club. I could have kept at it with the AAU/TAC. But it was just too much. The AAU/TAC was going nowhere. If they had done certain things then, I would have stayed coaching at Greater Boston probably to this day. And I would have had a separate women's coach, like what did happen right after me. But I would have stayed."

As a coach, especially at GBTC, Squires does acknowledge that his approach may be considered somewhat unorthodox for its comedic, loose manner, but that by no means meant he sacrificed professionalism, expertise, and results. "I know that what I coached worked because I'd done it. And each time in practice I would turn the screw a little bit more. And I always kidded and joked so that they'd think I was wacky, because every other coach was vanilla ice cream; I'm sorry, but I'll say it. You need a little flavor. You've got to be fun. You can't have a frown on your face. And don't blame the athlete. They're trying like hell. I hate it when a coach blames an athlete. It's you, the coach, if they don't improve; it's you! You're there to improve them and not to kill them. You've got to be on the same wavelength with them, and a lot of times you'll find out the athletes are working a second job or their father beats up their mother or they have kids at home. It's important to know. I knew so much about my kids because we'd drive in my car back and forth to meets all the time and we'd always talk. Sometimes you'd be one-on-one with a kid and you'd talk about things at home or at school. If you're going to be successful, you have to *know your athletes*; not know your *team*—that's a lot of crap. Know your athletes! Those are the individuals. And be fun."

One of his most important and everlasting impacts, even beyond the stellar lineup of championships and champions, is the number of athletes who became coaches. At one count, from Boston State and GBTC, it was 50, including about 40 in high school, and the others at the college and club level. "That was something I thought was important because I didn't think there were enough good coaches out there when I was in school and when I coached in high school. There just weren't, to be honest. And I'll clue ya, you can run all your life, but you can only race for anywhere between five to eight years, post-college. And some may go for a second Olympics, but after that, you can't really make a living off the roads. But as a coach, you have a better chance and you're helping out the sport and you're developing the younger kids. That's important. At Greater Boston, a lot of them didn't understand what was going on at the time. They'd do what I said, but they didn't get the overall picture of what I was doing. They were good athletes, but they didn't see it like a coach. But then I watched some guys taking other guys in Group 3 and actually bringing them along and training them on the side. I could see the improvement. That was good because that meant those guys figured it out. They knew what I was going for. They got it."

Some of his athletes who had that understanding and went on to coach included Bill Clark, Bob Hodge, Dick Mahoney, Greg Meyer, Don Ricciato, Alberto Salazar, Bob Sevene, Randy Thomas. "I liked being a part of all of that at Greater Boston," Squires reminisced. "I was watching history being made by our club. I knew this. We won every possible road championship in America, every single one. I was watching running history take place. I enjoyed it. I enjoyed the camaraderie, and it didn't matter where—on the track, at meets, on the road, at the Eliot. Oh, there was always something going on at the Eliot!" One night in particular at the Eliot Lounge, Squires noticed someone sitting in his Coach's Corner seat. He looked familiar from a distance, as most people do with Squires. When he got closer, he recognized it was actor Kelsey Grammer, who at the time, on the Boston-based "Cheers" television sitcom, portrayed Dr. Frasier Crane.

"I told him he was in Coach's Corner but that it was okay. He was going to get up, he and his lady friend, but I said it was all right. Eddie Doyle, the bartender at the [Bull & Finch Pub] 'Cheers' place, told him about the Eliot. So Kelsey asks me about the place, if there's a lot of novelty things here with the runners and stories and bar-type things that go on. I said, 'Oh, yeah. One day I brought a horse in.' He goes, 'What!' And he laughs." Squires detailed the various games played at the Eliot— such as a rolling contest on the floor, where people in supine positions moved fast across the floor; banister beer, where patrons slid beers down the banister to see whose traveled the farthest—but it was the horse story that intrigued Grammer. Depending on who you ask but according to Squires, one Columbus Day Monday, a holiday that featured a city parade and the Bonne Bell Mini Marathon, he was on his way back to the Eliot after a run when he came across someone riding a horse. "It was a big white horse with spots, very nice. I talked to the guy and he says they were in the Columbus Day Parade and he was going to get some water for his horse. I said, 'Come on with me.' We're going along and I say, 'How would you like a beer?' And he said, 'Sure.' It was about quarter to 12, and with it being a holiday, there weren't that many people in the Eliot, so I walk in alone and I ask for a pan of water for a horse. They say, 'Coach, what the hell is up? Cut it out.' I said, 'No, really. I have a horse and he needs some water.' They look out the window and they see the horse. So I said, 'The horse needs some water, and I also need a beer for the guy.' They say they can't bring beer out to the street."

With this in mind, Squires informed the rider that water was on its way but not the beer. He looked for a tree or something to which they could hitch the horse, but nothing was suitable. "I ask the guy, 'Can you get the horse in?' He said he could. I open the door and the guy ducks down as he rides the horse in to the Eliot. There were about a dozen people in there and they all look over and they can't believe what they're seeing. Some of them come over and pet the horse, and the guy's talking to everyone. They fill up a thing and the horse is slopping it all up. Then a guy goes, 'I bet it'd like beer.' And the rider says, 'Yeah, a little, but not too much.' So we gave it some beer." As the horse drinks its water and beer from containers on the floor, Squires walked to an Eliot regular who basically lived there, so much so that every night someone either called him a cab or walked him home. He was one of the fixtures. "I think the guy just put his paycheck on the bar each week. He lived pretty close. I even walked him home a few times. His head was down and I don't think he even saw the horse come in. So I go over to him, the horse is a few feet away, and I get the horse to come over right next to the guy. His head is right next to the horse's head and I nudge the guy. When he opens his eyes and looks up, right into a horse, he screams! That was the funniest thing. And I said to him, 'This is a horse for you.' He couldn't believe it. We finally get the horse out, which took a lot. He was stubborn. But later, I started to think about it. I guess it wasn't the best thing to do. I mean health-wise with the board of health, you can't even bring dogs in. But it was funny."

In addition to equine, politicians, celebrities, notables, marching bands, and the famous and not-so famous to visit the Eliot were also various members of Boston's pro sports teams. In the mid-1970s it was not uncommon to see Red Sox pitcher Bill Lee enjoy his libation. On game days! "He'd always come in. Especially during rain delays. He'd sneak out of Fenway, usually in his uniform, and get to the Eliot while the game was still delayed. We're that close to the ballpark. And Tommy'd have a beer ready for him. I'll clue ya, you could always hear him coming with those damn cleats. I think he may have put a jacket on, but you could always tell it was him—it was his Red Sox jacket!" A fan favorite, nicknamed "Spaceman" for seemingly obvious reasons, the outspoken and unconventional 1973 all-star pitched for the Red Sox from 1969 to 1978, which included the 1975 World Series. There was a photo on the Eliot wall of Lee, outfielder Bernie Carbo, and fellow hurlers Ferguson Jenkins, Jim Willoughby, and Rick Wise, known collectively as the Buffalo Head Gang for their oft-public disagreement with manager Don Zimmer. "I'd tell him about running; he'd show me how to throw a curveball. He had names for them, his pitches!"

CHAPTER 14

BOSTON

Squires's impact, connection, and relationship with the Boston Marathon and its governing B.A.A. is multifaceted and never-ending. He joined the B.A.A. in the 1950s, competed for them into the 1970s, coached numerous winners in the 1970s and 1980s, guided the invited elite athletes in the 1990s and 2000s, and continues to field questions and requests about the 42 kilometers stretching from Hopkinton to Boston.

During his tenure at GBTC alone, he produced an unprecedented string of remarkable achievements in the Boston Marathon. In the 11 editions while he coached GBTC, from 1974 to 1984, seven were won by Squires-coached runners. Seven! Three of those years featured a stunning accomplishment never seen before nor since, and most likely never will again: six of the top eight places in 1978; four of the top 10 in 1979; the top four in 1982. Collectively over his 11-year span, 27 athletes who Squires coached had top-10 finishes. In eight of those 11 years, the first American to finish was at one time coached by Squires. Not only was there the great number of wins, but there were the times. Up to and including the 2010 Boston Marathon—nearly three decades after Squires left GBTC—four of the top five on the All-Time Top American Men at Boston list ("who have run the fastest times," according to the B.A.A.) and four of the top seven on the All-Time Top Times by American Men at Boston list ("the fastest times run by American men"), were coached by Squires! And as of the 2019 Boston Marathon—35 years after his GBTC retirement—four of the top 10 on the All-Time Top American Men at Boston list and four of the top 11 on the All-Time Top Times by American Men at Boston list, were coached by Squires. And regarding team titles, GBTC under Squires won two and came in third once. No other club, team, coach, or even *country*, can claim all of these distinctions.

At one time, while in his 20s, Squires was one of the B.A.A. members who helped with the mail and Boston Marathon applicant envelopes and assisted the typist with the entrants—name by name—and aided Jock Semple. Thanks to Walter A. Brown—B.A.A. president and Boston Garden manager who owned the Celtics and Bruins—Semple was also the trainer of both teams and had an "office" in the Garden. Squires often saw Semple come in and out of the rooms as he collected the entry fees and grumbled in his hard Scottish accent that the number of predicted finish times on the applications never came close to the final results. "He was funny. He wasn't a coach—he'd just tell his guys, 'Run hard. Run hard.' And he wasn't a certified trainer, he was grandfathered in, but he eventually got to be an assistant on the road games. But his duties were to control the B.A.A. Marathon and the B.A.A. runners, and give them water and a rubdown and make sure they got to the races. That's what Walter Brown said. He said, 'My father (George V. Brown) was big in this, and I'm taking over, so Jock has to do this. I'm more of a hockey guy, so it's up to Jock.' And that's what he did. Even when there was a fire at the old Boston Arena, where Jock was, Walter made sure there'd be space for him at the Garden."

Squires, Semple, and other staff were squirreled away in little spaces at the Garden where Semple administered those rubdowns and massages. During this time, the B.A.A. did not have an official location (the clubhouse was razed in 1961, years after the B.A.A. filed for bankruptcy and sold it to BU), so Semple's place of work doubled as Marathon headquarters. But that was manageable then, since the fields for decades were small. "I'd take the applications and money into Celtics' coach (and general manager Arnold) 'Red' Auerbach's office because he had the safe in there. And Red would say, quickly, 'Hi, kid. How ya doin'?' And I'd tell Red that Jock wanted me to put the money and applications in his office, and Red would joke that he'd take a few of them out. Jock's office was at an angle to Red's, so you just walked in. And I'd see all the guys there, too. Tommy Heinsohn and Jim Loscutoff of the Celtics liked Jock, and all the Bruins loved him. I'd see Bobby Orr in there all the time because he was always banged up. And Johnny Most was always around."

Hired in 1953 by Walter A. Brown and Auerbach to replace Curt Gowdy for radio play-by-play, Most was the animated and cigarette-smoke-induced raspy-edged voice of the Celtics for nearly 40 years. A permanent fixture at the Garden and its replacement—two months after he retired, and two years before he died, his microphone was affixed near his regular broadcast spot in his honor—the former World War II B-24 gunner also hosted a radio show. And Squires was often a guest. "Those were good shows, about two hours, and we'd get calls in. One caller was [World Golf Hall of Famer Pat Bradley's father] Dick Bradley, who joked around about all the times he let me run on his golf course in Winchester and that I should thank him for my success. Johnny loved it. Another time, I went on the show and one of the first things I do is ask Johnny about being the backup quarterback at the University of Alabama. He liked that and said that it didn't last and he eventually played as a linebacker at Brooklyn College. 'Pretty good for a little Jewish kid,' he said. Later on we talked about the war because we both were involved in the air wing in one way or another. He said he flunked the pilot's exam, but was small enough to be able to crawl into the gunner's seat, which is what he was. And he was on about 30 combat missions and he got several medals. I mean, this is Johnny Most! The guy everyone knows with the gravelly voice on the games! And most people didn't know some of the things he did for this country. He was a great man."

Another fixture Squires often saw at the Garden was John Kiley, the decades-long organist who provided the music for the Bruins and Celtics games, as well as at Fenway Park for the Red Sox. At one hoop game in particular, Squires brought his eldest son to Game 7 of the 1965 NBA Eastern Division Finals, between Boston and Philadelphia (the game in which Most made his famous call of John Havlicek's game-saving steal for Boston). "For games, I was always able to get in and find a seat, even if it was sold out. Didn't matter. For this game, we got in, but there was nothing around. Nothing! Kiley ends up walking by and I introduce him to my son, and John says we can come up and stay with him while he plays. And he has a great view of the Garden from his corner. He can see everything. So he tells my son, 'Okay, what you're going to do is people are going to throw notes down to me to play, and some will have money with it. I get requests all the time.' Sure enough, we get there and all night long there are pieces of paper and dollar bills and things being thrown down from the seats above because you can't really get to him easy, so all these things are being thrown down to him. It was crazy! But my son would line them up on the organ and Kiley would mostly play by memory. And of course, as the trivia question goes, he is the only person to play for the Red Sox, Celtics, and Bruins. And the game was wild, of course. We won!"

As the Boston Marathon began to steadily grow in the late 1960s, so did the concern for its integrity. In addition to Squires's official and unofficial input and involvement with his acts of benevolence over the years—mile markers; certified course race officials; wheelchair entrants—there are the always-controversial qualifying time standards that can be partially attributed to Squires (unofficially), Semple (officially), and Cloney (officially). For the 1970 race, to reduce the number of entrants to those who could actually successfully complete the 26.2 miles, introduced for the first time was a qualifying standard: a runner had to show medical proof he could finish Boston within four hours. When that did not quite work—the measure actually increased interest and the field—the following year was introduced a qualifying standard of having to run a previous race within a certain allotted time: either a marathon under 3:30, a 20-miler under 2:30, a 15-miler under 1:45, or a 10-miler under 1:05 (Squires explained that the accommodation of shorter distances was due to the lack of marathons at the time). "I'm sure there are more people saying, 'That son of a bitch! He did that?' I started that with Jock and Cloney. We bitched about it to have people run a certain time to get into Boston because we saw so many guys that would go out like crazy and they would be picked up by a car and that would be the end. They'd go as far as six or seven miles and have their fraternity friends pick them up. It was a sin! This is a real, real, honest, big race. People are coming from all over the world to finish in the top five. That was a big thing in the world and they knew it was the toughest. And we've got applejacks out there; guys with Superman outfits on! So that was it. Also, I didn't want anyone to die out there. I thought Boston was that hard, especially on a hot day. Just imagine the 'Run for the Hoses' in 1976 when Jack Fultz won. It was over 100 degrees out and almost half of the field of about 2,000 quit. How many more would there have been if they were untrained? I also bitched about having coaches with the charity programs. Those runners would never make the standards, so I kept at it to get coaches for them. And now they do. That's good."

Then there were the scarce course amenities. When Jerome Drayton won the 1977 Boston, he publicly commented afterward about the lack of mile markers and water stations, a long-standing fact of the race. Having it aired was embarrassing enough, but when it came from the newest Boston champ and three-time Fukuoka Marathon winner, it was time it should be addressed. The only official mile markers on the course appeared at distances such as 4.25 in

Ashland, 9.75 in Natick, 17.75 on Commonwealth Avenue at the beginning of the Newton hills, largely due to the early years when checkpoints aligned with train stops along the course for easy accessibility for race officials to get on and off the train. "I'll clue ya, the Marathon was run as an afterthought. It was like, 'Oh, the B.A.A. track meet's over with. It's the spring? Time for the Marathon.' It didn't take much planning back then. And most guys that ran the Marathon figured out certain landmarks along the way—10K was somewhere near Framingham Square; 10 miles was in Natick Center; 30K was before Heartbreak Hill. But Drayton waited until he won it to say something. He said that having run internationally, he'd seen that they put down the kilometer or mile marks. And the press is eating this up because they have a story. It was Drayton that forced the B.A.A. to put down mile markers. But they didn't do it right away." Squires did. "Yeah! We did this on a Sunday. I got a five-gallon bucket of white paint and I got two of my cross-country/steeplechase athletes and we cleared the odometer of my car and left from the start. We didn't do anything at the start or anything until three miles. We painted a three, a five, and so on—fairly good-sized numbers on the flat area of the road, the crown, so everyone could see it. We finally get down to Brookline with about three miles to go—around 23 miles, somewhere in Coolidge Corner—and some guy comes out and yells at me, 'Hey, what are you doin'? I'm calling the cops on you!' I didn't care. If they jailed me, it's already done. And we were actually only going to do one more by then—at 24 miles. We weren't going to do one with one mile to go because everyone knows that one. So we were done by then. And we were pretty close with the markers because when the B.A.A. did it the next year, it was close."

Squires was also able to run Boston several times after his first one in 1961. Ten years later, he returned in 1971 with a 2:57:51 for 210th place overall (he only lost about a minute a year). In 1978, after the governing amateur rules were relaxed, he once again ran Boston. But the reason this time was different. This time it was on a dare with his GBTC athletes that originated where most things of import did back then—the Eliot Lounge. "We were talking about this guy somewhere in Western Massachusetts that ran a marathon in 2:58 and I made some comment like, 'Well, that's okay.' Then they said he was 42 or 44 years old, and they asked if I thought that was good. And I said, 'Yeah.' Then they asked what I thought I could run it in and I told them that I could run it in at least three hours. And I meant it." Squires was 45 and this was December 1977—*four months* before Boston. "I said, 'Yeah.

The beer ain't talking. I can do it.' And when they asked if I could do it in Boston, I said I could. They told me I couldn't, so I said, 'If I do, it'd be worth my money. Twenty dollars a head.' And with that we grabbed the spittoon from above the bar, which they had to dust off, and they all put an IOU in with their names and I had my wallet and I put my money in."

Even though it was Squires who coached many of them to prominent times and results, they still felt incredibly confident he could never run a sub-3:00 Boston Marathon. At 45! "Anything I say [for workouts], I've done it and can do it. They were saying that I never do any of the stuff they do, like on the long runs I just warm up with them and jump in my car and go back to meet them later. Well, that was it. The bet was on." And so was the training. One constant was that Squires made sure he trained over the Newton hills. He knew every inch of them. "I figured I'd have to live on the course twice a week, but I'm not going to go over to my guys when they were out there because I didn't want them to think they helped me at all. And I'd pray that I wouldn't see Rodgers or anyone on the course. So I'd go up there at night. I'd park in Newton and I'd run all the way to the course and I'd run down Market Street—a bitch of a mile down—and I'd cut over to my car. It was a 13-mile run and it was hard. We didn't have the clothes we have now, so I'm wearing double sweats, at night, and by myself. I finally talked this guy into running long runs with me on Sundays. And my guys would ask me about my training and I'd tell them it's going well. They'd ask me where was I training and I said it was a secret." He laughed. "Oh, boy! It was on!"

One New England winter day in early February 1978, Squires scheduled a 20-plus-mile out-and-back from his home in Everett to the outskirts of Nahant, along the Atlantic Ocean's Massachusetts Bay shorelines of Broad Sound via Revere Beach. On his drive home before the run that Monday, February 6, TV news forecast a blizzard, which had reportedly already begun. But as the skies did not seem threatening at the time, Squires brushed it off with typical Puritan aplomb. "I wanted to get a hard run in and that afternoon they said we're *into* a blizzard. I kind of laughed. A blizzard could be anything—10 inches, a foot, two feet. The weather guys always say that to cover themselves. One guy did go out on a limb, but all the other guys didn't. When I started at four o'clock in the afternoon, there was maybe a quarter-inch of snow on the ground. I did the shortcut down to the beach and then it started coming down like fluff. Big flakes." As he continued, it occurred to him how cold and overcast and snowy it quickly became. His thin gloves were no match for the onshore winds. But as a hardy New Englander, he thought the cold, windy, and snowy conditions along the water were not out of the ordinary. He thought no more of it until the cold turned to a chill; the flakes of snow began to heavily multiply; and the wind rapidly picked up. Still, as a runner in these parts, mileage through snow is par for the course. "I was dressed warm, but then it was sleeting and the wind was blowing in my face. I just wiped my face off with my gloves. When I hit Revere Beach, to pass the time I started to think about a person that I like, friends of mine, and I figure no one goes straight up to heaven [without help], so I say to myself that I'm offering this run up to this person or that person. I do this every day. And usually it's always someone I knew in the running community. And I think about them as I run and I think of some funny things, to pass the time."

On this particular run, who came to mind was Jim Hayes, a childhood friend who at the time was dying of cancer. As each frigid and snow-filled mile went by, pockets of memories of his pal surfaced. Good memories. "My hands are freezing and I was going to turn back at the end of the ocean. It was a bitch at the ocean. And there were no cars! I kept wondering why there were no cars—I saw, maybe, 10 cars in total—and people would tell me, 'It's an emergency!' I'd see a plow occasionally and I'd see the blue lights of the police around. So I'm wondering if I should go on the causeway there, so I stayed on the opposite side because the tide was coming in and waves were slapping up against the storm wall." Snow steadily accumulated; wind continually pushed; and the cold grew more bitter. He decided to turn around halfway down the beachfront. To top it all off, his thin gloves became solid as sweat and melted snowflakes solidified. "I had frostbite in college, so I know what that feels like. I could feel it coming. But I was looking forward to having the wind and snow at my back as I go home. So I'm talking to my buddy, you know, I'm talking to Jimmy about my hands and whatever and I look to the ground, and I swear on my mother's honor, I see something blue on the ground up ahead. It's a large mitten! And then just a little bit ahead is the other one. I pick them up and they're dry. I take my gloves off and I put them on. Oh, boy, were they dry! Inside was fur-lined or something like that. Jimmy Hayes—divine intervention with those gloves!" Any thoughts of turning back were replaced by a newfound shot of adrenaline and determination to finish what he started. And so he continued. All the way to the US Coast Guard Station on Short Beach along Nahant Bay and Broad Sound. "I said to myself, 'Well, there's no excuse now for me not to finish.' The minute I turned, the wind was at my back. I'm running and running and I am exhausted. I think I was running for three hours."

When he finally returned home, he discarded his double set of wet clothes, and in his draws turned on the radio and dropped into bed. He half-listened to the snow-emergency announcements that cars will be towed and classes that evening and the following day cancelled. When he awoke nearly 14 hours later, it was late Tuesday morning. Unbeknownst to him, while he slept, it continued to snow. "I had the day off from teaching at BoState, so I went out to get the paper and I couldn't open my friggin' door! I was snowed in! I had to go out through a window in the back. The snow was so high that I'm going through part of a snow tunnel out my window. I finally get out, but then I realize I don't have a shovel. It's in my car. Then I can't find my car. It wasn't there, so I climbed back into the house and I got snow all over the floor. I put on the radio and I hear about the blizzard. The Blizzard of '78, they call it."

And it was deadly. According to the National Oceanic and Atmospheric Administration, it snowed for nearly 33 straight hours in the Boston area, which received a 107-year snowfall record of just over 27 inches. Gusts of wind peaked at nearly 80 mph and tides were above normal levels by 16 feet. Motorists were stranded on highways; homes and buildings severely damaged; widespread power outages occurred; and public transportation was at a standstill. A state of emergency was declared by Massachusetts Gov. Michael Dukakis. In addition to the various towns, cities, and state services, further assistance was provided by the Federal Emergency Management Agency, US Army Corps of Engineers, American Red Cross Disaster Services, and the Massachusetts National Guard. Squires finally found and dug out his car. He also responded to the call for people to help those in need, as the Revere Beach area, like most oceanfront locales, was hit hard. The majority of the protecting seawall was damaged or washed away, as were numerous residences and businesses.

Just hours after his long run and sleep, "I remember seeing, literally, fish and lobsters and shells in the snow and on top of these big piles of snow on the sidewalks and streets. No kidding! And all these people were putting them in bags to eat. The fish were all frozen, so why not? There were so many people whose houses were just gone. They needed anyone who could get out of their house to report to the striptease joint at the corner of the beach. That was where you reported to help rescue people. The strip club! I went in there and it was so cluttered. They had cleared the big round bar area and the stage to bring in the people. We went over to houses in those military boats to get people. We'd yell out from the boats if there were any disabled people or veterans or kids. We'd go back and forth—we'd pick them up and bring them back to the strip club. The guy who ran it, along with the Red Cross there, had warm soup and coffee and muffins and blankets. The guy served what he had until there was nothing left. And the dancers were there helping out and they still had on their flimsy outfits, but they were covered up. Everyone pitched in." Food at home for Squires consisted of soup, bread, and peanut butter and jelly. (About eight weeks after the Blizzard of '78, Jim Hayes at 42 succumbed to cancer. Eight years later, Squires met up with his widow and daughter for dinner. "I had washed the mittens and put them in a box. I told them the whole story of my run in the snow and the perfectly warm and dry mittens on the ground. I gave them the box and I said, 'Can you believe this? Something Jimmy sent me.' I was thinking of the daughter, actually. She opens it up, and it was like a rainstorm—we all cried.")

As the 1978 Boston Marathon grew closer, and the training more difficult during a record New England winter, Squires refocused. It then occurred to him, quite ironically, in fact, that he had to qualify. He was worried about that because of his lack of training. "I thought to myself that I have a predicament. I wasn't ready. I knew I could get a waiver, but I'm the damn guy who helped put the time standards into Boston! Who could I ask for a waiver?" He settled on the Plodders Marathon in Foxboro, southwest of Boston. And it turned out to be yet another horrible winter day to run. "After all the snowstorms, we did have a pleasant few weeks. But that morning there was about half an inch of snow on the ground and by the time I got there, probably an inch. It's blowing, it was very cold, and there was sleet. I dressed well—double sweats, three layers on top, and Jimmy's mittens. But it got slushy on the course, which went around a lake about five times. I was overly rested because of snow days. I didn't really tone down for the race. I think I had a 12-mile run that Wednesday with two days of recovery on the Marathon course."

The beginning of Plodders was difficult to handle because of the freshly fallen snow and developing slush. Wind off the lake blew snow onto the course, the loop of which grew worse with each lap. "Everyone seemed to follow the tracks of whoever broke the path. We were all running on one little path. No one wanted to go into new snow because then you'd be getting a drag. By the second or third lap it was muddy and slushy. So I just stayed with a guy for the first few laps. And with each lap I would throw off a piece of clothing. There was a guy there giving out times at each lap and there was a pile of clothes near him. I felt bad for the bare-legged runners because all the slush and mud would get kicked up on their legs." For the last two laps, with about nine miles remaining, Squires picked up the pace. It was also a bit easier to run at this time because runners were more spread out along the course, and other than the occasional passing of a runner, the path ahead was clear. The sun started to appear and the snow melt, so more people came out to watch. After the final lap the course veered off the lake and through a gate for the last half-mile to the parking-lot finish. "The minute I come off the gate, the timing guy's cheering me on. Then there's a police car there with his lights on and when he sees me he puts on his siren. I'm 45 years old at the time and I know I'm going to win the masters division, and geez, he's going to make a big production out of it. People are coming out to watch me now and I finish and I break a tape at 2:50:03. I look at my Mickey Mouse watch and I see that the time's wrong. Oh, well!"

When he finished, Squires had no time to waste. He had a scheduled construction side job in Boston at the WBZ-TV station on Soldiers Field Road. Time was of the essence. He walked to the building near the finish line and was greeted by a few runners who asked how he did. "I told them I didn't know because the timer out there is wrong, but I won my division. Now I have to get to my car and get to work at 'BZ by two o'clock. I only had about an hour and a half to shower, change, and to get to Boston." Although he cleaned up afterward, Squires looked dirty because he changed into his old beat-up work clothes. But he finally confirmed he did indeed beat three hours. "After I found that out, I had to go. I started to leave and they asked me where was I going. I told them I have to get to a job, and they said I couldn't go. I said, 'Look, one of you guys can take home my masters trophy and I'll get it later.' They told me again that I couldn't go." As he tried to leave, Squires was summoned for pictures, so he quickly made his way to the awards area and notified the organizers that he really had to leave after the photos. "They said, 'Oh, no. You can't go now. You won the race.' I said, 'I know. I won the masters.' He says, 'No, you *won* the race!' I told them I thought there were guys ahead of me that I didn't catch on the last loop. They said they were behind me, and some guys dropped out. I ran 2:50:03 and I won! I win the thing!" Suddenly, Squires was at a loss. The victory began to sink in, but so was the importance of not being late, especially since he had the only key to get into the offices once inside the building.

Ninety minutes later, he was in Boston with sledgehammer in hand for heavy demolition work. While he helped destroy the station's interior, he reminisced to himself about another side job he had at WBZ-TV years earlier. It was during the days of the "Big Brother Bob Emery" show in the 1950s and 1960s, which started in the 1920s as a radio program by Claire Robert "Bob" Emery, whose "Small Fry Club" show in the 1940s was one of the first-ever network television children's shows that aired each weekday; and "Boomtown," a western-themed children's show on weekends from the 1950s to the 1970s that was produced locally and hosted by the legendary Rex Trailer. "Back then [during those shows] I had a great job driving the films back and forth three nights a week. I would pick up the film canisters at the airport—which at that time only had three terminals—and then bring them to the studio where those shows were filmed. And I'd see all the stars, and even Rex's horse that was there. Rex was an old-time rodeo guy that worked with Gabby Hayes from the movies. And he had his 'Rex Trailer's Boomtown' show there. And you know the name of his horse? It's Goldrush. Ol' coach knows all." He laughs.

After the Plodders win, much to the delight of Squires the results were published in the newspaper. At the following regular GBTC session, he played it cool, knowing full well that his guys read all about the surprise victory. "As we warm up at the Tuesday practice, when everyone usually talks about their war stories from what everyone did over the weekend, I wait a little bit before I say anything. Then I walk up to them and everything goes quiet. And I say, 'How we doing? So, you read anything in the papers?' They all looked around at each other and then we all laughed. Then they say it probably wasn't measured right or it was a short course and so on." Still in the moment, Squires goes down the line of those gathered, which included Rodgers, Thomas, Hodge. "So I say, 'Okay, I won a marathon. Rodgers—you've won a few. Randy—you won one. Hodgie—no, you never have. Well, keep at it.' They were all laughing and then they said I'd never break three hours at Boston. Little did they know, I was on the hills on the course twice a week."

At the 1978 Boston Marathon, Squires ran an impressive bet-winning sub-3:00 time of 2:48:29 for 1,011th place. At 45 years of age, his time was just 43 seconds off his 1961 result, when he was 17 years younger. As was customary,

Squires and company met up at the Eliot Lounge for their post-race gathering. While he made sure there was no advance billing in the newspapers of him being in the Marathon, at the Eliot afterward he certainly made sure everyone knew about his result. "I didn't want to have that in the papers in case I screwed this up. Well, when I came into the Eliot, I went to my guys and they all asked how I did. And I told them 2:48. They go, 'What?' I said, "Yeah, and I screwed up. I should have done 2:45.' They're all looking at me and they're saying nothing. And they're probably all thinking that I'm never going to let them forget about this. Which I didn't. You see, they never thought I'd do it. But it was all in fun." And it occurred to him that most of his guys had forgotten—conveniently—about the pile of IOU notes. "I get the spittoon that we were putting our money in. I dump it out and there was, like, one 20 and two 10s, and the rest were the friggin' IOUs. And the 20 was mine! I'm like, 'You bastards! You had 12 weeks!' I said to them, 'I was going to give a hundred and you were going to have the horse's laugh. So I've got the horse's laugh now.' And they were like, 'Oh, Coach, we'll buy you the drinks tonight.' I said, 'You're damn tootin' you're buying tonight.' They all laughed."

Squires actually successfully coached himself, a feat not that common or successful in running circles. He coached himself in training and during the race, and he benefited from the countless hours and miles he spent on the course as a runner and a coach. And this included his many unorthodox yet well-known experiments and analysis, such as his tangent test. Years earlier, one Sunday morning with GBTC, Squires wanted to show where best to run the various undulations of the course. In Wellesley Lower Falls, he used a tennis ball to visually explain his theory. "They always wanted to run in the middle of the road. Frig that! The middle is useless. The middle has a crown. It's the highest point of the course. I told them I wanted to prove they had to go to the left side or the right side of the route, depending on the curve or the hill. And after a while, you can train your eyes to look over and know where you want to run. I said to these guys, 'You people are in the top 10 or 12, you're not in with the nerdlings!' They said they wanted to hang with that line [on the road]. 'To heck with that line.' I told them to go where you're going to get flat roads." On Washington Street, between miles 14.5 and 15 of the Boston Marathon course, he bent over and released the tennis ball, and along with his athletes watched it follow the natural slant of the road. "It started down the middle of the course and then it went toward the right side and then eventually it went to the curve. I proved it. I said to them, 'You see

where that ball is going?' And I remember them saying, 'Oh, cut it out. Now you're going to be a scientist!' But I explained to them they don't want to have their feet going up and down, up and down. Find the flat areas."

Four years after his 1978 run was another watershed Boston for Squires, but as a coach. Four of the pre-race favorites for the 1982 Boston Marathon had coaching ties to him: Beardsley, John Lodwick, Rodgers, Salazar. The tight head-to-head duel was predicted to be between Rodgers and Salazar. Despite the fact Rodgers was third the previous year, he was still "King of the Roads" with four Boston wins. And Salazar came off two New York City Marathon victories. Between their Boston and New York wins alone, the two former GBTC runners shared the previous six New York titles (Rodgers won 1976-79, Salazar 1980-81) and Rodgers won three of the previous four Bostons (1978-1980). Fittingly, the bib numbers at Boston reflected their standings: Rodgers, 1; Salazar, 2. But it was the wearer of bib number 3 who was in the battle at the end. Beardsley, a lanky farm boy from Minnesota who caught the attention of Squires, had cracked the 1981 *Track & Field News* Men's Marathon All-Time US Top 10 Rankings (fourth) and World Top 10 Rankings (ninth). "I remember sending Dickie shoes in 1979 when I first started working a little with New Balance then. I contacted New Balance about him and I told them he's not good enough to be on the radar yet, but he needs good shoes. Anytime I'd see anyone that looked fairly good, I'd mention it to them, like I did with Dickie."

While he worked part-time at New Balance, some of the services Squires provided included instruction at seminars and clinics, and occasionally he answered questions that were sent to the shoe company's information network. "When I finally met Dickie in person, he told me he had already asked me a few questions over a period of time on the New Balance network. I didn't remember them. But Garry Bjorklund asked me to keep an eye on him and help him out. Dickie couldn't even get the low-end $25,000 contract with his times, but he's following me around and talking to me all the time." Squires became Beardsley's coach. And they also became the best of friends. In an early stage of their relationship, when they shared a house with other runners for the Falmouth Road Race in Cape Cod, Mass., the night before the race Squires discovered that Beardsley decided to stay awake the entire night due to a lack of an available bed. He gave his to Beardsley, who later found out that Squires slept in the bathtub! "He had to run the next day," said Squires, "not me."

Beardsley also told him that Bjorklund mentioned Squires could get him into the 1980 New York City Marathon and that Squires could put together a successful training program. This was news to Squires. But it was also possible. "This was in August! And New York was in late October! So I gave him Billy-boy's nine-week program. I based it on that the kid had to do long runs with pickups, baby tempos, and that was all—don't go with Bjorklund doing speed! I talked him through it so he could see what he had to do to move up to the next thing—six minutes steady; then seven minutes steady, which is tempo; then 10 minutes steady, which is when you're three-quarters of the way through the race when you can start with the small pickups. Then he would be able to increase his speed because he'll be able to run when he's tired and still do these one-minute, two-minute drills. But I told him he had to follow exactly like I have it. And he said fine." With Beardsley in Minnesota, which was not ideal, most training was delivered via phone and mail from, as Squires recalls, "my 'office' phone at the Eliot Lounge—their payphone. And I wrote a lot of things on their napkins and mailed them to Dickie."

Squires also instructed Beardsley to call him every three weeks to check in with updates, which he faithfully did. And the exuberance over the phone was palpable as Beardsley excitedly informed Squires of marked improvements in the training and race wins, to the point that Beardsley always found it difficult to go to bed after the calls. "He would call me and he would be high with excitement. He'd often say that when he hung up, he couldn't wait to run. I remember him saying that he didn't want to call me too late at night because then he couldn't get to sleep because he was all ready to run."

When it got closer to New York, Squires with Beardsley traveled to scout the course. While this was the 11th year for the New York City Marathon, it was only the fifth time the route traveled through the five boroughs of the city. "I had to do that at night; the course! At night! I'm going along, with Dickie in my car, and I'm getting honked at all the time. These people are used to parking in the middle of the street, driving wherever they want. There are some places you just don't want to be at night in New York. There are a lot of nice areas, but there are also places we just didn't want to stop." Race day, Beardsley was among the likes of champions Amby Burfoot, Drayton, Fultz, Kardong, Rodgers, and Salazar, the latter of whom brazenly predicted a sub-2:10. Squires waited along First Avenue in Manhattan, some 16 to 18 miles in. "I had my trusty transistor radio with a little earpiece in, listening to the race. And then I hear there're some runners down—the leaders—and I'm like, 'Oh, geez!' That happened over the bridge—someone had tripped and a few guys went down. But they got up." Beardsley was indeed among those involved, and subsequently lost some ground when he fell on the Queensboro Bridge. And instead of gradually reclaiming his place, as Squires would have preferred, Beardsley stepped it up to get back to where he was within the lead pack that included Salazar, Rodgers, and Jeff Wells, among others. Awaiting on First Avenue, Squires finally saw the leader exit the bridge. It was Beardsley!

"I had my AAU official's jacket on, so I pushed my way underneath the rope, ran out to Dickie on the course, and said to him, 'Dickie, what the hell are you doing?' He tells me he's feeling great. I say, 'Dickie, you've got nine, 10 miles to go, now use your head.' I didn't like him trying to catch up after going down because he had all those miles to go. I was running with him on First Avenue, telling him these things, and then I realize I don't know where I am when I finally stop." At the finish, two of the top five, and three in the top 10, were runners Squires had coached: Salazar (first at 2:09:41), Rodgers (fifth), Beardsley (ninth).

A few months after New York, Squires answered a call from England. In what started out as a solicitation for Rodgers to run a first-time marathon in London turned into a once-in-a-lifetime opportunity for Beardsley to make his mark internationally at the inaugural London Marathon, to be held in March 1981. On the other end of the call was Chris Brasher, its founder/race director. "He asked if Rodgers could run it, and I told him that he was all locked up in Boston. When he asked if I had anyone else, I told him about Dickie. I told him that he came from 2:28 to running 2:14. I said that he is raw, but I really feel he can run very, very well. And I said to Chris, 'I am so sure of him that if he bombs out, I will send you back the cost of his plane fare.'"

Squires learned about the new course, which was relatively flat, but included some narrow portions and even a stretch of cobblestones near the Tower of London. The finish was on Constitution Hill, at Buckingham Palace and Green Park. "Cobblestones beat the heck out of your legs, and if it ever rains or sleets, you're done. So I started to intensify the program for Dickie. I didn't have to worry about the distance because he's another distance freak that would go 110, 120 miles a week. But I didn't incorporate anything on the track then. That would come later because he needed groups to run with and times when he could only run on his own. I would give him August to November in how I would integrate speed. But Dickie had vision. He could see where the training was going. He could see it coming together. And he had natural strength—I think it was all farmwork from lifting hay, grain, baby heifers. And he ate right."

Squires did not make the trip to England with Beardsley, but he advised him to stay in the top five throughout the race and to remember the workouts, especially [how it feels] when he was within the last 10 to 11 minutes of speedwork. He coached that it *will* translate to the marathon. And in a superb 2:11:48, Beardsley and Norwegian Inge Simonsen held hands and simultaneously crossed the finish line to share the first win. Soon thereafter, Brasher phoned Squires with the good news. "He calls me and I go, 'I hope I don't have to send you Dickie's plane fare.' And he just starts to laugh. He put Dickie on the phone and he tells me all about it. He did a good job. And he finally got a contract from New Balance." In 1981 alone, Squires's marathon training helped power Beardsley to CR wins in London and Grandma's in Minnesota, two second-place finishes in Houston and Stockholm, and third place in Beppu-Oita in Japan. And three months before the 1982 Boston Marathon, he was second at Houston. But that was not enough. In March 1982, he came on location to train for Boston. "This was after I had him heat-trained in Atlanta to get him used to the heat. When he was here in Boston, he stayed with me in Everett."

With the lack of sufficient hills in Minnesota on which to train, Squires was forced to be creative to replicate the course's inclines. But once with Squires, it was all hills for Beardsley. The day after he arrived, they awoke to a heavy training day on the Newton hills. "I had this workout dreamed up just for Dickie. We were going to go to the course at Boston College. I'd run with him from the reservoir to Lake Street at BC, where the stores are as you go down after Heartbreak Hill in the Marathon. Then he'd go up Heartbreak Hill easy, the opposite direction of the course, turn around and then go hard up Heartbreak in the right direction—*eight times!* That's 16 friggin' hills! And I built this workout up for him, that no one else had done it before and it was unique. He loved it. He was eating it up. Well, that night it had started snowing. And it snowed and it snowed. I get the car ready in the morning and we're going to BC and he still wants to do it. It's crazy out there! I can't even see where I'm driving. I couldn't even drive up the hill! But he wanted to do it. He's used to tough winters in Minnesota. He loved it."

In the snow, Squires warmed up and cooled down with Beardsley, but left him on his own for the actual workout. While he waited, Squires endeavored to find a cup of coffee and some company. "There were no cars on the road, BC was closed, and only part of the roads were plowed. After we warmed up together, Dickie started at Lake Street and went up and down Heartbreak to Centre Street, turned around and went up Heartbreak and back down to Lake. That was one of eight. His recovery was when he was going up the hill the opposite way, but I wanted him to push it up the hill in the right direction as if he was running the Marathon. The snow was so bad that I was hoping he wouldn't be too tired afterwards because I'm going to need him to help me push my car out of the snow! The only thing that's going was the trolley." To alleviate the roads of cars as snowplows cleared the way, the city's subway system was still working. One end of the BC Line—the Green Line subway—is located near the stores at the beginning of Lake Street. Other than the occasional police car, snowplow, and subway trolley, the only other movement on the streets was the lone figure of a runner. And his coach. "The trolley driver sees this and he says to me, 'What are you doing?' I told him I have a guy training for the Marathon. The guy shakes his head and says, 'You guys are crazy.' This was, like, 7:30 in the morning and there's about half a foot to a foot of snow. When Dickie finishes up, he came in like a snowman. I think I gave him my gloves, a dry shirt, and a hot chocolate. His face looked frosted, and I go over and wipe his face off like I was a corner man of a prizefighter. Another trolley guy comes over and he asks us what were we doing? I told him we were training for the Boston Marathon, and he says, 'You guys *are* crazy!' His buddy probably told him about us."

In the pre-race hours on Patriots' Day, even with Beardsley's marathon wins and top finishes, he still slid in under the fans' radar; so much so that Squires had to sell his importance in Hopkinton just hours before the start of the 1982 Boston Marathon. "On the morning of the race, I didn't want Dickie over with all the other guys and the reporters, and everyone talking about the race. I didn't want him to get scared. And I couldn't find the house number where he was supposed to stay in Hopkinton, so I'm walking along with him and I'm trying to remember it. Dickie then says to me, 'I see some of them [runners and reporters] are over there with the regular people.' I said, 'You're number three! They'll be all over you, driving you nuts. No. Here's what we're going to do. I'll find you a room.' See, he didn't know I forgot where the house was. They described it as a Cape Cod house that was white with blue shutters. For chrissakes, every Cape Cod house is white with blue shutters! They're all the same!"

With about three hours until the noontime start, they continued to walk around the streets along Hopkinton Town Common in search of a place of refuge. Squires eyed a nice-looking house, left Beardsley at the street-end of the walkway, and climbed the stairs to the front door. He cleared his throat, turned on whatever charm he could muster, and knocked. "I say I'm a B.A.A. official and I have with me a person that may win this race. I tell her he's a young fellow from Minnesota. I turn around and Dickie's standing there looking around like he's in trouble. I told her what he needs is to just get off his feet because he'll be on them for a long time. And I said, 'You're going to be watching him! You put your TV on and you'll be seeing him in front.' She says, 'Of course. Come in.' She was very nice. She gave him tea, she went upstairs and turned the bed for him, and asked if he wanted some music to relax, some water. She asked him what time did he need to leave. She was a sweet lady. Later on, Dickie tells people that I was giving this spiel like a salesman, like I was selling housewares or something." Squires was used to dealing with all kinds of personalities. While Beardsley was loose and friendly, like Meyer, for instance, Salazar was more wound up and intense, like Lesley Welsh, who in 1982 became the first woman to win in the same year the NCAA and the TAC cross-country titles. Having at one time or another coached all four, Squires knew how to work with athletes of varying temperaments.

"Starting on the day before a race, and right till the gun went off, Al would put on his game face. He'd warm up. He'd try to stay away from people and get ready. He'd be so focused, *I* wouldn't even approach him then. He got it into his head that he was going out to win the battle. He believed that running was a battle. But with that kind of mindset, he would often do more during the week. I'd try to keep him down, but he'd always sneak in extra mileage. He wouldn't always tell me, but I could tell. And I'd say, 'Don't make me call your mother because she'd tell me you were out longer.' I can tell." Salazar, who in the fall of 1980 had joined Nike's Athletics West, arrived about a week earlier to a large group of reporters at the airport, thanks in large part to his proud father's pre-arrival phone calls to the media. Unlike Beardsley, an out-of-stater with minimal local ties, Salazar stirred hometown interest. The Salazar family from Cuba had moved to the Bay State, where the young Alberto attended and ran for Wayland High School. They lived less than 20 miles west of the Boston Marathon finish line. "When he got here for Boston in 1982, about five days before the race, he stayed with his parents. He even went down to the diner where he used to wash dishes during high school. But he snuck out on the course. It was easy to get there for him."

Marathon Monday, April 19, 1982, was bright and hot. The race became known simply as the "Duel in the Sun." Since most of the favored runners had at one time subscribed to the Squires school of Boston training, interest lay in seeing the execution of the when, how, and who. When the dust settled from the early miles, it was Salazar and Beardsley in shoulder-to-shoulder action from before the Newton hills to the finish. "That race was a mental as well as a physical test. It was around Natick that Salazar and Beardsley separated themselves from the others. I had surge moves in my training and Dickie tried them all. The last surge move, and he made it, was a big one. It was a three-minute move he did around 23 miles in Coolidge Corner. That gave him maybe eight or 10 yards. But Salazar knew the crowd would be there at Kenmore Square and he moved like hell to catch Dickie by Kenmore, and both of them ran together." Heading eastward in the point-to-point course, each runner glanced downward to the road ahead to see each other's shadow bobbing before him, which provided positional insight. No quarter was given. It was relentless. After Kenmore Square, near Fenway Park with about a mile to go, in particular, and especially over the final yards to the finish line, both men pushed hard and strong. All the while, Squires, in a makeshift television studio of scaffolding at the finish line, was watching the race in his familiar role of TV commentator dispensing on-air color. As coach of some of the top marathoners in the world, and especially in this very race, his viewpoint was insightful, unique, and entertaining.

"I see that Dickie would look to the crowd and look away; and Salazar just looked straight ahead. I kept saying that I thought that Salazar's really, really tired, but I know what he was going to do. I knew he was going to fire hard through the hills. He did, but they kept the same pace together. The sun was bright, which gets in your eyes with the sweat. Al didn't have a hat, but Dickie had the hat that I gave him. That morning, they were passing out cotton painter's hats before the race and I grabbed one, and with a ballpoint pen I perforated some holes in it to let it breathe. I had told Dickie to wet that hat with some water. He wore that for most of the race and I saw him throw it off to the side to some kid toward the end. It had done its job."

By two seconds, Salazar (CR 2:08:52) edged Beardsley (2:08:54) for the win as they were the first pair in the same race to run sub-2:09s. "I go into the finish area and there're interviews and reporters, and they're giving Al intravenous because he was dehydrated terribly. All of a sudden I get a hand on my shoulder and a man says, 'Coach, what the hell did you do? You almost killed my son.' It was Alberto's father, Jose. I asked if he was okay, and he said he was. He also said that Dickie was a nice boy. They were interviewing Dickie and he kept saying all these nice things about Al, like 'He's a better runner than I am,' and 'I gave it all I had and he beat me,' and so on. The father could see Dickie was honest. I saw Dickie first and he asked if Al was okay. I told him he was. And I said to him, 'Well, the ol' coach was right again. I said you'd be second or better. You're the best second I have ever seen. The [second] closest finish in the history of this race!' He said he did everything and he tried everything he could, and he said he thought Al was tired. I told him he raced Al into the ground. And I'll clue ya, Al got a lot of cockiness kicked out of him at that race." In a selfless show of respect immediately following the finish, Salazar had earlier, while still on the winner's podium, motioned Beardsley to join him. When he did, Salazar raised up Beardsley's arm in recognition of this great feat in an instant reaction of honor.

"The thing is, they were so different. Al really was such a serious guy into running. He got into running when he was a freshman in high school, and then really went at it at the University of Oregon. Dickie had visions of being an outdoorsman, which he did later as a fisherman and a hunter. But he went to a small agricultural school, the University of Minnesota Waseca, before he started to run seriously. And he had great rhythm. But if it wasn't for Al pushing that race, the times wouldn't have been there." When the media finally noticed Squires, they approached him with the question of how low times could be headed in the marathon. Two of his athletes just ran under the previous Boston Marathon course record. If there was anyone with a qualified answer, it was Squires. "I said they'd run about 2:06. And one of them in the back goes, 'He's crazy.' I remember that word. I said, 'I heard that! And I'll tell you why 2:06. I make my living out of this. When I have a guy, a rested guy, that can run 27:20 for a 10K, it's a 2:06. Not on this course—maybe a 2:07—but at another course.' The 10K is the benchmark." (Squires was right. Four years later saw Rob de Castella's victorious 2:07:51 at the 1986 Boston, and winning times of Cosmas Ndeti's 2:07:15 in 1994, Moses Tanui's 2:07:34 in 1998, Robert Kipkoech Cheruiyot's 2:07:14 in 2006 and 2:07:46 in 2008, before Cheruiyot's 2:05:52 in 2010 and Geoffrey Mutai's World Best CR 2:03:02 in 2011.)

About an hour after the 1982 Boston finish, Squires talked with Salazar. It took that long for Squires to finish his wrap-up television program and for Salazar to finish his IVs. "He says to me, 'I don't know how you do this. This farm kid, I never heard of him two years ago.' I told him the kid's a good listener and a very, very tough competitor. And Al said, 'He proved it.'" After that race, the two men suffered dearly, both in the short-term and long-term, due not only to their gut-wrenching run but also from the year's worth of hard training and competition. They still continued to excel before an eventual downfall. All of the hard miles and hard races did not sit well with Squires. He was extremely disappointed. Despite their great success, he knew, and had forewarned them, of the potential physical dangers that could, and most assuredly would, result in the body breaking down. "I didn't care for that," he said of the magnitude of miles, meets, and marathons. "It's kind of a natural tendency with athletes because their minds are blown out by everyone wanting them to come to an 'easy' race and make money. They're all beat up after a marathon race. Even a half-marathon can take it out of them. You need an easy month. I mean, Dickie ran Grandma's about two months after Boston!"

Squires's time was being shared between the club, school, as an advisor, and with outside athletes. The 1983 Boston yet again fielded several Squires runners, which included Greg Meyer (1st), Wells (9th), and Rodgers (10th). "After 1980, Greg started to think about marathons. He was running with these guys and he was seeing he was faster than these guys. So he asked me about training him for the marathon. At the time, in my head, I really thought I might be able to get him to run the Olympic 10K in 1984. But with an athlete, if they have a goal, I will help them. So I told him about an easy marathon he could run in Detroit. I didn't want him to run around Boston because I didn't want the press to build him up. He didn't need that." Squires informed Meyer that he himself had run the Detroit Marathon a few times with his training groups, in the neighborhood of three hours because he ran back and forth from group to group. "I just want him to get a feel for it and learn. I want him to come away from Detroit so we can really go into training. I want him to win and feel he's a star and feel he can beat up people. I wanted to keep adding and doing things a little different. Just keep adding on."

In a CR 2:13:07, Meyer won the 1980 Detroit Marathon. In April 1981, he added one second to that for a 2:13:08 at Boston for 11th. And by the 1982 Chicago Marathon, Meyer's progress via Squires's training surges was evident when he won in 2:10:59. With seven months between the Chicago win and the 1983 Boston, Squires continued the surges, Fartlek (training of varying speeds), track work, and road races. "With Rodgers being away a lot with all those races, Greg would be like a group leader with the Greater Boston guys in the workouts. I would intensify some practices because they could handle it. It wasn't a killer, and they would say they could do more, which is what I love to hear. That means I didn't drain them. I was building up a 10-minute surge, a 20-minute surge, and a 10-minute surge on the Marathon course. I was breaking up the course. We'd start at the two-mile mark and eventually we'd start at BC and we'd go back to Natick Square. From Natick on, toward BC, we'd break into groups with guys like Randy Thomas, Bob Hodge, and Tim Donovan. And Greg knew what the order was and that I wanted him to lead this thing to get the feeling of a race. When he hit his watch at, say, the 10-minute surge mark, he'd turn back and pick up the group and the guys would go back and get rounded up again. The rest pattern would be a 5:50 [mile pace]. This way, he's running in clusters—back to what we call 'normal pace pattern,' and then do another surge under five minutes, and so on. What good would it be if he went off for a 10-minute surge with the group and then run the rest of the way alone. No good."

Instead of the accumulation of hundreds of simple miles on the road—a common approach some coaches incorporated that infuriated Squires—in 1983 he cast a wide net for Meyer that included a healthy mix of track events and road races at various distances. And there was another workout in April, usually two, in fact, at BC that preceded Boston as a confidence booster. It was multi-dimensional. "I'd have them do some fairly fast mileage on the track at BC, then go out the backdoor of the track to St. Ignatius Church [at Commonwealth Avenue on the course]. Then they'd go up Heartbreak Hill from the opposite side [of the direction of the race], go to the top, cut through the campus on College Road and then follow the outside of the campus on Beacon Street, and take a left back onto the track. And I'd be there with my stopwatch. After running a little faster than a marathon pace on the track, they'd have surges of a two-mile, a mile, a three-quarter mile, and they'd finish with a mile. They'd move on the hill fairly well, and work the other roads. We'd have different guys leading up the hill each time. And they wouldn't know what distance they were going to run until I told them when they came back in each time. This was to give them the effects of being out there in the Marathon. Each group would work this, and they loved it. They'd talk about it like it was the greatest workout of all time. And this was after having already warmed up for three miles."

It was also inevitable that each runner strived to better the other. So much so that the giants of the past were mentioned in the same breath as these workouts—what did Rodgers do; did Salazar run this 8 or 10 times; didn't Beardsley do this workout in the snow? There were always comparisons. "Yeah, there was plenty of that. And then they'd ask if I had done these workouts myself, and I'd tell them I did, but not as fast. I didn't have me to coach me. These workouts were a true measurement. It showed them they could hold 65 [per lap], they were able to run under 4:20 [per mile], they were able to run under 4:40 [per marathon mile], they were able to run 63 [per lap] for three quarters, and then do their last mile in 4:16. This was *real* mileage, *real* times."

At the 1983 Boston Marathon, Squires thought to himself that Meyer could, and should, finish within the top two. He did not add to Meyer's pressure by divulging this to him, but he nevertheless predicted first or second. "Greg had way more speed than Beardsley, and Dickie came in second. But then again, having that kind of speed, there's been a lot of speed guys on this course that blew up. But I knew that Greg could run 2:10. He was a solid hill runner and he was very good on them." In addition to Meyer, other former and current Squires-coached runners included John Lodwick, Duncan McDonald, Rodgers, Dan Schlesinger, and Wells. And sure enough, over the familiar GBTC training ground of the Newton hills, Meyer took over the race. "Greg shot through the hills. He ran the hills pretty damn hard. I thought that was a smart move. Benji Durdin wasn't bad then, but Ron Tabb went back pretty quick. My guys can go over the hills—from the fire station to BC—in 50 minutes. These guys are going 4:50 [per mile] between those hills. But back then, there was no crowd control. Heartbreak Hill was a zoo for the kid. He ran about the last six miles by himself. And he would have broken the record, but he was waving to the crowd."

Two seconds off Salazar's CR, Meyer won in 2:09:00. With Meyer's victory, four of the top five fastest American men times at Boston—the first four on the list at the time—were coached by Squires: Salazar (CR 2:08:52 in 1982), Beardsley (2:08:54 in 1982), Meyer (2:09:00 in 1983), Rodgers (AR CR 2:09:27 in 1979). It stayed that way for 11 years until Bob Kempainen of Minnesota ran 2:08:47 in 1994; and whereas his time was for seventh place, Squires's four runners turned in three wins and one runner-up.

At the 1984 Boston Marathon, Squires coached Gerry Vanasse, whose bib number 5933 reflected his anonymity. "We had 11 months until Boston, and I was coaching him to run Boston specifically. He ran the hills I was emphatic about that. The more times you can run over these hills, the better you'll be. And that's what I did with Vanasse." During the week before Boston, newspaper sportswriter Joe Concannon, who covered the running beat and was the one who had turned Squires on to Vanasse, spoke with him. The two friends still had their jobs to do—Concannon writing pre-race stories, Squires coaching his athletes. "We talked about the race and how Gerry was doing. And Joe had asked me what I thought of Vanasse; what if he had Greater Boston when he was in college. And I said, 'He'd a been a friggin' killer!' He would have! But I ask Joe to just put Vanasse down in the paper as a footnote. I said, 'I know you have this story in your back pocket, but please don't build the kid up.' He said, 'I know. You never like to build up your guys before the race.' Which is true. At the pre-race press conference, I didn't go because I knew I'd be asked about the guys. But for Joe's story, I told him that I thought Vanasse would be no worse than 12th—between 8th and 12th. I said, 'Just say he'll give it his best, and write the old sonnet that he's a local kid, he's very serious, he wants to go into education, and so on. Do a nicey-nice piece, but it's only his second marathon!' And I'd talk to the press like that. I told them they can turn a kid to mush with the pressure from big stories and things."

For the 1984 Boston Marathon, Squires once again provided on-air color commentary for the live television coverage. And once again, there were several Squires-coached participants in the field. When he first saw Vanasse among the top runners, the other commentators did not even know his name, and referred to him only by his large bib number. "I hear them say, 'Well, we've got number 5933 near the top.' And I go, 'Holy, geez!' They hear me and they ask me about him, and I say that I coached this guy. And they go, 'Oh, good. We have to play this up.' I told them it was okay now since he was already out there, so I talked about him and said he was running pretty well. He wasn't leading, but he was running well. And then I said something about if the Boston College crowd [at Mile 21] was as good as the Wellesley College women [at Mile 13], that would help. Everyone had those little transistor radios then, and I was hoping to get the BC spectators cheering him on because I think he was around sixth at that point." On wet roads in raw and cold conditions, and for the eighth time in the previous 12 Bostons with GBTC as a club, a Squires-coached athlete was the top American when Vanasse finished second (2:14:49). "I saw him as being good, but I never saw him as getting second place at the Boston Marathon! But he had a good runner's frame and he had nice mechanics. He didn't have overt speed, but the speed came out with endurance. And the crowd pulled him in. Vanasse did tell me afterwards that he couldn't hear because the crowd was so loud."

In 1996, Squires ran the Boston Marathon on its centennial celebration. His run was partly due to the commemoration and partly to accompany former *Boston Globe* sportswriter Leigh Montville of *Sports Illustrated*, who via Leonard had requested Squires's accompaniment over the course. "He was a smoker and had played basketball, but was never a runner. So I put him through my usual simulation program, but downsized for him." An estimated record 38,000 entrants packed the streets of Hopkinton for the 100th Boston. As the noontime start loomed, Squires could not locate his charge; that is, until he caught the uncommon whiff of cigarette smoke. It was Montville, off to a corner, calming his nerves. "I just shook my head. He said he had quit, but then only had a few at a time. But he needed this one. Anyway, we went off toward the end. It took us about 24 minutes to cross the start line after the gun went off. It didn't matter." Along the course, every 50 minutes they would stop. "He had to take his shoes off and massage his feet. I'd say we lost at least about 15 minutes from that. But I think we just broke five hours," Squires noted of his 20th overall marathon, which he finished in a chip-time 4:59:22. "It was worth doing. Something special. It was the hundredth! And I'll clue ya, this was my ninth Boston and it was very different from the first few Bostons I did. The biggest thing were the water stations—they were at about every mile—and clocks at every mile. We never had anything like that back then."

With all the changes to the Boston Marathon that Squires had either witnessed, directed, or caused, there is one more on his wish list that he fears will remain a pipe dream. It is probably the last of the B.A.A.'s sacred cows, the number of which has dwindled since the inclusion of qualifying standards, women, increased fields, sponsors, prize money, waves, and an earlier start. "Sunday! The Marathon should be on a Sunday so it can be covered by the whole 'real' world and so everyone can sit at home and watch. Because on a Monday, they don't. The rest of the world is working! They don't have Patriots' Day! It's a waste! New York, Chicago, London, Berlin—they're all on a Sunday. On TV!"

CHAPTER 15

STAYING SHARP

The mid-1980s to the early 1990s introduced a new phase of coaching for Squires. No longer was he involved with the structured schedule of a running club or academic setting. He had retired from GBTC and Boston State/UMass Boston. He was free to roam, so to speak, and coach at will. But one thing that did not change was his approach to his athletes. "A lot of coaches will do it one day a week in person with their athletes, and verbalize the other days on the phone. But if you are a coach, to get good results you've got to be there! It seems that athletes perform for coaches. They do. I was there all the time [consistently in person and on the phone for the entire program]. And I can sit down and ask you four things and I can give you a program that'll work. I've done it! But I wrote it on napkins and scraps of things. I didn't want to use a nice piece of paper because that can be duplicated and I still didn't want my stuff to get out. That's the truth! People lose the napkins and scraps of paper more than a big sheet that they'd keep."

Squires was now a self-employed coach-for-hire. Paid a flat fee plus a percentage of winnings, his criteria was simple and strict: sub-2:13 male and sub-2:40 female marathoners. And he did not disappoint. The list of accomplishments his athletes achieved over the ensuing years included a stunning number of top-name marathon wins, national and world championships, and various appearances at Olympic Trials and Olympic Games. Some of his runners during their time with Squires included Jacqueline Gareau, who in 1983 was third at the Boston Marathon (2:29:27), fifth at the World Track & Field Championships in Finland (2:32:35), and second at the Marathon of the Americas in Illinois (2:31:36); Sue

King, 10th at the 1984 US Olympic Trials in Washington (2:34:29); Phil Coppess, first at the 1985 Twin Cities Marathon (CR 2:10:05); Kathy Kanes, who qualified for the 1992 US Olympic Trials in 3000 meters; Jonathan Little, who qualified for the 2007 US Olympic Trials Marathon in New York City (2:33:03); and Zika (Rea) Palmer, who ran a 2:41:06 PR at the 2005 Twin Cities Marathon and also qualified for the 2008 US Olympic Trials.

After having worked for New Balance part-time in 1981 while still at GBTC, it was not until about six years after his resignation from GBTC, and a year or two removed from any coaching at the club, when Squires fully joined the Boston-based New Balance Athletic Shoe Company as an advisor for its New Balance Running Team. Previously, in the late-1970s while he was the Boston State and GBTC coach, he would at New Balance put in about 10 to 12 hours a week on his off days, which soon grew to a part-time advisory role. While he simultaneously juggled the two non-academics, Squires attempted to keep his hands clean in regard to the selection process of members of the New Balance Running Team. By his doing, there would be no creation of any jealousy or undue pressures within the ranks. "I was doing what I called their grassroots program, and I had someone else pick the athletes. I told them I couldn't pick the athletes. I have a stable of 18 studs at Greater Boston and I'm going to pick only three—no more than three in a year, usually—and the other ones will look at me and ask 'What about me?' No. No way. I'm going to coach. I will guide my guys if the company says fine. Which they did. And that's what I did. But it was a terrible conflict of interest. New Balance expected me to tell the athletes to wear New Balance shoes. But I told them if the kids want to run in some other shoes, I'm not going to say they *have* to wear New Balance shoes. The kids around here, to them, New Balance was a fine shoe, but they wanted Nike; adidas; the Japanese shoes, Asics—they wanted a big-league contract that these outfits would give them. They'd give them $25,000, and New Balance at that time couldn't do that. They were the new company on the block, along with Nike, but Nike had a lot of money in them and a lot of great athletes that were wearing those shoes that got the young people going."

His early part-time commitment with New Balance blossomed when he eventually agreed to commit as a coach on a full-time basis. "They did have a coach in Kevin Ryan, a 2:11 marathoner from New Zealand. He wanted to be a designer and he learned the trade. But before that, he was the guy that would give out free shirts, talk to the runners, appear at running stores, and do these little clinics on how he became a good runner. What I had done was I had sold New Balance on a program that they better get the youth interested in their shoes. The people that really wanted New Balance to succeed—the higher-ups that wanted the company to be in the in-crowd, because Nike was *the* shoe company—would tell me the names of high school kids that were doing well. Now, they couldn't sell shoes to that kid, but they could get in the good graces of the family when we would give them a discount on the shoes and sell things to the kid's mother and father. The spin-off was good. It worked." Squires enjoyed handing out free shirts and shoes and clothing to the kids and their families while also lending coaching advice either in person or via a direct line to potential future prospects. "I loved that job. My phone line was always full. And on my days off, I'd come over to New Balance in Brighton (Massachusetts) and talk to runners. I think they liked that I was a runner, too."

Since he still ran, Squires could run and relate with athletes. But his athletic ability also attracted the occasional challenge. In November 1988, at Coach's Corner inside the Eliot Lounge, Squires was confronted by Paul Fetscher out of New York. A frequent visitor who Squires knew from his B.A.A. competitor days, Fetscher suggested the coach run his age. "I was 56 years old and Paul said I should do what a lot of people do when they run their age. He said I should run 56 miles. Fifty-six miles? It's all I can do to run 26 and finish a marathon! Then Freddy Doyle, one of my old Greater Boston guys, said how about 56 seconds." A compromise was settled on a quarter-mile *under* 56 seconds—still an amazing feat for Squires, especially at his age—at BC's outdoor track. And all Fetscher had to do was beat him. "He had a couple of decades advantage! I think he was 30. And the loser would have to buy a round at the Eliot! For everyone! I think it started out as a beer if I lost and a hundred bucks if I won. Something like that."

The time and date agreed upon was in five months, the morning of Sunday, April 16, 1989—the day before the Boston Marathon. Leading up to the bet, both Squires and—separately—Tommy Leonard, prepared in their own way. During one of his training days at the BU indoor track, Squires met up with Randy Thomas. "I needed to do some fine-tuning. It was two laps to a quarter at BU, so I asked him to go out and pace it for me. He went out too fast, so I yelled to slow down, and we settled in. I ended up doing a quarter in about 54, 55, which was, I think, a record." Meanwhile, unbeknownst to Squires, Leonard and company decorated and celebrated the event with as much pomp and circumstance as possible, and that included for Squires 56 gold and green balloons, a nod to his Notre Dame colors; 56 pieces of pizza from Balducci's House of Pizza in Quincy; 56 bottles of Sam Adams beer; a subscription to the *New Yorker* magazine, which, of course, added up to 56 issues; 56 tea bags; a pre-event fun-run mile called the Squires Stroll for friends and former athletes of Squires who Leonard summoned; and taped musical airings of two of Squires's favorites—the Notre Dame fight song ("Notre Dame Victory Song") and "Heart" (more commonly known as "You've Got to Have Heart") from the musical "Damn Yankees."

The day of the bet arrived with rain and wind; and much to the dismay of Squires, a 14-paragraph write-up in the sports section of the *Boston Globe* newspaper by Michael Madden, with the headline, "Paying Their Bill—Today's 'Event' at BC a Tribute to Squires" for all to see. "Great, with the article in the paper there were about 200 people out for this. That meant if I lost, I'd have to buy a round for all of them. I only had about a hundred bucks on me. I had to get more money just in case. With the rain, you never know if you're going to fall or something. Anyway, Paul never showed up. I ran by myself and ran a 66." Even though Squires failed to hit 56, the no-show by Fetscher got him off the hook. Back at the Eliot, with a line out the door and the lounge all festooned in the theme of 56, Fetscher paid up. "He did show up, but it was later; after I ran. And the round was on him. The place was packed. And there were all these balloons and pizzas and 56 bags of tea—all 56 of things!" The date was also proclaimed by Boston Mayor Raymond Flynn, as Billy Squires Day. And 16 days later, on May 2, in the first session of the 101st United States Congress in Washington, D.C., the recognition was read and added into the official Congregational record by US Senator John Kerry of Massachusetts.

In the mid- to late-1990s, shortly after he left New Balance, Squires for the last time coached a club; two, in fact—the new Sisu Running Club of men; and the trailblazing Liberty Athletic Club of women.

At the nepotistic behest of son Gerry Squires, Sisu was formed with about a dozen members; and as head coach, his father recalls of the moniker, "I remember reading running magazines and I would always see with the runners from Finland they'd say they had a lot of *sisu*. The way it was used in the magazines, I thought it meant courage or something like that, but then I found out it was also a slang word that means 'having guts' or 'balls.' So I liked that." For a few years out of the Braintree High School track, from 1992-94, Sisu featured Rachied Bahi,

Vin Connolly, Paul Croft, Tony Daroche, Dermot Fitzpatrick, Ray Flores, Jamie Goodberlet, Lou Ristaino, George Ross, and Gerry Squires, whose combined collegiate talent came from the likes of Bates College, BC, BU, MIT, and UMass Amherst. "It started with three guys, including my son, and the word got out and we had a good bunch of guys come out. They were good runners—good regional runners—in track and also low-key road races. And I turned them right around to do 10Ks and big-league meets." In road races, cross-country, indoors, and outdoors, Sisu incorporated the same preparation and determination for which the elder Squires was known. "We had about a dozen guys, including three masters. It was a project, but we killed everyone because the other teams were doing the same stupid stuff that had been done for 30 years. I told my guys that I will improve them. It isn't running miles and miles and miles; that's going to get them slow. I want more quality in their runs. I have it that when they finish the workouts, they're ready for that race."

In its short history, Sisu won the NETAC Cross-Country Championship; was second in the New England District Series, from distances of 5K to the marathon; and came in fifth at the 1992 NETAC Outdoor Track and Field Championship. At the outdoor NETAC, the 10,000 was ruled by Sisu, led by Gerry Squires in first. For indoors, at the 1992 Alden Invitational/NETAC Indoor Track and Field Championships, Sisu earned two of the top six spots in the 3000. "I had decided that we were going to go with the New England TAC series of the 5K, 10K, 20K, 25K, marathon, and the crazy 10-miler, and they were also going to run in cross-country and track. I told them they were going to train and race indoors; sharpen up their speedwork; keep the Sunday workouts; speedwork on Tuesdays; and if we race on Saturday, we won't race week to week. We'd look over the schedule, train accordingly, and stay sharp. These guys knew what to do. They'd done it already. It was different. And after a few years, it kind of disintegrated because guys were getting jobs and it went down to a few people. That was it. But it was good."

Around the same time, Squires became part of the Liberty Athletic Club—the oldest all-female running club in the United States—started in 1948 by Robert "Bud" McManus, a fellow Arlington High School sprinter. "He was the coach of what was called the Red Diamond Athletic Club, I think, from the 40s, and he wanted to do more so he started Liberty for girls under 18. His wife mentioned the name; something along the lines of him being free from Red Diamond that he finally felt good, like he got his liberty, which is a military term. It also sounded nice and Patriotic. So, Bud came up to me sometime in the 50s when he started it and asked if I could help him with some ideas for training. Which I did until I moved to Wakefield, and then I'd only see him occasionally. He also lived in Wakefield, but the club was out of Lexington. And credit John Babbington for continuing the club into the 70s after Bud. Title IX came and more women wanted to run, so Liberty accepted women over the age of 18."

In the early years, only individual members competed in open championships. Liberty did not send teams. However, from about 1973 to 1984, when there was enough talent to submit teams, they won seven NETAC track championship titles, and seven times made First Team in the NTAC Junior Cross-Country (1976-78), Senior Cross-Country (1978), 10K (1978, 1984), and Marathon (1984), championships. Over the ensuing years of steady growth, to maintain and enhance the training experience at the club, it was necessary to form separate groups of youths (ages 10-14), juniors (14-18), and college/adults (18 and over). "The youth girls would run until they got to high school, and then their school coaches would most likely take over. The juniors could run more races, and then when they went to college, a lot of them got scholarships. Some would still run during college, and when they got out of college they'd run for a shoe company perhaps, and then get married. But there was nothing that worked up *through* the groups. They didn't have a program that advanced the runner, like what I always use." Enter Squires. In 1989, just after Liberty's 40th anniversary, the 56-year-old came on board to helm the club. The initial connection was made more out of Squires's benevolence in the club than club interest in him. "That's right. Bud had died, and then later on, John left the club. So I began to think about it; that this was the oldest club for women; and plus, I liked what Bud had done. So I went over there to talk to them about it. When I got there, they had a few thousand dollars in the treasury, mostly from dues and a road race they had as a fundraiser, and I think there were about a dozen runners at the time. And they had moved from using the Lexington High School track to the track at Harvard University, which John had let them use."

Liberty was thrilled with who walked through its door. "They were very organized. And I told them I didn't want to take any money. I always wanted it to stay within the club, just like at Greater Boston. Keep it in the club! But I had to take something because of insurance reasons. I said I'd work for a dollar, but they ended up paying me 12-hundred, which was a hundred bucks a month. Anyway, they had a list of about 70 club women from over the years, and they said they ran a race on New Year's Day out of Winchester, and they advertised a little. That was about it. I asked them what was the nature of the club, and they said they wanted to keep it a track club more than a road-running club. That was fine." Squires then laid down Coach's law: workouts Tuesdays or Wednesdays, and as the season progressed, twice a week. With the majority of the club's demographic older than 40, he impressed upon them the importance of recruiting. And he stressed that he would strengthen Liberty for the next decade, to its 50th birthday, as long as they recruited members. If they did that, he stated, the club would be successful. Also, he wanted the club to train in Wakefield instead of Harvard. "I told them if they didn't do the recruiting for me—because I was good enough as a coach to get them to be champions—that I'd have to leave. I was doing too much with other things to spend time recruiting. And that was okay with them. I never had to worry about them doing what I said. They knew it would work. I never worried."

Liberty had a new direction. The next decade held great promise if, and only if, as Squires pointed out, certain actions were taken. The message was clear. "At that first club meeting, I told them I'd improve them. There was no doubt. No doubt! But I told them I'd need younger talent; under 30. I needed people like young moms, college gals, and if they'd run a little bit in high school, that's all the better. If they ran in college and they stopped and they want to start up again, that's fine, too, because they'll understand what's going on. But the club was so far away from this kind of thing. I think all they did was run and do a few strides and exercise and go home. The more I talked, I could see they were digging their trenches in. They didn't want new people coming in." The first thing Squires did was get their heads wrapped around his new approach and instill in them that each member was going to compete in the upcoming NETAC Championship. It had been years since Liberty had last tasted championship victory, and he wanted to reacquaint them with that feeling. "I told them that everyone in the club will be there! And I said they *will* PR. I said, 'And if you don't PR, it'll be my fault. Not yours. But guess what? I'll have you ready.' And we were ready."

In outdoors, Liberty immediately won the 1992 NETAC track and field championships—in which they beat the likes of GBTC, B.A.A., Falmouth Track Club—behind wins from Tina Anderson (400) and Chris Anderson (5000-meter walk). Other individual highlights included top-10 results at the 1993 USATF-NE track and field championships. For indoors, Liberty won the 1992 Alden Invitational/NETAC track and field championships with a commanding 23-point margin over—ironically—GBTC. A highlight of improvement was in heat one of the 800 with the fourth-fifth-sixth Liberty finish of Caroline Mitchell, Rita Cecil, Tina Anderson behind future US Olympian Amy Rudolph in third. Even more top-10 results came at the Alden Invitational/USATF-NE track and field championships in 1993, 1994, and 1997. And in national events, from 1991-95, Liberty was First Team in the NTAC Masters Cross-Country 8K (1991-93, 1995), World International Veteran's Cross-Country 8K (1992); and Second Team in the NTAC Open 5K Championship (1993).

Liberty seemed to respond to the structure and direction that Squires introduced. His time-tested workouts, which he adjusted for women, succeeded. "When I told them we were going to go against some good clubs in the nationals, they kept saying how better everyone was, and this and that. And I joked, 'Yeah, I heard they have three legs and four arms. No kidding! And they're gonna kill us!' And they'd relax and start laughing. I told them, 'Look, you are the New England champions. You *are* good! What were you the last few years? The I-should-a-beens, the I-would-a-beens, the I-could-a-beens, and the I-wasn'ts. You were nothing on that level. And now? You're going to do your best, whatever's in there, and you're going to learn how to run with the big girls!' That's what I told them to get into their heads. I'd push them because I believed in them, and I'd joke with them."

At the 1993 US Women's National Half-Marathon Championship and National Masters Championship, run in conjunction with the Fairfield Half-Marathon in Connecticut, Deb Bullerjahn of Liberty won the national women's masters crown. "Deb was a mother of three, and she was 47 years old! She ran pretty good. It was great for her." As the team gathered at the car and prepared to leave, Squires walked by a seemingly ordinary-looking man in street clothes and a map of Ireland under a cockney hat. The gentleman loudly cleared his throat to catch the attention of Squires, who finally looked over and recognized longtime friend and European and world champion runner Eamonn Coghlan. They then conspired against the team. Squires introduced the man as a runner who does not know what it takes to be a half-marathoner, but has run a few mile races in his lifetime. He asked him the amount of miles per week he runs, to wit the response was around 60. "Yeah, 60! Not that many," Squires retorts with a wink. The conversation turned to the man's specialty as being the mile. He asked if he has at least broken five minutes. "He says, 'Yeah, many times.' Then I start again and say that I don't want him to give us any fibs. I ask him if he's ever run a marathon." The gentleman responded that he had—once—yet neglected to add it was the 1991 New York City Marathon in 2:25:13 for 42nd place at the age of 38 for a 5:32 mile pace. "So I say, 'Okay, so you're not a marathoner—only one—and you don't do much of any of these half-marathons.'" The women begin to grow restless at the "non-runner." But for some reason, Squires persisted. When Squires "finds out" he is 41 years old and still running the mile, he scoffs at the notion of this master competing in a young man's distance. "I say to him, 'And you're still running the mile?' He says he is. Then I ask him how many has he run under five minutes, and he starts to think about it and adding it up in his head, and he goes, 'Ah…maybe…300.' I say, 'What? Did the leprechaun beat you or bite you? Get the heck out of here!' And I kind of start to laugh."

In a final indignity, Squires asked how many mile races he has run under four minutes. When the response was in the neighborhood of 80, Squires yelled that the only man who has ever done that is Eamonn Coghlan, "The Chairman of the Boards," who seven times won the Wannamaker Mile in the Millrose Games at Madison Square Garden, the last at age 34. "And I say, 'What? Are you trying to impersonate Coghlan?' And he says, 'Well, maybe I am.' Then I turn to my runners and I say, 'So, what do you think of Mr. Eamonn Coghlan?'" The reaction was expected—wide eyes, open mouths, and jumps of excitement. They surround Coghlan and asked for his autograph, pictures, and more stories, all the while they ignored Squires and pushed him aside. "That was fun. And when we came back home, they were all talking about it at the usual Tuesday workout. They were retelling the story to the other members, saying, 'And he's doing his crazy stuff, and we meet Eamonn Coghlan.' I love doing that." (Eight months later, in February 1994 at a scheduled specific mile race during a state high school meet on the indoor track at Harvard, Coghlan became the first man over the age of 40 to run a sub-4:00 mile, with a masters WR 3:58.15.)

Under Squires at Liberty, membership peaked in the high twenties. And that included quarter-milers, half-milers, milers, relay teams, and cross-country runners. "We filled in nicely with the events. We'd win the quarter, the half, the mile, the two-mile, and then we'd package together the relay teams. And we'd win! And some of them would also run the 110 or 200. But I'd give away the field events again. I could coach the long and triple jumps, and I'd improve them, but it'd exhaust me. I'd need another coach for the field events, so we'd give those away and focus on the track." Squires also "classed up" the membership application. It now included the Liberty Athletic Club history; philosophy; practice and competition schedules; goals; previous championships; biographical accomplishments of its coaches—Squires and Ken McKenna; and positive words of encouragement. In 1998, Liberty celebrated its Golden Anniversary at a party with nearly 70 former and current members; family, spouses, friends, and Squires. "It was a very nice evening of dinner and dancing and an awards ceremony. And it was funny, but they're all dressed up there, so when I began to speak, I opened with a joke, of course. I said, 'I'm astounded. I've never seen you people with your clothes on.' Right away the place goes nuts and everyone laughs. Then I use another line I've used before. I say, 'I feel like a mosquito at a nudist colony. I don't know where to start.' Hey, it's the ol' Coach, here!"

Also around this time, Squires was brought into the marathon fold in a way that would occupy more than a decade of his life as a result of a decision with which he was not even involved back in 1986. After they painfully resisted for years, the B.A.A. finally succumbed to the inevitable when they acquiesced to the demands of sponsorship money for their beloved Boston Marathon and signed Boston-based John Hancock Mutual Life Insurance Company as the principal sponsor of the race. One of the many offshoots spawned from the deal was the 1996 formation of the John Hancock Running and Fitness Program, which provides seminars, clinics, and expert coaching for John Hancock employees who are allowed to run without the need to qualify. Held by coach Fred Treseler III of the global sports marketing and event management firm, TRACS, Inc., he soon approached Squires, who he had come to know at GBTC (as a member), BC (as the women's cross-country and track coach), and the local television station where both worked during the Boston Marathon (Treseler III as a coordinator; Squires as commentator). "He had already started the John Hancock program the year before he contacted me. So that summer, in 1997, we talked about the program and I told him I've done it in 12-13 weeks, to get people ready for Boston. But with these people that he said would be coming from three different Hancock buildings and also after work, we're going to need more time. So I wanted to use a four-month program, so we backed it up."

Once Squires learned the types of people involved—neither top athletes, elite marathoners, nor college-level talent he was used to in the past—he designed proper training programs to be adapted and adjusted accordingly. "The programs I had were so different than anyone else's. I was thinking of how to get the most effectiveness out of their bodies. And I was also thinking of the pollywogs—the beginners. We had three different groups: the beginners, the intermediates, the veterans. If we did it generically, with no groupings, I bet we'd lose the beginners in three to five weeks. It'd be too much for them." Instead, Squires broke it down to those who have never run a marathon (beginners); those who have never run a marathon but have raced other distances before, or those who have run marathons but not that fast (intermediates); and those who have run several marathons for fast times (veterans). Beginners required everything possible in terms of proper training; intermediates knew how to train and have the running experience, but can still learn enough to improve; and veterans just wanted to get faster. Based on a runner's experience and fitness level, plus a completed information form, Squires placed each runner in a beneficial corresponding group. He was most proud that the average percentage of finishers in the program was between 95 to 98, which included a few years at 100 percent. And times ranged anywhere from 2:38 to just under six hours. As a coach, Squires continued to maintain high standards, whether he coached rookies or veterans.

CHAPTER 16

HONORED

In his eighth decade, years removed from actively coaching, Squires is never far from athletes and running. He always dispenses advice at the slightest request, and always preaches the good word at seminars and clinics. While he steadfastly strived to remain in the background to his athletes, honors and recognitions nevertheless followed. In 1995, the first Squires Bowl was awarded to the winning team of his Boston Mayor's Cup Cross-Country meet. In 2004, he received great praise from Arthur Lydiard, at one of the last public appearances by the legendary New Zealand coach and friend. One month prior to his passing, at an appearance at Regis College in Massachusetts hosted by GBTC and its coach, Tom Derderian, Lydiard boasted about Squires. It was a special moment between two old friends. "It really was," said Squires, his eyes filling up at the memory. "He says to everyone, 'You don't know how good this guy is. I know! I go through this in my country; they don't know how good he is. Look at his athletes, look at his training—he's one of the greatest marathon coaches you'll ever see!' That was very nice of him to say. And I had given him an advanced galley of my last training book months earlier and he said something like that when he reviewed it. That was very, very nice of him."

If he added up the number of foot strikes since he first began to run, Squires said it would be in the millions. That's because he really has not stopped running. "I haven't. I haven't officially stopped running. And thank God, because being born with a bad heart, I didn't know how helpful it was at the time." That beneficial running paid off greatly on several occasions. Shortly after he ran the centennial

Boston Marathon in 1996, he underwent his regular physical exam, which included several heart tests. Since childhood, he always felt blessed with his "borrowed time." There were instances when he was reminded of the tenuous nature of his heart; of his good fortune to live beyond his life expectancy of adolescence. But he also was under the impression that one way or another, everything would mostly correct itself. "I always thought I had something like a heart murmur that you outgrow as you get older. I always passed all the physicals I've had. But at the same time, I'd also have these flashbacks of me in a dark room as a kid and not being able to do anything. For a kid to realize, when he was two or three, that he's being treated like a vegetable—stuck in a room all alone to watch his friends play outside; to be pushed around in a baby carriage when you're old enough to walk; when you hear your parents talk about you to doctors and you're not being told what's going on—it stays with you forever."

In the spring of 1996, at the repeated insistence of his physician, Squires finally subjected himself to various heart tests, including an echocardiogram and electrocardiogram. "I remember he said to me that no one at the age of 63 should have a pulse rate of 39 to 41. The average athlete would be just under 60 to 65, and the average guy would be around 70. With that, I took the tests. And then hopefully I'd also find out why I had tasted blood when I raced." At another hospital, which featured cardiovascular specialization, Squires was notified that a separate EKG revealed he was experiencing a heart attack. Devastating news indeed. But it was not true. In fact, he was used to this kind of response because with previous exams throughout his life, doctors unfamiliar with his medical history often came to this conclusion without the full knowledge that one of his four heart valves was abnormally reduced. "That always happened. I'd heard it all before. If that was true, I'd have more heart attacks than I could count. But this time, at my age, the doctor wondered how I was still alive. He said I'd need stents. He had thought before that I'd need one or two valves replaced, but I never got things checked out when he suggested it. But he said I was like an old car—if one cylinder goes, the car could still run but we wouldn't let it go too fast. So I saw a specialist. I didn't tell anyone. I don't want people worrying about me. If I'm going to die, I die. I don't worry about death. If I go, I go."

About a month after he ran the 100th Boston, Squires underwent surgery for a stent. The procedure entailed the insertion of a tube into the reduced valve to open it up wider to increase the flow of blood. There was also the great possibility he would require two. After what he thought was about an hour's time in the operating room, he slowly awoke in recovery to receive the update. "They didn't do anything! They opened me up and took a look and said they couldn't put a stent in. I was groggy and kind of out of it, but that's what they told me. The doctor said, 'You know the old adage—if it ain't broke, don't fix it? I went in, we looked it over very close—within inches—at your heart, and that valve is sealed over and is now the size of a little bit bigger than the inside of the end of a ballpoint pen. The other three valves are overly open, about the size of dimes.' He said that was phenomenal, those three valves. He told me to keep doing what I've been doing all my life—the running. But he didn't want me to run anymore marathons," recalled Squires, who was given a dilating pill to keep the smaller valve open as much as possible. "At least I found out why I tasted blood when I ran. It only happens when I ran a lot at once, like three or four events in one track meet. The blood was backing up because only three of the four valves were fully working. I never saw blood or coughed it up. I could just taste it as it went back down."

But twice in 2008—February and August—he was hospitalized. The first time, "I felt lightheaded, like I was going to faint. I had shortness of breath and I started feeling, like, a burning sensation in my left arm. I tried to relax. I just sat there to relax. I thought I was having a heart attack. I was just so weak. My whole body felt weak." At the ER they checked his medical bracelet for emergency contact information, and quickly began the examination. "That was the first time I thought that was it, that they'd have to use that info. But then I did start to feel better, actually. And after they did some tests, the doctor came out and told me that I've had two heart attacks, silent heart attacks, that he saw in my chamber. He could see the scar tissue of them and he said that they were old. I didn't know I had a heart attack. Or two of them. That was a shock. And this one, too, in February. It wasn't silent! *It was noted!*" He was discharged the following day. After some rest and regular checkups, he began to resume his daily life. But six months later, "In the middle of the night, I had another *thing*. I was lightheaded again, I had real shortness of breath—and I don't usually have that this much. They checked me out again and I was told to rest. I couldn't run for a while, but I did start to feel better."

While he was advised he could eventually require a pacemaker, he was still allowed to run shorter distances on his own or in a race. In fact, in only his third race since the surgery, at the Camy 5K Run & David 5K Walk, in Walpole, Mass., in November 2008, Squires won a third-place age-group medal, all the while on the course he regaled those around him with stories and tales as he ran. Six months later, in May 2009, he laid down at home one Friday evening and awoke two days later to the door-banging sounds and immediate assistance of neighbors and medical personnel. Exactly two weeks after the Boston Marathon, in a groggy state of mind, Squires sat up in a bed at the hospital not quite grasping the fact he suffered a stroke.

Extensive examinations further revealed that at the age of 76, and after three heart attacks and a stroke, Squires had cardiomyopathy—the deterioration of the heart muscle itself. Specifically, he recalled being informed he had an LBBB—left bundle branch block—which he says was explained to him as when the left ventricle contracts later than its counterpart on the right. This, in part, stemmed from his childhood heart valve abnormality. "With another look, one of my arteries was still all sealed up. He said I have a big heart, which is normal [for a marathoner]. And mine's a muscle heart. But nothing had changed. It was getting worse. These episodes were happening more often now. Some days I couldn't run. I didn't feel like it. But sometimes I still did." To Squires, running *was* life. "If I didn't get into running, I probably would have been dead when I was 25. It just shows that the doctors when they tested me every year, because I was running, they automatically said I was okay. And when I went into the service, same thing—that I was okay. Except at the end of the service, there was this one air force doctor. He said I should have never gone into the service. He asked me to jump up and down, run up and down, and so on. He asked me if I knew what my heart rate was, and I said it was around 41, 43. He said it was under that. He asked me what branch was I in the service and what did I do, and I told him I was in the air wing and we didn't use oxygen masks. He said with the high altitude, he didn't know what would happen. What he was doing was he was scaring me in case I wanted to stay in. He said I could get 30 percent salary for the rest of my days because they screwed my heart up. I told him they said they thought I had a heart murmur. He said, 'No way.' He said I had something drastically wrong with my heart." That was 1958! Squires did not follow up.

Finally, in early December 2010, Squires received a pacemaker. The results were astounding. His health improved as well as his spirits. He even discovered he could run faster. He ran the *Runner's World* Classic Celebrity Mile in 2016 and the DMSE Sports Classic Celebrity Mile, organized by Dave McGillivray, his former

GBTC runner, at Merrimack College in North Andover, Mass., in 2017. "I'll clue ya, if it wasn't for Dr. Ed Carroll, who saved my life as a kid when I was with my mother and he had me run to check my heart, and then told me I could go out and play; and Dr. Charlie Tifft, who pushed me to get those tests, I don't know where I'd be," said Squires, who then continued after a short pause. "Yes, I do."

Squires continued to receive numerous honors, most of which embarrassed the man who often preferred to slip into the background. Some were unique, some were "normal." At the Suffolk Downs horse racetrack in Massachusetts, a thoroughbred by the deliberate name of Billy's Choice was so designated by a former GBTC athlete. He was also awarded by the National Distance Running Hall of Fame the distinguished Bill Bowerman Coaching Award. In another recognition of his commitment to the sport and his athletes, a commemorative plaque was dedicated on the Nike Walkway of Fame in its Beaverton, Oregon, campus headquarters. And in addition to various GBTC ceremonies, at the 20th anniversary of the club he was among those awarded the Paul Revere Silver Bowl; and soon thereafter, the inclusion of the Bill Squires Invitational Mile at the GBTC Invitational, held annually at Harvard. Also, the Coach Squires Award, annually presented at the Camy 5K Run & David 5K Walk, is awarded to the runner whose finish place is that of Squires's age at the time. And he has been inducted into several halls of fame, among them the Arlington (Mass.) High School Hall of Fame, Boston State College/University of Massachusetts Boston Hall of Fame, Massachusetts State Track Coaches Association Athletes's Hall of Fame, and in 2017 the prestigious USATF National Track & Field Hall of Fame.

Upon receipt of such honors, Squires always recalls Charlie Leverone, who he credits as the one who pushed him into running when all he wanted to do was play football. "If it wasn't for Charlie in high school, I don't think I would have gone out for track or cross-country. He was a senior when I was a junior, and it was Charlie that got me onboard!" And however truly nice and complimentary the recognitions are, Squires steadfastly points with never-ending pride to his family as what is most important to him. "I love them all. I know I've made some mistakes in my life, but they're the best things to ever happen to me—Sally and my kids. My brother, too, but he wasn't up to me." He laughed.

In regard to the creation of a coaching legacy, he never thought of his accomplishments in those terms. Whatever he did, it was for his athletes. In the forefront was always the goal that was set not for him as a coach, but for the athlete he coached. But he is most proud of being part of a lineage of coaching from his high school coach William "Doc" McCarthy to his college coach Alex Wilson to himself to those he coached who became coaches, including Dick Mahoney, Bob Sevene, Randy Thomas, and the former Rookie—Alberto Salazar (whose pool of Olympians includes Dan Browne, Mary Cain, Mary Decker, Mo Farah, Adam Goucher, Kara Goucher, Sifan Hassan, Dathan Ritzenhein, Galen Rupp, Alan Webb, to name a few). "I learned from all my coaches, especially Doc McCarthy, who gave me great tips for running and for racing that I used as an athlete and still use as a coach. From Doc and Alex, I learned things you should do and things you shouldn't do. I found out what worked and what didn't work, mostly by doing things myself. I experimented on myself. I cannot fault any of my coaches. I always pour over the workouts, and people improve. And don't say it's just my personality. Anyone that's worked under me knows that when we get down to the track, it's all business. I'll fool around when I get you to a meet; and after the race, I'll fool around then. But I always simulate every damn thing. You can't simulate a track—a track is a track. You have to run a simulator for weather, for terrain, for the time of day of the race. You have to get up and eat and do exactly what you're going to do the day of the race. You have to train for what you're going to run. You've got to so you can feel what your body will go through in the race."

During an Olympic event in the twilight years of old friends Squires and US Olympian Arnie Sowell, the collegiate contemporary succinctly capsulized Squires's post-Notre Dame career. He told the former Fighting Irish that he and his Pitt Panthers always saw him regularly run three, four, even five events in a meet. They thought among themselves that that workload surely must have gotten to Squires, but they never saw an outburst. Squires recalls of their conversation, "Arnie said, 'I bet you got so mad at some of the things you were doing then that you wanted to prove that you knew all this stuff about running. And you proved it.' He said that he had the Olympics and all that, but after it was over, that was it. He told me to look at all the Olympians I've coached and all the people I'm coaching. He said he has a job [military career; state housing authority] and he has a couple of meetings a year and meets up with the other Olympians in his area. But he said that I was living the life of helping to develop other people. That was nice of him to say. Believe it or not, I had never framed it like that."

At the conclusion of a recent Boston Marathon expo seminar panel discussion that featured Boston winners Greg Meyer, Catherine Ndereba, Bill Rodgers; broadcasters Larry Rawson, Toni Reavis; and coaches Fred Treseler III and Squires, while Squires signed autographs, posed for pictures, and answered questions onstage, he delivered advice and tips as if on a game show. He told those in line, "Run the course whenever you can. Your knees hurt? Check your shoes. Don't wear anything new in a race, even if your girlfriend or grandma gets you something special to run with. You run slow? Try quarters on a track. Wait a minute, I'll write something down to do. Anyone got a napkin?"

ABOUT THE AUTHOR

Paul C. Clerici is the author of five books—*Images of Modern America: The Boston Marathon*; *A History of the Falmouth Road Race: Running Cape Cod*; *Boston Marathon History by the Mile*; *Journey of the Boston Marathon* (Chinese-language version); and *History of the Greater Boston Track Club*. He has been covering the sport of running and the Boston Marathon since 1988. A freelance journalist, writer, photographer, and former newspaper editor and sports editor, his accomplishments are recognized in *Marquis Who's Who in the East*. He is a recipient of the Albert Nelson Marquis Lifetime Achievement Award.

A lecturer and historian, Paul is often invited to guest on radio and television programs. He has written for the *Brockton Enterprise, Foxboro Reporter, Medfield Press, Sampan* (Chinese-English language), *Walpole Hometown Weekly, Walpole Times* newspapers; *Boston College Chronicle, Bostoniano* (Italian themed), *Level Renner* (running), *Meter/Tracksmith Journal, New England Patriots Weekly, New England Runner, North End Magazine* (Italian themed), *Orlando Attractions Magazine, Running Times, State Street Journal* magazines; and has produced and hosted shows at Milton Cable Television and Walpole Community Television. A New England Press Association and Massachusetts Press Association award winner, he was also a regular contributor to *Marathon & Beyond* magazine for several years up to its cessation.

Race director of the Camy 5K Run & David 5K Walk, he competes in nearly every distance from the mile to the marathon—including two triathlons, 43 marathons (the Boston Marathon 23 times)—and has won numerous age-group and Clydesdale division awards. He is a graduate of Curry College in Milton, Mass., a Walpole High School Hall of Fame member, and resides in Massachusetts.

APPENDIX: OTHER VOICES

"Coach Bill Squires turned a bunch of wacky, individualistic Boston runners into marathon elites in part because he shared the same traits – he's wacky and individualistic. And very, very smart about training for road-race success. I only got to train with Squires and the Greater Boston Track Club a couple of times in my career, but those workouts were among the hardest – and most fun – I ever did. I'll never forget those runs."

–Ambrose "Amby" Burfoot, 1968 Boston Marathon winner, Runner's World editor-at-large, author

"Coach Billy Squires, as we affectionately called him, is a remarkable human being as well as a brilliant coach. He is always generous with his time and we've had many conversations over the years. I know him as a very thoughtful and articulate man with a sense of humor. Not only did he train Alberto Salazar, Dick Beardsley, Bill Rodgers, and Greg Meyer, to name a few, but he takes time to chat with many of us in the running community. I remember him at the Boston Marathon year after year and we'd sit and talk about the old days and the new days. I never had a coach, but if I had, I would have wanted it to be Coach Squires. He often said he wished he'd known me 40 or 50 years ago, and I'd smile. I always look forward to our chats and wish there had been more of them. He's a great coach and a wonderful person. I have a huge amount of respect and affection for him."

–Roberta "Bobbi" Gibb, three-time winner of the Boston Marathon (1966-68) and the first woman to finish the race

"Bill Squires was the first great marathon coach in the United States that did for marathon racing and training what University of Oregon coach Bill Bowerman did for distance runners on the track. Bill Squires mentored and influenced a lot of future runners and coaches with his training methods. No other marathon coach in the United States before or after Bill Squires has coached as many world-class runners in the marathon. He, along with my high school coach Don Benedetti and University of Oregon coach Bill Dellinger, were largely responsible for whatever success I had as a runner or as a coach."

–Alberto Salazar, three-time New York City Marathon winner, 1982 Boston Marathon winner, former Nike Oregon Project coach of Olympic medalists, author

"In the fall of 1973, my junior year at Boston State College, I approached my teacher, Bill Squires. Bill was my physical education health and fitness instructor. Classes were always full of engaging conversation, and no one missed them. Bill was also the coach of the Greater Boston Track Club as well as for Boston State College. After class, I asked Bill if he would coach me to do the first National Wheelchair Mile the following summer. The record was under seven minutes (6:53). I thought I could do it. He looked at me, shaking his head, 'Do you know what that is? That's four back-to-back quarter miles … in a wheelchair!' I told him I could do it. Bill gave me a workout schedule and told me to see him in the spring. I followed up in the spring and told him I was ready. He realized that I was committed and gave me a track program and told me to keep in touch.

"The day before I was to leave for the Mile, I saw him in the hallway at school. I called his name and he turned and smiled. He said, 'Look, I've sent two guys to the nationals, the third coming back a champion. Here's what you're going to do. Someone is going to break away; don't worry. Tuck in, say, around fourth place. At 300 yards coming out of the corner, sprint to the finish.' To my amazement, it happened just like that. I broke the record by four seconds (6:49). I was so proud wearing my Boston State College uniform and Converse running flats that he had given me.

"After doing the World Championship, I went to Bill again about doing the Boston Marathon. He told me I was nuts, but he gave me a distance training program. As part of this training, I did part of the Marathon route during a race in February called the Washington Day Marathon. Bill followed me in his station wagon – encouraging me and stopping traffic. He was spinning around in a very dangerous intersection, flapping his hands, stopping traffic in all directions, urging me to come through. He looked like a scarecrow! When I was approaching Heartbreak Hill, he got out of his car and waved me to stop. He yelled, 'You did it! You did it! It's all downhill. You did the Boston Marathon!' He presented me with a medal, which I cherish to this day. Eventually doing the actual Boston Marathon, Bill helped me accomplish my goal of breaking three hours in 1975 (2:58:00) and receive a certificate for all future entrants (but the beef stew was gone). All with the encouragement of my coach, Bill Squires."

–Bob Hall, pioneering two-time Boston Marathon winner, 1977 National Wheelchair Championship WR-setter, former Boston Marathon Wheelchair Athlete Liaison

"I first met [Bill Squires] in 1974, I think, at a track meet, of course, when Vin Fleming, a teammate, introduced me and told him that I had joined the Greater Boston Track Club. I was surprised that he knew a lot about me and my running, and he was very encouraging. The Boston-area track and field community was tight, and everyone seemed to know everyone else. I was learning. Looking back, it is clear to me that his success came from his love of running and track and field. Just being around it – translating all his practical knowledge into specific workouts, many individualized, and watching his athletes perform – was exciting and he put his life into it and never looked for anything in return other than sincerity.

"There are many, many stories of Coach's generosity, from giving money to Bill Rodgers to buy bread and milk when he was on food stamps to giving up his bed at a road race to Dick Beardsley and sleeping in a bathtub with a shower curtain for a blanket. He would give fatherly advice as well, urging me to return to college and finish my degree after a cross-country trip of nearly a year. He told me, 'Bobby, I'm glad you quit picking daisies and got serious.'"

–Bob Hodge, seven-time Mount Washington Road Race winner, 1979 Boston Marathon third-place finisher, Greater Boston Track Club

"Billy Squires was a high school miler, runner, and champion at the national level. He went to Notre Dame and competed for them and was at a very high professional level post-collegiately for a while and [several times] ran the Boston Marathon.

"He coached Boston State College and he made the Greater Boston Track Club the highest-level distance running group ever organized in Massachusetts. Billy helped all of us in GBTC to improve and reach higher levels, and of course those runners include people like 1983 Boston Marathon champion Greg Meyer, 1982 Boston Marathon champion Alberto Salazar, and many other high-level runners such as 2:08 marathoner Dick Beardsley, 2:11 marathoner Randy Thomas, 2:10 marathoner Bob Hodge, and the list goes on and on. Billy inspired all of us and motivated all of us because we could see how much he loved our sport – that was the ultimate key to the success of the Greater Boston Track Club.

"It was an honor to introduce Coach Squires at his induction into the USATF National Track and Field Hall of Fame in 2017. Coach Squires is known across the country and certainly is one of – if not the – best marathon coach of all-time. Not only that, he is a great guy. And to this day, I still hear his former athletes talk about their work with Coach Squires. He also played a powerful force in the first running boom in the United States, which might be his greatest contribution to the sport. We all like the Coach."

–*Bill Rodgers, four-time Boston Marathon and New York City Marathon winner,* Marathon Man *co-author*

"Sporting endeavors and the people in them are in the same world as the politics, sociology, and economics of the times. Coach Squires came along at a turbulent time for America. The 60s and 70s, when Coach Squires worked, were times of discontent with protests against Vietnam and the rising second wave of feminism. Young people did not trust the 'establishment.' His first runners were young men of draft age. Previously, coaches were of the quasi-military persuasion. They saw themselves as taskmaster or drill sergeant. Many had delusions that they were commanding officers in the field of battle, demanding do-or-die unquestioning obedience. Squires was not like that. He did not demand loyalty with a firing-squad threat, but attracted true loyalty with humor, wit, and a willingness to listen to the athletes. Coach Squires brought a refreshing counterculture idea to track and field and long-distance running. His runners returned the affection. For him, it was not 'my way or the highway,' but rather 'we are on this journey together so let's run hard together like wild horses and have some fun while we go.' My favorite Coach Squires summation of coaching: 'Get the horses together and let them run.'"

–*Tom Derderian,* Boston Marathon: Year-By-Year Stories of the World's Premier Running Event *author, Boston: The Documentary executive producer, Greater Boston Track Club current coach*

"As a serious and ambitious runner, one of the wisest things you can do is surround yourself with great advisors. In the fall of 1977, I was in the very middle of a scholarship commitment at Providence College. I knew that I did not want to continue as an English education major but was still a little uncertain as to what other route to take. My high school coach, Alex Vyce, back in Chicopee, Mass., was a very good coach from a motivational point of view but knew baseball much better than distance running. My coach at Providence knew even less. During this time, Coach Squires was having tremendous success coaching Bill Rodgers, Randy Thomas, Bob Hodge, and a solid stable of 'horses,' as he liked to call them. So I decided to take some time off from school and go up to Boston to join Greater Boston Track Club.

"Randy Thomas and Vin Fleming had a small apartment near Cleveland Circle and were kind enough to let me crash there for a few months. Bob Hodge was also a frequent guest on the couch, but we also shared the apartment with many guests of the insect variety. During this time, I took a fulltime job in the Brighton (Mass.) New Balance Factory; minimum wage, making shoes – the semi-toxic smell of the glue and primers was something that could get you a free out-of-body experience. I ran there each morning and either ran back to the Cleveland Circle apartment or to Boston College for GBTC track workouts.

"Under Squires, and with the help of my GBTC teammates, my progress was dramatic. At the Trials for the US World Cross-Country team in February, Randy and I tied for first, and Billy [Rodgers] also made the team. It was a huge breakthrough for me to say the least. The following week at the GBTC workout, Coach pulled me aside and put his hand on my shoulder to give me this sage advice: 'Kid, you're doing great. But don't get too comfortable here. You need to get yourself back down to Providence and finish up that degree of yours.' The word 'comfortable' rang in my head for a minute or two. I knew he was well aware of my living situation – no sponsors; working long days in harsh conditions; having little money for food; sleeping on the floor of a roach-infested apartment. I did end up making it back to Providence [and] a few months later finished a business degree, and thanks to Coach, even making All-American a couple of times. He was never too busy to pick up a phone and make sure I was doing okay with training and classwork. I knew that I had a home with the GBTC once I graduated. Thanks, Coach!"

–Dan Dillon, seven-time US World Cross-Country team member, Providence College All-American, Big East champion

"It was a privilege to meet Coach Squires back in 1980. We New Zealand athletes considered him a legend then. Coach of the world-famous Greater Boston Track Club, coach of Bill Rodgers, Greg Meyer, Dick Beardsley, Bob Hodge – this list is very impressive. I was drawn to Coach because he was close to running a four-minute mile. It's a fantastic journey over this time to share with Coach Squires. Great coach, great friend, great community leader, great inspiration. Gotta love Coach."

–Rod Dixon, New Zealand Olympic 1500-meter medalist, 1983 New York City Marathon winner, 3:53.62 miler

"Coach Squires had the ability to make average runners good, and good runners great. His unique training mixture of long intervals, hill work, long runs, and of course his trademark 'Squires Simulators,' were what separated his athletes from the rest of the pack. He always had an uncanny knack for prescribing the best workout at the appropriate time. The workouts were administered with his trademark sense of humor, and the guys were given creative nicknames and put into groups like Sturdlies, Horses, Polliwogs, or the ultimate insult, Guppies. This sense of humor prevented boredom from setting in during the long workouts. Phrases like 'he couldn't make a dog bark' were bestowed on those who mistakenly thought they knew more than they did. He was and is an excellent coach, mentor, and friend."

–Fred Doyle, Greater Boston Track Club, Athletics East VP/co-founder, former Saucony VP, former Nike US commerce director

"I had the great fortune to run at Boston State College and Greater Boston Track Club with Coach Squires and am forever in his gratitude for life lessons on and off the track. He approached coaching and mentoring through an innovative lens. His 'simulators' prepared athletes for success at every level of competition [with] training concepts used today by Olympic champions. To Coach Squires, every athlete presented unique individual talent and motivational challenges. In his own style and language, Coach Squires was dedicated and focused on athlete improvement, building confidence, and having fun.

"Coach Squires enjoyed creating opportunities. As an example, wheelchair racing grew from the vision of Boston State student-athlete Bobby Hall and Coach Squires. They adapted innovative track workouts and engaged GBTC athletes to support the inclusion of wheelchairs in major races. Breaking barriers for disabled athletes – my favorite Squires life lesson.

"During practice, Coach Squires would frequently walk under the stands at Boston College while athletes warmed down. What was he doing? Collecting clothes left by runners or spectators. After a BC training session, he gave me a ride home but needed to make one stop … the Pine Street Inn [homeless shelter]. Years later, many of his athletes entered sports businesses, sending Coach apparel and shoes. However, when we'd see Coach, he'd be wearing old gear. Where were the new clothes and shoes? Pine Street Inn. Giving back as part of [a] legacy!"

–*Mark Duggan, Boston State College, Greater Boston Track Club, former Nike Bauer Hockey CEO*

"I remember very clearly when I first met Coach Bill Squires. It was near the 17-mile mark of the Boston Marathon course in 1976 when I was about to pass two runners and move into second place. It was hot, though I don't remember being overly distressed about the heat. Suddenly, from the side of the road, out ran this guy with outstretched arms, matching my stride and offering me two handfuls of ice cubes. 'Here!' he said. 'Rub these on your arms and neck, they'll help cool you down.' Or something to that effect. His words and actions possessed such an authoritative resonance that I didn't hesitate to obey his 'command.' As I soon thereafter passed those two runners, Coach Squires's refreshingly cold but quickly melting ice cubes served as an added weapon of sorts in my arsenal for this competitive battle. Though my initial thought – as I offered what was left of those little morsels of aid to one of the two runners – was to keep the playing field level and share the limited resource that Coach had provided, a twinge of psychological warfare crept though my mind; 'Here, you need this more than I do.'

"Years later, when I'd moved to the Boston area and trained occasionally with Coach Squires and the Greater Boston Track Club, I came to realize my action of psychological warfare at our initial meeting was just the sort of tactic he was preaching to his charges. Such actions, and a bar napkin full of would-be workouts, defined Coach Squires's somewhat zany but always inspiring coaching methods. They are still hard to describe, but the results speak for themselves. The level of accomplishments achieved by the runners he coached would most assuredly not have been near the exceedingly high-water mark they were without his wisdom, guidance, support, encouragement, and love of the sport and his athletes."

–Jack Fultz, 1976 Boston Marathon winner, Dana-Faber Marathon Challenge training consultant/coach

"I met Bill Squires after being second in Boston in 1983. He was very open to share his knowledge, so while I was vacationing, he visited me and my husband at a restaurant in Kennebunk Beach. He explained to me some fun workouts to do that included some speed included in an endurance run. Some kind of well-scheduled types of fartlek (slow/fast running) done on the road that prepared me well for my 1983 World Championship Marathon in Helsinki, Finland, where I ended up fifth. He also told me to do those different workouts in a cycle of 10 days, which made sense to me. I continued that kind of training by myself, and since I'm a bit of a wild horse, I preferred to go by instinct instead of following a coach's plan. It's probably not a very wise decision for an athlete like me who can easily overdo it, but that's the way I was and still am; and like Edith Piaf, said, 'No, I regret nothing!' I'm really thankful for Bill Squires's help. I'll always remember him as a great empathic coach."

–Jacqueline Gareau, Canadian Olympian, Boston Marathon winner (1980) and runner-up (1982-83)

"Having first met Coach Squires when he taught science at my junior high school (Wakefield, Mass.), and having run with the Greater Boston Track Club in the 70s and 80s, I have been privileged to see all sides of him. They are all good.

"As a theoretician, he has been one of the great innovators in the techniques of how most effectively to approach long-distance training and competition, especially in the marathon. As a coach, he has helped athletes develop the courage and tenacity to find more in themselves than they might ever have thought they had, as well as the wisdom to tailor his teaching to best suit their own capabilities and style. Whether it was Bill Rodgers floating or Alberto

Salazar nearly shuffling, they came away with what it took to win. And while his speaking style can be colorfully elliptical, the message always comes through, delivered with honesty and integrity – often at the track and on the roads; occasionally at the Eliot Lounge.

"The measure of his impact comes not only in athletic performance, but in the deep connections he has formed with the athletes who he has so deeply affected. The connections are lifelong. Some of his athletes continue to this day to join him for regular breakfasts and lunches – such is the well-earned respect and affection that he has generated. He is a singularity, and the world of running is the better for it."

–Tom Grilk, Boston Athletic Association Board of Governor and CEO, Greater Boston Track Club

"Among other things, Bill Squires is an expert on the Boston Marathon course. No one else is close. However, his lasting contributions to running is his willingness to share that knowledge. Match that with his disarming wit and sense of humor and you have a memorable character."

–Tim Kilduff, 26.2 Foundation founder, former Boston Marathon race director

"(Regarding the Greater Boston Track Club and Bill Squires's early impact on the Falmouth Road Race) Bill Squires brought down all the horses! It was Squires. He said he was going to bring down all the big boys to help us out. They gave us some dignity, some class. It was incredible. All the Greater Boston Track Club guys that came down, they really gave us some integrity. They made it a race. They were an elite track club. They were just a great band of brothers; they were gentlemen, I remember that distinctly."

–Tommy Leonard, Falmouth Road Race founder, Official Greeter of the Boston Marathon (taken from previous interviews with the late founder)

"I met Coach Squires right after I had completed my 3,452-mile Run Across America in 1978. I wanted to join the Greater Boston Track Club mainly to become faster and more competitive but was convinced I wasn't good enough. The first thing Coach said to me was, 'Well, with that cross-country run, I would think you have a pretty good base now!' Ha. You think? He then gave me the nickname Long Run and has called me that ever since. I truly realized that the Coach was the best when he said to me, 'Whatever speed you can do eight-repeat miles at on the track, you can run 30 seconds slower per mile in a marathon.' I was doing repeat miles at 5:10 at that time. The next marathon I ran, I did a 2:30. What is that per mile? Yup, 5:40 per mile! The Coach nailed it. It was then I realized he really was a genius when it came to running and coaching!"

–Dave McGillivray, Boston Marathon race director, author, endurance athlete

"Coach Squires was ahead of his time! While he was a solid athlete at Notre Dame, his greatest successes came from the athletes he coached. From Bill Rodgers, Randy Thomas, Bob Hodge, and me with the Greater Boston Track Club, to Alberto Salazar and Dick Beardsley, he produced some of the greatest distance runners of that era. He also kept the egos in check that allowed the Greater Boston club to be the dominate running club in the US, if not the world.

"Bill had an intuitive sense of what was needed to succeed. Today, those practices are backed up by science, but he just knew what to do. He also knew how to adapt to the talents of the individual runner. Luckily, I was an example of that, and it was his commingling of my need for hard hills and intervals developed under my college coach Ron Warhurst, with his sense of long runs, surges, and tempo runs that led me to winning Boston. There was no coach who knew how to prepare for Boston better than Coach Squires. Just look at the winners and top results during the 70s and 80s, and Bill's fingerprints are all over them.

"While it seems all great coaches are a bit quirky, Bill was no exception. His broken sentences of instructions which needed to be interpreted, to his nicknames for some of the groups, like 'guppies' and 'sturdlies,' still makes me smile. What never lacked was his communication for his love of running and the athletes he coached, and for that myself and the sport benefited beyond measure."

–Greg Meyer, 1983 Boston Marathon, 1982 Chicago Marathon, and 1980 Detroit Marathon winner

"To know Coach Squires is to know greatness. His compassion for, and knowledge of, training runners of all abilities is unsurpassed. His unique ability to size up a runner, to see the individual, and to challenge him or her to improve through innovative work, is legendary in our sport. Never one to shy away from a situation, Coach is tough and results driven, all the while operating from a place of respect and admiration for the individual athlete. Coach clearly loves what he does and is ready to tell you so, through an incredible story or memorable personal experience. His legacy firmly intact, many remain eager to listen to his collected words of wisdom from a long and storied career, often accompanied by smiles or a hearty laugh!"

–Guy Morse III, Boston Athletic Association Board of Governor, former Boston Marathon race director

"The legend of Coach Squires writing training programs on the back of a napkin at the Eliot Lounge is true. I experienced this firsthand in the summer of 1979 as a recent Cornell grad living over the Bill Rodgers Running Center, eager to soak up as much running knowledge as possible. We were leaning against the bar, talking about preparing for the national cross-country championships, and Coach pulled out a pen. He wrote down three weeks of training, including an innovative interval workout on a golf course. Greater Boston Track Club won the cross-country title by a landslide that November. Coach shared much wisdom in the coming years, including marathon simulation workouts that I still remember. Thanks, Coach!"

–Pete Pfitzinger, 2-time US Olympic marathoner, 1984 US Olympic Marathon Trials winner, Athletics New Zealand chief executive

"Among the many very impressive talents of Coach Squires was his accomplishments in high school and at Notre Dame as a miler. In discussions with him, I was struck with how few miles his high school and college coaches had him run. Training was between 20 to 30 miles a week, and yet he still ran 4:21 in high school and 4:07 in college! He never reached his full potential as a miler. In conversations with Coach, he told me in college he felt he could run 48 seconds for a 440-yard leg on a relay. With speed like that, proper coaching, and more mileage, I believe Bill Squires could have been America's first sub-four-minute miler."

–Larry Rawson, two-time ESPN National Emmy Award winner, race commentator

"Great coaches in any sport tend to think out of the box while being perfectly content to exist in a space not yet embraced by their mainstream colleagues. Their singular belief in their program's design and the ability to transmit that belief to a cadre of winning athletes is what separates them and eventually confers their greatness. Coach Squires embodied all those qualities in a uniquely personal style that made him a legend whether at Boston State College or later with the Greater Boston Track Club."

–Toni Reavis, Running USA Hall of Champion broadcaster, race commentator

"Bill Squires is one of the most significant coaches in running history. His inventive energy was part of the fuel that powered the great running boom. Most remarkable about Squires was the range of runners his mentoring skills helped, from raw college students through eager club runners to the superstars whose triumphs he helped to create – Rodgers, Salazar, Beardsley, and more."

–Roger Robinson, When Running Made History *author, scholar, historian, 1985 Boston Marathon and 1980 New York City Marathon masters champion*

"I did not know Coach Squires all that well; however, he seemed to know me well. As a college runner, I think he saw my potential before I did. He talked as fast if not faster than I ran. He talked as fast as most of his runners ran. Coach always seems to have a smile on his face and a tip of advice to offer. A very personable guy. He also seems to be omnipresent in New England and national track circles. A legend!"

–Joan Benoit Samuelson, inaugural 1984 Olympic Women's Marathon gold medalist, two-time Boston Marathon winner, multiple world, course, and age-group record-setter

"October 1978. Purchase, New York. Diet Pepsi National 10K Championships. The Greater Boston Track Club contingent flew from Boston to New York early Friday morning. Coach took a later flight. We had a Friday evening banquet and Coach was a guest speaker. He walks to the podium, looking great – his clothes are matching, no plaids and stripes; he even has matching socks. Looks great and captivates the crowd. Saturday morning, we race. Following the awards ceremony, we return to the hotel to shower and catch the hotel shuttle back to the airport. The shuttle is scheduled to leave in 10 minutes. Bobby Hodge and I walk to Coach's room to make sure he is getting ready to check out of the hotel. We walk into his room and once again he looks great, matching outfit, suit and tie. We say, 'Let's get going, Coach.' He replies, 'Yup, Yup.' He picks up his suit carrier and starts walking out of the room. Hodgie notices he has left a tie on the bed. Hodgie says, 'Coach, you left your tie on the bed.' (Now this is a second tie, as he is already wearing one.) Coach replies, 'Balls,' picks up the tie and ties it up around his neck. He walks out of his room wearing two ties. Checks out wearing two ties and takes the shuttle to the airport wearing two ties. He checks in for his flight wearing two ties and boards the plane, people just staring at him. We arrive in Boston and he deplanes wearing two ties. A friend meets him in the lobby and says, 'What's with the two ties?' He looks down and replies, 'Balls.'"

–*Randy Thomas, former multiple world and America record-holder, Boston College women's track & field and 16-time NCAA champion cross-country head coach*

"For over four decades, Coach Bill Squires has been an inspiring coach and mentor. Coach generously shared his experiences of and insights on both running and human physiology with everyone who had the good fortune to meet him. Perhaps Coach's greatest gift was taking the time to understand what makes someone tick and then helping that person believe in themselves to unlock their best self. He was truly a master on the mental aspects of athletics, which really put him decades ahead of the sports scientists. My wife and I will never forget working with Coach for New Balance at the 1984 Los Angeles Olympics – 10 consecutive days and nights of track and field craziness that we will always cherish. Coach Squires has lived and breathed every aspect of the sport of running and we have all benefited from his generous nature and selfless support, perhaps none more than myself. Thank you, Coach!"

–*Fred Treseler III, coach, TRACS Inc. president and CEO*

Cover design: Andreas Reuel, Annika Naas
Interior design and layout: Andreas Mann

Cover photo: Getty Images
Interior photos: © Paul C. Clerici, unless otherwise noted

Managing editor: Elizabeth Evans
Copyeditor: sarahcomms@btinternet.com